CHOPIN AND HIS WORLD

CHOPIN
AND HIS WORLD

EDITED BY
JONATHAN D. BELLMAN AND HALINA GOLDBERG

PRINCETON UNIVERSITY PRESS
PRINCETON AND OXFORD

Published by Princeton University Press, 41 William Street,
Princeton, New Jersey 08540
In the United Kingdom: Princeton University Press,
6 Oxford Street, Woodstock, Oxfordshire OX20 1TW
press.princeton.edu

For permissions/credits, see page x

Library of Congress Control Number: 2017935498

Cloth ISBN: 978-0-691-17775-5
Paper ISBN: 978-0-691-17776-2

British Library Cataloging-in-Publication Data is available

This publication has been produced by the Bard College Publications Office:
Mary Smith, Director
Irene Zedlacher, Project Director
Karen Walker Spencer, Designer
Text edited by Paul De Angelis and Erin Clermont
Music typeset by Don Giller

This publication has been underwritten in part by a grant from Roger and Helen Alcaly

Printed on acid-free paper. ∞

Printed in the United States of America.

1 3 5 7 9 10 8 6 4 2

The editors would like to dedicate this book to the master pianists of the Golden Age: those who flourished and were trained in the years 1850–1925. From their teachers, they inherited the memories of Chopin's world, the sounds he knew and recomposed. Their Chopin recordings, which stretch back to the dawn of the recording era, are a priceless legacy, and we are forever in their debt.

Contents

Acknowledgments

The editors wish to thank above all the president of Bard College and artistic co-director of the Bard Summer Festival, Leon Botstein, for inviting them to be scholars-in-residence at the 2017 festival, *Chopin and His World*, and to edit this volume. His team—and our friends—Christopher Gibbs, artistic co-director, Byron Adams, program committee, and Irene Zedlacher, executive director, have been unfailingly warm and friendly throughout this process. A crown of laurels to Paul De Angelis, of Paul De Angelis Books, who edited the editors and kept things organized, sane, and on track from the very beginning. His sober guidance and eagle eye made this very complicated project somehow manageable, and we are much in his debt. The entire team assembled by the Bard College Publications Office —Mary Smith, director of publications; Erin Clermont, copy-editing; Don Giller, music typesetting; Karen Spencer, design; Scott Smiley, indexing— and at Princeton University Press have produced a handsome volume, and we are grateful to collaborate with them on this project.

Above all we would like to thank our contributors, in alphabetical order: Leon Botstein, Jean-Jacques Eigeldinger, Jeffrey Kallberg, David Kasunic, Anatole Leikin, Eric McKee, James Parakilas, John Rink, and Sandra Rosenblum. The opportunity to work with international Chopin scholars on this project has been a gift indeed.

Permissions

The following copyright holders have graciously granted permission to reprint or reproduce the following images:

National Museum, Poznań/Culture-images/Lebrecht for *Chopin's Polonaise (Ball at the Hotel Lambert in Paris)* by Teofil Kwiatkowski, Figures 1 and 2 (pp. 17, 18); Fryderyk Chopin Museum, Warsaw/Ullstein bild via Getty Images for *Chopin at the Piano* by Teofil Kwiatkowski, Figure 3 (p. 19); Hamburger Kunsthalle, Hamburg/Bridgeman Images for *The Musician's Dream* by Caspar David Friedrich, Figure 4 (p. 30); Musée de la ville de Paris, Musée Carnavalet, Paris, France/Bridgeman Images for Fan depicting George Sand and friends by Auguste Charpentier & George Sand, Figures 1 and 2 (p. 113); Bibliothèque Polonaise, Paris, France/Archives Charmet/Bridgeman Images for portrait of Fryderyk Chopin by Maria Wodzińska, Figure 2 (p. 301); Pictures from History/Louis-Auguste Bisson/Bridgeman Images for daguerrotype of Fryderyk Chopin by Louis-Auguste Bisson, Figure 5 (p. 304); Musée de la vie romantique, Paris for photographs of the plaster and bronze casts of Chopin's left hand by Auguste Clésinger, Figures 6a and 7b (pp. 305 and 306); National Museum, Kraków/Princes Czartoryski Museum Kraków for the photograph of the bronze cast of Chopin's left hand by Auguste Clésinger, Figure 8a (p. 308); Fryderyk Chopin Museum, Warsaw for drawings by Albert Graefle, Figures 6b and 9 (pp. 305 and 310).

Credit is extended as well to the publishers of *Eras of the Dance: The George Verdak Collection* (Montgomery, AL, 1976) from which we have taken *La menuet de la Cour*, attributed to Le Couteur, Figure 1 (p. 188) and to wikimedia for the painting of a polonaise being danced (circa 1790) by Jean Pierre Norblin found at http://commons.wikimedia.org/wiki/File:Jan_Norblin-_Polonais.jpg.

The authors, editors, and publisher have made every effort to trace holders of copyright. They much regret if any inadvertent omissions have been made.

CHOPIN AND HIS WORLD

Introduction

HALINA GOLDBERG AND JONATHAN D. BELLMAN

The life of Fryderyk Franciszek Chopin (1810–1849), the child of a French emigrant to Poland and a mother from impoverished Polish nobility, was framed by key historic events that defined his worlds in Warsaw and in Paris, exerting a profound impact on his professional and personal choices and on his art. In 1807, less than three years before Chopin was born, Napoleon Bonaparte established an eastern outpost in Warsaw in preparation for his Russian offensive. As a consequence, the Napoleonic campaigns cast a shadow over Chopin's earliest years, though Warsaw began to flourish after the 1815 Congress of Vienna. Similarly, the Revolutions of 1848, in particular the overthrow of the July Monarchy in France, darkened the composer's last years; he suffered a dramatic loss of income as his students and audiences fled the political turmoil in Paris, and it became impossible for him to sustain himself. These circumstances and the nasty breakup in 1847 from George Sand (the successful French writer who had been his consort for nine years), necessitated the ill-fated tour of Great Britain, which—given his fragile constitution at the time—undoubtedly hastened his demise.

Other political upheavals left indelible marks on Chopin's biography, too: just as he was entering adulthood, the Revolutions of 1830 shook Europe. The one in Paris was successful; it established the the July Monarchy that held sway during most of Chopin's years there and empowered the social circles that were later amply represented among Chopin's students and audiences. The revolution in Warsaw, however, which was intended to restore sovereign Poland, failed. This forced Chopin, about to start a concert tour, to become a permanent exile from his native country, and defined his mature personal and musical identity as that of Polish political émigré in France. The historical events culminating in the Polish revolution of 1830–31, known as the November Uprising, explain much about Chopin, his music, and his world.

Sixteenth- and seventeenth-century Poland, at the height of its political and military power, comprised the territories of much of today's Poland

and large parts of western Ukraine, Belarus, and Lithuania (with which it had had a dynastic union since 1386 and formed the Polish-Lithuanian Commonwealth in 1569). It fended off hostile neighbors—especially the Teutonic Knights, an ostensibly religious order founded to protect pilgrims in the Holy Land but better known for its territorial incursions into northeast Poland and the Baltic lands, which were characterized by brutality toward civilians and the use of mercenaries—and contributed to important military and diplomatic efforts of its allies. The most famous of these events (usually regarded as one of the proudest moments in Polish history) was the 1683 defeat of the Ottoman army at the Battle of Vienna, where the Polish King John III Sobieski, in command of the combined forces of the Polish-Lithuanian Commonwealth and the Habsburg-headed Holy Roman Empire, decisively halted the seemingly relentless northward expansion of the Ottomans.

Thereafter, though, Poland slipped into an unstoppable decline. Starting in 1772, Poland's territory was gradually dismantled by its neighbors—Russia, Austria, and Prussia—in a series of three partitions, the last of which (1795) obliterated Poland's name from the map of Europe for more than a century. A few heroic efforts to stop these events—the Constitution of the Third of May 1791, which intended to rectify the political corruption that caused Poland's decline, and the Kościuszko Insurrection in 1794, an uprising led by the Polish general, Tadeusz Kościuszko, who earlier had distinguished himself fighting in support of the colonists in the American Revolutionary War—had little long-term effect, and only in 1918 was sovereign Poland reinstated and ratified in the Treaty of Versailles, at the close of the First World War.

When Napoleon entered Prussian-occupied Warsaw in 1807 he was cheered by the locals. With him were the Polish Legions—military units of Polish exiles, formed in Italy under the leadership of General Jan Henryk Dąbrowski—which had fought under the Little Corporal since 1797. Bonaparte recruited them with guarantees of restoring sovereign Poland, a promise unfulfilled beyond the establishment of the Duchy of Warsaw, a puppet state encompassing the territories immediately around Warsaw. In place of sovereignty, Poland saw economic ruin, as Napoleon's forces drew resources from local industries and agriculture, and suffered massive devastation brought upon by his reckless military campaigns. Among the thousands of Polish soldiers who perished under his command was the revered nephew of the last King of Poland, Prince Józef Poniatowski, who won numerous battles for Napoleon but died tragically during the 1813 Battle of Leipzig. Conditions in Warsaw were doubtless dismal in this precarious time, which was when Chopin's father, Nicolas (Mikołaj), received a teaching post there and relocated his family (including the infant Fryderyk) to the capital city.

The Congress of Vienna (1814–15), convened to address Napoleonic damage, forged a new agreement concerning Poland. Most of the historically Polish lands were to remain occupied by the powers that annexed them in the previous century; Kraków was given the status of Free City within Austria; the Grand Duchy of Poznań was granted limited independence from Prussia; and the territories around Warsaw became the semi-sovereign Polish Kingdom under the control of Russia. Although the Polish Kingdom was promised limited self-governance, with control over matters of religion, culture, education, and economy, even this semi-sovereignty was often violated by tsarist authorities. Still, the Polish intelligentsia in the Kingdom seized opportunities to restore Poland's cultural and economic assets by implementing beneficial policies and establishing the necessary institutions to carry them out.

Chopin's later childhood and adolescence in the Polish Kingdom took place during a period of relative stability. Warsaw prospered both economically and culturally, and Chopin was able to attend the highly regarded Warsaw Lyceum, where his father taught French, and the just-established Warsaw University. His musical skills were honed at the new Warsaw Conservatory, one of the first such institutions in Europe, and he participated in a thriving Varsovian musical scene that included concerts by international stars such as Johann Nepomuk Hummel, Angelica Catalani, Henriette Sontag, and Niccolò Paganini, and productions of internationally acclaimed operas, sometimes within a year or two of their world premieres. Polish operas were also performed, the most substantial of these composed by the talented but often adversarial co-directors of the National Theater, Karol Kurpiński and Józef Elsner—the latter Chopin's beloved composition teacher.

The rise of Polish national opera was part of a larger movement toward the articulation of Polish national identity. After the loss of the monarchical framework that had fostered polity and culture in the Polish lands, newer ideas of identity-based statehood, emanating from Germany, appeared particularly attractive to the Polish intelligentsia, who perceived that a language- and culture-based community could preserve and nurture Polishness in the absence of a territorially sovereign country. The most conspicuous products of this early nationalism were massive cultural undertakings such as the multivolume *Dictionary of the Polish Language* compiled by Samuel Bogumił Linde, a friend and neighbor of the Chopins, and the patriotically charged operas that employed Polish language, historical Polish subjects, and included folkloric music. The earliest of these was Jan Stefani's *Cracovians and Highlanders* of 1794, the premiere of which helped to arouse the masses, serving as a prelude to the Kościuszko Insurrection. The most beloved patriotic operas of Chopin's childhood included Kurpiński's *Jadwiga, the Polish Queen* of 1814 and Elsner's *King Łokietek* of 1818.

Numerous grassroots initiatives sought to foster a sense of Polishness among the populace. For example, the magazine *Diversions for Children*, intended to propagate the Polish language and to encourage children to write in that tongue, was well known in the Chopin household and especially treasured by Chopin's beloved younger sister Emilia—a girl with uncommon literary talents who in 1827 died tragically at age fifteen. To familiarize children with Polish history, the venerated poet Julian Niemcewicz wrote the *Historical Chants*, a cycle of poems about Polish historical heroes and events, which were set to music by amateurs and professional composers. Children of Chopin's generation learned and internalized these songs; indeed, Chopin improvised on *Historical Chants* at the piano well into his adulthood. Elsner and Kurpiński promoted the use of the vernacular within Catholic services by composing accessible settings of sacred texts in Polish for parish use, and they also advocated the use of patriotic songs, which started to take on new significance in the last decades of the eighteenth century, to honor the Polish heroes and historical events of this tragic era. These patriotic works included the Kościuszko Polonaise, the Dąbrowski Mazurka ("Poland Has Not Yet Perished"), the Poniatowski March, and the Polonaise of May the Third. In this new, intensely national context, Polish dances—*krakowiak*, mazurka, and polonaise—acquired new importance. The mazurka began as a fashionable ballroom dance and an occasional folkloric accent in Polish-themed operas, but after the November Uprising—and mainly through Chopin's influence—it came to symbolize Poland itself. The polonaise, on the other hand, had already acquired a mythic significance in the first decades after independent Poland fell, and by the time Chopin composed his mature pieces in the genre it had been enshrined by the poet Adam Mickiewicz as a nostalgic and mythic recollection of the noble traditions of Poland before the partitions.

Mickiewicz was the most important Polish proponent of the new Romantic trends that were closely related to the cultural phenomena taking place in Germany, England, and France. With the publication in 1822 of his *Ballady i romanse*, he stirred the imaginations of young poets and writers, many of whom were Chopin's friends, and Chopin's imagination as well. Polish Romanticism soon became intertwined with the nascent nationalism and the political aspirations aimed at reestablishing autonomous Poland, a sentiment that became more urgent in 1825 after the sudden death of the progressive Tsar Alexander I. Political conditions in the Polish Kingdom worsened under his reactionary successor Nicholas I. Armed revolt was brewing, and on 29 November 1830, only four weeks after Chopin's departure from Warsaw to embark on a concert tour, it exploded in the rebellion known as the November Uprising.

After a lengthy period in Vienna and several German cities Chopin arrived in Paris just as thousands of Polish exiles began to flood the French capital after nearly a year of bloody battles and the ultimate failure of the revolt. Beyond military and political repercussions, the historically Polish territories under the Tsar's control lost any semblance of cultural autonomy, and hosts of insurgents willingly or forcibly became exiles as part of the Great Emigration. More than five thousand emigrated to France, which—although sympathetic to the Polish cause—had not provided the support that the leaders of the Uprising had anticipated. The losses of human capital were crippling, as Poland's intelligentsia, writers, and artists settled in Paris. Among them were many of Chopin's friends and acquaintances: Józef Bohdan Zaleski and Stefan Witwicki, poets whose texts were often used in his songs; and such Conservatory colleagues as Antoni Orłowski, who established himself as the music director of the opera in Rouen (where Chopin gave concerts in 1838), and Julian Fontana, who remained his trusted amanuensis (though one who, in private, bitterly resented his famous and successful friend's selfishness). Chopin also made new connections among the émigrés, including those frequenting the gatherings at the Hôtel Lambert, residence of Prince Adam Czartoryski, which served as the center of Polish émigré life in Paris. Among these new acquaintances was Adam Mickiewicz, whom Chopin had admired as an adolescent and who proved an inspiring, even if at times frustrating, presence in his adult life. But his closest Polish friend was Adalbert (Wojciech) Grzymała, an exile who had held a prominent political function with the insurrectionary government, who with the patience of an older, wiser brother attended to the composer's emotional and practical needs.

Paris during King Louis-Philippe's July Monarchy (1830–48) became the European capital of music. Since 1795 the city had been home to the Conservatoire de Musique, the first modern-style institution of musical learning, and this plus the presence of affluent audiences, continually hungry for new musical talent, drew the greatest virtuosi to the French capital. When Chopin arrived there, the giant among Parisian pianists was Frédéric Kalkbrenner, but his fame was about to give way to a new generation of virtuosi—Sigismond Thalberg, Franz Liszt, and, of course, Chopin himself, who after the first few years of his career seldom performed publicly, but instead supported himself and maintained his reputation through teaching and private concerts in salons of his influential friends and patrons (many of whom were also his piano pupils). He also made money through publishing, mainly through the printing house of Maurice Schlesinger, one of the most successful among the host of Paris publishers. Next to performances by instrumental virtuosi, the other major draw for Parisian audiences was opera. Several opera houses premiered works by the foremost composers of the era; most notably, Meyerbeer and Halévy dominated the world of the Opéra, while the Théâtre-Italien belonged to Donizetti and Bellini (whose meteoric rise to fame was interrupted by his untimely death in 1835), though revivals of favorites by Rossini were also common. Chopin, devoted to opera since his Warsaw years, regularly attended performances, and drew inspiration from operatic melodic styles, dramatic strategies, and the genre's developing harmonic language. He also cultivated friendships with singers, most notably with the multi-talented Pauline Viardot.

Soon Chopin found himself in the cenacles of Parisian artistic luminaries; he frequented the same salons as writers whose work resided in the heart of French Romanticism—Alphonse de Lamartine, Honoré de Balzac, Victor Hugo—and even the usually cynical Heinrich Heine showered his performances and compositions with unfeigned praise. Starting in 1838, Chopin's liaison with George Sand, a successful woman of uncommon intellect, offered additional opportunities to interact with notables. The most welcome visits involved such close friends as Eugène Delacroix, the painter who in the mid-1820s imbued his works with a new Romantic intensity of expression. Delacroix often stayed at Sand's estate in Nohant, where the Sand-Chopin "family" (the couple, plus her two young children) enjoyed fresh air, relaxation, creative vigor, and marmalade-making during their lengthy summer sojourns. These were joyful years when their feelings and commitment to each other were strong, before strains revealed fissures in the family structure they built and caused it to implode, ultimately setting the ailing composer on a path of descent from which he never recovered.

Thus Chopin stands like the protagonist of his own opera, an exiled Polish patriot whose tragic personal life is seen against the turbulent historical events of his time, while (paradoxically) his career continued to flourish in the warm glow of the July Monarchy, fading with the onset of the 1848 revolutions. Yet, as his gaze remained turned to the country of his childhood and the loved ones who stayed behind, many of his pieces spoke for and of Poland. So there is probably no better introduction to Chopin than one of the most famous passages in Polish literature, which describes a vision of Poland's history as expressed through music.

This is Jankiel's "Concert of Concerts" (Koncert nad koncertami), or simply "Jankiel's Concert" (Koncert Jankiela), as it is known in Poland, which comes from the twelfth and final book of Adam Mickiewicz's *Pan Tadeusz*. Written during the author's Parisian exile in the grim 1830s realities that followed the November Uprising, *Pan Tadeusz*—considered Europe's last epic poem—is a nostalgic, idyllic vision of life in Poland-Lithuania in, roughly, 1811 and 1812. By 1811 Poland, partitioned among Russia, Prussia, and Austria, had suffered multiple failed political and military attempts aimed at keeping and restoring sovereignty. From the vantage point of 1830s Paris, however, the still hopeful era of two decades ago seemed idyllic indeed.

The scene in the "Concert of Concerts" is the highlight of the climactic and most joyful event of Mickiewicz's story, the celebration of the young protagonists' engagement. Jankiel—a Jewish innkeeper and Polish patriot who is also a fabled master of the dulcimer—is implored to perform. In some 120 verses, Mickiewicz describes how Jankiel musically narrates significant events in Polish history, starting with the hopeful unveiling of the Constitution of the Third of May in 1791 and ending in 1807 with the victorious return to Poland, alongside Napoleon, of General Dąbrowski's Polish Legion. The music that evokes both these joyful events and the traumatic setbacks taking place in the interim uses well-established musical topoi connoting battle, suffering, sadness, and triumph. Moreover, Jankiel also makes use of familiar tunes associated with the depicted events, such as the Polonaise of May the Third and the Dąbrowski Mazurka. The reactions of Jankiel's listeners, detailed in the poem, demonstrate their deeply emotional response to these topoi and song quotations whose narrative significance they immediately grasp.

Possible models for Mickiewicz's Jankiel include Michał Józef Guzikow, a Jewish virtuoso on the "straw-fiddle" (a simpler predecessor of the modern xylophone), who was known to perform improvised fantasies on Polish songs, and Chopin himself, who often performed improvisations on patriotic themes in intimate private gatherings. An idealized amalgam of such improvised performances seems most likely, and this would have allowed Mickiewicz—highly sensitive to music as he was, and passionately nationalistic—to imagine a musical account of Poland's recent history, so rendered that the patriotic ardor of Jankiel's performance would likewise ignite a room full of joyous wedding guests. Here, then, is how one of Poland's greatest poets conceived the effect an improvisation such as Chopin's would have had.

The "Concert of Concerts" is immediately followed by a description of the guests dancing the polonaise, a passage that was likewise destined to become iconic for generations of Polish readers, and sets the stage for Chopin's heroic polonaises.

"Concert of Concerts" and "The Polonaise"

by Adam Mickiewicz
Translated by Kenneth R. Mackenzie
(New York: Hippocrene Books, 1992), 562–70.

For none would dare
To play on [the dulcimer] in Jankiel's presence there.
(The winter no one knew where he had been;
Now he was suddenly with the Generals seen.)
All knew that on that instrument was none
To equal him in skill or taste or tone.
They urged him on to play, but he refused;
His hands were stiff, he said, and little used,
He dared not play before such gentlemen,
And bowing crept away; but Zosia then
Ran up; in one white hand she brought with her
The hams used to play the dulcimer,
And with the other Jankiel's beard caressed;
She curtsied; "Jankiel, play for me," she pressed,
"It's my betrothal, Jankiel, won't you play,
You said you'd play upon my wedding day!"

Jankiel was very fond of Zosia, so
He bowed his beard, his willingness to show.
They brought the dulcimer and fetched a chair,
And sat him in the middle of them. There
He sat and, taking up the instrument,
He looked at it with pride and deep content;
As when a veteran hears his country's call,
Whose grandsons take his sword down from the wall,
And laughs: it's long since he has held the blade,
But yet he feels it will not be betrayed.

Meanwhile two pupils knelt before the Jew,
And tuned the strings and tested them anew.
With half-closed eyes he sat still in his chair,
And held the hammers motionless in air.

At first he beat out a triumphal strain,
Then smote more quickly like a storm of rain.

They were amazed—but this was but a trial,
He suddenly stopped and raised the sticks awhile.

He played again: the hammers on the strings
Trembled as lightly as mosquito's wings
And made a humming sound that was so soft
'Twas hardly heard. The master looked aloft
Waiting for inspiration, then looked down
And eyed his instrument with haughty frown.

He lifts his hands, then both together fall
And smite at once, astonishing them all.
A sudden crash bursts forth from many strings
As when a band of janissaries rings
With cymbals, bells and drums. And now resounds
The Polonaise of May the Third. It bounds
And breathes with joy, its notes with gladness fill;
Girls long to dance and boys can scarce keep still.
But of the old men every one remembers
That Third of May, when Senators and Members
In the assembly hall with joy went wild,
That king and Nation had been reconciled;
"Long live the King, long live the Sejm!" they sang,
"Long live the Nation!" through the concourse rang.

The music ever louder grew and faster,
Then suddenly a false chord—from the master!
Like hissing snakes or shattering glass, that chilled
Their hearts and with a dire foreboding filled.
Dismayed and wondering the audience heard:
Was the instrument ill-tuned? or had he erred?
He had not erred! He struck repeatedly
That treacherous string and broke the melody,
And ever louder smote that sullen wire,
That dared against the melody conspire,
Until the Warden, hiding face in hand,
Cried out, "I know that sound, I understand;
It's *Targowica!*" Suddenly, as he speaks,
The string with evil-omened hissing breaks;
At once the hammers to the treble race,
Confused the rhythm, hurry to the bass.

And ever louder grew the music's roar,
And you could hear the tramp of marching, war,
Attack, a storm, the boom of guns, the moans
Of children, and a weeping mother's groans.
So splendidly the master's art resembled
The horror of a storm, the women trembled,
Remembering with tears that tale of grief,
The Massacre of Praga; with relief
They heard the master's final thunder hushed,
As if the voices of the strings were crushed.

They've scarce recovered from their marvelling,
The music changes and a murmuring
Begins: at first a few thin strings complain
Like flies that struggle in the web in vain,
But more and more come up and forming line,
The scattered notes in troops of chords combine;
And now with measured pace they march along
To make the mournful tune of that old song:
The wandering soldier through the forest goes,
And often faints with hunger and with woes,
At last he falls beside his charger brave,
That with his hoofbeat digs his master's grave.
A poor old song, to Polish troops so dear!
The soldiers recognized it, crowding near
Around the master; listening, they recall
That dreadful hour when o'er their country's fall
They sang this song, and went to distant climes;
And to their minds came memories of those times,
Of wandering through frosts and burning sands
And seas, when oft in camps in foreign lands
This Polish song had cheered and comforted.
Such were their thoughts, and each man bowed his head.

But soon they lifted up their heads again,
The master raised the pitch and changed the strain.
He, looking down once more, the strings surveyed,
And, joining hands, with both the hammers played:
Each blow was struck so deftly and so hard,
That all the strings like brazen trumpets blared,

And from the trumpets to the heavens sped
That march of triumph: *Poland is not dead!*
Dąbrowski, march to Poland! With one accord,
They clapped their hands, and "March, Dąbrowski!" roared.

The player by his own song seemed amazed;
He dropped the hammers and his arms upraised;
His fox-skin hat upon his shoulders slipped;
His floating beard majestically tipped;
Upon his cheeks two strange red circles showed;
And in his eye a youthful ardor glowed.
And when at last his eyes Dąbrowski met,
He hid them in his hand, for they were wet.
"Our Lithuania has waited long for you,"
He said, "as Jews for their Messiah do.
Of you the singers long did prophesy,
Of you the portent spoke that filled the sky.
Live and wage war!" He sobbed, the honest Jew,
He loved our country like a patriot true.
Dąbrowski gave the Jew his hand to kiss.
And thanked him kindly for his courtesies.

Time for the polonaise. The Chamberlain leaves
His place, and, throwing back his flowing sleeves
And twirling his moustaches, makes a bow
To Zosia: Would she start the dancing now?
Behind the Chamberlain they form a line,
As he leads off the dancing at a sign.

His crimson boots upon the greensward flash,
His saber glitters and his rich-wrought sash.
Slowly he steps as though from listlessness,
But from each step and movement you could guess
The thoughts and feelings that his breast inspire:
Now he has stopped as though he would inquire:
He bends his head to whisper in her ear;
She turns her head away, too shy to hear;
He doffs his cap to her and humbly bows;
She deigns to glance, but ne'er a word allows;
He slackens pace, his eyes upon her bent,

• 11 •

And laughs at last—with her reply content.
He dances faster now, and, looking 'round
His rivals, pulls his cap with feathers crowned
Down on his brow, now thrusts it to the rear,
Then, twirling his moustache, cocks o'er his ear.
All envy him and follow him along.
He would have gladly stol'n her from the throng.
Sometimes he stops and with his hand raised high
Politely bids his rivals pass him by;
Sometimes he tries to draw aside, perchance
By changing course he may elude the dance.
But they importunate pursue him yet,
Entangling him within the dance's net;
Angered whereat his hand to sword-hilt flies,
As if to say: Plague on your envious eyes!
He turns about with proud defiant stare
Straight at the dancing throng: they do not dare
Stand in his path and, changing all about,
Set on again.

On every side they shout:
"Perhaps he is the last—you may not see, young men,
Such leading of the polonaise again!"
The pairs proceed in turn with merry noise,
The ring contracts and then again deploys,
As when the folds of a huge serpent curl,
The varied colors of the dresses whirl
Of ladies, soldiers, gentlemen, and gleam
Like golden scales lit by the sunset's beam,
Against the quilted darkness of the ground.
On goes the dance and shouts and toasts resound!

PART I

Contemporary Cultural Contexts

Chopin's Oneiric Soundscapes
and the Role of Dreams in Romantic Culture

HALINA GOLDBERG

[A composer's] logic . . . is the dreamlike logic that combines
the most daring and contradictory visions, and yokes them
together. To understand it, one must be dreaming oneself.

—Józef Sikorski

The notion of dreaming in music immediately brings to mind Chopin's
nocturnes.[1] Indeed, this genre's explicit association with the night invokes
the oneiric realm, the domain of dreams. Yet, as we investigate listeners'
responses to Chopin's music more closely, we discover that they repeatedly refer to dreamlike episodes in his compositions in other genres, and
that in addition to timbral representations of nocturnal haziness Chopin
employs other compositional techniques that bring about the experience
of dreaming.

Modern-day scholars' responses to the perceived dreamscapes in
Chopin's compositions follow on the heels of a long tradition of hearing
his music as a dream, a tradition that originated with his friends and contemporaries.[2] While other modern scholars, for example James Parakilas
in this volume, highlight the compositional and stylistic language of
Chopin's dream world and seek to interpret the experience of hearing
it, my task in this essay is to explore the cultural milieu that shaped the
composer's penchant for oneiric soundscapes and his contemporaries'
responses to it. What were the cultural reasons for the increased interest
in oneiric visions? Under what circumstances would Chopin have been
exposed to these cultural trends? What was music's role in portraying
oneiric experiences? What qualities of Chopin's music evoked dream
images for his audiences? What significance might dreams and dreaming
have held for Chopin and his audiences?

Chopin's Peers on His Musical Dreamscapes

Chopin's contemporaries frequently commented on the dream sound-scapes they heard in his music. Needless to say, the nocturnes most often elicited such responses. Indeed, in the first extensive Polish assessment of Chopin's music, published in Poznań in 1836 by Antoni Woykowski, we read that Chopin's nocturnes, in contrast to John Field's works that are "dry and dull," are "true dreams of a tender, pure soul, violently moved by the emotions of a silent night."[3] Around the same time Gottfried Wilhelm Fink, in his review of Chopin's Nocturnes, Op. 27, described their character as that of "The Dream, who revels in round dances with Longing [Sehnsucht]."[4] Fink's evocative image relates Chopin's dreamy soundscape to Sehnsucht, that quintessentially Romantic concept of longing for the Unattainable, the Infinite, the Ideal. At face value Woykowski's comment appears to highlight the intense emotionalism of Chopin's nocturnes, placing them in a sphere of Sentimentalism, but in full context it becomes clear that Woykowski also understands these pieces as offering an insight into the ideal realm, for in the same essay he describes Chopin's music as "a magical art that gives man a glimpse of his higher origins and lifts him instantly from this vale of tears to the happier lands above."[5]

Reviewers also invoked oneiric imagery in relation to Chopin's other works. An 1842 article in *Revue et gazette musicale de Paris* offered a general observation that Chopin's compositions are "a dreamy pleasure which shuns noisy outbursts and penetrates the soul with vague melancholy."[6] More specifically, in 1837, in his review of the A-flat Major Etude from Opus 25 performed by Chopin, Robert Schumann remarked that "when the *étude* was ended, we felt as though we had seen a radiant picture in a dream which, half-awake, we ached to recover."[7] Aleksander Jełowicki, who befriended Chopin in Paris, heard his friend's improvisations as dreamy memories of Poland. He recalled that when they were together, missing home and remembering old times, Chopin would sit at the piano and his music made Jełowicki "dream of home, and wake up dreaming."[8]

In their descriptions, the listeners to Chopin's music place themselves in diverse relationships to the dream: in some instances, exemplified by Jełowicki's account, they are dreaming while listening to the music; in others, represented by Schumann's description "half-awake," they remember the dream; others still, for example Woykowski, witness a memory of someone else's (the composer's?) dream narrated by the music. For Jełowicki, an ardent Polish patriot and a veteran of the November Uprising of 1830, dreaming and memory are intertwined with nostalgia for Poland, a mode of listening that I have described

Figure 1. Teofil Kwiatkowski, *Chopin's Polonaise—Ball at the Hôtel Lambert*, (formerly *Polonez—Rêve de Frédéric Chopin Pianiste*), watercolor, 1857. Muzeum Narodowe, Poznań.

elsewhere.[9] This interplay between dream, night, memory, yearning, and nostalgia appears time and again in descriptions of Chopin's music, perhaps most beautifully captured by Fink, who with his characteristic eloquence, observes that Chopin's "forms are always bathed in a twilight, from whose hazy fragrance shadows of memory now softly arise and play with longing, now rage by in a tempest, terrifying and eerie."[10]

Such dreaming and remembering, tinged with nostalgia, are the topic of one of the most famous paintings representing Chopin, by Teofil Kwiatkowski. The title usually given to this work is *Chopin's Polonaise— Ball at the Hôtel Lambert,* but before it became known under this name, the painter showed this watercolor in 1859 at the Salon under the title *Polonez—Rêve de Frédéric Chopin Pianiste*. The work dates from around 1857, and thus was painted by a close friend of the composer just a few years after his death. The image is composed of three groups of figures: on the left are easily identifiable members of the Czartoryski family, who serve as hosts of the event (hence the reference in the better-known title of this painting to the Hôtel Lambert, Prince Adam Czartoryski's Parisian residence and a synecdoche for the political faction associated with him); on the right, a group of artists and intimates surround Chopin at the piano, among them the poet Adam Mickiewicz, Chopin's student Princess Marcelina Czartoryska, George Sand, and Kwiatkowski himself; in the center allegorical and historical figures (including the celebrated fifteenth-century knight Zawisza Czarny) are dancing a polonaise.[11]

In Kwiatkowski's painting, apparitions and allegorical figures conjured up by Chopin's music mingle with real persons, contemporary and

Figure 2. Detail of Chopin at the piano surrounded by friends and
allegorical figures, *Chopin's Polonaise—Ball at the Hôtel Lambert* .

historical: an allegorical peasant girl, invoking the "pure" Polish folk,
stands by the piano; to the right of the composer two angels listen closely
to the music; among Chopin's intimates gathered behind the composer, a
figure of *guerrier gaulois*, representing the primeval spirit of France, looks
on from the shadows. The winged figures appearing throughout the
room are historical rather than allegorical: they are the Winged Hussars,
members of the elite Polish cavalry associated with King Sobieski's victory
over the Ottomans at Vienna. Temporal and spatial frames are likewise
conflated: the informally dressed Chopin, at an upright piano, exists in
the same time and space as the illustrious and formally clothed hosts.
Standing to his right, Mickiewicz, by the late-1830s already famed for
his description of the polonaise in his epic *Pan Tadeusz* (reproduced in
the introduction to this volume), seems to beckon the ladies to dance.
The Polish bard is aptly dressed in *kontusz* and *żupan,* the archaic traditional attire of the Polish nobility, which was strongly associated with the
polonaise and belonged to the nostalgically recalled era of sovereign eighteenth-century Poland (a cultural trope that is addressed in Eric McKee's
essay in this volume).[12] Not only does historical time coincide with con-
temporaneity, but even the modern figures in the painting reference

Figure 3. Teofil Kwiatkowski, *Chopin at the Piano*,
watercolor, 1847. Muzeum Chopina, Warsaw.

a variety of time frames: Chopin and Mickiewicz, who at the time the painting was completed were already dead, are placed in the same time frame as new members of the Czartoryski family, such as Princess Maria Amparo, who only in 1855 married Prince Władysław. The pose of Kwiatkowski is a visual quotation from his well-known painting representing Chopin's last moments in 1849.[13] Likewise, the image of Chopin is reproduced nearly verbatim from an intimate, impromptu watercolor Kwiatkowski made in 1847 (see Figure 3). The actual Hôtel Lambert was a luxurious and bright residence dating from the period of Louis XIV, and designed by an architect and artists closely associated with the king. The space depicted by Kwiatkowski, however, is defined by murky Romanesque arches supported by columns crowned with medieval capitals, which imbue it with an air of mystery and timelessness.[14]

This disjointed, conflated sense of time and space is characteristic of dreams and memories. But Kwiatkowski leaves much to the viewer's imagination. He makes us ask: Who is the dreamer? Is it Chopin dreaming about (remembering?) Polish history while improvising? Are his listeners dreaming (remembering?) in response to his music? Is it Kwiatkowski dreaming about (remembering?) Chopin's dreams of Poland's past? Or is it all taking place concurrently—memories and dreams being endlessly reflected in mirrors of time?

Chopin's "Dreamlike Logic": Musical Vocabularies of Memory, Nostalgia, and Dream

In Chopin's music, as in Kwiatkowski's painting, the states of dreaming and remembering overlap and share similar musical vocabularies, and nostalgia for his homeland meets Romantic longing. In recent decades scholars of memory have ascertained that our memories distort the recalled experience through the fading, blurring, and fragmenting caused by a weakening of neuron connections in our brains.[15] These scholars often turn to Marcel Proust's *A la recherche du temps perdu* as the paradigmatic artistic representation of memory.[16] Long before Proust, however, the composers of the early nineteenth century—especially Beethoven, Schubert, Schumann, and Chopin—mastered the art of capturing in their music the distorted experience of a recalled past. In Chopin's compositions, we hear techniques beyond the fragmentary recall of a theme or a motive: he renders us subject to temporal distancing through auditory distortions—fading, blurring, and fragmentation. These distortions, especially in combination with the national connotations of the mazurka genre, invoke nostalgia in its original sense: as a spatial and temporal displacement from one's homeland.[17] Thus when Jełowicki speaks of Chopin's improvisations as dreams of Poland, he references this patriotic mode of nostalgic remembering and dreaming. But for the Romantics nostalgia also carried an association with a broader concept, *Sehnsucht*, an existential yearning, a longing for the Unattainable. In genres that did not specifically reference Poland, such as the etudes or nocturnes, Chopin's contemporaries heard musical dreams and memories that reflected these broader Romantic ideas. Therefore, when Fink references memory and dreaming in relation to Chopin's Nocturnes, Op. 27, and Schumann refers to these concepts in relation to Chopin's first etude from Opus 25, they do so not in the patriotic sense, but within this broader Romantic framework.

Both mental states—dreaming and remembering—are characterized by fragmented thoughts and images, which throughout Chopin's works are suggested by thematic and motivic fragmentation. On a subtler pianistic level, both can likewise be evoked by the fading and blurring of sound that Chopin achieves through soft dynamics, the use of pedal points, drones, or non-chordal tones, rubato, and his masterful shading of pianistic sonorities, including, of course, his exquisite use of the pedals, both damper and *una corda* pedal.[18] In the coda of the B-flat Minor Mazurka, Op. 24, No. 4, for example,

> the tempo slows down and the volume fades out at the end, leaving only a faraway reverberating specter of a mazurka. He indicates a performance that imitates the experience of receding sound through copious expressive comments— *ritenuto, diminuendo, calando, mancando, sempre rallentando*, and *smorzando*—that accompany repeated *pianissimo* markings. A blurring that heightens the sense of distancing is further achieved through harmonic means and a lingering pedal (note, especially, the last four measures). The melody, which alludes to an inner voice motif from the opening, echoes with repetitions, closing as an eerie, Phrygian fragment.[19]

While there is an overlap in compositional strategies that invoke dreams and memory, some of the techniques point more directly to the experience of dreaming than remembering. In music that uses topics associated with the nocturnal, such as the nocturne, berceuse, or barcarolle—not just in pieces in these genres but also in others that reference them as topics, for example within the ballades and scherzos—particular groupings of compositional devices, such as the blurring and fading gestures, or fragmentation and distortion of musical ideas, seem to point more specifically to night and dreaming. The F-Minor Nocturne, Op. 55, No. 1, illustrates such a convergence of the nocturne genre and compositional devices that evoke dreaming and memory. The opening section has all the topical markings of a funeral march (the F-minor tonality, duple meter, the "walking" accompanimental figure, dotted rhythms in the melody), but the soft dynamics that Chopin sustains throughout the march make the listener experience it as an expression of private rather than public grief. The middle section introduces a different topic: dramatic, stormy, and restless. The minor mode, rapid unison figurations, chromaticism, chordal exclamations in dotted rhythm, and overall loud dynamics place it firmly in the *tempesta* tradition, well entrenched in operatic and instrumental writing by the time of Chopin.[20] It is the section that follows the "storm," however, that gives this piece an entirely unexpected turn. After the turbulent episode, the opening returns, but it is truncated, and the first phrase of the theme is never completed, quickly dissolving into waves of soft, chromatic figurations that soar upward, ever softer and faster. Kleczyński sums up this moment by saying that in the end "everything disappears like a frightful dream, and you cannot be sure whether you saw apparitions or living men."[21] The oneiric quality of this piece results from the particular convergence of the subjective quality of the grief expressed in the opening, the nightmare-like moments of fright that follow in the *tempesta* section, and the fragmentary return of the opening dissolving into a blurry, ethereal conclusion, all within a private genre that is directly associated with the night.

In some of Chopin's pieces, unexpected juxtapositions of dissimilar topics and ideas happen in fast succession, with incomplete themes taking turns through unexpected and barely prepared modulations. The phantasmagoric experience results from precisely these compositional features. In his 1865 article introducing a new volume of Chopin's late works, Józef Sikorski, a Polish music critic of Chopin's generation whose extensive and illuminating essay of 1849 commemorating Chopin's death has been included in this volume, perceptively sums up the aesthetic context for such successions of musical ideas in Chopin's works.[22] Sikorski notes that a great composer's "dreamlike logic . . . combines the most daring and contradictory visions, and yokes them together." In such compositions, he continues, "the bizarre, dreamy details never reappear in the same constellation—nothing but the background stays the same."[23] Indeed, Chopin, who started to use the compositional strategies that conjure up the experience of remembering or dreaming in the 1830s, had mastered them in the last decade of his life. James Parakilas, in his interpretation of the Mazurka,

Op. 56, No. 3, as a dream, focuses on just such bizarre details and moments of discontinuity (incidentally, the Opus 56 Mazurkas were part of the volume reviewed by Sikorski). He points out the unpredictable harmonic shifts, unexpected interruptions of themes and textures, and frequent fadeouts of musical ideas. Through these strategies, and by withholding and manipulating the generic markers of the mazurka, Chopin makes us experience "not so much dance music as a dream narrative in a mazurka rhythm."[24]

Examples of the compositional strategies described above abound in Chopin's oeuvre. In one of his mature works—Mazurka in B Minor, Op. 33, No. 4—the composer offered a performing direction that confirms such an understanding of the piece: in the autograph we find the word *risvegliato* (awakened) written over the two-measure gesture concluding the piece.[25] But we find astounding occurrences of dreamlike moments in his works such as the ballades, fantasias (consider, for instance, Opus 61), and, of course, nocturnes. In his essay in this volume, Anatole Leikin places Chopin's Preludes, Op. 28 and the Nocturne in B Major, Op. 32, No. 1, within the context of the nocturnal aesthetics of the Gothic. Literary genres, the Gothic novel among them, are indeed an important component of the cultural background against which we can understand Chopin's and his audiences' fascination with dreams and dreaming.

Dreams in Romantic Literary Genres

Dreams have appeared in literature throughout its entire history, beginning with such early examples as the Book of Job, Penelope's dream in *The Odyssey*, and Enkidu's dream in the *Epic of Gilgamesh*. Here they serve to illuminate divine mysteries and transmit prophecy. Likewise, writers of the late Middle Ages and early modern era—most notably Dante, Shakespeare, and Milton—presented their readers with memorable and dramatic dream sequences. In the late eighteenth century, however, the advent of the Romantic movement led writers to engage dreams in their works with renewed interest and intensity.

For Romantic poets, dreams fulfilled an important expressive function. At first, ample models for their representations of the nocturnal could be found in the fashionable Gothic novels that appeared in England in the 1760s and soon spread to the continent. By the early nineteenth century the works of English poets William Blake, Percy Bysshe Shelley, John Keats, William Wordsworth, Samuel Taylor Coleridge, and others prominently featured dream sequences.[26] These poets were fascinated by the potential for dreams (natural or opium-induced) to enable them to venture beyond the boundaries delimited by the senses. Their dreamy visions also evoked the aura of mystery that characterizes medieval sagas and folktales, and served as a means of exploring the creative process. In some of these works, most notably those by Blake (who also left numerous images depicting dreams), dreams and prophecy inhabited the same space; the poet's imagination thus echoed divine creativity.

On the continent, the Fantastic literature of German and French authors became the ideal vehicle for Romantic dream visions. E. T. A. Hoffmann's oeuvre is rich with discussions of dream states and descriptions of dreams experienced by his characters (of course, Hoffmann's original *Nutcracker* story, far more grim and disturbing than the ballet version we all know and love, is a child's phantasmagoria).[27] By the late 1820s Hoffmann's works had been translated into French and gained the following of leading French writers, including Charles Nodier, who wrote about dreams throughout his career. For Nodier, the Fantastic was a form of philosophical inquiry, a vehicle to explore the ideal, to venture beyond reason, science, and religion.[28] "Only in dreams," he tells his reader, "can the universe of imagination be mapped. The universe of sense-perception is infinitely small."[29] Nodier and other French writers who made the oneiric experience central to their oeuvre—Théophile Gautier, Honoré de Balzac, Charles Baudelaire, Victor Hugo, Gérard de Nerval—understood dreaming to be not just as important, but conceivably of even greater value than awakened consciousness.[30] They also frequently linked dreaming with somnambulism, hallucinations, and madness.

Perhaps the most succinct summation of the significance dreams held for Romantic writers comes in the opening canto of Byron's 1816 poem "The Dream":

> Our life is twofold: Sleep hath its own world,
> A boundary between the things misnamed
> Death and existence: Sleep hath its own world,
> And a wide realm of wild reality,
> And dreams in their development have breath,
> And tears, and tortures, and the touch of Joy;
> They leave a weight upon our waking thoughts,
> They take a weight from off our waking toils,
> They do divide our being; they become
> A portion of ourselves as of our time,
> And look like heralds of Eternity;
> They pass like spirits of the past,—they speak

Like Sibyls of the future; they have power,—
The tyranny of pleasure and of pain;
They make us what we were not,—what they will,
And shake us with the vision that's gone by,
The dread of vanished shadows.—Are they so?
Is not the past all shadow?—What are they?
Creations of the mind?—The mind can make
Substance, and people planets of its own
With beings brighter than have been, and give
A breath to forms which can outlive all flesh.

In these eloquent verses, Byron acknowledges dreams' relationship with waking experiences, reminding his reader that not only our "waking toils" find echoes in our dreams, but also that dreams are remembered in our "waking thoughts." By claiming that dreams "pass like spirits of the past,— they speak like Sibyls of the future," he sets up a parity between two kinds of dreams: those that act as recollections of bygone occurrences, and those functioning as visions of events that are yet to come. Thus, for Byron, memory and prophecy are mirror images of each other that coexist in dreams. In dreams we freely traverse several dimensions without being subject to the physical restrictions of time and space. We break out of our corporeal confinement and are subject to experiences unconstrained by the imperfections of our senses. But the most important qualities of dreams possibly have to do with their liminality, their positioning between life and the beyond, or, as the poet says, their being "a boundary between the things misnamed death and existence." In dreams this boundary does not limit us, because dreams reveal the important truth that there is no division between the spiritual and the corporeal, that "the mind can make substance." Ultimately, dreams are a vehicle for the transcendental experience: they demonstrate that the mind can "give a breath to forms which can outlive all flesh." They are the "heralds of Eternity."

The ability of dreams to transcend the senses had been noted as early as 1781 by Jean-Jacques Rousseau in his *Confessions* (and it likely influenced the use of the dream topos in French literature). However, the understanding of dreams as a state in which the absolute is channeled resonates most directly with concepts that are central to German Idealism, and found most direct expression in the writings of German philosophers around 1800. These ideas were transmitted to France, mainly through the agency of the philosopher Victor Cousin, and continued to influence the arts in France and throughout the Western world for decades to come.

Dreams in Idealist Philosophy and in Science

The *Frühromantik* (early Romantic) writers placed great importance on dreaming and what were understood to be related liminal states of consciousness—somnambulism, recollecting, hallucinating, and prophesying. These ideas received the most extensive treatment in the writings of the highly influential natural philosopher Friedrich Wilhelm Joseph Schelling and the poet and philosopher Friedrich von Hardenberg, better known by his pseudonym Novalis. Writings of Friedrich Schlegel were also important, as he articulated many of the Frühromantik aesthetic ideals, as did the novelist Ludwig Tieck and the art historian Wilhelm Heinrich Wackenroder. Their preoccupation with the liminal states was rooted in core concepts of German Idealism.

Stemming from internal tensions within the German Enlightenment, Idealism initially sought to rescue the key principles of the *Aufklärung* from their inner conflict. In their effort to formulate criticism without skepticism and naturalism without materialism, Immanuel Kant and his Frühromantik followers sought to convey a new understanding of the relationship between the subjective and objective, between the ideal and the real. Though their specific interpretations of these concepts varied, many writers belonging to the generation active in the last decade of the eighteenth century embraced the notion of *Naturphilosophie*, an organic conception of nature as a living force that could be manifested as both the subjective and objective, the ideal and the real. This living force was externalized in the objective and the real, and internalized in the subjective and the ideal. Within this view the mind and the body were completely interdependent.[31]

The Idealist view privileged intuiting over reasoning, and by acknowledging the limitations of an epistemology built on reason and empiricism, these writers also had to recognize the limits of our ability to express the ideal through a philosopher's language. They considered the metaphoric language of the arts, however, especially suitable for this purpose. For them, the aesthetic experience became "the criterion, instrument, and medium for awareness of ultimate reality or the absolute."[32] In such art the subjective and objective were merged. The artist's ability to express his subjective feelings and desires was not so much the source of his claim on metaphysical truth as was the idea that his activity was "continuous with and an integral part of, nature as a whole."[33] The Frühromantiker pointed out that in such art not only "the activity of the artist . . . is being expressed; it is also the activity of the absolute that expresses itself through him."[34] In particular, the Frühromantiker elevated poetry to a metaphysical status, along with its even more perfect sister art, music. Music more than any other art—and even more aptly, *instrumental* music—had the power to bring us closer to an understanding of the absolute and give us a glimpse of what must remain inscrutable to our minds.

Dreams and reveries, like other borderline phenomena—prophetic inspiration, clairvoyance, presentiments and déja-vu experiences, animal magnetism and telepathy, and somnambulism—held particular significance for Frühromantik philosophy as moments "when forces of life are in repose, when the boundaries between matter and spirit are blurred."[35] Thus, in their writings, we frequently find themes of night and dreaming. For instance, in *Der blonde Eckbert*, first published in 1797, Ludwig Tieck uses descriptions of dreams and dreamlike states to destabilize the reader's sense of reality, to blur the boundaries of human experience and put into question the validity of our perception of the world.[36] Most notably, though, we find these topics in the writings of Novalis: in his *Hymnen an die Nacht* (1797–1800, published in the journal *Athenaeum*, founded by Friedrich Schlegel and his brother August, who was a poet and a translator), where they help him conceptualize a transcendental domain that exists outside of time and space, and in his unfinished novel *Heinrich von Ofterdingen*, in which the prophetic dreams of this medieval poet reveal a higher world.[37] From these writings, oneiric topoi made their way into later works, most notably E. T. A. Hoffmann's "Der goldene Topf" ("The Golden Pot") and "Der Sandmann," where they are merged with related concepts from science.

The eighteenth century saw renewed and deepened interest in the exploration of magnetic and electric phenomena, which led to epoch-making discoveries and, ultimately, to the harnessing of electric energy. Electricity and magnetism also caught the attention of eighteenth-century physicians, who were interested in the curative potential of these phenomena. Most famously, in 1766 a Viennese doctor, Franz Anton Mesmer, published *De planetarum influxu in corpus humanum* (On the Influence of the Planets on the Human Body), in which he laid foundations for the doctrine of animal magnetism. According to his theories, planetary energy was connected by the way of a fluid to energy fields of all living creatures, and ailments caused by disturbances of such energy could be healed through making the individual's energy field whole again. As part of his therapy, Mesmer induced hypnotic states by laying his hands on patients, or by requiring his patients to hold magnets or supposedly magnetized protrusions of a vessel known as the *baquet*, a procedure often accompanied by the sounding of a glass harmonica. In the ensuing years, the talk of magnetism and mesmerizing permeated a wide range of discourses, whether it was a humorous reaction to the fad, as in Mozart's reference to magnetism in *Così fan tutte*, or a serious fascination, as in the case of followers of esoteric movements such as the Rosicrucians and Freemasons. Mesmer's theories had an impact on diverse communities, from serious scientists to swindlers who held the unwitting public in their greedy embrace, to poets and philosophers—most notably Coleridge, Schelling, and Friedrich Schlegel.[38] Although Mesmer's ideas were viewed as highly problematic by much of the scientific community, they brought about a new focus on the interrelated phenomena of mesmerism, hypnosis, somnambulism, and madness. And by forcing scholars to interrogate the boundaries between consciousness and unconsciousness, Mesmer opened new paths of inquiry for the emerging field of psychology.

While Mesmer's argument was still grounded in the materialism of the Enlightenment, a circle of scientists, poets, and philosophers who gathered around Novalis and Schelling, which included Gotthilf Heinrich von Schubert (naturalist and physician), Johann Wilhelm Ritter (chemist-physicist), and Franz von Baader (physician turned geologist), reframed the significance of "magnetic sleep," somnambulism, and other liminal experiences as revealing the transcendental. Ritter's work with galvanic reflexes gave the other members of the circle a much sought-after confirmation that their mystical interpretations of somnambulistic states had a basis in science. Schubert's 1806 series of lectures on "The Nocturnal Aspects of the Natural Sciences" made a profound impression on his contemporary writers and philosophers, from Madame de Staël to Friedrich Schlegel. In the most influential of his publications, *Die Symbolik des Traumes* (The Symbolism of the Dream) of 1814, Schubert focused on the language of dreams, which he called the hieroglyphic language, and argued that in oneiric states the soul—freed from the confines of the body, space, and time—speaks a language of images it shares with poetry and prophecy. In this book Schubert laid foundations for the study of the subconscious; Freud's theories and modern psychology were later built on those foundations. More immediately, Schubert offered scientific underpinnings for conceptual and artistic explorations by eminent Romantics who were intimately acquainted with his work—Goethe, Schelling, and E. T. A. Hoffmann among them. Franz von Baader's work made the most direct connection between magnetic voyance and the arts. When creating a work of art, claimed Baader, the artist draws from the divine creative energy that brought about living beings; in somnambulistic states the artist makes contact with that cosmic force. Thus Baader linked the roles of the "true artist" and seer, giving priority to the irrational and unconscious in shaping the artist's ability to convey in his work the oneiric visions of the mystic realm.[39] In *Der Traum des Musikers* (The Dream of the Musician), Caspar David Friedrich, the famous Romantic painter who was personally acquainted with several of the Frühromantiker and shared their ideas, attributes such an ability to engage with the otherworldly to a musician. In the charcoal drawing shown as Figure 4, Friedrich portrays a vision of angelic music making that comes to a lute player in a dream.

This circle of thinkers helped perpetuate the fascination with mesmerism into the nineteenth century. And though they influenced popular imagination and everyday parlance, an imprint of their theories can be also found in philosophy, literature, and aesthetic writings. It is not surprising, therefore, to find terminology related to the concepts of Mesmer, Schubert, and Baader in descriptions of Chopin's performances. Chopin's early biographer Hippolyte Barbedette tells his readers that Chopin was able to give the piano a soul: "It was an unrivalled charm, a sort of magnetism one could not escape."[40] Likewise Louis Enault, when explaining how Chopin's music evoked passions, says that "he established a sort of an invisible magnetism between the soul of his listeners and the sonorous vibrations of the instrument."[41] Barbedette invokes magnetism, perhaps metaphorically, to explain the hypnotic hold that Chopin's performances had on his listeners. But Enault references the interconnected scientific and aesthetic theories more specifically. By linking the physical phenomenon of sound made by Chopin's piano to the soul of his listeners, he draws attention to the core principles of Naturphilosophie, according to which the phenomenal and noumenal realms were organically joined. Magnetism was the means through which this connection could be made real, and artistic creation played a central role in this mystical process.

Chopin Among Philosophers, Artists, and Charlatans

Without a doubt the talk of dreaming—poetic, musical, transcendental, or hypnotic—surrounded Chopin in Warsaw and in Paris. References in newspapers, literature, and personal writings demonstrate that Poland was well acquainted with the mesmerism craze. Animal magnetism was discussed, debated, practiced, satirized; and the terminology related to mesmerist practices entered the common vocabulary. Warsaw musicians offered humorous responses to the fad: in 1820 the National Theater in Warsaw staged a vaudeville by Józef Damse titled *Klarnecik magnetyczny* (Magnetic Clarinet); and in 1829, the same stage hosted a production of *Lunatyczka wiejska* (A Village Sleepwalker) by Walenty Kratzer, Chopin's singing teacher at the Warsaw Conservatory.

Figure 4. Caspar David Friedrich, *Der Traum des Musikers*, 1826–27.

Chopin's letters indicate his own awareness of animal magnetism. In an 1830 letter from Warsaw to Tytus Woyciechowski, he uses the term "magnetize" in jest as a means of supernaturally compelling his unwilling friend into action.[42] In the last summer of his life, the mortally ill Chopin became an unwitting participant in a series of events that unfolded in the manner of a farcical opera when a parcel containing a large sum of money from an unnamed benefactor was delivered to the composer's apartment, and then disappeared. Suspicion fell upon the lady concierge, who swore up and down that she had not laid eyes on the ill-fated bundle. After much ado the clairvoyant (*somnambul*) Alexis was consulted and thankfully was able to intuit the location of the lost parcel using a lock of hair obtained by Chopin from the concierge under a clever pretext. Chopin detailed the entire story in a lengthy letter to his friend Wojciech Grzymała. "Believe now in magnetism," concluded Chopin, though in the subsequent letter, admonished by Grzymała, he retreated to a position of sensible skepticism.[43]

Chopin kept company with major artistic figures who flirted with animal magnetism. His intimates George Sand and Eugène Delacroix attended magnetic séances in 1839–40, when these practices were under intense scrutiny from the Parisian scientific establishment.[44] In fact, the clairvoyant who solved the mystery of the lost parcel was none other than the famed Alexis Didier, whose magnetist *cénacles* included the likes of Alexandre Dumas père, Théophile Gautier, Victor Hugo, the pianist and composer Louis Adam, and Delphine de Girardin, the wife of a powerful press publisher and an accomplished author herself.[45] Chopin frequented Madame de Girardin's famous salon, where aesthetic judgments and artistic reputations were decided. Specifically, in September of 1847, Chopin was invited by Madame de Girardin to attend a séance of "*la somanmbule* who falls into ecstasy under the influence of music."[46] A year or two later David Koreff, an eminent authority on animal magnetism who cured the melancholy of Chopin's friend Marquis Astolphe de Custine, became one of Chopin's physicians.[47] Koreff developed his interest in mesmerism under the influence of the Naturphilosophie of Schelling and Baader. He was also a close friend of E. T. A. Hoffmann, and later of several Parisian luminaries. The preoccupations of Chopin's associates and his physician have a good deal to say about Chopin's cultural milieu, and are suggestive of his familiarity with oneiric themes in literary and philosophical writings.

The Warsaw intelligentsia had been exposed to the views of Frühromantik philosophers early on, before Chopin was born. During the years 1795 to 1807, the portion of partitioned Poland that included the capital city was under Prussian administration, and among the Prussian officials stationed there, three were known as ardent and vocal champions of the new Romantic ideas—Julius Eduard Hitzig (first cousin of Felix and Fanny Mendelssohn's mother), Zacharias Werner, and E. T. A. Hoffmann. Hoffmann was directly involved with Polish musicians and music lovers while organizing the activities of the Harmoniegesellschaft, and among his most enthusiastic colleagues in this endeavor was Józef Elsner, destined to became Chopin's composition teacher a couple of decades later. Shortly after leaving Poland, Hoffmann embarked on the path of music journalism and in 1810 penned his landmark review of Beethoven's Fifth Symphony, widely understood as the paradigmatic exposé of instrumental music's role within transcendental philosophy.[48]

In the meantime, the major Polish cultural centers, in particular Warsaw and Wilno (Vilnius), were ignited by the fires of Romanticism. The most courageous public statements of the new trends came in an 1818 publication, "O klasyczności i romantyczności tudzież o duchu poezji polskiej" (On Classicism and Romanticism as well as the spirit of Polish poetry), of Kazimierz Brodziński, who a decade later became Chopin's literature professor at Warsaw University. After the publication in Wilno of Adam Mickiewicz's Ballady i romanse (1822) and Forefathers' Eve parts II and IV (1823), the debates that until then had remained mostly private exploded into the public sphere. Among the younger generation, the loudest and most eloquent voice publicly explicating and supporting the new trends was that of Chopin's friend Maurycy Mochnacki.

Seven years Chopin's senior, Mochnacki embodied Romantic restlessness. Even as a teenager he engaged in subversive political activities, and his participation in the November Uprising led to his exile in France and premature death at the age of thirty-one. But Mochnacki was also a talented pianist and a gifted writer, who, mostly as literary and musical critic, put his pen in the service of propagating Romantic ideas in Poland. In their Warsaw days, Chopin and Mochnacki traveled in the same circles of young Romantics who met in favorite cafés or the salons of the Mochnackis and the Chopins. It was Mochnacki who extolled Chopin's pianistic talent in published reviews of his friend's Warsaw concerts.

Mochnacki's writings reveal the strong influence of the German Frühromantiker, especially Schelling, though he was clearly also familiar with Kant, the philosopher Johann Gottlieb Fichte, the Schlegel brothers, the writer Jean Paul (born Johann Paul Friedrich Richter), Novalis, and Gotthilf Heinrich von Schubert. The extent of Mochnacki's extraordinary erudition is revealed in the references he makes throughout his writings to a broad range of German, French, and English literary, philosophical, and scientific texts. Mochnacki articulated a Romantic program based on

Frühromantik concepts for the young generation of Polish writers, often using their poetic works as vehicles for his expositions. He embraced core precepts of Schelling's Idealism, specifically Naturphilosophie, and like Schelling, considered aesthetic theory a branch of Idealist philosophy. But he also redirected some of the aesthetic impetus toward specifically Polish manifestations of the Romantic. Unafraid to defend with passion his aesthetic beliefs and the work of artistic friends in public forums, Mochnacki used his writings as a bulwark against the attacks of the conservatives who sought to discredit the new trends.

Not surprisingly, Frühromantik ideas concerning art's relationship to the unconscious, with attendant links to the science of magnetism are crucial to Mochnacki's aesthetic arguments. He even quotes Schelling's formulation of this principle: "It was long ago perceived that, in Art, not everything is performed with consciousness; that, with the conscious activity, an unconscious action must combine; and that it is of the perfect unity and mutual interpenetration of the two that the highest in Art is born."[49] Mochnacki's seminal text *O literaturze polskiej w wieku dziewętnastym* (On Polish Literature in the Nineteenth Century), drafted during the time he associated frequently with Chopin and published just after the onset of the November Uprising, further refines his aesthetic views, while dedicating a remarkable amount of space to explicating Schubert's scientific underpinning of Naturphilosophie, magnetism, and clairvoyance.[50] It is significant, though not entirely unexpected, that a focal essay devoted to Polish Romantic literature emphasizes so strongly the scientific findings related to animal magnetism, since by the time Mochnacki's article was published, the influential Wilno literary circles had received considerable exposure to mesmerism through *Pamiętnik magnetyczny wileński* (The Wilno Magnetic Diary), a journal issued between 1816 and 1819.[51] Thus irrationality and liminality abound in the aesthetic and literary works of Chopin's Polish friends and contemporaries, taking the guise of nocturnal references, dreams, and otherworldly phantasms.

These subjects make their first appearances in literary works written in Poland during the 1820s; after the failure of the November Uprising in 1831, nearly all of the young Romantics found themselves in exile, where they continued to engage with these ideas. We find them in masterpieces by Adam Mickiewicz (for instance in *Forefathers' Eve*, 1823 and 1832), Zygmunt Krasiński (*The Un-Divine Comedy*, 1833), Juliusz Słowacki (*Balladyna*, 1839), and in the poetry of Chopin's friends Stefan Witwicki (*Edmund*, 1829) and Seweryn Goszczyński (*The Castle of Kaniów*, 1828). For Polish writers, as for their German, French, and English counterparts, the liminality of the oneiric realm offered a glimpse of the otherworldly.[52] It would be a mistake, however, to imagine Polish writers solely as passive recipients of aesthetic ideas from abroad. Not only did the Polish Romantics reframe the concepts they received from the West in specifically Polish terms, but in Paris they imparted their version of Romanticism to their French counterparts. Most widely attended by the Parisian literary elites were the lectures (or, as some have called them, performances) of Mickiewicz, the bard of the Polish émigré community. These presentations were dedicated to a broad range of topics, from literature to philosophy, politics, and religion and took place at the College de France between 1840 and 1844. Chopin and Sand—by this point his companion—also attended Mickiewicz's lectures. Moreover, Sand published articles on Mickiewicz's lectures and poetic work, and maintained close social contacts with the Polish poet.[53]

Thus in Paris, as in Warsaw, Chopin mingled with prominent literati in whose writings dreams appeared with astonishing frequency. These circles included Polish poets residing in the French capital, but also the French literary elite: Nodier, Hugo, Balzac, and Lamartine among them. Sand's own novels often contained scenes conspicuously focused on dreams and visions (*Consuelo*, for example). In her fantastic story *Histoire d'un rêveur*, a little-known work from 1830 bearing the stamp of E. T. A. Hoffmann's influence, Sand makes a particular case for music and dreams connecting the real and ideal realms. In her tale, a traveler hikes up Mount Etna in search of the meaning of life. On his journey he encounters a mysterious genderless and ageless being who sings in a beautiful, uncanny voice. Throughout the story the experiences of both characters unfold through dreams, and at the end of the tale, the traveler wakes up, as if the entire episode has been a dream. Within this profusion of hazy dreamlike events, one asks: Who is the dreamer in the title of the story? The protagonist? The mysterious singer? The reader? Music assists the oneiric visions in destabilizing our sense of reality, as Sand's language vividly conveys the auditory experience of the mysterious voice and the sounds of nature. She describes these intertwining sounds as "human voices that mingle with the groaning of the wind in the old oak trees in the forest."[54] As in several of her later narratives, in *Histoire d'un rêveur* Sand calls attention to the link between music and the fantastic, between music and dreaming, between music and the ideal.

Dreaming Through Music

Musical compositions did not lag for long behind the literary arts in incorporating oneiric imagery. Starting around 1800, musical works highlighting dreams and altered states of dreaming captured the public's attention. The topic of sleepwalking became central to numerous musical stage works, beginning in the late 1820s and culminating in 1831 with Bellini's wildly successful *La sonnambula*. Moreover, throughout the 1830s and 1840s numerous instrumental works, such as Berlioz's *Symphonie fantastique* and other symphonic and piano pieces on fantastic themes featured reveries and phantasmagoria.[55] Even in stage works that did not directly focus on such topics, dreaming (or sleepwalking) sequences appeared in key moments.

Operatic works started to feature spectacular dream sequences during the first decade of the century. In 1804, when Jean-François Le Sueur's *Ossian ou les bardes*, based on James Macpherson's epic poem, premiered at the Paris Opéra, audiences were wowed by a fourth-act dream sequence that revolutionized operatic sensibility. In this scene, which has no equivalent in Macpherson's epic, the imprisoned Ossian, behind a scrim, dreams of ancient heroes to the accompaniment of mysterious-sounding choral music.[56] In 1818, perhaps under the influence of Le Sueur's work, Chopin's teacher Józef Elsner included an iconic dream sequence in *Król Łokietek*, his opera about King Władysław the Short, who restored partitioned Poland at the end of the fourteenth century. The opera became well known to and admired by Elsner's famous pupil. In the second act, as one of the opera's main characters falls asleep, he is first subject to ghoulish nightmares, and then experiences a prophetic dream that takes him through the next five centuries of political events in Poland and foretells the heroes who would define them. Elsner's music skillfully underscores the macabre and blissful moments of the dream, marking the prescient appearances of more modern heroes with the patriotic tunes that are associated with them.[57]

Although dream sequences underscoring a specific narrative in stage works would have provided important models for Chopin, his compositions offer moments of purely musical dreams. Allowing instrumental music to express the subjectivity of the dream world was a novel concept: the nocturnal lulling and romancing would have found predecessors in works such as Field's nocturnes, but it was for compositions such as Karol Kurpiński's Fantasia *Chwila snu okropnego* (A Moment of a Frightful Dream), published in 1820, to convey a recollection of a nightmare (see Example 1).[58] By giving prominence to chromatic melodic lines, extremes of register, and loud dynamics in this brief improvisatory, prelude-like piece, the composer captures in a single musical gesture an emotional intensity and subjectivity that are fundamentally Romantic.

The novel usage of music to express the otherworldly went hand in hand with technological innovations in the construction of musical instruments. The recently invented glass harmonica, so readily used by Mesmer in his séances, found its way into musical moments of madness and the uncanny, as in Donizetti's *Lucia di Lammermoor*.[59] Around 1800, the newly developed variants of the Aeolian harp—a string instrument sounded by natural breeze, which had roots in antiquity—became fashionable, first with poets and then with the general public. As a manmade device channeling the sounds of nature, the Aeolian harp served as a metaphor for that unity of human and natural forces defined by Naturphilosophie. One must also consider the variety of timbres that could be achieved through the use and various combinations of the pedals available in early nineteenth-century pianos—damper, *una corda*, moderator, and numerous others. Performers and listeners would have welcomed the piano's ability to produce such otherworldly, hypnotic sounds.[60] Schumann, after hearing Chopin's performance of the first etude from Opus 25, described the dreamlike expressive effect as a layering of sonorities akin to the sound of the Aeolian harp, achieved by Chopin through the undulations of a chord sustained "with the help of the pedal."[61]

Chopin's Dream Worlds

Surrounded by a culture in which dreams and dreaming held such a prominent place, Chopin frequently experienced his waking hours as reveries. His nights, too, were sometimes given to frightening visions. The accounts of his intimates and his own correspondence preserve ample record of such experiences and traces of the composer's thoughts about them. The latter have been gathered and contextualized in a beautifully insightful reading of the composer's mindset as revealed in his letters by the Polish literary scholar Ryszard Przybylski.[62] "At the age of barely twenty," says Przybylski, "Chopin began to depart the world—into dreams."[63] Przybylski quotes instances from Chopin's letters that support his view that for Chopin recollection of the past and visions from dreams acquired equal measure of implausibility. In a letter from 1831, reflecting on mementos from the past, Chopin summed up his feelings: "I have the impression that these recollections are a dream; I give no credence to that which actually occurred."[64] Earlier that year he reported his sense of

Example 1. Karol Kurpiński, Fantasia *Chwila Snu Okropnego* (1820).
Errors in mm. 14 and 23 of the original printed music have been corrected.

Example 1 continued.

alienation from the reality of visiting with friends: "And I laugh, I laugh, but in my soul, just as I write this, some terrible presentiment befalls me. It seems to me a dream, a daze, that I am with you and dreaming what I hear."[65] At times the dreams and phantasms would become particularly terrifying, most famously when Chopin imagined himself a corpse in morbid visions he recorded in September of 1831 on the pages of the so-called Stuttgart Diary.[66] Many years later, in 1848, he wrote from Scotland to Solange Clésinger that he experienced hallucinations while performing the B-flat Minor Sonata, Op. 35, seeing "emerging from the half-closed case of the piano the accursed apparitions"; this might account for the unexpected break in the performance mentioned by a critic in the *Manchester Guardian*.[67] We are told by George Sand that during their ill-fated stay in Mallorca during the winter of 1838/39—the oft-invoked backdrop to the creation of the Preludes, Op. 28—phantasms that appeared in his dreams frightened Chopin out of his wits. "No longer able to distinguish dream from reality, he had calmed himself and played the piano drowsily, persuaded that he had died himself."[68]

In these stories and in his letters, we encounter a Chopin who inhabits the boundary between life and death, between the real and ideal; whose sense of time—past, present, and future—is hazy. The trustworthiness of these accounts is irrelevant; whether they are factual or invented, they tell us plenty—not simply about what Chopin experienced, but about his sense of self: his feelings of alienation, his bifurcated consciousness, his forays into the realm of imagination, or as he called it—the *espaces imaginaires*.[69] They tell us that he comprehended the liminality of the oneiric experience in terms similar to those of Romantic poets and philosophers; and that in the moments when he sensed a blurring of boundaries between reality, dreams, and hallucinations, he often turned to the piano. They also tell us that when Chopin's contemporaries placed him in the liminal realm—as ailing, moribund, or on the edge of madness; when they heard dreams and visions in his music, they were acknowledging him as a seer, a "true" artist capable of channeling the transcendental.

Given the centrality of oneiric realms to Chopin and his Romantic peers, it is only fitting that he sought to convey them in his compositions: through the sense of haziness; the feeling of disjointed flow of time; the impression of shifting between conscious and unconscious states of mind. For Chopin's listeners, these passages awarded the dreamlike experience of the ideal. The last word here belongs to Józef Sikorski, who in his extended eulogy for Chopin, reproduced in its entirety in this volume, eloquently sums up a reaction to encountering this "mysterious world" within Chopin's musical dreams:

> Fantasy in disarray leads us, in unfathomable phrases, as if in a dream from object to object, from thought to thought. And as in a dream we succumb to a force, incomprehensible to us when awake, that, binding that which never is bound, shows the interweaving of all things: thus captivated by Chopin's dream, despite the resistance of our vigilant senses,

we follow him across the depths and the heights; yielding to the magical sway, we comprehend the logic of feelings, we understand the fantasy turned into reality. After the magical notes fade away, we still dream in the same direction, and struggling to break free from the power of the mysterious world to which the poet has subjected us, we ask, upon waking, whether it was a dream or reality?[70]

NOTES

1. The epigraph is from Józef Sikorski, "Przegląd muzyczny," *Tygodnik Ilustrowany* 325 (1865): 253–55, quoted from *Chopin and His Critics: An Anthology*, ed. Irena Poniatowska (Warsaw: Fryderyk Chopin Institute, 2011), 68. Translation by Piotr Szymczak. I am grateful to my gentle old-soul dog Freddie for loving me and taking me for uplifting hikes during the arduous time of writing this essay and editing the book.

2. Among modern writings that explore the oneiric quality of Chopin's compositions, the most notable are Michael Klein, "Chopin Dreams: The Mazurka in C♯ Minor, Op. 30, No. 4," *19th-Century Music* 35/3 (Spring 2012): 238–60; Charles Rosen, *The Romantic Generation* (Cambridge, MA: Harvard University Press, 1995), 338–42; and James Parakilas, "Disrupting the Genre: Unforeseen Personifications in Chopin," *19th-Century Music* 35/3 (Spring 2012): 165–81.

3. F. Antoni Woykowski, "Chopin," *Przyjaciel Ludu*, nos. 28–30, 1836, quoted from Poniatowska, *Chopin and His Critics*, 52. Translation by Piotr Szymczak, amended by me.

4. Gottfried Wilhelm Fink, "Rezension der 2 Nocturnes op. 27," *Allgemeine musikalische Zeitung* 38, 1836, quoted from Poniatowska, *Chopin and His Critics*, 264–65. Unless otherwise indicated, translations are mine. I am grateful to Kristina Muxfeldt for her help with Fink's challenging German.

5. Woykowski, "Chopin," quoted from Poniatowska, *Chopin and His Critics*, 50. Translation by Piotr Szymczak, amended by me.

6. Anonymous review, *Revue et gazette musicale de Paris* 16, 1842, quoted from Poniatowska, *Chopin and His Critics*, 355.

7. Robert Schumann, review of Opus 25 in *Neue Zeitschrift für Musik* 50 (1937): 199–200, quoted in Jean-Jacques Eigeldinger, *Chopin: Pianist and Teacher, As Seen by His Pupils*, ed. Roy Howat, trans. Naomi Shohet, Krysia Osostowicz, and Roy Howat (Cambridge: Cambridge University Press, 1986), 69.

8. Aleksander Jełowicki, *Moje wspomnienia*, 1839, quoted from Poniatowska, *Chopin and His Critics*, 54. Translation by Piotr Szymczak. In his *F. Chopin* (1852), Liszt also references the topos of dream in Chopin's music.

9. Halina Goldberg, "Nationalizing the *Kujawiak* and Constructions of Nostalgia in Chopin's Mazurkas," *19th-Century Music* 39/3 (Spring 2016): 223–47.

10. Gottfried Wilhelm Fink, "Rezension der *Sonate b-Moll* op. 35, des *Impromptu Fis-Dur* op. 36 und der 2 *Nocturnes* op. 37," *Allgemeine musikalische Zeitung* 42 (1840), quoted from Poniatowska, *Chopin and His Critics*, 282.

11. Anna Rudzińska, "Teofila Kwiatkowskiego *Polonez: Rêve de Frédéric Chopin pianiste*," in *Epoka Chopina: Kultura romantyczna we Francji i w Polsce*, ed. Andrzej Pieńkos and Agnieszka Rosales Rodriguez (Warsaw: Wydawnictwo Neriton, 2013), 137–38. Rudzińska makes a strong case for the relationship between the specters dancing the polonaise in Kwiatkowski's *Polonaise* and Julian Niemcewicz's *Historical Chants* which are known to

have inspired Chopin's improvisations. But given the allegorical dreamlike atmosphere of the painting, a comparison to Józef Elsner's dream sequence in *Król Łokietek* is inescapable. Kwiatkowski left multiple versions of this painting (dated over several years); my references are to the one at the National Museum in Poznań, reproduced here.

12. Also see Goldberg, "Nationalizing the *Kujawiak*," 237–38.

13. Rudzińska, "Teofila Kwiatkowskiego *Polonez*," 137–38.

14. In fact, in another version of this painting, now at the National Museum in Warsaw, Kwiatkowski places the polonaise dancers in an elegant, aristocratic ballroom.

15. Daniel L. Schacter, *Searching for Memory: The Brain, the Mind, and the Past* (New York: Basic Books, 1996), 76–79.

16. Ibid., 26–28.

17. Goldberg, "Nationalizing the *Kujawiak*," 236–43.

18. Although there are no instances of *una corda* notation in Chopin's manuscripts or published scores, witnesses provide ample testimony of his use of the left pedal. See Eigeldinger, *Chopin: Pianist and Teacher,* 130n122.

19. Goldberg, "Nationalizing the *Kujawiak*," 243.

20. For a discussion of the *ombra* and *tempesta* topics, see Clive McClelland, "Ombra and Tempesta," *The Oxford Handbook of Topic Theory* (Oxford and New York: Oxford University Press, 2014).

21. Jan Kleczyński, "Fryderyk Chopin," *Tygodnik Ilustrowany*, new series 106:13–14, 107:32–34, 108:42–43 (1870), quoted from Poniatowska, *Chopin and His Critics*, 74. Translation by Piotr Szymczak, amended by me.

22. The first Polish "complete edition" of Chopin's works (Gebethner i Wolff, 1863–67) was organized chronologically in six volumes, and volume 5, which was reviewed by Sikorski in the article quoted here, contained Opp. 46–58.

23. Józef Sikorski, "Przegląd muzyczny," *Tygodnik Ilustrowany* 325 (1865): 253–55, quoted from Poniatowska, *Chopin and His Critics*, 68. Translation by Piotr Szymczak.

24. Parakilas, "Disrupting the Genre," 176.

25. Ibid., 169. The composer obviously started exploring the idea of moving between reality and dream early on, as the term *risvegliato* appears in the manuscript and early editions of the Mazurka in E Major, Op. 6, No. 3, and in the last movement of the F-Minor Concerto, Op. 21.

26. Of the vast literature on this topic, two books stand out: Jennifer Ford, *Coleridge on Dreaming* (Cambridge: Cambridge University Press, 1998); and Douglas B. Wilson, *The Romantic Dream: Wordsworth and the Poetic of the Unconscious* (Lincoln: University of Nebraska Press, 1993).

27. A fairly comprehensive list of Hoffmann's works related to dreaming is found in Diana Stone Peters, "The Dream as Bridge in the Works of E. T. A. Hoffmann," *Oxford German Studies* 8 (1973): 60–85.

28. Matthew Gibson, *The Fantastic and European Gothic: History, Literature, and the French Revolution* (Cardiff: University of Wales Press, 2013), 2–4. Nodier's essays have been gathered and published as *De quelques phénomènes du sommeil* (Bègles, Fr.: Le Castor Astral, 1996).

29. Quoted in Tony James, *Dreams, Creativity, and Madness in Nineteenth-Century France* (Oxford: Oxford University Press, 1996), 51.

30. Ibid., 9.

31. This interpretation of German Idealism is based on Frederick C. Beiser, "The Enlightenment and Idealism," in *The Cambridge Companion to German Idealism*, ed. Karl Ameriks (Cambridge: Cambridge University Press, 2000), 18–36; and Beiser, *The Romantic Imperative: The Concept of Early German Romanticism* (Cambridge, MA, and London: Harvard University Press, 2003).

32. Beiser, *The Romantic Imperative*, 73.

33. Ibid., 76.

34. Ibid., 77.

35. Glyn Tegai Hughes, *Romantic German Literature* (New York: Holmes and Meier, 1979), 16.

36. Ibid., 32–33.

37. Ibid., 71–78.

38. Laurie Johnson, "The Romantic and Modern Practice of Animal Magnetism: Friedrich Schlegel's Protocols of the Magnetic Treatment of Countess Lesniowska," *Women in German Yearbook* 23 (2007): 10–33; Frederick Burwick, "Coleridge, Schlegel and Animal Magnetism," in *English and German Romanticism: Cross-Currents and Controversies*, ed. James Pipkin (Heidelberg: Carl Winter Verlag, 1985), 275–300.

39. Gwendolyn Bays, *The Orphic Vision: Seer Poets from Novalis to Rimbaud* (Lincoln: University of Nebraska Press, 1964), 53–58. In describing the Romantics' view of the aesthetic experience, Frederick Beiser prefers the term hyperrational to irrational (*The Romantic Imperative*, 61).

40. Hippolyte Barbedette, *Chopin: Essai de critique musicale* (Paris: Leiber, 1861), quoted from Poniatowska, *Chopin and His Critics*, 365.

41. Louis Enault, "Frédéric Chopin," *Le Papillon*, 10 March 1861, 103, quoted from Poniatowska, *Chopin and His Critics*, 382.

42. Chopin to Tytus Woyciechowski, Saturday, supposedly 4 September 1830, in *Chopin's Polish Letters*, trans. David Frick (Warsaw: Fryderyk Chopin Institute, 2016), 174. The erotic overtones of the passage in which this comment appears require separate commentary and cannot be addressed here.

43. Chopin to Wojciech Grzymała, 28 July 1849 and 3 August 1849, in *Chopin's Polish Letters*, 488–90 and 491–92.

44. Françoise Alexandre, ed., *Sand Delacroix Correspondance: Le rendez-vous manqué* (Paris: Les Editions de l'Amateur, 2005), 229–30.

45. Bays, *The Orphic Vision*, 111.

46. Camille de Courbonne to Chopin, 21 September 1847, quoted in Marie-Paule Rambeau, "Chopin et le salon du marquis de Custine," in *Chopin's Musical Worlds: The 1840s*, eds. Magdalena Chylińska, John Comber, and Artur Szklener (Warsaw: Narodowy Instytut Fryderyka Chopina, 2008), 67.

47. Chopin mentions Koreff in his letter to Grzymała, 18 June 1849, in *Chopin's Polish Letters*, 480.

48. The relationship between instrumental music and philosophy has been given in-depth discussions in Mark Evan Bonds, *Music as Thought: Listening to the Symphony in the Age of Beethoven* (Princeton: Princeton University Press, 2006); and briefly addressed in Tomas McAuley, "The Impact of German Idealism on Musical Thought, 1781–1803" (PhD diss., King's College London, 2013), 16–17.

49. From Mochnacki's essay "Myśli o literaturze polskiej" (Thoughts on Polish Literature) first published in *Gazeta Polska* in 1828. Modern edition is Maurycy Mochnacki, *Rozprawy literackie* (Wrocław: Zakład Narodowy im. Ossolińskich, 2000), 123. English translation from Friedrich Wilhelm Joseph von Schelling, "On the Relation of the Plastic Arts to Nature," *The German Classics*, 20 vols., trans. J. Elliot Cabot (New York: German Publication Society, 1913), 5:112.

50. Mochnacki, *O literaturze polskiej w wieku dziewiętnastym* (On Polish Literature in the Nineteenth Century), vol. 1 (Warsaw: Józef Węcki, 1830). The passage directly referencing Schubert and the famous case of Fredrike Hauffe, a clairvoyant and somnambulist, can be found Mochnacki, *Rozprawy literackie*, 186–97.

51. Alina Kowalczykowa, "Romantyczne zaświaty," *Problemy Polskiego Romantyzmu*, ed. Maria Żmigrodzka (Wrocław: Zakład Narodowy im. Ossolińskich, 1974), 240.

52. Polish literary scholars have spilled much ink describing the centrality of these phenomena. See in particular Kowalczykowa, "Romantyczne zaświaty"; Halina Krukowska, *Noc Romantyczna (Mickiewicz, Malczewski, Goszczyński): Interpretacje* (Białystok: Dział Wydawnictw Filii UW w Białymstoku, 1985); Maria Piasecka, *Mistrzowie Snu: Mickiewicz, Słowacki, Krasiński* (Wrocław: Zakład Narodowy im. Ossolińskich, 1992); and Maria Janion, *Projekt krytyki fantazmatycznej: Szkice o egzystencjach ludzi i duchów* (Warsaw: PEN, 1991).

53. Zygmunt Markiewicz, "Mickiewicz i George Sand: Dzieje przyjaźni i jej odbicie w literaturze," *Pamiętnik Literacki* 52/3 (1961): 51–76.

54. David A. Powell, *While the Music Lasts: The Representation of Music in the Works of George Sand* (Cranbury, NJ: Rosemont Publishing, 2001), 190–205. Quote from Sand's *Histoire d'un rêveur* is found on page 196. The source used by Powell: "Histoire d'un rêveur," ed. by Thierry Bodin, *Présence de George Sand* 17 (June 1983): 9–39.

55. For discussion of these works and their cultural context see Francesca Brittan, "Berlioz, Hoffmann, and the Genre Fantastique in French Romanticism" (PhD diss., Cornell University, 2007).

56. Jean Mongrédien, "*Ossian, ou Les bardes,*" *The New Grove Dictionary of Opera*, Oxford Music Online, http://www.oxfordmusiconline.com.proxyiub.uits.iu.edu/subscriber/article/grove/music/O004454, and James H. Johnson, *Listening in Paris: A Cultural History* (Berkeley, Los Angeles, London: University of California Press, 1995), 176.

57. This compositional strategy is described by Karol Kurpiński in his essay "On the Historical Songs of the Polish People." Kurpiński also singles out Elsner's dream sequence as a prime example of this practice in "On Musical Expression and Mimesis." Both essays are included in this volume. The subject is also discussed in depth in Halina Goldberg, "Descriptive Instrumental Music in Nineteenth–Century Poland: Context, Genre and Performance," *Journal of Musicological Research* 34/3 (Summer 2015): 224–48.

58. The descriptive title under which Kurpiński's Fantasia was published, given some four years after it was first composed, indubitably stems from the composer. On the piece's history, see Halina Goldberg, *Music in Chopin's Warsaw* (New York: Oxford University Press, 2008), 89n48.

59. Philip Gossett, *Divas and Scholars: Performing Italian Opera* (Chicago: University of Chicago Press, 2006), 434–35.

60. Something of this sort has been suggested in relation to Haydn's keyboard music by Tom Beghin. See his *The Virtual Haydn: Paradox of a Twenty-First-Century Keyboardist* (Chicago: University of Chicago Press, 2015), 199–201.

61. Robert Schumann, review of Opus 25 in *Neue Zeitschrift für Musik* 50 (1937): 199–200, quoted in Eigeldinger, *Chopin: Pianist and Teacher,* 69.

62. Ryszard Przybylski, *A Swallow's Shadow: An Essay on Chopin's Thoughts,* trans. John Comber (Warsaw: Fryderyk Chopin Institute, 2011); first Polish edition 1995.

63. Ibid., 203.

64. Chopin to Alfons Kumelski, 18 November 1831, quoted in Przybylski, *A Swallow's Shadow,* 204.

65. Chopin to Jan Matuszyński, New Year's Day 1831, quoted in Przybylski, *A Swallow's Shadow,* 205.

66. Chopin to Solange Clésinger, 9 September 1848, in *Chopin's Polish Letters,* 231–33.

67. Quoted in Przybylski, *A Swallow's Shadow,* 220.

68. George Sand, *Story of My Life,* quoted in Przybylski, *A Swallow's Shadow,* 206.

69. This expression is used by Chopin in the oft-quoted passage from a letter to his family, 18–20 July 1845, in which he contemplates the spatial disunity of his consciousness. *Chopin's Polish Letters,* 369.

70. Quotation taken from the final part of the fifth section of Sikorski's essay, included immediately below.

Józef Sikorski's "Recollection of Chopin": The Earliest Essay on Chopin and His Music

TRANSLATED BY JOHN COMBER
INTRODUCED AND ANNOTATED BY HALINA GOLDBERG

"Recollection of Chopin" by Józef Sikorski is the earliest extended essay on the composer's life and works.[1] The author's emotional language captures the immediacy and poignancy of the response to the news of Chopin's death in the composer's Warsaw circles. A close reading, however, also reveals striking similarities between Sikorski's effusive prose and the overlapping metaphoric vocabularies of German Idealism and Polish political messianism: the figurative language is deployed to locate Chopin and his artistic achievement within these two philosophical frameworks. Moreover, Sikorski was among the first critics to offer perceptive analytical observations on Chopin's compositional strategies and his innovative musical language.

Penned during the first weeks following Chopin's death, the essay appeared in the December 1849 issue of *Biblioteka Warszawska* (The Warsaw Library), a periodical "dedicated to scholarship, the arts, and industry." The reports of the composer's death in his Paris home, on 17 October 1849, reached Warsaw within days and caused a great stir among people close to Chopin and his family: "Chopin passed away!—The news, like a watchword of grief, today makes the rounds of our city by word of mouth," wrote the pioneering ethnographer Oskar Kolberg, whose brother Wilhelm was a close friend of Chopin, in an obituary that appeared in the same issue of *Bibioteka Warszawska* as Sikorski's essay.[2] In fact, many contributors to *Biblioteka Warszawska* (established in 1841) had known Chopin during his Warsaw years. Among them were Kazimierz Wójcicki, a historian and acquaintance of Chopin who served two non-consecutive terms as the journal's editor-in-chief; the university professor Feliks Bentkowski, whose history lectures Chopin had attended in his university years; and Fryderyk Skarbek, the godfather of the composer, also a professor, and a onetime pupil of Mikołaj Chopin. Indeed, Chopin was born at the Skarbek estate in Żelazowa Wola.[3]

• 45 •

The author of the article, Józef Sikorski (1813–1896) is remembered today mainly as the originator of professional musical criticism in Poland and the founder, in 1857, of the periodical *Ruch muzyczny* (The Musical Movement). Three years Chopin's junior, Sikorski followed the same educational path as the composer, from Warsaw Lyceum to the Warsaw Conservatory, though the impecunious Sikorski did not interact with or travel in the same circles as Chopin. The expert eye of Chopin's composition teacher Józef Elsner immediately spotted the musical potential in Sikorski: he mentored the young man through the Conservatory program and taught him composition free of charge. Sikorski's participation in the failed November Uprising derailed his professional plans, however, making it prudent for him to lie low in the countryside for a few years. After returning to Warsaw he became a successful piano teacher. His journalistic career was launched in 1843, when he was invited to contribute an article to *Biblioteka Warszawska*. This and other early articles, which astounded the journal's editors and the public, launched a remarkable writing career that stretched over half a century. In a cultural environment in which music and musical performances were viewed as entertainment, Sikorski assumed the responsibility of elevating music to the rank of high art and teaching the public how to become attentive listeners with refined tastes.[4]

The educated and informed readership of *Biblioteka Warszawska* represented the small segment of Polish society that at the time of Chopin's death would have had some familiarity with his music. But Sikorski felt that even they needed to be taught what was exceptional about Chopin's genius, and what made his published compositions stand apart from the hundreds of lesser piano publications that would have been familiar to them.

The essay is divided into seven sections. Section I serves as an introduction and sings praises of Chopin's genius. In Section II, Sikorski provides the most extensive biography of the composer to date, emphasizing his Warsaw years. This information is particularly valuable since the author had access to the family and friends of the composer. The most illuminating parts of Section III place Chopin's pianism within the history of nineteenth-century piano virtuosity and contextualize contemporary music within the post-Napoleonic era's events and trends that include the awakening of national feeling. In Section IV, the author develops a rationale for including Chopin in the pantheon of great composers, as the heir to Beethoven. The ensuing sections offer analytical comments on Chopin's works: Section V focuses on the diverse genres in which he composed, and Section VI on the individual characteristics of his style. Section VII returns to Chopin's pianism. Section VIII serves as a conclusion, comparing Chopin's music to an important early Romantic poetic novel, *Maria*, by Antoni Malczewski.

Although Sikorski does take up the question of national character in Chopin's music, he is far from claiming his compositions exclusively for Poland. Nor does he see the Polish attributes of Chopin's pieces as being of utmost interest. If at first glance it seems that he dedicates an inordinate amount of space to explaining Chopin's music in singularly hagiographic terms, upon closer reading we recognize the language of his ornate descriptions as strikingly similar to that employed by E. T. A. Hoffmann in his celebrated 1810 review of Beethoven's Fifth Symphony. For example, Sikorski's claim that Chopin's performances invoked "spirits inhabiting the unfathomable world" resonates with Hoffman's oft-quoted depiction of Beethoven drawing the listener into a "wondrous spirit-realm of the infinite."[5] Indeed, it becomes apparent that the exceptionally well-read Sikorski deliberately references Hoffmann's famous review and the writings of Friedrich Schelling and others from his circle. Sikorski's aim is to define Chopin in accordance with Idealist concepts as an ideal Romantic composer through whom the transcendental is expressed, and whose music awards listeners with a foretaste of "the world of mystery."[6] This prophetic role overlapped with the function assigned to selected artists (*wieszcz*) by the proponents of Polish political messianism, a doctrine according to which the crucified Poland would be resurrected, its sacrifice having brought about universal salvation.[7] Contemporaries assigned Chopin this role as early as 1841; understood in these terms, rather than merely religious or panegyrical ones, Sikorski's descriptions afford a portrait of Chopin as a quintessentially Romantic and Polish master composer.

The image of Chopin and his music that Sikorski sketches was later eclipsed by that offered by Franz Liszt (and his unacknowledged co-author, Princess Carolyne zu Sayn-Wittgenstein) in the feuilleton series titled *F. Chopin*, which first appeared in 1851 in *La France musicale*. Sikorski's article was neither translated nor disseminated abroad and was mostly forgotten, even in Poland; Liszt's feuilleton, on the other hand, was later slightly expanded and published as a book. And whatever *F. Chopin* lacked in biographical information and analytical observations was more than made up for by belleletristic literary effusions and elements of travelogue. These stylistic embellishments and the international fame of its author guaranteed its popularity with readers.[8] Subsequently, *F. Chopin* was translated into many languages, including Polish.

Some of the information from Sikorski's "Recollection of Chopin" was indeed absorbed into the writings of Chopin's later Polish biographers Marceli Antoni Szulc (1873) and Maurycy Karasowski (1878), and from their books into biographies and studies of writers who followed. But these subsequent borrowings reflected the historical and aesthetic preoccupations of these later authors: on the one hand, the ethnic (even racial) and folkloric Polishness that sprung up in the aftermath of the tragic January Uprising of 1863–64, and on the other, the shift in the vocabulary of musical criticism away from the metaphoric language of Idealist aesthetics.[9] In the process, Sikorski's insightful analytical observations and his highly metaphoric discussions of aesthetics, which sounded foreign to more modern ears and in any event would probably have been dismissed as old-fashioned *Schwärmerei* (excessive sentiment), were lost. Later tastes notwithstanding, Sikorski's essay is really the only critical discussion of Chopin and his music with deep roots in his own lifetime, his own country, his own musical circles, and in contemporary aesthetic contexts. The translation here is the first complete publication of this crucially important essay in English.[10]

Recollection of Chopin
Józef Sikorski

[Note: Arabic superscripts refer to editorial glosses in the endnotes; lower-case roman numerals indicate footnotes in Sikorski's original.]

> Let my song of Aldona's fate
> Be sung by the angel of music on high,
> And by the tender listener in his soul.
>
> —*Konrad Wallenrod*

I.

So henceforth only recollection! . . .[11] No one had the compassion to cancel the wretched news that has long since loomed over us! It was thought once before that he had died; perhaps now too he had simply fallen asleep! . . . Ah! No doubt it is an endless sleep, when so much grief cannot break it! Yet happy the man who thus falls aslumber, who, before dying, has freed his spirit from its bodily chains, who, like Chopin, has long since inhabited an unearthly land, visiting us only from time to time, like a traveler from distant lands, to bring us news therefrom, to console us in our woes and augur a better future. Oh, that future—of which death is the beginning and eternity the limit; which man, out of a sense of grandeur or a need to believe in divine compassion, has called immortality—is revealed to us by the geniuses, like prophets inspired. Without their help, barely would we be able to stir beneath the crushing yoke of mortality that weighs us down; to not be a mollusk oblivious to the precious pearl enclosed within its shell. When prophets die, how will humanity keep from weeping? In any case, we have always too few of them! It is fortunate that their inspired voices have unsuppressed strength; they will not be lost in limitless space, for having touched the heavens in their flight, with the heavens' blessing they flow down into our hearts; our noblest sentiments greet them with an echo and will continue to augment the inspired voices' might until the time comes when all will be drowned in a single sound. And that which we only dream sometimes when we heal our wounds with the balm of religion, seek to shield in philosophy against the missiles of adversity, or shelter from pain beneath the solicitous wings of art will become real and everlasting. In [religion, philosophy and art] we find salvation, consolation, sympathy. So happy is the one who has gained the friendship and protection of one of these Three Sisters; so great is the one who has been made the steward of the boons of one of them: all the greater in that under her sign he distributes the treasures of the other two as well. Their source is one, as is their purpose; from them, man draws the conviction that he is made in the image and likeness of God. That is what faith, reason, and feelings teach him, and he seeks happiness elsewhere in vain. So the one through whom humanity receives them from the repository of grace is called a genius; and sooner or later, once he has been acknowledged, tears are shed for his loss, as for a guide who carried forth the torch of salvation in the darkness of life; as for a prophet who showed tormented souls the expanse of immortality that would soon receive them. Blessed the generation from whose midst he emerged; blessed too the land that rocked him with its songs, fed him with its bread and sent him to mankind—another gift added to so many others! Rich are the lands along the Vistula where they have such harvests; rich is the life of the nation when its prophets lead the emissaries of other nations in the great science of the great future. And it is the finest of riches! All can use it; and it will replenish itself even as it is used, like the wine in Cana; it will multiply miraculously, like those five loaves of bread in the wilderness. Since the times of Piast,[12] it is not the first miracle in the rich history of Poland, and God grant that it not be the last! . . .

And lo! today the world is weeping its heart out for our fallen prophet. Chopin experienced what befalls few men of genius: he was acknowledged during his lifetime. Let no one claim that it attests to his inferiority compared with those misprized by their peers, understood solely by relentless posterity; let no one wrong the unfortunate geniuses who went before Chopin when granting him superiority, a power that prevailed over the meager rivalry of his contemporaries. Instead, among its many virtues, our epoch should also be granted the ability to appreciate geniuses in the artistic profession; such is the progress it has already made in its inner life that it grasps the nobility of feelings and understands the meaning of the words of the divine lawgiver: "My kingdom is not of this world." Apparently Chopin came at a propitious time for himself and for his art, since he was universally acknowledged; apparently he found music already sufficiently advanced that he could, with its help, speak of wonders to the people, and apparently thanks to him it expanded so copiously, since he became unrivaled, although so many imitate him. He is our pride and a cause for tears all the more abundant in that he took from the heart of our nation all that he dazzled with; in that he spent half his lifetime among us, the half in which grows everything that bears fruit in the future; and that in that fruit we recognize the harvest of our own land. Yet he is not ours alone, for a genius is the property of the whole world, and whatever nationality he is, people of all nations can see themselves in him as in a mirror; that is why all hearts today are mourning Chopin. For humanity, the death of a man like him is too great an occurrence not to resonate powerfully among the greatest events. Thus today many voices are speaking about the artist and the man, as if the great chorus of universal admiration had not dared to awaken until after the mortal frame of the idol of hearts had crumbled:

For the finished bell shall rise,
When the form in pieces lies.[i]

---

i. Schiller in the Bell, translation by the late J[ózef] D[ionizy] Minasowicz. [The Song of the Bell, trans. Margarete Münsterberg, in Münsterberg, ed., *A Harvest of German Verse* (New York: 1916). Ed.]

Setting down a few words here to the eternal memory of our great compatriot, we sense the enormous difficulty of the undertaking. That difficulty lies in the nation's love, in the greatness of the man, and in the impossibility of explaining in ordinary language the divine speech with which Chopin moved our hearts.

Too great for us Poles is the loss that we have lately suffered with his death, and we as people are touched too strongly by what he was for us to be able to defend ourselves easily against the impact of the dual love for things national and for art. We should beware that the tears we shed for him into the general fount not veil our questioning gaze. So are we to become our own tormentors? Tear out our hearts so that they might not remind us what they have so often felt? Leave to the mind's cool reason the assessment of that greatness created with the heart, raised for the heart and best comprehended with the heart? Indeed not! . . . Let us expose ourselves to the accusation of an excessive attachment to everything that belongs to Chopin, since it is ours as well, rather than rid ourselves of such a valiant guide as the heart, so as to at least explain, if not appraise, the heart fed by our emotions and watered by our tears. Our great poet counsels us:

"Have heart and look to your heart" ("Romanticism").[13]

Chopin, as a great example for current and future music, constituting an epoch in the history of that art in Poland and in Europe, is all the more difficult to assess during a period that itself does not yet belong to history, since it has not yet been covered by a new stratum of history. Historical greatness can only be accurately represented when seen within the broad framework of history. On the other hand, where might we find the grounds for judging current times, if today, in the field of aesthetics, old assumptions have withered and we do not know whether new ones will ripen; if new ideas even undermine one another? And how can we speak about a man who expands aesthetics and advances history without considering those two foundations? So we must rely on our shared conceptions, which are too broad for a new criterion not to find for itself a thread linking it to older ones; as for history, we must rely on what we already know, and only with our reasoning and presentiment reach into the future, occasionally illuminated by the lightning bolts which the present, moving into it, sends for reconnaissance; we sense in advance the inaccuracy of the picture that might have been drawn today. Instead, we will merely evoke a few features, having recourse to sentiment, prepared to submit to it entirely if it undertakes to enlighten the mind.

May that same sentiment and inner conviction, long since affirmed by research, give us strength to at least hint at the magic of musical language! . . .

II.

Fryderyk Franciszek Chopin was born on 1 March 1809 in Żelazowa Wola, a hamlet some two miles from Sochaczew, and around six from Warsaw.[14] Men of genius are usually ascribed, while virtually still in their infancy, an attraction to that which with time will make them stand out. Nothing of the sort can be said about Chopin; perhaps only that the delicate and sickly child showed, with his tears, a remarkable sensitivity to musical sounds. That impression, too strong for his nerves, quickly noticed by his parents, was doubtless not painful, and soon he began to evince such a distinct attraction to the piano that in his seventh year the child was given a teacher; on account of his tender age, his elder sister shared an hour's tuition with him. Żywny (†1840)[15]—a native Czech who had moved to Poland during the times of King Stanislaus Augustus—was the first and only guide of the musical aptitude developing so quickly in Chopin, and soon, at his young pupil's request, he was writing down Chopin's ideas. Sometimes the child would subsequently alter them, as if seeking the best means of conveying his ideas; that augured the meticulousness with which the future great artist would finish his works. In his ninth year, he had made such progress that he played a concerto by Gyrowetz in public, in a concert for the poor. The press of the day, the *Gazeta Warszawska* and *Korrespondent*, carries mentions of that first performance under the date 24 February 1818. Also dating from that time is a march arranged by him for piano, published in Warsaw, but with the composer's name not given. Thereafter a musical personality numbered among the ranks of the child prodigies, he was a frequent guest in the illustrious homes of Warsaw, namely those of the Duchess of Łowicz, the Princes Czartoryski, Sapieha, Lubecki, and Zajączek, the family of Count Skarbek, Wolicki, Okołow,[16] and many others. There, he became accustomed at an early age to the luxury that later surrounded him in Paris. He displayed aptitudes in other disciplines almost on a par with his musical gifts: enrolled in the fourth year at the Warsaw Lyceum, where his father taught French, he could boast of two public awards in recognition of his avid work and impeccable conduct (in the years 1824 and 1825). He continued his musical work with irrepressible zeal; even when weak and confined to bed, he would caress the piano, which was moved to his bedside. His sole guide, his enthusiasm, led him so ably that in his sixteenth year he again performed in public. In the *Kuryer Warszawski* of 27 May and 10 June 1825, we find a mention of Chopin performing in amateur concerts given at the former music conservatory. The eagerness with which he worked to overcome the mechanical difficulties of the piano may be gauged from the accounts of witnesses to his practicing. Struck by the beauty of a chord with an upper tenth (a tenth, an interval two notes wider than an octave), yet prevented by the slenderness of his hand from reaching and striking it, he sought a way of achieving the desired span for his hand, and to that end would place objects between his fingers that pushed them out, like wedges; and he would spend nights with that apparatus in place. He did this not for vainglory at the span of his hands; he subjected his fingers to voluntary torture not in order to surpass others in the execution of new difficulties for pianists; he was led to it by the difference in beauty he had observed between the sound of chords in closed and open positions, which he made common in his compositions. The musical world, which probably long before had assessed these chords, now, inspired by Chopin's example, regarded them as practicable; today, they are by no means considered at odds with the nature of the hand. This pursuit of wide-spanning chords clearly manifests the refinement of Chopin's musical sense; to a greater extent than was assumed they represent the boundlessness of the spirit encompassing space, penetrating infinity: all these are characteristics of the works of Chopin. More on this in the appropriate place.

His musical fame grew with each day that passed, because he worked on it every day. To have Chopin in one's home, to hear him playing, was one of the greatest delights that Warsaw had to offer at that time; and Brunner and Hoffmann, inventors of the aeolomelodicon (see *Biblioteka Warszawska*, 1848, vol. 2, page 367), in order to raise its worth in the eyes of Emperor Alexander, entrusted its presentation to Chopin.[17] Yet neither a diamond ring received from the monarch nor universal adoration could halt him in his work, which just shows his great modesty and his need to conquer a world that was hitherto accessible to no one. By then, his work as a composer was also wresting him away from purely mechanical work; besides a Rondo dedicated to Mrs. Linde[18] (Op. 1) and the *Rondo à la mazur* (Op. 5), published by Brzezina of Warsaw, he wrote virtually everything he performed both in his farewell concerts in Poland and in his first concerts in Vienna, Munich, and Paris. Those works were now occupying him entirely, and to those urging him to rest, he replied that he could not break off that which would determine his future. Among his close friends and music lovers, he also found a considerable number of inspiring figures, among whom we will mention here just Tytus Woyciechowski,[19] since Chopin remembers him as his best friend in his last letter to his family. All the finest professional musicians in Warsaw featured in Chopin's life; among the many we will mention here the pianist Aleksander Rembieliński,who died in 1826,[20] and Fontana,[21] now living in New York, as well as former teachers at the music conservatory in Warsaw: Ernemann, Czapek, and Jawurek, an elderly gentleman of worthy memory who was a frequent guest in the home of Chopin's parents.[22] In a sense, the counsel and examples of some and the rivalry of others had to compensate for the lack of a constant guide in his work at the instrument. He was taught composition by Józef Elsner, the teacher of virtually all those who sustain Polish music today. Although a genius is his own best teacher, Chopin first had to be a pupil in order to reach the point where the efforts of our predecessors have led us, so that from there he could lead the world forward and become himself a teacher. Hence we regard it as fortunate for the pupil and a credit to the master that the works and teachings of past centuries, summarized in a system via Elsner as the mediator, were assimilated by Chopin. To be a pupil of Elsner was to be sure that one would not overlook anything that formed the core of the discipline; to be the teacher of Chopin is to have a claim on historical memory almost on a par with Elsner's other claims to be inscribed in history by posterity.

Gathering together everything that might be regarded as having influenced the formation of this young man, who progressed virtually unaided, we also cannot forget his journeys beyond the Polish borders. The first, taken in 1826 to the waters in Reinertz, Silesia, cannot be counted, since it was made solely in order to bolster the health of the young man, weak by birth and further enfeebled by his work. On his trips to Berlin in 1828 and to Vienna and Prague in 1829, Chopin appears to have been on a par with the best and to have been superior to many, though no one knew about it, since he did not perform anywhere in public and there was no opportunity to compare. His musical individuality was already half-matured, and the models that he might have encountered here and there could teach him little. He had already long since assimilated what he found in them to his advantage, and in many things he followed his own path. The trip to Berlin was most memorable in that, on stopping in Poznań, Chopin acquired one more admirer in the person of the late Prince Antoni Radziwiłł (the composer of music to Goethe's *Faust* and an excellent cellist), and when staying a while on Radziwiłł's Antonin estate, he worked on the Trio (Op. 8) which he subsequently dedicated to the prince.

And so in our account of Chopin's life we have arrived at the threshold of the era in which he began to live publicly, so to speak, with the farewell concerts given in Warsaw in 1830. He performed as a virtuoso and a composer unique of his kind; both those attributes were acknowledged in him already by Warsaw before foreign voices hailed his greatness, as if in defiance of the opinion—alas all too true—that we only appreciate what others have acclaimed. From the *Kuryer Warszawski* of 16 March 1830, the eve of his concert, we learn that interest in hearing Chopin was so great that there were not enough loges for the admirers who applied. There were 880 people at that concert, "which proves that our public was wont to reward true talent. The young virtuoso pleased those in attendance; it was opined that he belonged among the foremost masters," etc. In the second concert, about which the same *Kuryer* writes on 23 March, the audience was 900 strong. "The virtuoso was greeted with tumultuous applause, which was continuously renewed; particularly after the performance of the *Rondo à la krakowiak*." This report goes on to mention Chopin's improvisation on familiar songs: "Świat srogi, świat przewrotny" and "W mieście dziwne obyczaje."[23] "The audience summoned the virtuoso with universal clamor, and one music lover cried out: "Hey, for pity's sake, give at least one more concert before you leave." The fervor generated by Chopin's music was manifested in various ways; here, mazurkas and waltzes were created from the motives of his concerto, fantasy, and *Rondo à la krakowiak*; there, poems were written in the artist's honor. We will quote the sonnet by Leon Ulrych[24] published in the *Pamiętnik dla płci pięknej* (volume II, fascicle 2), reprinted in the *Kuryer*:

To Fryderyk Chopin, Playing a Concerto on the Piano

O what noble song stirs my sleeping heart
And kindles so many feelings in my breast?
I feel my blood seething, in my eyes burns a flame,
And my thoughts, midst the crowd, forget the whole world.
Suddenly, a song of hope beguiles my sullen soul
And in tender rapture sheds a tear of longing;
Then a native air dampens all emotions
And ignites a sacred feeling in my Polish bosom.
The soul, pulled upward by the strength of these songs,
Flies to the heavens on harmony's wings,
There to consort with angelical choirs;
Yet one emotion binds it to the world,
And from the edge of the skies it returns to the earth
To caress your songs.

In the final concert, wreaths of native flowers fell at the artist's feet, and Chopin's family has kept one of them to this day, in memory of the omen so marvelously fulfilled. In the autumn of 1830, Chopin left Warsaw; eminent artists and amateurs representing the capital saw him off to Wola and placed the city's heartfelt wishes in a souvenir prepared specially for him. His first foreign port of call was Vienna. He gained popularity there with his famous Variations (Op. 2) on "Là ci darem la mano," a theme by Mozart, always a favorite with the Viennese; and the Polonaise for piano and cello (Op. 3). It was not until later, in 1831, that he left Vienna and, at the end of that year, passing via Munich, he arrived in Paris. His reputation from Germany, and especially from Vienna, preceded him; nevertheless, although the latter city had not yet ceased to pass judgment on artists in general, and musicians in particular, Paris already held its own opinion too highly to immediately accept a newcomer; it was too great a vortex, in which stiff rivalries were fought, for a foreigner to easily make his name. One of the coryphaei of the piano at that time, Kalkbrenner, lived there permanently and presided over all those who had devoted themselves to that instrument. Thus it was his recognition and support that Chopin sought; and so much of it did he gain that the Parisian grandee undertook to protect the newcomer, on condition that the somewhat intractable talent that he had brought with him from Poland be curbed in the French fashion through a three-year course of study. The young man, holding a modest opinion of himself and grateful for the master's offer, honored him with one of his masterworks (the Concerto, Op. 11) and wrote home for advice. Although well aware of the worth both of his former pupil and of the one who had thrust himself forward as teacher, Elsner vigorously deterred him from that step and thereby, if not rescuing Chopin's individuality, already too outstanding to be lost, at least prevented it from being halted in full flow. Meanwhile Chopin, already honorably acknowledged in the musical salons of Zimmerman and Pleyel, soon became the delight of art lovers, a model for artists, and within a short space of time the idol of almost everyone, just as today, with his premature death, he has filled all hearts with mourning.

His time in Paris was interrupted only by short excursions: now to the south of France; now to Rouen; now to the waters at Carlsbad, taking the opportunity to visit Leipzig and Dresden (in 1836); now to Spain and one of the Balearic Islands (in the company of George Sand); now to London, which he visited twice. Having won tributes from what is now the musical capital of the world, he traveled also to its commercial capital, London; but there he did not reveal his greatness in public until 1848, when political unrest in Paris and France, disrupting his habits, drove him again to that capital city. After the election of 10 December, he returned to Paris, where at 2 a.m on the night of 16–17 October 1849 he departed, to dwell forever in the worlds described so many times in his works.

It will befall the future biographer of Chopin to trace his relations with people of great genius, importance, or wealth; his opinions, minor details of his life, and incidental circumstances. Here we will mention some of the personal attributes widely ascribed to him by those who knew him well. He possessed all those irrefutably necessary to be beloved of men: ungrudging charity, of which he himself was occasionally in need, complaisance to anyone seeking his recommendation and advice, tact, noble-mindedness, dignified comportment; and, as will no doubt surprise those familiar with his works, fleeting mirth, bordering on frivolity, and a Garrickian ability[25] to imitate people in their speech, movements and physiognomy, which shows acute observation.[ii] He performed rarely in public, and on such occasions he would mostly play his shorter works. That is regrettable, since the tradition of the understanding and interpretation of his larger works will not be widespread and may be distorted once it reaches our land, its primary source. Yet Chopin left many pupils and therefore no fewer admirers and friends—not counting others. Who could fail to comprehend the wonderful sympathy that links a pupil to a teacher, when the former is intelligent and sensitive and the latter need only be a guide! That bond is as sweet as the one that ties parents with their children. Tenderness and solicitude on one part and trust and gratitude on the other merge in a common environment of love for the art. Two beings fused into a single ideal through egoistical feeling can come to love each other. When the turn comes for one to withdraw into eternity, the other becomes its swansong and, on the wings of the art beloved by both, raises it onto immortal heights and, as if lamenting the temporal divide, strives to revivify its cold remains with ardent tears. Thus ended the master, who himself had once lamented a pupil. The name of Carl Filtsch,[26] who died in his fifteenth year, often strayed across his lips, in a feeling of profound grief.

III.

The few biographical details that we have noted here from the accounts of family and friends and from reports in periodical publications belong mostly to the half of his life that Chopin spent among us. Separated from

---

ii. When playing in the family home, he did not greatly participate in the riotous sports of his peers, but preferred quiet jokes and little pranks.

the second half geographically, we have clutched with familial interest at details brought to us by familial business. Yet those vague bits of news were lacking either certainty or some connection with corresponding events in his life, which no doubt influenced his artistic works to a greater or lesser extent. With time, after scattered fragments come together into a single whole—both those known today and those that await more than one death to be freed from the seal of mystery—the light will grow bright and flood the whole figure. Today, it sinks into the numerous gaps, and that which might illumine the inner life itself needs kindling by the same. This is because a biography is written in the hand of the author himself, spread across his works. A work of art, like almost every work of man, reflects the moment that inspired its creation; hence a succession of works—that is, a collected body of work—is a concentrated echo of various moments in life; anyone able to read it will discover the entire path taken and will count the notches on the artist's heart; such a biography never misleads, although it is concealed beneath an unusual form. After all, a person's face hides behind a mask in vain; the shrewd observer's eye will spot a flash or two of the countenance and find its bearings. Expression dresses up thoughts to no avail; if just once the mantle falls, the truth will be seen. To give one last comparison: in vain has our earth overlaid its history with strata, covered the kingdom of flora and fauna with mineral deposits, built towering tiers of rock upon them, and even occasionally laid history under the sea to render them unrecognizable; man came along and understood all those tricks, counted its years, described the disorderly scenes and, with proof in his hands, accused it of destroying gardens and streams and the creatures that populated them. Yet we do not venture here to assess and dissect Chopin's works; that is a huge task, requiring gigantic forces, and could easily fill whole volumes. And even that biography of the heart, which, as we said, could be read from his works, would be premature. For that, time is needed to establish the conviction that one has not just espied individual moments, but also discerned the chain that links them together; to show how one is born of the other and gives rise to the next. Such a genealogy of emotions, ramified into various shades that are perhaps still concealed in hidden and unpublished works, cannot be hastily elaborated. What remains, therefore, is a brief survey of the most conspicuous moments; from them will emerge the nature of Chopin's genius, and at least in part his services to mankind and to art.

As a virtuoso and a composer, Chopin devoted himself almost entirely to the piano, about which it was maintained that of all the musical instruments it was the least capable of speaking to the soul. Chopin condemned to oblivion that way of seeing things, teaching us how to exploit its nature, so that it could be used to work virtual wonders. His artistic profession is so closely linked to the history of the piano that the latter should be related here in brief; that is, during the period preceding the appearance of Chopin. A few words will suffice.

Schools of piano playing date from the times of Clementi,[iii] who is known as the father of the piano, and his contemporary Mozart; the first of these can boast Field[iv] and Cramer[v] and the second Hummel.[vi] Soon other schools also sent rivals into battle; the Parisian school (the Conservatoire) sent forth a pupil of [Louis] Adam, Friedrich Kalkbrenner,[vii] and the Prague school launched Moscheles,[viii] a pupil of F. D. Weber. By 1830, the time when Chopin's talent had matured and he was about to emerge into the musical world, Field and Hummel were already beginning to depart the scene, and virtually nothing was heard of Cramer; meanwhile, the rivalry between Kalkbrenner and Moscheles led the experts to despair when it came to awarding one of them the palm; it was usually the last one

---

iii. Muzio Clementi, born in 1752, in Rome. In 1780, after spending six years in England, he performed in Paris, then in Vienna, where he was a rival to Mozart. On returning to London, twenty years later, in 1802, he again embarked on a journey around Europe, taking with him Field, whom he left in St. Petersburg. His other outstanding pupil was Ludwig Berger, who approaches Chopin with the fleeting spirit of some of his works. Clementi's *Gradus ad Parnassum* (1817) summarizes all the difficulties of the piano and shows that the author followed the instrument's development.

iv. John Field, pupil of the above, born ca.1780, in England, settled in Russia. He performed even mere trifles so admirably that, as the experts maintained, he left even Hummel behind. In harmony, he was weak. In 1832, he traveled from Moscow to London, Paris, the South of France and Italy, then returned to Russia.

v. [Johann Baptist Cramer,] born in 1771, in Mannheim. Cramer did not exert any great influence on the virtuosi, since, residing continuously in London, he only traveled to Paris briefly, in 1834, and remained unmoved by the progress in musical execution. He made his name with piano exercises, which were long used more than all others and remain essential still today.

vi. Johann Nepomuk Hummel, ultimately Kapellmeister at the court of the Grand Duke of Weimar, born in Pressburg in 1778. As a pianist, a pupil of Mozart, from 1795 of Albrechtsberger (a celebrated contrapuntist of recent times), and later of Salieri; under their guidance, he became one of the most brilliant composers, particularly for the piano. From 1820, he was known throughout Europe as a virtuoso and an improviser.

vii. Friedrich Kalkbrenner, in composition a pupil of Catel. In 1802, as a fourteen-year-old boy, he won the first two prizes at the Paris Conservatoire for piano playing and composition. From 1823, he traveled around Europe, and despite the rivalry of others he was considered the best. In 1834, he toured Germany.

viii. Ignaz Moscheles, born in Prague, in 1794; besides [Friedrich] Dionysius [Bedřich Diviš] Weber, who was rector of the Prague Conservatory, he was also, like Hummel, a pupil of Albrechtsberger and Salieri. As a pianist, he was almost as famous as Kalkbrenner, and in composition surpassed him.

heard who received it. As for their technique, the two adversaries worked on it doggedly, as if they were only beginning to seek to make a name for themselves; and whereas Moscheles never allowed his fingers to rest, beleaguering them on a dumb keyboard even when traveling so as not to lose time—or rather to make of it double use—Kalkbrenner recommended to Europe, astonished by his technique, his *guide-mains*, on which he himself worked relentlessly to emancipate his fingers, equalizing their naturally various strengths.[27] These and similar efforts took finger technique (not so much hand technique, since that—except for octaves—is a newer art) to its ultimate level, just as admirable in the epoch of the two coryphaei as the heroic conquests of the new virtuosi today. The art of the protagonists of those times, like that of their predecessors Clementi and Mozart, mainly cultivated works in which it could manifest itself to best effect; and each artist selected those difficulties which could show his technical predispositions to the greatest advantage. In order to convey the gradation of those difficulties, or rather their spirit, one might say in general that they were initially replicated in scales and common arpeggios; thence in double passages; Kalkbrenner even readily used fuller chords, whereas Moscheles dazzled with audacious leaps. The introduction of intervals greater than an octave was opposed so much at first (although composers, for instance [Jan Ladislav] Dussek, did employ them from time to time) that Field's first works written specifically for them proved unpopular. So much for the mechanical side; that it was excellent is clear; and by recalling the use of all this in compositions, one easily divines their splendor and bravura. Who could forget them? Yet that usage did not occur so infelicitously as it does today; composers did not exaggerate to such an extent as they often do today, by turning a secondary element into a principal one; the right moment was chosen more carefully. And if on the one hand a generous handful of spice was sometimes thrown into compositions calculated for public performance, on the other hand, thorough and sometimes lengthy studies of counterpoint undertaken with strict past masters taught them fondness and aptitude for other kinds of composition—that to dazzle was not the purpose of music—and the same virtuosi left excellent works in other genres. Their texture still betrays the habit of dazzling display, marked by luxuriousness of ideas and connections, but they do not lack passages genuinely devised from the heart and at times so typical of serious works that they can be called society [chamber] music. That name is so accurate that, from knowledge of the society of those times (under that one word we understand both the German *Gesellschaft* and the French *salon*, although there are differences between them) the spirit of that music can be divined, and the spirit of society discerned from the music.

In the almost unbroken peace in Europe following the settlement of political relations and extending from the Congress of Vienna up to the year 1830 (and the appearance of Chopin), all estates began to breathe more fully again; after the lengthy disturbances of war, there emerged a trust in the new order of things. All nations were reminded of the notion of their own strength, since over the course of the drawn-out fighting all, if sometimes vanquished, had also been victorious. Thus national pride was inclined to support everything of worth that was found at home, so as to stand up to rivals in that domain as well. Rummaging through national treasures turned up much that was foreign: here out of date, there carried by new storms. There ensued a period of extensive historical-purifying research, gilded with a new philosophy. What it isolated, it joined together: industry, commerce, and art, satisfying the general needs of people, in whose experience the ancestral patch had become too restrictive. Now was the time for the glory and rewards that had befallen mostly people of war and politics to begin to pass to scholars and artists, who had been exasperated at their extended sojourn in the shadows: everything was done to ensure them of the blessings for a long time to come. Agricultural, industrial, and commercial work soon boosted depleted fortunes and built new ones on strong foundations; and the blissful state of affairs was disturbed by neither the voices of the alarmists nor the initial endeavors of a few malcontents. The cities began to savor prosperity and the pleasures of life, to which the arts contributed greatly, thus occupying a substantial place. Instead of standing beneath bloodied flags or worrying their heads with politics as before, people young and old rushed to their favorite rendezvous, to relieve the monotony of their peaceful occupations. Sweet feelings of love, friendship, contentment, and hope, shaded with a light veil of longing, animated people's lives. Only occasionally did a little cloud of remembrance seem to move against the rosy background, blown by sighs rather than tears, before some blast of triumph or joy would chase it away again.

Such is the thread from which the musicians of those times wove their pictures; it was a heyday for duos, trios, and larger music ensembles. Beethoven, already flourishing and esteemed, albeit not yet entirely understood, supported that current with the full weight of his imposing genius. Many people helped him, and they worked so effectively that he is liked still today, particularly in Germany; although the spirit of chamber compositions has altered like the spirit of the times, primarily under the influence of Onslow.[28]

Beethoven, a man not belonging to any school as regards his later works, a coryphaeus of instrumental music, an increasingly profound or, as was said, increasingly great skeptic and eccentric, was in a sense in almost complete isolation, a representative of the incredulity with which keener observers (and perhaps people with steadfast intentions) beheld the rosy times; hence he became isolated. Yet the line of thought he represented did not long remain broken off by his death (1827).

IV.

That line was taken up by Chopin, who led it through his times; the closer in time to Beethoven, the more similar Chopin was to him (although at first more autonomous than the former, who was clearly influenced by Haydn and Mozart); the further from him, the more distinctive he became, and the more accurately he portrayed his epoch in his works. That epoch was characterized first by a calmness perturbed by inner storms or audacious ideas, and finally a widespread crumbling of the floodgates holding back humanity as it flowed toward the great ocean. So Chopin, straddling two eras, gently rocked by one and swept up by the welter of the other, left traces of both in his works—traces more profound of the [era] which for a longer time bore witness to his development. He was its child to such an extent that he fell as it fell, not without a prophetic glance into the future. Yet that future cannot and does not foretell the events to come, since art is not fact, but reflects the impressions to which it gives rise. That future is rather a foretaste of eternity, in which a caring bosom will gladly clasp all those who in this mortal life see no consolation for themselves.

It is impossible to disentangle the strands in question here, just as one cannot grasp ever fleeting time, which at once both dips into the past and glances into the future. To see those strands, it is enough to compare Chopin's first works with his middle period works, the young man with the finished article. Although they are linked by the same individuality, unstintingly faithful to itself, that individuality is nevertheless guided by the action of time; and this is exactly what determines the possibility we discussed earlier: that of extracting the artist's inner history from his works. The human spirit succumbs to the influences of a dual world: the outside world that consists of memories, souvenirs, general and particular aspirations, friendships, family, and the great family known as the people; and the other, inner, world which, peopled by the faculties of the mind and the heart, arrays the former in reflection. A person's individuality, being sensitive to the continuous influence of those two merged worlds of thought and of deed, is forged by that influence. It cannot shield its work from that influence or alter itself, because even if the action of the two worlds were to take a new direction, the resulting amalgam would cover a ready-made construction, and the old forms would not be lost. A trace of the old influences always remains, just as the effects of an organism's turmoil caused by a serious, albeit cured, disease will remain; the evil has been removed, but experience has recorded its existence and looks back at the first pages of its journal even while continually adding new pages to those from which it arose. Seen from this perspective, Chopin's works display a unity that with the passage of time turns into an infinite variety.

It is interesting to see how his spirit gradually wriggled free from under the sway of the schools on which he was raised as a composer. Not subjected to the exclusive guidance of any of the then hallowed musical grandees, he voluntarily took advantage of them to develop models for himself. This is evident in his very first works: now in the overall form, now in the structural design, now in the texture of the ideas. This applies to his concertos, rondos, sets of variations, fantasy on Polish airs, polonaise for piano and cello, and trio. Yet at the same time, they betray bold and new ideas, autonomy of design and great inventiveness, which immediately set him in first place among composers. His individuality mixed youthful elegance with sensitivity, tenderness with energy, soaring hope with dolefulness; and all of that with a prodigality which at once revealed virtually inexhaustible yet barely touched treasures. Indeed, the wealth of his ideas was so vast that—other than a few passages of his own device—it seems no one has found the same thing twice in his numerous works, and even then not without alterations, and rarely repeated. The first works already show Chopin as an autonomous virtuoso, using his mighty will to break through the walls against which the efforts of his predecessors had hitherto foundered. Having opened wide the path for those covetous of freedom and shown them how to gain access to it (the Op. 10 Etudes), he began revealing to people the treasures that lay alongside it, while the hotheads kept on running. There is no doubt that these first works were somewhat contingent upon the general trend in music at that time; under familiar and popular forms, they would open up for him the temple in which the magi of the piano had installed themselves, and also introduce new ideas to the world, as if under the passport of general consent. Yet, having accomplished his aim, Chopin soon freed himself as well from those confines of form, and renewed form in the same way he renewed the distinctive content that he entrusted to it. We do not wish to maintain here that he invented entirely new forms; that is impossible, since all forms develop from one first form, based on the phi-losophy of art, which will always remain unique, and it is sufficient, being extraordinarily flexible. We wish merely to mention that where the lot of composers was to employ well-worn formulas to press their fantasy into what might be called pigeonholes, the vastness of Chopin's fantasy reached both further and deeper than hitherto and could not develop within such strictures. So Chopin shattered them, not in order to show himself as origi-nal and exceptional (as those misunderstanding his ideas maintained), but because the original and exceptional character of his ideas forced him to do so. Suffice it to invoke as evidence here the Larghetto in the full-of-pathos Second Concerto (Op. 21), or the *Andante spianato* before the Polonaise (Op. 22). Chopin even filled out the lean form of the mazurka with the gold of his ideas, turning it into a fantasy; for example, in Opus 58. And we witness with him what happens to everyone who speaks with great feeling: the more he says, the more he has to say, for what heart-felt subject could ever be exhausted? In this inundation of thoughts and concepts one pushes the other, at times turning the work into almost an enigmatic compression (the Ballade Op. 38, the first Polonaise Op. 26); it crashes down with such a torrent of powerful ideas that the interpreter needs to show persistent repetition in order to merge with a work, in order to possess it, to separate it, in order to grasp the whole having seen the single part. Yet there is no disarray in this tumult: it conceals a logic, despite the bold elision of entire ideas. There is a limit even to the emotion, which we know from what we have heard to be limitless; the material end must be fixed, but the listener, having grasped the content, will long continue in the same spirit.

That spirit that already haunts the first works of Chopin, beguiling us with the purity of its view upon God's world, yet penetrating us here and there with a plaintive voice, gradually delves ever deeper. Enriched by its achievements, it passes through all the shades of suffering, from melancholy to despair, tormenting itself with the ascetic rapture of the penitent. Whether it be experience, the separation from his family and his loneliness amid the hurly-burly, the suffering of his wasting organ-ism or perhaps all of that together, suffice it to say that from Chopin's works we see a gradual departure from the world and a closing up within himself. The free or forced relinquishing of one world must have expanded the other; deed was transformed into thought, impracticable ideals turned into fantasy, drama into lyricism, and these translated to an instrument full of resources, increased by Chopin's inventiveness, spread forth with increasing might. Hence the chords, initially accompanying in chorus, resolve into voices quivering with autonomous life (e.g., the third

Mazurka Op. 50 or the second Nocturne Op. 55); like the worm that, cut into pieces, gives life to each of them through the strength of its suffering. Hence the urgency of spirit, rejecting everything that stands in the way of the principal element of the sound (melody; the *unisono* in the finale of the Sonata Op. 35); hence that mysticism strewn over so many pages; hence the bleakness of the blissful images; hence the refined ideal of maternal song—the Berceuse (Lullaby)? Op. 57—or the dreaming, perhaps remembrance, of the delights of a gondola (the Barcarolle Op. 60). The composer himself must have discerned this spirit in his works. Marking some with only a word indicating the form—e.g., rondo, concerto—he included in others both form and content—e.g., mazurka, bolero. He gave a characteristic name to most of them—Nocturne, Ballade, Scherzo, or Barcarolle.

Chopin's reflective character had to foster inside him early on, as indeed it did, a tendency to seek a trusty companion in the piano. At an early stage, he was already guided by the germ of a split between the two worlds of thought and deed, which he later developed beyond measure; and it was that disjuncture that stopped him from turning his hand to vocal composition, which forces one's fancy to submit to the will of someone else's inspiration—although he did attempt setting poetry to music at the outset of his compositional career. His songs, written mostly to words by Witwicki,[29] still remain among us, in the possession of a privileged few; the composer evidently thought little of them, asking his family to consign them to oblivion. He was even less suited to dramatic composition: besides the inconvenience of a text, a drama hangs emotions on the frame of actual life, as if on display, and it relies on many individuals both in the creating and in the performance; it was too onerous a solidarity for the shrinking Chopin. Although the optimism of youth gave him the courage to use an orchestra, later he deigned merely to summon the assistance of a single cello of elegiac sound. He came to love the piano as an instrument full of charm and intelligence, providing him with so much delight that he raised it to the greatness which, in hallowed moments, allows one to dispense with people. He was also rather reluctant to play for them, except when they bonded with him through some singular disposition, although that could not occur very often, and he tended to invoke spirits inhabiting the unfathomable world. It was in their company that he found pleasure as he became increasingly deep, increasingly detached; and while still of this world, he left it increasingly often and for longer periods of time. And yet that other world did not give him a single moment of genuine good cheer or a single flash of wit or humorous trait; it was rather that he raised the worldliness of all this, having ennobled it with his suffering, to an ideal, in keeping with his individuality as an artist. With him, merriment is a song soaring over the stars, the thoughts of a mother leaning over her child's crib with hope and prayer; some triumph born of suffering; at times, it is a smile of melancholy, merriment that has nothing in common with the riotous life of our world. Such is exuded, for example, by some of the polonaises and mazurkas. Wit becomes clairvoyance, recognizing the influence of the spiritual world to which he so willingly submitted; it created some of the nocturnes and the ballades. And humor, that characteristic feature of the percipient spirit so strongly developed in Chopin, did not veer into satire, irony, or sarcasm, for those are practical instances of agitated humor. With him, who condemned himself voluntarily to heart-rending suffering, the inseparability of that for which he yearned and that which befell him turned into bloody derision, the abuse of the world, invested with a swarm of sufferings; and it gave rise to a Scherzo, the name used solely for the want of any other (the sonatas also have similar features). This is a struggle between two elements, two opposing forces that cannot defeat each other, but tear asunder every heart drawn into the whirl of their battle. Features of this sort are too salient in Chopin's works to be singled out here; they are raised to an intensity all the greater in that sometimes they lie right next to features of angelic mildness, of youthful sensitivity and tenderness. They characterize his compositions, particularly those next to last, with increasing intensity, and they instruct us that their general character lies in the notion of battle.

The principle of art—art for life and through life—disseminated nowadays in the place of former principles, in this respect finds plenty of support in Chopin's works. Due to the inseparability of those two worlds—the real world of life and the fictive world into which the great artist leads us—it appears that this principle cannot be applied; yet that is merely an ostensible opposition. In his artistic vision, Chopin was under the influence of the ordinary world, like a body chained to it; and although he created his own ideals, he could not, on entering their realm, leave his individuality on its doorstep. This important world adds elemental force to the dream world: the latter is the former's reflection. The bright spheres floating in the ether above our heads and the clouds suspended in the heavier element closer to us will sink, in image, into the depths of the watery looking-glass when we gaze at them. They will perhaps sparkle less lustrously there, the clouds will perhaps seem gloomier, depending either on the bottom of that mirror or on the atoms dissolved within it; it is enough that the image looks thus and not otherwise. After all, an ideal does not cleanse reality of that which offends us; it is not supposed to be a mere lie or semblance but a lifting of the veils of falsity, a luminous truth, as if raised exponentially. And we see such an ideal life in the works of Chopin; we find the models in the actual world, on its surface and all around us. What we call civilization is gradually raising, or rather altering, everything. Thanks to it, people have already achieved incredible things: they have explored the earth and seen into the sky; they have fixed the air and mastered fire; they have plundered the depths of the oceans and can even weigh the sun's rays! And what have they gained from this for the heart, or even for existence? The wise man says: to know yourself is the greatest wisdom; so humanity has made vast progress in wisdom. It sees its degradation ever more clearly, its increasingly dreadful abyss. That is the reality! And its ideal lies in the works of Chopin. With them he seems to have done more for humanity (if it could only learn how to understand his works) than the praxis and theories of the philanthropists, which quake and crumble with every strike of the hammer. If you loved your neighbor like yourself, there would be less evil in the world; so all you heartless people, go to the works of the great artist for a single drop of love; he will show you suffering, show you despair; his own example will teach you. Go and behold what you do not know; and on making its acquaintance, you will ache with someone else's despair and you will come to love the genius who ennobles your hearts. All the sufferers already love him as a brother!

Herein lies the secret of that near-deification of the artist by those who have understood him even though they did not know him, for here is proof of that goodness of heart and effusiveness about which those closest to him cannot say enough. Truly! man creates in his own image and likeness. Herein too lies the most crucial achievement of music, thanks to Chopin. No musician before him penetrated human emotions so deeply; as if not wishing to deprive himself of the illusory delights of reality, as if not deigning to raise the ignominy and horror strewn across the world on which we tread as if on a soft carpet. Chopin stirred it and showed that it was woven from venomous adders; he gave himself up to them as prey, in order to warn humanity. So should the redemption that religion has already brought us be supported by redemption through art?

Beethoven, in his *Fidelio*, had already espied the same path, and he pursued it across an abyss of abstract woe; but he grew frightened of it and refrained from tempting it further. So he remained alone, ahistorical in that respect and misunderstood; he shackled himself to drama, which, as reality transferred to the stage, he did not succeed in elucidating, and the composer himself was evidently unable to leave any commentary to his thinking. Chopin's pure lyricism shed light on his predecessor's ideas and affixed them to the history of the meanderings of the mind; at the same time he joined with Beethoven through spiritual affinity and, sufficiently developed, himself entered the historicity of an idea. Thus far we have not seen to whom his mission might have passed. Shrouded in the spirit of the times, spurred by his example, numerous musicians grasp the magic wand, but it crumbles in their hands, sullied with the mud of earthly deeds. Their voice is the mimicking of a wail, an inversion of pain, a sickly breath of emotion, cowed by the body and striving to regain its rights. It is not their lot to be prophets!

V.

A consideration of Chopin's works could lead one to almost lose oneself in the multitude of observations that reinforce one another and make up the overall impression! Here, we have set down just a few features; a book would not suffice to detail and demonstrate them all, were it indeed possible to calculate them. Having indicated some features, whose source could be shown, we omit explications. Although the indeterminate language of music and the personal fantasy of everyone who gazes more deeply hinder such justifications, they facilitate the task of all those willing to approach masterworks through faith. Faith is so necessary for considering every work of art, and it is most necessary of all in music, on account of music's inexpressible depth, its innate Romantic nature, if one may put it like that, the mystery undisclosed to the dull inquiry of common practice. Anyone to whom faith is alien has neither the mental capacity to delve beneath the stratum of the ordinary view of things nor a heart trained to ponder the sufferings of the heart; he will not understand Chopin there where he is at his loftiest.

If an overview of our compatriot's works provides numerous ideas, many other tangible ideas ensue from a survey of the genres—or more accurately the forms—in which they developed. Most numerous are those which are akin to *song*, such as those derived from dance forms: mazurka, waltz, polonaise, *krakowiak*, tarantella, bolero; the etudes, preludes, improvisations (impromptus), and nocturnes also belong here. Considering them individually shows how they outgrew their typically small dimensions; the restricted dance rhythms of a bolero or a krakowiak, for example, turned into more or less expansive fantasies. We see this to best effect in the native *mazur*; let him who knows say what it became. Initially called upon to fill out a more extensive form (*Rondo à la mazur*, Op. 5), in the very next work,[ix] and thereafter appearing very often on its own account, it is nearly always in spirit a poem, and so substantial and varied that a hefty tome would be needed to describe Chopin's mazurkas alone. Most common in these native dance forms are features of a buoyant merry-making, while truly humorous features supposedly should be sought only in some of the mazurkas. Are we to enumerate here as well the qualities with which they enchant both us and the world? If we knew the words with which that might be done we would not gladly thus proceed with other genres. Endeavoring to reveal the features of some mazurkas only, we do so only in order to show off our kin's achievement in a public forum; for in lamenting the loss of one's beloved, it is impossible to deny in one's mind the notion of what made him beloved.

Chopin's preludes (Op. 28) are a handful of ideas, some of which are lacking the development to form self-contained entities (e.g., Nos. 2, 7, 20), others are close to an independent song (like No. 15), some are rhapsodies (18, 22), others etudes (3, 5), some more extensive (19, 24), and then there is a threnody (6). Without exception they are not the normal preludes; that is, an introduction, preparing the listener for what is to follow. In Chopin's preludes, there is too much substance, for that is what lies in the nature of his idea; the content is too deep, and the character, although not developed, captivates us too strongly for us to relinquish it without regret, to assume with indifference the bidding of another spirit. Only the lack of artistic completion fills us with some sadness: a longing for rounded form, or even its extension more appropriate to the greatness of the ideas.

The same variety of character is possessed by Chopin's etudes, and to many one may easily apply various names of songs that we mentioned in relation to the preludes; for example, to Op. 10, No. 11, or to Op. 25, No. 7. There is a striking similarity between some of the finished etudes and ideas cast forth in the preludes; the Preludes Nos. 1 and 8, for instance, are clearly akin to the Etude Op. 25, No. 3.

Among earlier composers, it was Field who was most admired in the nocturne, and he bestowed many a rapturous moment upon lovers of

---

ix. We assume that Chopin sent his works to publishers as and when he composed and completed them, although we know that there could have been, and indeed were, exceptions to this rule. Thus, for example, the second Concerto, only later published as Opus 21, was begun, but not completed, before the first (Op. 11). That may sometimes explain why, when surveying the works as indicated by their ordinal numbers, we waver in the assumption we make regarding the gradual change of their spirit. We will not list the other supposed reasons for this confusion; they can be found by anyone.

music. When Chopin's nocturnes appeared, it was claimed that he derived them from Field; it was even maintained, no doubt on the strength of some similarity and proximity between Poland and Russia, where Field was living, that Chopin was a pupil of his (Gustav Schilling, *Universal-Lexikon der Tonkunst*, s.v. "Chopin"); and mediocrity and envy, pursuing the young and humble genius, ventured to belittle (*Iris*, Berlin)[30] that which in the small musical forms previously preferred by Chopin best revealed, through a small number of features, the spirit of his poetry, which only later became entirely freed in other forms. Comparing the nocturnes of Field and Chopin, we see not the superiority of one over the other, but their separate aspirations: although one cannot deny that some of Chopin's first nocturnes are very close in spirit to the fruits of the other, one can identify a difference in Chopin's characteristic depth and in the beguiling phrases, even more characteristic of him, the wondrousness of which reveals, with a single crisp stroke, the profundity of feeling over which he glides. Yet Chopin's nocturnes in general cannot be compared with Field's in terms of their number and spirit. If musical substance could be expressed in words, we would say that the Field *notturno* was in general a soft, sweet, gentle image, quiet contemplation disturbed only occasionally by a flash of fantasy that fades away almost without regret. The name "serenade" that is sometimes given to nocturnes is very apt for these songs of Field's. Chopin's nocturnes, meanwhile, are for the most part pictures on a dark background; spirits flowing down to the earth at night appear and disappear here mysteriously. Fantasy in disarray leads us, in unfathomable phrases, as if in a dream from object to object, from thought to thought. And as in a dream we succumb to a force, incomprehensible to us when awake, that, binding that which never is bound, shows the interweaving of all things: thus captivated by Chopin's dream, despite the resistance of our vigilant senses, we follow him across the depths and the heights; yielding to the magical sway, we comprehend the logic of feelings, we understand the fantasy turned into reality. After the magical notes fade away, we still dream in the same direction, and struggling to break free from the power of the mysterious world to which the poet has subjected us, we ask, upon waking, whether it was a dream or reality? Boundless riches in a concise form; each note gives rise to swarms of others, like a cloud of atoms from a bursting drop. There is a whole there, albeit unuttered; and when the notes inevitably cease, obeying the earthly laws of matter, the tumult of infinity overwhelms us and suspends us in anticipation.

Nearly every work of Chopin's exerts the same, or similar, influence over us, particularly since it is impossible to break free of it; one must believe its evidence, or at least yield to it, even when putting up resistance. That resistance is generated in the listener by certain places in his works—most strongly in the ballades. Let us take the first good example that comes to mind, Opus 38, one of those through which Chopin most deeply penetrated the world of mystery. This is a sumptuous legend! Not like our gentle, playful national legends, taken from the mouths of the common folk by the genius of Mickiewicz, but menacing and overpowering, like ineluctable fate. This trait is characteristic of German ballades, in Bürger,[31] for example; a relic of hard feudalism almost unheard of in Poland, of a superstition born of the Germanic character. There, you find necessity foretold and inescapable; here circumstance; there, grief and dread; here submission, bound up with hope. There the anguish of mystery; here the openness of fantasy; there, poison, graves, skeletons and phantoms; here water nymphs, capers, and at worst a little devil who can easily be cheated; and there, to close, numb despair—with us, sentient faith. The image of our legends lies in more than one Chopin mazurka; his ballades have nothing in common with them and merely illuminate the path along which imagination strays, withdrawing into itself, forced by suffering to withdraw into the jail of itself. This is what created the Fantasy (Op. 49), softening the dark coloring with a native theme; and, merged with the dolors of a scherzo, gave rise to the sonatas, which have yet to see their equal as regards both distinctness of ideas and boldness of presentation.

Chopin's depth, his immense variety of ideas and their audacity, all but overflowing the confines of the form with a breath of infinity, make him almost peerless as a composer for piano among the thousand musicians of his day whose names are preserved in publishers' catalogues as composers for that instrument. He had imitators, but they, losing heart after their very first attempts, had to resort to fabrications: fantasies, that is, stitching other people's ideas together; transcriptions, rewriting them note for note; arrangement, that is, dressing them in a different, more fashionable gown; such was the domain of their rivalry. Chopin's fecundity and innovation sometimes stimulated them; he wrote, for example, a sonata, a ballade, a scherzo; so others at once set about writing sonatas, ballades, elegies, scherzos, and even—who would have thought it?—mazurkas! Occasionally, those imitations are marked with the stamp of truth, for they were also produced by people; yet more often they remained so much merely people that they failed to raise themselves to the loftiness of divine emotions. Yet the example given from above halted the flood of modern trash and will serve as its dam for a long time to come.

VI.

Having revealed the spirit of whole poems by Chopin as far as we could, we would gladly dissect them; that may prove useful for gaining a better idea about them. May no one expect us to reveal here the means by which the genius arrives at certain solutions; if anyone could do so, the world would surely hail him as a benevolent sorcerer, as the ultimate and supreme genius; then anyone could become a genius. Yet that will never come about. Nature gave the musician sound and movement to use in accordance with his needs, and he did not err in their use; it deposited the formulas in his organism—in his voice, in his hearing, and in the coursing of the blood to his heart. In that heart, it set feelings, for him to portray them, and by linking the heart with the brain, the seat of all the faculties, it entrusted him with judgment over the feelings of the former and the latter; this judgment called taste is so indulgent that it acknowledges everything the heart needs and assimilates and with which, via the intermediary of sound and movement, it appeals to other hearts for sympathy. That is the whole natural theory of musical composition. How a person is to go about it is his business—on condition that he remain faithful to the laws of nature. Humanity has long since been familiar with and used them according to its needs; it is man's genius that determines the loftiest notion and best application of them. Thus anyone who assumes that geniuses like Beethoven and Chopin have destroyed all prescriptions is mistaken; they were not prescriptions, but phantasms that had extended their tyranny to other ends. These two geniuses merely led the withering art out of its exhausted role into new, virgin territories, which they discovered much as Columbus discovered America, driven by the conviction of their existence and guided by the compass of feelings better conceived. Who knows? Perhaps these new pastures will also turn barren with time, wasted by humanity's hunger and a craving for rich harvests; then, under the command of later geniuses, humanity will again discover new, untouched domains, for nature has more in its possession than it has thus far distributed. Yet before we need to have recourse to its munificence, long years of plenty will repeatedly glorify Chopin with their bountiful harvest. Let us now try to examine his works when broken down into their constituent parts.

His melody, varied in accordance with different inspirations, is always refined. At first gamboling freely, scampering about like the first flush of youth, refined in its elegance, resplendent and readily sparkling, it fills Chopin's earliest works. Soon afterward, however, it is more serious, tender rather than passionate, often close to the Italian in its songful and elaborate character, bending in alluring shapes and graceful phrases; here it sprays gently in a shower of melismatic drops, there it ponders on a longer note; it is usually cheerful and limpid, even when jolted by an impertinent rhythm or when the harmony clouds over. Such melody is the reflection of the most wonderful season in a person's life, when the heart seems to beat more strongly for all that is beautiful and great, when the mind is not yet overcast with bitter experience, although already it whispers arguments sowing timidity and doubt in the heart as it thrusts itself into the world's embrace. Rich stores of such melody are the first Concerto (Op. 11), the first nocturnes and some of those published later; in addition, the mazurkas, and especially the *Rondo à la mazur* (Op. 5). This is also the time when humor appears, as the increasingly experienced mind perceives better, and the heart has not yet suffered enough to descend into tears. So the melody is often capricious, mocking, coarse; and it sometimes forgets itself to such an extent that God knows where it might end up and a more moderate harmony has to take it in hand (Op. 17, No. 4). Yet those features are increasingly rare; sullenness prevails, the clouds gather, rumble with a storm and send down lightning; the melody erupts and groans, yet sheds no tears; only sobbing can be heard, and the complaint can hardly force its way through (Sonata Op. 35). Then again it takes revenge for the freedom it has lost, for the torments it has suffered, and it grows impetuous, violent and cruel (Scherzo Op. 39); at times, it swoons from exhaustion (Op. 54), and one can barely tell that it lives. The history of Chopin's melody is the history of his works, and even of himself.

Yet the generally predominant, albeit not exclusive, coloring of this melody is its nationality, although anyone assuming that Chopin's melody —let us speak more generally, that his music—is always Polish would be mistaken. Chopin was too frequently cosmopolitan in his outlook not to free himself from exclusive influences, at least in his views, if not in spirit; we would be inclined to agree with one author that deeds based on the partial spirit of some people is already national. Yet Polish music should be sought not just in Chopin's mazurkas, krakowiaks, and polonaises. It is not only our native rhythm that can be found where we least expect it; for example, a mazurka rhythm in the second variation of Op. 12, a *kujawiak* (*obertas*)[32] rhythm in the finale of the same work; Polish song can be found concealed here and there, intertwined with passages of the overall warp: such, for example, is the theme of the Fantasy, Op. 49 and that melody, of a Slavonic rather than exclusively Polish nature, in the Nocturne, Op. 62 (p. 10)[33] How can it be recognized? Who can say how to recognize the (non-dance) song of the common folk, even when it has strayed onto marble floors? Who can explain the violet's scent? But never mind that feelings are hard to describe in words. When Chopin appeared among foreigners and played for them in our style, the peoples listening to him asked in amazement: "What is that song so charming, so strong and simple, so lofty and new?" And the peoples learned that it was a Polish song! Oh! It's not new anymore; the world ought to know it by now!

The harmony in Chopin's works shares the fortunes of his melody. Fated by dint of the very nature of the art to occupy a secondary role in music, it rises from its previous post and stands virtually at the forefront, on an equal footing with melody through its worthiness, so to speak, its zeal in supporting the melody and its depth of combinations, justified by the spirit of the whole and so woven with the naturalness of simplicity. Here harmony serves the melody, there supports it, now wraps a caring arm around it, now shows it around its own domain; then again, penetrating the melody's realm, it extracts its treasures in all directions. Sometimes it clarifies it, and very often, fighting with melody, wounding it with mighty blows, brings it to despair; harmony teaches melody impetuosity, saps its strength in fruitless struggles, almost kills it, and usurps it with triumph. And then, filled with rancor, it gently stirs its motionless victim or else, shaking it despairingly, rouses melody from its lethargy. More briefly, but perhaps less forcefully, one might say that Chopin's harmony possesses gentility, strength, depth, activeness, daring, and other attributes more highly advanced than anyone has developed since the times of the great Bach,[x] Beethoven excepted. Beethoven does not even measure up to Chopin as far as the abundant use of all the resources harmony can offer, although as a composer mainly for orchestra, he stands higher than the latter in the emancipation of the individual voices of harmony (polyphony); in this he was surpassed by Bach, albeit in a different spirit. Bach, that creator or rather the father of harmony—since he did not create it, but nurtured it—in some way, ensured its status; Bach was the only composer whose works lay for a long time on Chopin's piano before his death. Chopin regarded him as the composer most worthy of study, the source of the most profound combinations, the stern guardian of artistic refinement. It is evident that he drew on Bach's music, yet not in the same genre (although one may enumerate here several of the examples given earlier), since he did not devote himself to developing

---

x. Of the many brilliant musicians of that name, belonging to one and the same family, the most outstanding was Johann Sebastian, cantor of Leipzig, born in Eisenach in 1685, who died in 1750. In 1736, he was appointed court composer to the Elector of Saxony, King Augustus II of Poland.

individual voices, but bade whole groups of tones to travel together, and therefore, naturally, with less adroitness and less relentless sense of direction. Thus, where in Bach the apparently convoluted is clarified by lines of distinctly led voices, in Chopin the apparently cheerful is clouded by layers of chords, arising as if out of some abyss, and after them the spirit of harmony, like Titans over the mountains, ascends to fight with melody. To match it, harmony moves all the forces of its dominion: now it inflicts such acute pain that a wail issues forth from melody's bosom; now pushed into a chasm, it perfidiously submits, seething with hostility, and on regaining strength launches a new onslaught.

One of the elements of harmony, chromaticism,[xi] is copiously unfurled in Chopin's compositions. It determines the storminess of the harmonic life, strongly influencing the direction, and thus too the spirit of melody. Chromaticism offers eternal resistance to diatonicism and disturbs the peace of the melody, draped over the latter; it is the eternal negation of the buoyancy of the principal voice, the groan that accompanies rapture, a pain distorting lips set in a smile. Diminished and augmented intervals, used now melodically, now harmonically, violently twist the trajectory anticipated by the ear as it waits for the nearest resolution, send violent blows through the ear to the heart, wounding it mercilessly. If we add to this the frequently changing, vacillating major and minor, we have a picture of the continuous wrestling that lends Chopin's later compositions, in particular their character, encapsulated in a single notion: battle.

To so many mighty elements must another be added? Here comes rhythm, no poorer, no weaker than the others. It is determined by a particle of eternity, time, cut up into small segments; it is the pulse of the musical life, it leads the above-mentioned forces, be they in concord or combat; rhythm itself sometimes sows discord and reconciles, incites, pulls, breaks, and soothes. It is what predominantly determines whether the melody cloaked in harmony is a mazurka, a krakowiak, or some other song. And Chopin was philosophically familiar with its properties: in the Sonata—Op. 4, as yet unpublished[xii]—dedicated to Elsner—he set down for eternity his explorations in $\frac{5}{4}$ Andante, and rhythm in general brings great variety to his works. It is rhythm that rocks the sleeping child to the beat of maternal song (Op. 57), rhythm that leads the loving couple out onto the ocean blue with a skillful oar and rescues them in the storm

---

xi. Antithesis of diatonicism, which results from employing tones belonging to a particular scale that has been chosen as a foundation.

xii. Also left in manuscript in Warsaw were completed variations for four hands on an original theme.

(Op. 60), rhythm that sometimes almost singlehandedly launches a bid for power or stands up to fight doggedly with the two components of the sound that deny it any such right, instigating indescribable combat. And when no willing adversary is at hand, it disintegrates into discrete parts that fight one another. At such times, the battle takes on a frightful character, because the opposing rhythms, like fire and water united by the artist's implacable will, can neither defeat one another nor tear away from the opponent's clutches (Sonata Op. 58) until the idea they are supposed to represent comes to an end.

That is not the end of the investigation for the curious student of the great composer's paths; it is all but impossible to exhaust them, for the deeper the exploration, the more new details it reveals to be admired; let us just touch on one more. To be conveyed in the right spirit, the originality and freshness of Chopin's ideas are often manifested in an original and extraordinary way. Let us take a look, for example, at the beginning of some of his works: he has not yet commenced, has only cast forth a few preparatory strokes, and we already know what to expect. Or it seems there was no beginning, that what we are hearing is a continuation of ideas previously occupying the artist. At times, his works also have no conclusion; to no avail the insatiate listener, after the last chord, wonders about the lengthy pause and waits: in vain! The stream issues forth from the heart of the mountain, but who knows where it really began or how far it has traveled underground before emerging into the light? Who knows where it has turned, whether it will run much farther, where the stream will suddenly descend, sinking into the heart of the earth as if into a grave? A great idea resembles that stream: only part of it emerges. What form can then contain Chopin's conceived and completed idea—which is not isolated or alone, but is akin to other great ideas, at times begets them?

VII.

The elements of music presented here, spread forth in Chopin's works lavishly and with great fantasy, proclaim with one voice that character we have endeavored to show in its entirety. Yet this voice must be heard in order for miracles to be believed. How to wield a magic wand in order for spirits to obey its every motion? Chopin revealed the answer to those fortunate souls who heard him play. According to them, his playing was generally gentle. We believe this, though not unconditionally. Mildness and tenderness befit only the smaller works (and not everywhere); they would spoil everything that is tempestuous, impulsive, violent.[xiii] We rather conclude that on account of his increasingly waning strength[xiv] he did not wish to expose himself to a double exhaustion of body and spirit, and for that reason did not play at least his great poems before witnesses; or perhaps he thought that he would not be understood and did not wish to ill-treat his noblest ideas. Whatever the case, one easily finds accounts of Chopin playing mazurkas, nocturnes, and even polonaises; no one mentions hearing a ballade, a scherzo, or a sonata.[34]

He was heard by many people in Warsaw before and during his final concerts;[xv] but those times are so distant now! Besides, how different in his compositions was the Chopin of those times from the later Chopin! It is the difference between a youth and a mature adult, so it must also have existed in the performance of his own works. So are the treasures that he revealed lost forever? Indeed not! His praises have been sung around the world for so many years, and his spirit has dwelled in our corner of the world as well, written out in musical characters; he has been

---

xiii. We draw the reader's attention to the dual notion of *strength*: absolute strength, in the case at hand, is puerile; relative strength merits attention in the performance of works not just by Chopin, but by any composer. Relative strength may depend on the personal powers of the player, on his state of health, the genre he is playing, the spirit of the work, and even the character of the venue, to say nothing of acoustic illusions.

xiv. This was his most important reason for not fulfilling the wish, expressed in one of his letters to his family, to visit Poland at least once.

xv. We [Sikorski] are also among their number; yet we were too young to retain more than a blurred impression. We have a better memory of an event (and there are others who remember it) which in our remembrance of our illustrious compatriot we wish to preserve as a legend.

During the times of the former university of Warsaw, every Sunday and feast day, a morning service was held for its students at the church of the Nuns of the Visitation, around 11 a.m. A choir, composed of pupils and alumni of the conservatory of the day, led by Elsner, would perform hymns with organ or with orchestra. During his last year in Warsaw, Chopin was a frequent guest in the choir, and he willingly played on the organ, be it fugues by various masters or his own improvisations. A difficult part of playing the organ is the skilled and rich use of the pedal; he had the utmost facility in it, and it occasionally led him almost to show off, which in turn led to the suitable stirring of the voices of the keyboard. And once, in an interval between the parts of a mass performed with orchestra, Chopin sat down at the organ and, in the manner of famous organists, took as his theme a motive from the foregoing section and began to pour forth from it a wealth of ideas so copious, flowing in an uninterrupted stream, that everyone, from the oldest to the youngest, pressed around the player's bench, became engrossed, swept away, oblivious to the place and the duties they had gathered to fulfill. Until they were stirred by the hurried steps of the sacristan, launching into his peroration as he ran: "And what the deuce do you think you're doing here? The priest has already begun the *Dominus vobiscum* twice, the boys have been ringing and ringing at the altar, and the organ hasn't ceased! The Mother Superior is livid."

loved and adored, not for his fame, but for his works; so they have been understood. Although this may be said solely about his smaller works, in order to understand the large works as well, one must only have the will and some preparation to commence the work. We are not speaking here about purely mechanical means, for the need to possess these is self-explanatory, and excellent means are normally required. We mean here a preparation that enables the breaking down into its constituent parts that which cannot be understood as a whole; its substance will become gradually visible, the sections distinguished, the contrasts revealed and the whole become clear, immense and comprehensible. We recognize this from a stronger beating of the heart, from the blood flushing the face, from a tingling all over the body.

With regard to the purely mechanical aspects of playing the piano, Chopin was almost as inventive as in his compositions. The very nature of his ideas led him to the discoveries I will refer to here. The previously mentioned account about the efforts he made to encompass a tenth led even further, so that he taught the left hand in particular to reach intervals and create from them chords and arpeggios of hitherto unheard-of dimensions. The innovation of those passages that characterized his music forced him to carefully select and order the fingers, something he frequently indicated here and there in his works in order to facilitate the surmounting of difficulties, which were in any case vast. In this respect, too, he broke with the habits of old routines; he appeared to proceed contrary to the natural configuration of the fingers, yet he achieved splendid facilitations. We will point to at least one example of this in the sixth etude from Op. 25. At times, he has entire successions of notes played by a single finger, thereby explaining the accent with which he wishes to distinguish that place better than with words and signs. We will pass over other details of this kind; they may result from the habits of his hands and the singular exercises to which he sometimes subjected them; but they are mostly based on pertinent observations regarding the nature of the hand and the fingers. As a teacher, no doubt he sometimes had the opportunity to give similar advice, and this subject was sufficiently close to his heart that he even prepared a manuscript designed to reveal and make easier to acquire his way of understanding playing action. Yet he delayed its publication until his ideas were so pithily condensed that they fit onto just a few pages. If, as we assume, he was intending to express them in a logical system, that would be one more invention of his, since, as far as we are aware, nothing like it has yet been produced.

As regards the universal means through which Chopin realized the spirit that he applied to all compositions, we would surely not err in discerning it in the use of the pedal that raises the dampers. Chopin was the first to bestow upon the pedal such extensive use that he calls it into continual action throughout entire compositions, and in some passages he has it change almost every note, according to the changes of harmony. This emancipation of the pedal, so to speak, shows that he had divined the nature of the instrument (indeed, many ingenious improvements still lay before pianos in this respect) and turned that to his advantage in order to transmit his ideas. What, if not the sustaining pedal, arrays the nocturnes in a veil of mystery? It seems that we can see the shadows of fleeting spirits, hear them rustling. What, if not the pedal, arrays individual notes in melancholy and contemplation? What brings out the singing? What musters scattered notes, orders them like soldiers beneath the banner of a single chord and sends them into mortal battle against melody, and occasionally to its succor? The pedal, always the pedal. The role it plays in Chopin's works is so important, the help with which it covers up the instrument's shortcomings so marvelous, that on rejecting its participation the spirit of music comes to resemble a faintly drawn picture. One finds there character, fantasy, and strength, but without the distinctness that overcomes materiality; the notes remain in the piano, but weakened, meager, diffuse.

VIII.

May this be an end to our survey of Chopin. We began in his name and in the name of the art of which he was and will remain one of the patrons; and although we endeavored not to leave out anything that would concern the subject directly or indirectly, we have the feeling that we have barely touched it from a few angles and our strength is already exhausted. So with one final effort, we wish to summarize, as we see it, the spirit of the monuments of art that he has left us, so as to seek for him a likeness, if not a faithful portrait, among our other prophets—and the author of *Maria* comes to mind.[35]

The works of Chopin and the poem by Malczewski exude the same breath. They betray the same gloominess in their images and the same tenderness, the same dolor in the most exquisite passages, the same mysteriousness, blowing misfortune from all sides, the same courage, terror, and ferment of battle, and the terrifying action of nefarious influences. Malczewski completed his poem, yet we would still be in need of a conclusion: not because the plot of the play should be taken further or the feelings better developed; but we need something to allay the agitation in which the poem has engulfed us, for the Sword-bearer's silent despair has crept into our souls, and they (alas!) must refer to heaven for a solution. Chopin also leaves us in suspense. And the suffering he spreads out before us is genuine and immutable, so tightly woven with all that is rapture that when timorous hope, having reached the end, has found nothing for itself, it returns to the path it has already trodden to begin rummaging again until it drops from exhaustion, rendering itself up to the Everlasting will.

The details of this comparison, presented here in general outline, could be extrapolated; yet we must forgo them here, since they would lead us to numerous quotations of both geniuses and, given the indeterminate meaning of musical expressions, to subtle arguments frequently based on the significance of the elements of music. We sense that even this would not lead to the desired goal, since matters of sentiment are indicated only to a degree and can never be uttered, being visible to sentiment alone. Here we will just mention that this similarity extends to minor aspects of form and enables us to infer about the spirit as well; for instance, bold expression, unexpected phrases previously all but unknown to the language (of both), energy that penetrates the depths of feeling like lightning with just a few words; and those minor ambiguities which an expert on two languages, although comprehending, would gladly see more transparent than condensed into one, would gladly find extended for the sake of better contemplation. [The similarity even extends] as far as expressions that confuse good taste, which is overwhelmed by effects and drowned in the idea that flows from them.

Yet this comparison has its limits: Malczewski left us a single narrative poem; Chopin more than a dozen [narrative works], and being ever original, and constantly new, he could pour himself out onto more numerous pages and reveal himself more precisely. Hence numerous works of his contain features which in Malczewski's *Maria* are lacking or less well developed. Yet in spite of this, the general spirit of the works left by both proceeds in fraternal embrace; and we suppose that if Chopin had placed his poetry in words and Malczewski expounded his in music, the similarity would remain the same, and perhaps only the relative development of the two would alter.

Let us not inspect the outward circumstances of their lives, Chopin the happier in that he was acknowledged during his lifetime and spoke in a language which the whole of humanity understands; yet of all peoples we Poles understand him best. May his voice never cease to fill our souls with a loftiness equal to the pain that overflows our hearts since his loss!

NOTES

1. Józef Sikorski, "Wspomnienie Chopina," *Biblioteka Warszawska* 4 (1849), 510–49.

2. O[skar] K[olberg], in "Doniesienia literackie" (Literary News), *Biblioteka Warszawska* 4 (1849), 436.

3. The baptismal document lists a different person, but members of Chopin's family always referred to Count Fryderyk Skarbek as the composer's godfather. Piotr Mysłakowski and Andrzej Sikorski, "Okoliczności urodzin Fryderyka Chopina: Co mówią źródła" (The Circumstances of Chopin's Birth: What the Sources Tell Us), *Ruch Muzyczny*, 2002, no. 20, 28–34. More extensive study of biographical documents related to the composer, his family, and friends has been published by the genealogists Mysłakowski and Sikorski as *Fryderyk Chopin: The Origins* (Warsaw: Fryderyk Chopin Institute, 2010). Scholars have long debated the conflicting details about Chopin's birth, however Sikorski's information seems accurate. See the beginning of Section II.

4. Elżbieta Szczepańska-Lange, "Józef Sikorski (1813–1896): Szkic biograficzny," *Muzyka* (1997): 31–69.

5. E. T. A. Hoffmann, "Review of Beethoven's Fifth Symphony," *Allgemeine musikalische Zeitung* (July 1810): 634.

6. An excellent introduction to the subject of German Idealism and music is found in Mark Evan Bonds, "Idealism and the Aesthetics of Instrumental Music at the Turn of the Nineteenth Century," *Journal of the American Musicological Society* 50/2–3 (1997): 387–420.

7. On Chopin and Polish political messianism, see Halina Goldberg, "'Remembering That Tale of Grief': The Prophetic Voice in Chopin's Music," in *The Age of Chopin: Interdisciplinary Inquiries*, ed. Halina Goldberg (Bloomington: Indiana University Press, 2004), 54–92.

8. On Liszt's book as a travelogue, see Virginia E. Whealton, review, "Franz Liszt, F. Chopin," *Journal of the American Liszt Society* 63 (2012): 81–88; and the chapter titled "Touring Poland: Nationalist Fantasies" in her forthcoming dissertation from Indiana University.

9. An extensive study of racialized reception of Chopin's music is found in Maja Trochimczyk, "Chopin and the 'Polish Race': On National Ideologies and Chopin Reception," in Goldberg, *Age of Chopin: Interdisciplinary Inquiries*, 278–313.

10. Short fragments of the essay have been translated in the indispensable volume *Chopin and His Critics: An Anthology*, ed. Irena Poniatowska (Warsaw: Fryderyk Chopin Institute, 2011), 60–63.

11. Sikorski provides as his epigraph the concluding verses of Adam Mickiewicz's narrative poem *Konrad Wallenrod* (1825–28), describing fictitious events that take place in fourteenth-century Lithuania. Polish contemporaries of Mickiewicz understood the poem as a veiled description of Poland at the time.

Here, and throughout Sikorski's text, the three dots represent suspension points from the original, *not* editorial ellipses.

12. Piast Kołodziej (the Wheelwright) was the mythical ninth-century progenitor of Poland's first dynasty, the house of Piast, which expired and was followed by the Jagiellonian dynasty in the fourteenth century. The Piast legend held special appeal during the Sarmatian revival of the eighteenth and nineteenth centuries, which emphasized the local rustic roots of Poland's early monarchs.

13. Sikorski quotes the closing line from the poem "Romantyczność" (Romanticism) by Adam Mickiewicz, which served as a manifesto for the Romantic generation of Polish artists.

14. Though the accepted date of Chopin's birth is 1 March 1810, both the day and the year have been questioned because of conflicting reports and historical records. The most recent scholarship supports the date of 1 March (the date always given by the composer and his family) over the oft-mentioned 23 February (the date on the certificates of his birth and baptism). The accepted year, 1810, however, appears to be incorrect. The date of 1809, given by Sikorski, reappears in numerous nineteenth-century publications

written under the watchful gaze of Chopin's mother and sisters, and the year 1810 was not introduced into writings on Chopin until Ferdinand Hoesick's book of 1904. Numerous other arguments in favor of 1809 as the year of Chopin's birth have been presented by the genealogists Mysłakowski and Sikorski in *Fryderyk Chopin: The Origins*, a thorough investigation of biographical documents related to the composer, his family, and friends.

The distances given by Sikorski are in historic Polish miles, one of which (in the nineteenth century) equaled about 8.5 kilometers.

15. The year of Żywny's death (†1840) requires a correction: Wojciech Żywny (also Vojtěch or Adalbert Živný) died in Warsaw in 1842. Żywny, Chopin's only official piano teacher, was born in Bohemia in 1756. After he relocated to Poland, he was at first in the employ of Prince Kazimierz Sapieha and then moved to Warsaw, where he became a popular piano teacher.

16. The first few families listed by Sikorski were among the most illustrious in Warsaw in terms of social standing and, in some cases, patriotic and cultural contributions. Two households mentioned in the list belonged to Russians: that of the Duchess of Łowicz (Joanna Grudzińska), a Polish woman married to Grand Duke Constantine, the brother of the Tsar, who resided in Warsaw as the as Chief Commander of the Polish Forces (since the morganatic marriage had cost him the Russian throne); and that of Jerzy Okołow, the Director of the Royal Accounting Chamber and a much hated agent of Russia. Konstanty Wolicki was a wealthy financier whose salon was notable for its music making. The Chopins remained close to the Skarbek family, the employers of the composer's parents, Mikołaj and Justyna Chopin, before their move to Warsaw. For further information on these salons, see Halina Goldberg, *Music in Chopin's Warsaw* (New York: Oxford University Press, 2008), 151–61; also, my "Musical Life in Warsaw During Chopin's Youth, 1810–1830" (PhD diss., City University of New York, 1997).

17. During the early years of the nineteenth century Europe experienced an increased interest in developing a household-size organ. In Poland the experiments of the taxidermist August Fidelis Brunner and professor of mineralogy Fryderyk Jakub Hoffman, as well as the piano builder Józef Długosz resulted in the construction of such instruments that are mentioned in sources under various names. Chopin was known to have performed on and even composed for these instruments (the two compositions are no longer extant). See Goldberg, *Music in Chopin's Warsaw*, 37–41.

18. Ludwika Linde (1800–1836) was the second wife of Samuel Bogumił Linde, the Rector of the Warsaw Lyceum, where Chopin's father taught French, and a professor at Warsaw University. Professor Linde was most famous as the author of the monumental *Dictionary of the Polish Language*. The Linde and Chopin families were neighbors and friends. An especially intimate relationship existed between Fryderyk's sister Emilia and the professor's daughter by his first wife, also named Ludwika. Mrs. Linde, daughter of the conductor of a military orchestra, received a solid musical education. She often played four-hands with the young Fryderyk, and it is to her that he dedicated his Opus 1, the Rondo in C Minor.

19. Chopin's confidant during the composer's teenage years, Tytus Woyciechowski (1808–1879), was the recipient of some of the most intimate and insightful letters written by the composer.

20. The private performances of the amateur pianist Aleksander Rembieliński (ca. 1800–ca.1828), who in 1825 arrived in Warsaw after six years of studies in Paris, elicited praises from Chopin. Rembieliński was also a composer of waltzes, mazurs, and two piano trios. Zofia Helman, Zbigniew Skowron, and Hanna Wróblewska-Straus, eds., *Korespondencja Fryderyka Chopina* (Warsaw: Wydawnictwo Uniwersytetu Warszawskiego, 2009), 136.

21. The friendship between Chopin and Julian Fontana (1810–1865) —a pianist, composer, jurist, and translator—went back to their conservatory years in Warsaw. After they reconnected in Paris, Fontana often served as copyist of his famous friend's works. The pursuit of his own pianistic career took him to Cuba and New York. After he returned

to Europe, in response to the request from Chopin's family, he served as the editor of Chopin posthumous works (Opp. 66–74).

22. The three pianists—the German-born Maurycy Ernemann (1800–1866), and the Bohemians, Józef Jawurek (Javůrek) (1756–1840) and Leopold Eustachius Czapek (Čapek) (1792–1840)—frequently associated with Chopin and are mentioned in his letters. The first two musicians taught at the Warsaw Conservatory, where Chopin was a student.

23. The song "Świat srogi świat przewrotny" (A World That's Harsh, a World That's Perfidious) came from the singspiel *Cud mniemany, czyli Krakowiacy i Górale* (The Supposed Miracle, or Cracovians and Highlanders) with music by Jan Stefani to a libretto by Wojciech Bogusławski, the "Father of Polish National Theater" and member of the conspiracy against Poland's occupiers. Premiered in 1794, the opera incited audiences to take up arms in the Kościuszko Insurrection. The political allusions hidden under the surface of pastoral comedy remained current for decades to come, and in 1816 Kurpiński offered a new version of the opera *Zabobon, czyli Krakowiacy i Górale albo Nowe Krakowiaki* (Superstition, or Cracovians and Highlanders, or New Cracovians), from which came the song "W mieście dziwne obyczaje" (Strange Customs in the City). Chopin's choice of these two arias as the basis for improvisation would have held patriotic significance for his audiences, but it did not bring the expected enthusiastic success.

24. Leon Ulrych (1811–1885), later famous for his translations of Shakespeare's works to Polish, would have known Chopin from gatherings of the young artists and intellectuals they attended together in the late 1820s.

25. The English actor David Garrick (1717–1779) revolutionized theater with his realistic acting that involved pantomime and vivid use of gesture. The Garrickian reform also had a profound impact on opera.

26. The life of Carl Filtsch (1830–1845), a pupil of Chopin, whose performances were greeted with admiration from the most illustrious musicians of his time, was cut short by tuberculosis. Chopin had great hopes for the gifted young man, in whom he found a kindred musical spirit.

27. The Romantic era witnessed a proliferation of mechanical contraptions intended to strengthen, stretch, and exercise the hand of a pianist. In addition to Kalkbrenner's device, others included Johann Bernhard Lodier's *chiroplast*, Casimir Martin's *chiro-gymnaste*, and Henri Hertz's *dactylion*.

28. George Onslow (1784–1853) was a French composer famous and highly respected for his numerous chamber works.

29. Chopin and the poet Stefan Witwicki (1801–1847) frequented the same circles of young Romantics in Warsaw, and already then Chopin set several of his songs to Witwicki's texts. Having served in the National Guard during the November Uprising, Witwicki had to leave the country after its failure. Their friendship continued in Paris, with Chopin setting a few more of Witwicki's poems and dedicating the Mazurkas Op. 41 to him. The letters written by Witwicki, Chopin, Bohdan Zaleski, and George Sand indicate that the poet and the composer remained close throughout their lives.

30. Sikorski is referencing Ludwig Rellstab's notoriously negative reviews of Chopin's published compositions, which appeared, starting in 1832, in the Berlin journal *Iris im Gebiete der Tonkunst*. With the 1836 review of the E-Minor Concerto, Rellstab's tone softened, and when he visited Paris in 1843, he reached out to Chopin with a letter of introduction from Liszt.

31. The ballads of the German poet Gottfried August Bürger (1747–1794), the most famous of them "Leonore," helped define the genre and had a lasting impact on Romantic poets and composers.

32. The *kujawiak* and *obertas* are Polish folk dances often mentioned in relation to the mazurka. A revisionist perspective on the kujawiak is offered by Goldberg in "Nationalizing

the Kujawiak and Constructions of Nostalgia in Chopin's Mazurkas," *19th-Century Music* 39/3 (Spring 2016): 223-47.

33. Sikorski refers to the theme that opens the *agitato* passage (measure 41) of the middle section of Nocturne in E Major, Op. 62, No. 2.

34. While there might be some validity to the claim that in his later years, when his health was failing, Chopin shied away from performing the larger works, there are numerous witnesses who report such performances in earlier years. For example, Georges Mathias and his father heard Chopin play the Ballade in G Minor, Op. 23. In 1838, Félicien Mallefille published a vision inspired by Chopin's performance of the Ballade in F Major, Op. 38; Chopin also performed this work during the 26 April 1841 concert at the Salle Pleyel. Even as late as 1848, he played his Sonata, Op. 35 to some English friends.

35. Sikorski refers to the Romantic poet Antoni Malczewski (1793–1826), whose reputation rests on a single work, his poetic novel *Maria* (1824). For the young Romantics, *Maria* was the model of poetic writing that embraced new content and style. Based on historical events that took place in the seventeenth century, *Maria* centers on the death of a young aristocratic woman, the beloved daughter of the Sword-bearer, who was murdered on the orders of her father-in-law. Like Lord Byron and Sir Walter Scott, Malczewski envelops the narrative in an atmosphere of mystery and horror.

Chopin and the Gothic

ANATOLE LEIKIN

Programmatic literary influences are common in Romantic music, but only three cases of direct literary connections can be established with any certainty in the works of Fryderyk Chopin. Tangible links exist between Chopin's Preludes, Op. 28, and Alphonse de Lamartine's poem "Les Préludes."[1] Chopin's Ballades have apparent bonds with Adam Mickiewicz's poetic writings.[2] Finally, Chopin's Nocturne in G Minor, Op. 15, No. 3, according to several contemporary commentators, was composed and perhaps even originally inscribed "after a presentation of the tragedy of Hamlet."[3] Interestingly, Chopin's literary choices follow a common thread that unites all three authors— Lamartine, Mickiewicz, and Shakespeare— despite their historical, geographical, and stylistic dissimilarities. This common thread is Gothic fiction.

The Gothic angle has not been explored as one of Chopin's probable literary inspirations. The main reason for such an omission is that until the 1970s most critics and commentators considered Gothic literature a sideshow of Romanticism at best or an embarrassing and destructive cultural phenomenon at worst. When the Gothic was not vilified, it was either politely ignored or offhandedly dismissed as a poor relation to the Romantic movement.[4]

In fact, Gothic literature had a rich genesis and an even more fertile history. It began with Horace Walpole's novel *The Castle of Otranto: A Story*, published in England under a pseudonym on Christmas Day, 1764. The novel instantly became so popular that it was reprinted the following year under Walpole's name and with a different subtitle: *A Gothic Story*. Walpole's success impelled several other authors in England to follow in his footsteps and publish novels with "Gothic" in the title, including Clara Reeves's *The Old English Baron: A Gothic Story* (1778), Richard Warner's *Netley Abbey: A Gothic Story* (1795), and Isabella Kelly's *The Baron's Daughter: A Gothic Romance* (1802).

Other literary titles published at the time did not include the word *Gothic*, yet the term eventually became a common reference to a literature of nightmare, terror, death, and, frequently, romance. In fact, in the late eighteenth and nineteenth centuries Gothic stories were often called "romances" to set them apart from "realist" novels.[5]

Walpole's first Gothic novel had predecessors. Walpole himself, in the preface to the second edition, pays homage to Shakespeare, drawing parallels between *Hamlet* and the novel. Not only Walpole but other Gothic writers revered several scenes from Shakespeare, particularly the Witches' and the Ghost's scenes from *Macbeth* and *Hamlet,* as prototypical for the genre.[6]

Another influential force was a group of poets who emerged in England in the eighteenth century. The impetus for a new poetic movement was inaugurated in 1721, when the poem "A Night Piece on Death" by Thomas Parnell (1679–1718) was published posthumously. The poem was soon followed by many other poetic works in the same vein, among them Edward Young's "The Complaint, or, Night-Thoughts on Life, Death, & Immortality" (1742–45), Robert Blair's "The Grave" (1743), James Hervey's "Meditations Among the Tombs" (1746–47), and Thomas Gray's "Elegy Written in a Country Church-Yard" (1751).

As is evident from their titles, all these poems were full of mournful reflections on the brevity of life, terror, loneliness, darkness, and ruins. The poets of this movement meditated on such topics deep into the night, usually amid tombs at a graveyard, which earned the group the name the "Graveyard School."[7] Many graveyard poets were clergymen who interspersed their thoughts of death with religious ponderings. The graveyard poets gained vast popularity in England and were translated throughout Europe.

Yet another influence on the future development of the British Gothic novel can be found in some lugubrious eighteenth-century French writings. One of them was Benedictine monk Dom Calmet's (1672–1757) *Traité sur les apparitions des esprits et sur les vampires ou les revenans de Hongrie, de Moravie, &c.* (Treatise on Apparitions of Spirits and on Vampires or Revenants of Hungary, Moravia, etc.). Published in 1752 in an expanded version and translated into English in 1759, it "served to popularize a subject which would eventually become one of the major themes of the Gothic."[8] Among other influential French texts, Terry Hale mentions a play by François-Thomas-Marie de Baculard d'Arnaud, *Les amants malheureux, ou le Comte de Comminge* (The Unfortunate Lovers, or the Count de Comminge), published in 1764 as an adaptation of an earlier novel by Mme de Tencin. It concerns two lovers, cruelly separated by parental edict and reunited in death in the somber cloisters of a monastery.[9]

Early Gothic writers in England eagerly absorbed and expanded the themes and the moods of their forerunners. The dramatic paraphernalia of Gothic tales included rambling old castles and abbeys; supernatural manifestations and apparitions; stark contrasts between pastoral landscapes at daytime and dreadful graveyard settings at night; characters consumed by love and haunted by death; mysterious occurrences and frightful hallucinations. English readers met new Gothic fiction with delight and a growing demand for more. The genre flourished. After Walpole's *The Castle of Otranto,* the throng of authors included Clara Reeve (*The Old English Baron*), Ann Radcliffe (*The Castles of Athlin and Dunbayne,* 1789; and *The Mysteries of Udolpho,* 1794), Matthew Gregory Lewis (*The Monk: A Romance,* 1796), and Charles Maturin (*Melmoth the Wanderer,* 1820), along with many others.

Gothic fiction thus became an integral part of Romantic literature. Anne Williams insists that "Gothic" and "Romantic" are not two but one poetic tradition.[10] Indeed, one of the most prominent Romantic authors in England who thrived on Gothic elements was Lord Byron (1788–1824). He read in depth a great number of Gothic novels, including those by Horace Walpole and Ann Radcliffe, and reused their notions ingeniously. Byron's *Manfred* and *Childe Harold* (especially Canto IV) both teem with Gothic details.[11] As Peter Cochran asserts:

> The Gothic literary tradition meant a lot to Byron in his writing as well as in his leisure activities. He derived from it a template for his more mysterious, alienated, sociopathic characters, and an encouragement for his preoccupation with ruins, and the inevitability of decay—decay civic, architectural, and human.[12]

English Gothic novels were widely translated into French and German. In France, for example, the number of translated English Gothic novels between 1767 and 1828 varied from one to ten a year (with the exception of 1790 and 1804, when no such titles were published in France). All in all, more than a hundred English Gothic novels were translated into French during that period.[13]

In the late eighteenth century, French and German authors began writing their own versions of Gothic tales, and these were also immediately translated into other languages. In Germany, the development of Gothic literature culminated in the Romantic works of Friedrich von Schiller (1759–1805) and E. T. A. Hoffmann (1776–1822). Schiller was "a pioneering author of Gothic literature,"[14] and his *Schauerroman* (shudder novel), *Der Geisterseher* (*The Ghost-Seer*, 1789), was widely read not only in Germany but also in translation in France and England. (Byron was deeply influenced by *Der Geisterseher*, which he read in translation, since he could not read German.)[15] Hoffmann had an enormous impact on French storywriters as well. His works were translated into French and had countless admirers in France.[16]

In the wake of the craze caused by translated English and German Gothic tales, French authors created their own version of horror fiction in the late eighteenth century, a genre that came to be known as *roman noir* (black novel). *Roman noir* flourished from the 1790s until the 1820s. In 1821, Charles Nodier (1780–1844), one of the founding figures of the French Romantic movement, published *Smarra ou le demons de la nuit* (Smarra, or The Demons of the Night), a fantastic fable filled with violent imagery and dream sequences. It marked a new development in French Gothic fiction, for which Nodier coined the term *roman frénétique*. The term *frénétique*, according to Nodier, refers to writers who, whether in prose or verse, "flaunt their . . . rage and despair over tombstones, exhume the dead in order to terrify the living, or who torment the reader's imagination with such horrifying scenes so as to suggest the deranged dreams of madmen."[17]

Between 1821 and 1848, more than two hundred novels and collections of short stories were published in France, excluding translations, and all could be categorized as *frénétique*. One of the most popular *frénétique* novels of the early 1820s was *Le solitaire* (The Recluse) by Charles-Victor Prévot, vicomte d'Arlincourt (1788–1856). Within a few months of its publication in 1821 it was reprinted a dozen times and translated into ten languages.

Any deliberation on the impact of Gothic fiction on Chopin is hampered by the fact that Chopin never discussed art and literature in his letters. We do know, however, that long before he moved to Paris he was keenly interested in poetry. In Dresden, Chopin attended a five-hour performance of Goethe's *Faust* and was deeply impressed by that poetic play. In Warsaw, he spent many days with his friends at the coffeehouse Dziurka (The Little Hole), talking for hours about Byron and Schiller.[18]

George Sand, Chopin's consort and one of his closest friends between 1837 and 1847, recalls that her mother read d'Arlincourt with passion. Sand herself read, with delight and terror, Ann Radcliffe (in French), felt overwhelmed by Byron's poetry, and read as well the *frénétique* authors

Eugène Sue (1804–1857) and Jules Janin (1804–1874). Sand enjoyed reading the novel *Fragoletta, ou Naples et Paris en 1799* (Fragoletta, or Naples and Paris in 1799), written by another popular *frénétique* writer, Henri de Latouche (1785–1851). Latouche was a close friend of Sand who helped advance her budding literary career.[19]

We also know that Eugène Sue visited Chopin at the composer's apartment in rue de la Chaussée d'Antin on 13 December 1836, and that Jules Janin was among a small number of invited guests at Chopin's concert at the house of Marquis de Custine on 8 May 1838.[20]

Perhaps even more important are Chopin's close personal connections with Polish émigré poets who exhibited strong predilections for the Gothic, particularly the "Three Bards" of Polish literature: Adam Mickiewicz (1798–1855), Zygmunt Krasiński (1812–1859), and Juliusz Słowacki (1809–1849).

The impact of Gothic aesthetics on Chopin's music is arguably most tangible in his Preludes, Op. 28. In reviews of a concert in which Chopin played several preludes for the first time in public, Franz Liszt and an anonymous critic both mentioned that Chopin's "poetic preludes" were "similar to those of a great contemporary poet Alphonse de Lamartine," evidently alluding to Lamartine's poem "Les Préludes."

Indeed, Chopin's Preludes have very little—if anything—to do with the innumerable didactic piano preludes published previously by various composers who were mostly piano pedagogues. Instead, the Preludes are, as Liszt put it, "compositions of an order entirely apart; they are not merely, as the title would indicate, introductions to other *morceaux*."[21] Chopin's Preludes have much more in common with Lamartine's poem than with their nominal musical namesakes.

Many aspects of Lamartine's "Les Préludes" are best comprehended within the context of Gothic fiction. These include stark contrasts between serene, sunlit landscapes, violent storms, and eerie night scenes, as well as the presence of a supernatural creature (*génie*, or Genius) who conjures sundry manifestations of death for the protagonist.

Most of these attributes can be found in Chopin's Preludes, to which the composer added other typical Gothic trappings—chiefly because of the surroundings and the atmosphere of the place where Opus 28 was completed: an abandoned Carthusian monastery on the Spanish island of Mallorca. Spain held a special attraction for nineteenth-century avid readers. The country was a popular exotic setting in quite a few Gothic works, such as Lewis's *The Monk*, Jan Potocki's *Manuscrit trouvé à Saragosse*

(*Manuscript Found in Saragossa*, 1804–10), Charles Robert Maturin's *Melmoth the Wanderer* (1820, translated into French in 1821), and Lord Byron's *Childe Harold's Pilgrimage* (1812–18). Prosper Mérimée (1803–1870) and Théophile Gautier (1811–1872) both defined Spain as "the romantic country *par excellence.*"[22]

The abandoned Carthusian monastery in Valldemossa, Mallorca, where Chopin, George Sand, and her two children spent the winter of 1838–39, epitomized a perfect Romantic—that is to say, Gothic—getaway. The monastery was (and still is) surrounded by breathtakingly gorgeous landscapes. As Elizabeth Durot-Boucé remarks, "Gothic stories usually open in the daylight in picturesque or sublime surroundings." However, all the important events in Gothic novels take place at night, especially midnight. In contrast to the bucolic daylight scenery that surrounds a castle or a monastery, night appears even more mysterious and menacing.[23]

Furthermore, as Fred Botting points out, the Gothic aesthetic was based on feeling and emotion, which made it particularly receptive to the atmosphere of the sublime, which is associated with grandeur and magnificence. Craggy, mountainous landscapes of Gothic tales aroused powerful emotions of wonder and terror.[24] Poetic landscapes are an essential component generally in Alphonse de Lamartine's works, and in particular in "Les Préludes." Although the poet depicts no mountains in it, mountain landscapes figure prominently in his other poems—for example, in "Milly ou la terre natale" from *Harmonies poétiques et religieuses* and in "La solitude" from *Nouvelles méditations poétiques.*[25]

Another part of the monastery that delighted both Chopin and Sand was the monks' graveyard, surrounded by the walls and windows of the cloisters and, in 1838, overgrown with grass. The reason a cemetery would hold so much attraction for the French voyagers is obvious. In a great many Gothic fables, a decaying, gloomy castle "was linked to other medieval edifices—abbeys, churches and graveyards especially."[26]

Chopin mentioned yet another morbidly Gothic feature in his letter to Fontana on 28 December 1838, saying that his cell was shaped like a tall coffin. Indeed, the high, vaulted ceiling of the cell gently sloped toward a flat rectangle, giving its occupant the troubling impression of looking at the lid of a coffin—from the inside. Apparently, every time the Carthusian monks lay down, they would contemplate the *memento mori* molded into the ceiling.[27]

One can only imagine how that architectural design could have affected Chopin's anxious imagination. He always had a peculiar attraction to the macabre; his correspondence contains many descriptions of coffins and corpses; he both dreaded and was fascinated by death and was haunted by constant premonitions and fears of his own impending demise.[28] In the nineteenth century, of course, this mindset was not at all unusual. In countless Gothic stories, "death proves an omnipresent element, haunting the characters either when, awake, they fear for their lives or, when, asleep, they conjure up nightmarishly gory scenes."[29]

After dark, the cloisters outside the visitors' cell became much more mysterious and sinister, having an unavoidable effect on the imagination. "I would challenge the calmest and coolest brain," Sand writes, "to preserve sanity here over a long period. . . . I confess that I seldom walked through the cloister after dusk without a feeling of mingled distress and pleasure."[30]

One more component puts the finishing touches on the Gothic setting at the Valldemossa monastery: frightening ghosts and nightmarish hallucinations. Like protagonists in Gothic tales, Chopin lived through these ordeals, too. Sand's ten-year-old daughter Solange played a role in shaping Chopin's belief that the ghosts of monks were haunting their cell. As a child who was spending time with the locals, she was the only one in the family who could have picked up the Mallorcan language, especially while her mother and brother Maurice (then sixteen), were running errands in Palma. It was most probably Solange who told Chopin that Maria Antonia, the only other tenant at the monastery, saw the ghostly procession of monks carrying a coffin to the cemetery, and that one of the monks said to her, in Mallorcan, "Tell him to prepare for this!"

And it was Solange who apparently told Chopin that her playmate saw the ghost of Father Nicolás, the monk who used to live in the same cell, sitting on Chopin's bed. Moreover, in one of her later letters, Solange gleefully described how she and her friend dressed up in monks' robes, which they found in the monastery, and "frightened Chopin out of his wits by creeping into the cell at dusk."[31]

Chopin, who almost never ventured for a stroll outdoors, spent his days and nights inside the monastery, composing and, occasionally, descending (or ascending, if you will) into hallucinatory states. Sand maintains that for Chopin "the monastery cloister was full of terrors and phantoms even when he was well."[32] She recalls that when she returned with her children from her nocturnal explorations in the ruins, she would find him "at ten in the evening, pale at his piano, his eyes haggard, his hair standing almost on end." It would take Chopin several moments to recognize them.

Death—an overriding notion in graveyard poetry and an omnipresent component in Gothic writings—is also a predominant concept in Lamartine's poem. How does the idea of death manifest itself in music?

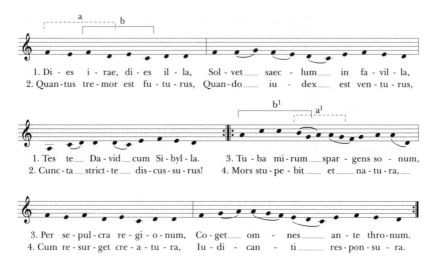

Example 1. *Dies irae* plainchant.

Funeral marches, of course, are the most obvious candidates for this role, and there is no shortage of funeral marches in Chopin's music, whether they are designated as such in the score or, far more frequently, not. But there is also another powerful musical symbol of death.

George Sand in her memoir offered an intriguing, if cryptic, observation, averring that several Chopin preludes bring to mind the visions of dead monks and echoes of funeral chants that besieged the composer.[33] My analyses of Opus 28 determine that all twenty-four preludes are thoroughly imbued with the medieval chant *Dies irae* (Day of Wrath or Judgment Day), part of the Catholic Requiem Mass for the dead (see Example 1).[34]

The Gothic appeal of the *Dies irae* is manifold. As many other typical Gothic elements, this prayer's origin is medieval and monastic. Even more important, it carries existential, even eschatological, and therefore profoundly Gothic inferences.

Depictions of Judgment Day are found in various Gothic tales. Thus one finds references to Judgment Day in Part 4 of Mickiewicz's *Dziady* (Forefathers' Eve), which depicts an ancient Slavic feast commemorating the dead. Zygmunt Krasiński's drama *Nie-Boska Komedia* (Un-Divine Comedy) is filled with medieval topics, death, madness, supernatural beings, and satanic forces; it also contains frequent references to Judgment Day.

In the *Dies irae* chant both the living and the dead are brought to the throne of the Judge, and the idea of life and death as two worlds with a fluid or even barely existing boundary between them is an ultimate Romantic—that is, Gothic—idea. Novalis (1772–1801) had already proclaimed the "dissolution of the differences between life and death," stating that "death is the romanticized principle of life . . . through death, life is laid bare . . . death frees the human."[35] Adam Mickiewicz, among other writers, expounded this notion in his *Dziady*. For example, the poem "Upiór" (The Phantom), which serves as a prologue to Part 2 of *Dziady*, is a symbol of oscillating connections between life and death, of a continuous interaction between these two worlds.[36]

Since the nineteenth century, the *Dies irae* chant has become one of the most potent and familiar musical symbols of death. Two notable secular compositions that include extended quotations of the *Dies irae* and precede Chopin's Opus 28 are Hector Berlioz's *Symphonie fantastique* (1830) and Charles-Valentin Alkan's *Trois morceaux dans le genre pathétique*, Op. 15 (1837). The *Symphonie fantastique* is clearly the more celebrated of the two, but it is difficult to assess how it influenced the Preludes. To begin with, in the finale of the symphony, *Songe d'une nuit du sabbat* (Dream of a Witches' Sabbath), the quote from the plainchant is an ironic reference to Roman liturgy, an exuberant, if mocking, depiction of a Black Mass. Berlioz's approach is far removed from the moods that prevail in Opus 28.

Alkan's treatment of the chant markedly differs from the one used by Berlioz. In his three-movement piano suite, the first two pieces are titled "Aime-moi" (Love Me) and "Le vent" (The Wind). The *Dies irae* is invoked in the third piece, "Morte" (Death). Here the chant is indeed a signifier of death. It is neither a church prayer nor a mocking caricature of one (and, in any case, Alkan was Jewish).[37]

The macabre atmosphere of "Morte" apparently did not sit well with Robert Schumann, who vilified the piece for being depressingly "black on black" and having "a considerable flavor of Sue and Sand."[38] Eugène Sue was, as mentioned, a friend of Sand and a prominent representative of the French Gothic.

Night imagery, associated with dreams and nightmares, anxiety and mystery, supernatural creatures and death, is of paramount significance in Gothic tales. It comes as no surprise, therefore, that Chopin's nocturnes serve as natural conduits for Gothic ambiance. His Nocturne in B Major, Op. 32, No. 1, is a fascinating case of a piece emanating precisely this Gothic aura.

Describing this nocturne, Lennox Berkeley writes that its "quiet, reflective character . . . is suddenly interrupted by a forceful and menacing recitative, as though the composer's thoughts had been put to flight by some sinister apparition. It is an ending that defies analysis, but compels acceptance."[39] For Herbert Weinstock, the Nocturne's conclusion defies logic—it is "a coda of apparently unrelated, recitativelike material that, with numerous uncertainties and pauses, . . . is an action worthy of a better composition."[40]

Indeed, quite a few editors and pianists have refused to accept the unusual minor-key ending of this B-Major Nocturne (see Example 3), despite the fact that the French, German, and English first editions all end the piece that way. Several later editors could not reconcile themselves with the idea that a major-mode piece would inexplicably close in a parallel minor key and "corrected" the closing chord from B minor to B major. These editions include those published by Carl Mikuli (1879), Theodore Kullak (1881), Karl Klindworth (1883), Herrmann Scholtz (1905), and Rafael Joseffy (1915). Arthur Rubinstein also concludes his recording of the Nocturne with a B-major chord.[41]

And here is yet another commonly misconstrued feature of this nocturne. Its soothing, gently undulating melody is occasionally interrupted by a *stretto* and abrupt *forte*, followed by stunned silence (see Examples 2a and 2b). Many performers nonetheless ignore Chopin's notation, apparently not seeing sufficient justification to ruin a lovely cantilena. A long list of pianists who smooth over Chopin's ostensibly eccentric markings includes Arthur Rubinstein, Grigory Sokolov, Daniel Barenboim, Maurizio Pollini, and Mieczysław Horszowski.

Indeed, it is rather difficult to rationalize both the strange recitative-like ending in the parallel minor and the odd disruptions of the melodic flow—unless we place the Nocturne into a Gothic context. Glimpses of something horrifying lurking in the dark, ubiquitous in Gothic tales, always create jolting, hair-raising moments that curdle the blood. In these circumstances, a sharp *stretto*, combined with a *forte* and a sudden long pause, depicts precisely an inescapable reaction to horror that makes the heart race and the lungs gasp for air (see Example 2a, measure 6). Only after a pause comes the realization it was all probably just a figment of the imagination. The feeling of threat recedes, anguish subsides, and the song resumes—at least until the next bloodcurdling moment.

Intriguingly, the third *stretto* moment (Example 2b, measure 35) lacks a *forte* indication in all of the first editions of the Nocturne—French, German, and English. In spite of that, many later publications added a

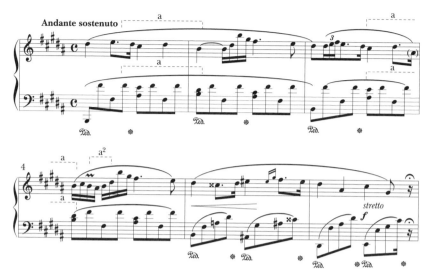

Example 2a. Nocturne, Op. 32, No. 1, mm. 1–8.

Example 2b. Nocturne, Op. 32, No. 1, mm. 28–35.

forte marking in measure 35, evidently for the sake of consistency. There are, however, a couple of copies of the French first edition belonging to Chopin's students (Camille O'Meara-Dubois and Jane Stirling) that have Chopin's autograph annotations in the scores. He corrected a few misprints, wrote down fingerings, etc. He also added several dynamic markings, but did not pencil in a *forte* sign in measure 35.

This creates an interesting musical sequence. After the first two loud cries of terror in the Nocturne's measures 6 and 18 (see Example 2a), the listener expects a similar reaction in the next *stretto*. Instead, the melody

Example 3. Nocturne, Op. 32, No. 1, mm. 60–66.

is unexpectedly interrupted with a soft gasp, which sounds just as much if not more terrified (Example 2b). Now the narrative in the Nocturne is clouded by uncertainty. Will the next *stretto* be introduced *piano* or *forte*? There is just one more *stretto* that occurs in the Nocturne, in measure 56, and it turns out to be loud after all.

The last five bars of the Nocturne, characterized by Berkeley as "a forceful and menacing recitative, as though the composer's thoughts had been put to flight by some sinister apparition," supplies a fitting closing to the Nocturne's Gothic discourse (Example 3). Curses and prophecies that spell doom for main characters are common in Gothic fiction. The music coming from nowhere at midnight in Ann Radcliffe's *The Mysteries of Udolpho* is said to warn people of their death. Eleanor Sleath's novel *The*

Nocturnal Minstrel (1810) features a mysterious soothsayer who begins his incantations deep at night.[42]

The Gothic atmosphere of the Nocturne would not be complete without an evocation of the Final Judgment. In the Preludes, Chopin systematically quotes the entire *Dies irae* chant (Example 1) not as one uninterrupted melody played from beginning to end, but broken into brief motives that undergo conventional permutations: inversion (a melodic phrase flipped upside down), partial inversion (only a portion of a phrase is inverted), retrograde (a melodic phrase replayed backwards), and retrograde inversion. Some symmetrical rearrangements of these motives can be found in the original plainchant, and *all* the symmetrical motivic reshufflings permeate Opus 28, essentially turning it into a monothematic composition.

In the B-Major Nocturne, however, only the two most recognizable motives of the plainchant are used. These two motives, marked by brackets and indicated as a, b, a^1, and b^1 in Example 1, commence each half of the chant. (Motives a and b, in various symmetrical modifications, are embedded elsewhere in the chant, but for our purposes it is sufficient to point out just two instances of their use at the beginning of each half). Motive a and its partial inversion, indicated as a^2 in Examples 2b and 3, appear several times in the text of the Nocturne, both in the treble and middle voice.[43] Motive a^2 does not occur in the original chant, but many entries of it are found in Chopin's Preludes, including the one that begins the bass line of Prelude No. 1.[44]

Motive b^1, a partial inversion of motive b, is also incorporated into the melody of the Nocturne. As in the chant, motives a and b (and their derivatives) dovetail with each other, that is, the last two notes of a preceding motive become the first two notes of the following motive (compare the interlocked brackets in Example 1 with those in Examples 2b and 3). Incidentally, motive a^1 in Example 1 is a retrograde inversion of motive a.

Chopin composed the B-Major Nocturne a couple of years before the Preludes were completed, in 1837—the year Alkan published his "Morte." Actually, Chopin had already been attracted to the *Dies irae* several years earlier. He arrived in Paris in 1831, met Berlioz the following year, and they became close friends for a period of time. By then, Berlioz's *Symphonie fantastique* was well known in Paris, and its inclusion of the *Dies irae* apparently gave Chopin the first impetus to quote the chant as well, albeit not in Berlioz's sardonic manner. The three Nocturnes Op. 15, completed in 1833, and especially the last one in this group, in G minor

Example 4a. Nocturne, Op. 15, No. 3, mm. 1–2.

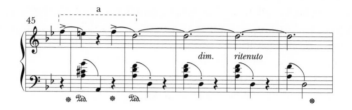

Example 4b. Nocturne, Op. 15, No. 3, mm. 45–50.

Example 4c. Nocturne, Op. 15. No. 3, mm. 91–92.

Example 4d. Nocturne, Op. 15, No. 3, mm. 97–100.

(the aforementioned "Hamlet" Nocturne), contain several quotations of motives *a* and *a¹* from the *Dies irae* (Examples 4a, 4b, 4c, 4d).

The strong presence of Gothic elements in the B-Major Nocturne has far-reaching implications for performance. Chopin frightens the listener with glimpses of hidden horror before arriving at the final pronouncement of doom. The Nocturne also contains segments from the *Dies irae*, embedded into melodic lines. Projecting all of these elements in performance dramatically enhances the emotional impact of the Nocturne on the audience.

Other compositions by Chopin display the Gothic traits that symbolize death—the *Dies irae* and funeral march—usually working in conjunction with other features often associated with Gothic tales. Thus Chopin's Second and Fourth Ballades (Opp. 38 in F Major and 52 in F Minor, respectively) both include numerous statements of motives *a* and *b* from the *Dies irae*. In addition, each ballade follows the general outline of a typical Gothic story: tranquil beginning leading through abrupt plot twists and violent episodes to a calamitous denouement.

Open fourths and fifths in slow tempo and low register evoke images of cavernous, echoing rooms in a castle or a monastery. When these dark soundscapes are combined with emblematic representations of death (through the *Dies irae*, or a funeral march, or both), Gothic associations come to the fore. In Prelude 2 (A minor) and the middle section of Prelude 15 (D-flat major) from Opus 28, hollow-sounding intervals in the bass are integrated with foreboding *Dies irae* motives.[45] The slow movement from the B-flat-Minor Sonata (Op. 35) and the C-sharp-Minor Nocturne (Op. 27, No. 1) blend such reverberant sonorities with a funeral march.[46]

Motive *a* from the *Dies irae* figures prominently in the Nocturne in G Minor, Op. 37, No. 1; Nocturne in B Major, Op. 62, No. 1; and *Polonaise-fantaisie*, Op. 61. In the G-Minor Nocturne from Opus 37, the *Dies irae* motives are combined with elements of funeral march, chorale prayer, and mournful sighs consisting of the 6th and 5th minor-scale degrees. In the B-Major Nocturne from Opus 62, multiple statements in the middle section of motive *a* from the *Dies irae* are trailed by exotic-sounding passages at the conclusion of the piece—exotic themes and locales are immensely popular in Gothic fiction.

Not all of the compositions listed above end in a minor key. Correspondingly, not all Gothic tales come to a tragic conclusion. In fact, it is customary to divide Gothic fiction into the narratives written by male or female authors. The Male Gothic, as Anne Williams points out, has a tragic plot. The Male Gothic protagonist fails and dies. He either loses his kingdom, like Manfred of Otranto (Walpole, *The Castle of Otranto*), or his life, like Monk Ambrosio (Lewis, *The Monk*). The Female Gothic formula, on the contrary, demands a happy ending, a concluding wedding. The Female Gothic heroine experiences a rebirth, being "rescued at the climax from the life-threatening danger."[47] Furthermore, in Ann Radcliffe's novels, apparent mysteries and supernatural occurrences, though profoundly horrifying during the course of an unfolding tale, almost always receive rational explanations in the end.

As far as we know, only Chopin's Preludes, Ballades, and the G-Minor Nocturne, Op. 15, No. 3, can be linked with the poems and plays of Lamartine, Mickiewicz, and Shakespeare. Chopin's other compositions that exhibit generic Gothic influences lack documented links with specific works of Gothic literature. Can such links be ultimately established? Perhaps, although it is doubtful. Moreover, it is not entirely certain that the efforts to find definitive connections between Chopin's compositions and Gothic masterpieces are even necessary. After all, visual artists produced Gothic paintings that did not derive directly from a single novel or a poem—Henry Fuseli's *The Nightmare* (1781) and Francisco de Goya's *Witches in the Air* (1798) immediately come to mind. Likewise, it is quite possible that, rather than invoking specific literary references, Chopin created his own original musical Gothic narratives that should be studied and performed as such.

NOTES

1. See Anatole Leikin, *The Mystery of Chopin's Préludes* (Farnham: Ashgate Publishing, 2015; repr. London: Routledge, 2016).

2. See a thorough and insightful discussion of these links in Jonathan D. Bellman, *Chopin's Polish Ballade: Op. 38 as Narrative of National Martyrdom* (Oxford and New York: Oxford University Press, 2010).

3. Jean-Jacques Eigeldinger, *Chopin: Pianist and Teacher, As Seen by His Pupil*, ed. Roy Howat, trans. Naomi Shohet, Krysia Osostowicz, and Roy Howat (Cambridge: Cambridge University Press, 1986), 79, 153n187.

4. Michael Gamer, *Romanticism and the Gothic: Genre, Reception, and Canon Formation* (Cambridge: Cambridge University Press, 2000), 8; Peter Cochran, "Byron Reads and Rewrites Gothic," in *The Gothic Byron*, ed. Peter Cochran (Newcastle upon Tyne: Cambridge Scholars Publishing, 2009), 1; Anne Williams, *Art of Darkness* (Chicago: University of Chicago Press, 1995), 4.

5. E. J. Clery, "The Genesis of 'Gothic' Fiction," in *The Cambridge Companion to Gothic Fiction*, ed. Jerrold E. Hogle (Cambridge: Cambridge University Press, 2002), 21–22, 28; Steve Clark, "Graveyard School," in *The Handbook to Gothic Literature*, ed. Marie Mulvie-Roberts (New York: New York University Press, 1998), 107.

6. Cochran, "Byron Reads and Rewrites Gothic," 3.

7. Clark, "Graveyard School," 107; Alexandra Maria Reuber, "Haunted by the Uncanny —Development of a Genre from the Late Eighteenth to the Late Nineteenth Century" (PhD diss., Louisiana State University, 2004), 20–21.

8. Terry Hall, "French Gothic," in *The Encyclopedia of the Gothic*, ed. William Hughes, David Punter, and Andrew Smith (Chichester: Wiley-Blackwell, 2013), 255.

9. Ibid., 256.

10. Williams, *Art of Darkness*, 1.

11. Christina Ceron, "*Manfred*, The Brontës, and the Byronic Gothic Hero," in Cochran, *The Gothic Byron*, 56, 168.

12. Cochran, "Byron Reads and Rewrites Gothic," 2.

13. Terry Hale, "French and German Gothic: The Beginnings," in *The Cambridge Companion to Gothic Fiction*, 70; "Translation in Distress: Cultural Misappropriation and the Construction of the Gothic," in *European Gothic*, ed. Avril Horner (Manchester, UK: Manchester University Press, 2002), 31.

14. Jennifer Driscoll Colosimo, "Schiller and the Gothic—Reception and Reality," in *Who Is This Schiller Now? Essays on His Reception and Significance*, ed. Jeffrey L. High, Nicholas Martin, and Norbert Oellers (Rochester, NY: Camden House, 2011), 287.

15. Ceron, "*Manfred*," 60.

16. Reuber, "Haunted by the Uncanny," 158.

17. Hale, "French and German Gothic," 78; see also Hale, "Roman noir" and "Frénétique School," both in Mulvie-Roberts, *The Handbook to Gothic Literature*, 189–93 and 58–63, respectively.

18. Tad Szulc, *Chopin in Paris: The Life and Times of the Romantic Composer* (New York: A Lisa Drew Book/Scribner, 1998), 44–45.

19. George Sand, *Histoire de ma vie*, in *Oeuvres autobiographiques* (Paris: Gallimard, 1971), vol. 1: 171–72, 644–45, 887–88, 1092; vol. 2: 8, 136, 147–48, 150–60.

20. Krystyna Kobylańska, ed., *Korespondencja Fryderyka Chopina z George Sand i z jej dziećmi*, vol. 1 (Warsaw: Państwowy Instytut Wydawniczy, 1981), 34, 39.

21. Frédéric Chopin, *Preludes, Opus 28*, A Norton Critical Score (New York: W. W. Norton, 1974), 91–92.

22. Joan Curbet, "'Hallelujah to Your Dying Screams of Torture': Representations of Ritual Violence in English and Spanish Romanticism," in Horner, *European Gothic*, 163.

23. Elizabeth Durot-Boucé, "Midnight Trysts: Minuit est la plus belle heure du jour," in *Etudes anglaises* 57 (2004/3): 306–7.

24. Fred Botting, *Gothic (The New Critical Idiom)* (London: Routledge, 1996), 2–4.

25. See Mary Ellen Birkett, *Lamartine and the Poetics of Landscape* (Lexington, KY: French Forum Publishers, 1982), 40, 51–52, and 89.

26. Botting, *Gothic*, 2–3.

27. Leikin, *The Mystery of Chopin's Préludes*, 35–37.

28. Jeffrey Kallberg, "Chopin's March, Chopin's Death," *19th-Century Music* 25/1 (Summer 2001): 22; Ewelina Boczkowska, "Chopin's Ghosts," *19th-Century Music* 35/3 (Spring 2012): 205; Szulc, *Chopin in Paris*, 45, 59.

29. Durot-Boucé, "Midnight Trysts," 306.

30. George Sand, *Winter in Mallorca* [1841], trans. and annot. Robert Graves (Chicago: Academy Chicago Publishers, 1992), 109.

31. Robert Graves, "Historical Summary," in Sand, *Winter in Mallorca*, 179–82.

32. George Sand, *Story of My Life*, ed. Thelma Jurgrau, trans. Tamara Alvarez-Detrell, Kristine Anderson, Sandra Beyer, et al. (Albany: State University of New York Press, 1991), 1091.

33. Sand, *Story of My Life*, 1091.

34. Anatole Leikin, "Chopin's *Préludes* Op. 28 and Lamartine's *Les Préludes*," in *Sonic Transformations of Literary Texts: From Program Music to Musical Ekphrasis*, ed. Siglind Bruhn (Hillsdale, NY: Pendragon Press, 2008), 13–44; Anatole Leikin, "L'unité cyclique des 24 Préludes op. 28 de Chopin: Implications pour l'analyse et l'interprétation," *Analyse Musicale* 62 (2010): 42–52; Anatole Leikin, *The Mystery of Chopin's Préludes*, chaps. 4 and 5.

35. Novalis, *Pollen and Fragments*, trans. Arthur Versluis (Grand Rapids, MI: Phanes Press, 1989), 69, 72, 75.

36. Lyudmila Sofronova, *Pol'skaya romanticheskaya drama: Mickiewicz, Krasiński, Słowacki* (Moscow: Nauka, 1992), 79–81.

37. At the time Alkan wrote "Morte" in 1837, he and Chopin were close personal friends and neighbors in the Square d'Orléans in Paris.

38. William Alexander Eddie, *Charles-Valentin Alkan: His Life and His Music* (Aldershot: Ashgate Publishing, 2007), 43.

39. Lennox Berkeley, "Nocturnes, Berceuse, Barcarolle," in *Frédéric Chopin: Profiles of the Man and the Musician*, ed. Alan Walker (New York: Taplinger Publishing, 1967), 178.

40. Herbert Weinstock, *Chopin: The Man and His Music*, 2nd ed. (New York: Alfred A. Knopf, 1959), 232.

41. The major-minor progression of keys in a single piece is unusual but not unique. Schubert's Impromptu in E-flat Major, Op. 90, No. 2, and Brahms's Rhapsody in E-flat Major, Op. 119, No. 4, both end in E-flat minor.

42. There is an almost inescapable parallel with the surprise recitative ending of Schubert's famous *Erlkönig*—a dramatic ballad involving the supernatural and death in the middle of the night. Schubert's recitative differs from that of Chopin save for the last two notes, an ascending semitone in both cases (though in different keys). The two concluding notes in Schubert's recitative are set to the words *war tot* (was dead). In the ending of the Nocturne's recitative, however, the first note of the semitone is repeated on the downbeat, A♮–A♮–B. Although just a conjecture, this repetition generates an extra syllable in comparison with the German text, which would fit a Polish three-syllable equivalent of the German *war tot: był martwy.*

43. The quality of the intervals in the quoted motives from the *Dies irae* is different from the original chant, but it is common in tonal music. When a melody moves from a minor to a major key and vice versa, minor intervals usually change to major ones, and so forth.

44. See Leikin, *The Mystery of Chopin's Préludes*, 67–69.

45. Ibid., 71–77, 113–15.

46. On elements of funeral march in the C-sharp-Minor Nocturne, Op. 27, No. 2, see Anatole Leikin, "Genre Connotations, Thematic Allusions, and Formal Implications in Chopin's Nocturne Op. 27, No. 1," in *Chopin and His Work in the Context of Culture*, vol. 1, ed. Irena Poniatowska (Kraków: Polska Akademia Chopinowska, 2003), 232–35.

47. Anne Williams, *Art of Darkness*, 99–104.

Revisiting Chopin's Tubercular Song, or, An Opera in the Making

DAVID KASUNIC

Anyone commencing a study of Chopin's music and biography will soon encounter several facts that have shaped the way his music has been received since his arrival in Paris in September of 1831: he was a Pole who arrived amid other Polish émigrés as Paris was championing the Polish nationalist cause; he had a nervous disposition that made him averse to giving public concerts, and thus earned his income from a combination of teaching wealthy pupils and composing; he suffered from a chronic chest ailment, which those closest to him understood to be tuberculosis; and he wrote lyrical piano music that encouraged many who heard him play to claim that he was an unparalleled "singer" at the piano—that he made his piano sing.

A crucially important but overlooked aspect of Chopin's biography is the link between his illness and his perceived singing, and that what seems to occasion this singing is a disease that progressively hollows out one's lungs. As such, Chopin as singer becomes a metaphor for the lyric creativity of the tubercular Romantic artist, which, as Susan Sontag observes, became such a cliché in the nineteenth century that "at the end of the century one critic suggested that it was the progressive disappearance of TB which accounted for the current decline of literature and the arts."[1]

The pathbreaking work of the French diagnostic pathologist René Laënnec (1781–1826) challenges this generalized metaphoric reading of the reception of Chopin. It does so by linking the sounds produced by a tubercular chest to the sounds produced by Chopin's piano as well as to Chopin's singing writ large. Laënnec's work thus provides the immediate medical-acoustic context for understanding more precisely how and why Parisian auditors perceived Chopin as, at once, tubercular sufferer and singer. From Laënnec, we learn of the phenomenon of tubercular singing, produced by female patients in the advanced stages of tuberculosis and afflicted by nervous agitation. The linking of Chopin's singing to the disease thus marks tubercular singing's first musical incarnation in a thirty-year migration from Laënnec's female patients in the 1820s to the operatic stage in Verdi's *La traviata* (1853). Whereas Donizetti had marked Lucia's wordless singing at the end of *Lucia di Lammermoor* (1835) as mad— read "nervous *in extremis*" and, as the century wore on, "hysterical"—Verdi's Violetta marks, at midcentury, a shift in the understanding of hysteria in which both it and tuberculosis were assumed to result from hereditary factors, from biology. The ecstatic florid singing of Violetta's Act 1 concluding aria, on repetitions of the word *gioir* ("rejoice," but in the sense of "enjoy life!") and ushered in with the word *follie* (madness), announces a temporary madness and the confirmation of her advanced-stage tuberculosis. The contemporaneous reception of Chopin's music must be understood in this context. Before reconsidering an influential strain of that reception in the writings of George Sand, we must first examine the relevant work of Laënnec that provides the framework for doing so.

Come the 1820s, Laënnec had revolutionized the understanding of tuberculosis and related diseases through case studies of patients he had examined, pre-mortem, by listening closely to their chests by means of his invention, the stethoscope.[2] These case studies as well as Laënnec's new invention were introduced to the public in the 1819 first edition of his treatise *De l'auscultation médiate* (On Mediate Auscultation). The stethoscope rendered tuberculosis as a musical illness, a series of sounds that the physician must listen to and interpret.

Early reviews of Laënnec's treatise focus on the diagnostic breakthrough that occurred when, through the use of the stethoscope on tubercular cases in the advanced stages of the disease, Laënnec discovered what he calls *pectoriloquism* or *pectoriloquy*. According to Laënnec, *pectoriloquism* is "a true pathogonomic sign of phthisis, and announces the presence of the disease sometimes in an unequivocal manner, long before any other symptom leads us to suspect its existence. I may add, that it is the only sign that can be regarded as certain."[3] He defines pectoriloquism by way of example:

> In the case of a woman affected by a slight bilious fever, and a recent cough having the character of a pulmonary catarrh, on applying the cylinder below the middle of the right clavicle, while she was speaking, her voice seemed to come directly from the chest, and to reach the ear through the central canal of the instrument.[4]

Often accompanying this so-called chest-speaking is a phenomenon Laënnec dubs *metallic tinkling*, in which "every word is followed by a sort of tinkling, like that of a small bell or glass that is finishing resounding, which dies away in the tube at a variable altitude."[5] In Laënnec's later brief essay devoted to metallic tinkling, published in 1826, shortly before he himself died of tuberculosis, he adds to this tinkling bell and ringing glass the sound of "the vibration of a metallic chord touched by the finger."[6] Pectoriloquism accompanied by metallic tinkling thus amounts to a speaking chest with musical accompaniment.

In describing the sounds he hears coming from tubercular chests, Laënnec draws on the same acoustic imagery—ringing glass, tinkling bells, and vibrating strings—that populates descriptions of Chopin playing his Pleyel piano.[7] The acoustic image that contemporary auditors most frequently invoke to describe the sound of Chopin playing is one that invokes Laënnec's "vibrating metallic chord," the sound of the Aeolian harp. Robert Schumann, Henry Chorley, Henri Blaze de Bury, and Sophie Leo all likened the sound of Chopin playing to that of the Aeolian harp, an instrument whose music is dictated by the wind and thus an instrument one cannot play. This image nicely captures both the distinctive sound of the Pleyel, rich in overtones, as well as Chopin's extremely light touch, so light that it often made listeners, such as Sophie Leo, wonder whether he was touching the keys at all: "He appeared hardly to touch the piano; one would have thought an instrument superfluous. There was no suggestion of the mechanical; the flute-like murmur of his playing had the ethereal effect of Aeolian harps."[8] Liszt, writing after Chopin's death, likened the sound of Chopin's Pleyel to another instrument rich in overtones and important to the Romantic musical imagination—the glass harmonica: "[His Pleyel] permitted him to draw therefrom sounds that might recall one of those harmonicas of which romantic Germany held the monopoly and which her ancient masters so ingeniously constructed by joining water and crystal."[9] In his review of Chopin's 21 February 1842 concert at the Salle Pleyel, Léon Escudier noted how Chopin "sings so sweetly, tenderly, and with such sorrow" before noting the qualities of the Pleyel itself, as played by Chopin:

> The magnificent instruments of M. Pleyel lend themselves admirably to these diverse functions. In listening to all those sounds and nuances which pour forth one after the other, weaving about each other to disengage and then reunite once more as they give shape to the melody, one cannot help but think he is hearing the faint voices of fairies sighing under silver bells or showers of pearls falling on crystal tables.[10]

The pieces on Chopin's program included two of his most famous compositions: the Etude in A-flat Major, Op. 25, No. 1, and the Prelude in

D-flat Major, Op. 28, No. 15. This etude comes down to us as the "Aeolian Harp Etude" likely because of Schumann's 1837 review of the Opus 25 etudes, which Schumann reviewed *after* he heard Chopin perform them. Schumann singles out the first etude for particular praise, likening its sound to that of an Aeolian harp. The prelude performed on that concert is commonly known by the nickname "Raindrop" Prelude, which, perhaps, echoes Escudier's dropping pearls on a crystal table, and thus Laënnec's ringing glass.

Scholars have not addressed the musical language of Laënnec's treatise.[11] And since they have drawn on either the first French edition or the redacted English translation of the second edition (published in 1826), they have not been alert to a remarkable discovery announced in the French second edition. Laënnec's clinical work from 1824 and 1825 brought to his attention an acoustic phenomenon related to tuberculosis, only hinted at in his earlier diagnostic work, that now compelled him to move from verbal metaphor to musical notation in order to describe and analyze it: a "song" (*chant*) coming from the carotid artery of certain female patients who are both in the advanced stages of tuberculosis and suffering from nervous agitation. The only scholar since the nineteenth century to discuss these additions to the 1826 edition is medical historian and Laënnec biographer Jacalyn Duffin, who calls this section of the treatise "the most disarming passage in his entire opus."[12] Anglophone scholars of Laënnec can be forgiven for relying on John Forbes's widely read English translation of the 1826 edition, which removes Laënnec's musical notations and accompanying discussions, radically streamlining Laënnec's eleven paragraphs into three.[13] In a footnote to this section, found in the 1834 (fourth) edition of the translation, Forbes misleads the reader into thinking that all that he removes are the melodic transcriptions: "The author records the exact *melody* in these cases, in musical notes, which I have omitted, as being a matter of mere curiosity."[14] At the same time, Forbes notes that both he and two other doctors have documented cases of the "musical bellows-sound," and that the case Forbes observed in a man under his care was "so loud as to be distinctly audible without the stethoscope, at a short distance from the person's body."[15]

Because Duffin's focus in her biography of Laënnec lies elsewhere, her discussion of this passage is understandably quite brief. I have thus translated the omitted passage and offer it here at length. The phenomenon at issue is the *bruit de soufflet musical*, the "musical bellows sound":

> This variety [of bellows sound] occurs only in the arteries, or
> at least I have never encountered it in the heart. The arterial

bellows sound frequently degenerates (especially in moments when the patient, for any reason, is more restless than usual) into a whistling sound similar to that made by wind passing through a pinhole or the resonance of a metallic string that vibrates long after being struck. The sibilant sound of the arteries can even perfectly imitate the resonance of the tuning fork that is used to tune keyboard instruments.

These sounds, never very intense, are, nevertheless, very appreciable, and one can easily find the notes they represent in a particular pitch; what is more, in these cases, rare though they may be, the resonance moves up or down in intervals of a tone or semitone, as if the artery had become a vibrating string on which a musician, advancing or recoiling the finger, would make two or three notes sound in succession. This fact being one of the most extraordinary of those presented to me by auscultation, I report here an outstanding example.

On 13 March 1824 I was consulted by a lady in whom I found some signs of pulmonary consumption. In exploring the region of her right subclavian artery, I heard a moderately intense bellows sound. I wanted to see if this sound was not also in the carotid artery on the same side. I was strangely surprised to hear, instead of the bellows sound, the sound of a musical instrument, performing a rather monotonous song, but very distinct and capable of being notated. I thought at first that the music was coming from the apartment below! I listened closely, I placed the stethoscope on other points: I heard nothing. Having thus ascertained that the sound was happening in the artery, I studied the song: it traveled over three notes, very nearly forming an interval of a major third, the highest note was a bit too low, but not enough to be marked with a flat sign. In respect to the value or duration, these notes were fairly equal. The tonic alone was prolonged, and formed a sustained note, whose [rhythmic] value varied. I notated this song accordingly as follows:

The sound was as weak and it was distant, a little shrill and very similar to that of a mouth harp, with the difference that this rustic instrument can execute only detached [*pointées*]

notes, and here, on the contrary, all notes were slurred. The transition from one note to another was obviously determined by the diastolic pressure, which, in the same sustained notes, rendered perfectly the slight shake musicians notate with a dotted slur. The weakness of the sound made me believe at first that it was happening in the distance, but by listening closely and touching the artery with my finger, I recognized that the sound was linked to a slight tremor of the artery, which, in its diastoles, seemed to rub, through its vibrations, the tip of the stethoscope. Moreover, from time to time the *melody* suddenly ceased and gave way to the sound of a very loud rasp. This alternation had the effect of which I can only give an idea, at the risk of using an odd comparison, by comparing it to a military march in which the sounds of military instruments are occasionally interrupted by the raucous sound of drumming.[16]

The next patient Laënnec examines is a woman who exhibits a bellows sound, who has "coughed for several months, sometimes spitting much blood," and who was "prone to experience a quite pronounced nervous agitation."[17] Laënnec continues:

Since that time, I have encountered two subjects whose carotid arteries whistled two notes at an interval of a tone:

and a third in whom the whistle, prolonged until the next diastole, then rose a semitone:

That is the extent of Laënnec's music notation. He then proceeds to describe a case from July 1825, when he was consulted by a thirty-year-old woman "with a very nervous constitution."[18] The left ventricle of her heart produced a "very strong bellows sound," and the "right carotid artery gave a slight sibilant breath similar to the sound of a tuning fork."[19] Laënnec even recalls hearing in this patient the "metallic tinkling," consequent of tuberculous evacuation, at the top of her lung.[20] And finally for our consideration, Laënnec begins his subsequent section, titled "Causes of the Bellows Murmur," by noting:

I have seen quite a number of subjects die from very varied acute or chronic diseases who—during the last days of
their lives, and sometimes for several months—presented
the bellows sound in a very clear manner, in the heart and in
various arteries. And upon opening up their bodies, I have
found no organic lesion that coincided consistently with
these phenomena, and that is not frequently found in subjects who present none of these phenomena.[21]

The *musical* bellows sound is thus a death knell, a swan song. And the
music that Laënnec listens to, notates, and analyzes is the song that arises
from a combination of nervousness and tuberculosis. Healthy bodies do
not produce this song: fatally diseased bodies do, though without apparent
physical cause—it is a wordless song whose very existence signals death.

The emergence of the phenomenon of tubercular singing in Paris,
starting in the 1820s, should make any Chopin scholar sit up and take
notice. For this means that, prior to Chopin arriving in Paris, a medical-
musical discourse was in place positing that melodies coming from the
chests of nervous women was confirmation that these women were dying
of tuberculosis. Whether, in the case of Chopin, that lyrical excess gets
translated as the distinctiveness and prevalence of lyricism in his music or
as a recasting of the brilliant style *fioriture* that still populated his music
through the 1840s, or both, the implications for an understanding of the
reception of Chopin and his music are evident.

Consider these known facts:

1. In 1832, thus not long after Chopin's arrival in Paris, the Irish pianist-
   composer John Field infamously deems the sickly, nervous, and
   often feminized Pole as "un talent de chambre de malade."
2. To the dismay of family, friends, and colleagues, Chopin eschews
   composing in genres such as opera and the symphony in favor of
   intensely lyrical piano pieces, the melodies of which—as played by
   Chopin on a Pleyel—elicit from his auditors the same timbral imagery used by Laënnec to describe the chest sounds that definitively
   announce tuberculosis.
3. Chopin plays these pieces with a softness and rhythmic subtlety
   that both fuse them to Chopin's style of playing (that is, outside the
   reach of imitators) and require his listeners to incline their ears to
   hear them.

In this light, we are challenged to revise our understanding of the
reception of Chopin's music to allow for a convergence of medical and
musical discourses in which contemporary listeners to Chopin assumed

the role of diagnostic physicians, with Chopin as their tubercular patient. Understood as such, the pronounced lyricism of Chopin's oeuvre amounts to the performance or externalization of the sound inside his body, an amplification of what one would hear were one to listen through a stethoscope applied to his chest. Indeed, the recorded responses of Chopin's auditors indicate that to diagnose Chopin's sound they had to engage in the same practice of close listening that the stethoscope demanded from physicians. That sound, coupled with Chopin's appearance and disposition, would have permitted them to pronounce a terminal diagnosis.

In other words, that the nervous, sickly, and feminized Chopin should write music marked by its lyricism is, in this medical-musical calculus, wholly appropriate. And this distinctive lyricism, which courses throughout Chopin's corpus, is now cast as his protracted swan song. Whether Auber or Berlioz, or neither, said it, the well-circulated observation that Chopin was "dying all his life" ("il se meurt toute sa vie") accounts for the perception, throughout his time living in Paris, that he was ill.[22] Our revised view of the medical understanding of tuberculosis during this period thus encourages us to review the list of recurring facts that one encounters when studying Chopin (with which I began this essay) to develop a more complete picture. The phenomenon of tubercular singing is one more puzzle piece, which permits us to return to the written record of Chopin's playing his own music and perhaps revise our understanding of it. This record allows for such a revision because its imagery, metaphors, and similes have always been multivalent, summarizing and registering several related impressions at once. It is our role, as those interested in Chopin, to try to decode this record, now inflected by this new medical understanding.

Regarded as his most lyrical compositions, soaking in both brilliant pianism and contemporary operatic practice, Chopin's nocturnes and his nocturne-styled passages in other genres are the obvious locus for considering tubercular singing.[23] The nocturne style served as musical shorthand for the composer; consider, for example, that it is the nocturne style that Schumann summons in his "Chopin" movement in *Carnaval*, Schumann's musical summary of his contemporary.[24] And as the most famous, verbally generous, and likely most frequent auditor of Chopin's nocturne performances, George Sand produced a rich written record of those private and public performances. Her letters, memoirs, and novels contain imagery that seeks to sum up Chopin as a nocturne singer. Two prominent images Sand deploys are the nightingale and Orpheus. Both images are sufficiently generic to resist scrutiny and could thus be easily passed over as common Romantic tropes. But as Sand was alert to their complex of literary, cultural, and operatic connotations, and as she bore an intimate knowledge of Chopin, her images more likely register something specific to Chopin, impressions borne of private knowledge yet commingled with Chopin's public image as the proud, mournful Polish patriot son in exile, and as the nervous sickly aesthete of the drawing room.

In what follows, I revisit Sand's fashioning of Chopin as both a nightingale and as Orpheus; this will enable us to focus on how these images, as applied to Chopin, register (less obviously) a terminal diagnosis from tuberculosis—a death sentence, in other words. In her early years with Chopin, Sand had to confront his tuberculosis head on.[25] One need only think of her account in *Winter in Majorca*, describing the disastrous trip Chopin's friends had urged him to take with her because of his consumption. Their subsequent relationship played out against the backdrop of his disease, often in the company of close mutual friends, such as the painter Eugène Delacroix.

Sand relates the following nocturnal scene, from January of 1841, in which Chopin is improvising at her piano as she and Delacroix carry on a discussion about aesthetics. The scene culminates in Sand and Delacroix stopping their conversation to listen to Chopin's playing, at which point they are pulled in and await the beautiful song of the nightingale (that is, Chopin):

> Chopin is no longer listening. He is at the piano and improvises as if haphazardly. He stops . . .[26] He resumes playing without seeming to recommence, so vague and hesitant is its musical outline. Little by little our eyes become filled with those soft colors corresponding to the suave modulations taken in by our auditory sense. And then the blue note resonates and there we are, in the azure of the transparent night. Light clouds take on all the forms of fantasy; they fill the sky; they crowd round the moon which casts upon them large opal discs, awakening their dormant colors. We dream of a summer night: we await the nightingale.
>
> A sublime melody arises.[27]

The source of the nightingale music, however, is the "sublime melody" coming from Chopin's piano, not a bird in a tree. From Delacroix's perspective, this distinction of place—Chopin was at his piano instead of in a tree—would have mattered. Writing after having arrived at Sand's Nohant estate in June of 1842, Delacroix hears the sounds of Chopin's piano blending with those of nightingales. The sources of these sounds remain geographically separated. Chopin is in his room, while the nightingales are in the garden: "From time to time you hear through the window that opens on to the gardens wafts of Chopin's music, as he works in his own room; this blends with the song of nightingales and the scent of roses."[28] One wonders what Delacroix would have written had Chopin, without Delacroix's knowledge, wheeled his piano into the garden and played it in the midst of the nightingales. Berlioz, it seems, would have been happy indeed:

> A Greek, on the invitation to go hear an individual who, through whistling, could perfectly imitate the nightingale, responded, "I'm not moving; I have heard the nightingale itself." I cannot comprehend how one could give such a response. My dear philosopher, I would have told him, it is precisely because it is not a nightingale that forms this song that it deserves to be listened to and admired.[29]

Perhaps Delacroix would have agreed. In any case, this is the tenor of Sand's praise of Chopin's nocturnal melody.

Sand does not go so far as to transform Chopin's body into that of a nightingale. But four years prior, in 1837, the painter Auguste Charpentier (1813–1880) came close to doing just that, rendering Chopin as a Siren— human head, bird body—perched not at a piano but on Sand's lap (see Figure 1).[30] Charpentier, who painted a now famous portrait of Sand that same year, collaborated with Sand and the illustrator Paul Gavarni (1804–1866) on this decorative fan. Charpentier painted the bodies, Gavarni the heads, and Sand the landscape (presumably Nohant). The legend accompanying the fan sets the entire scene, ascribing roles to all of the depicted personages, with the "incomparable nymph Sandaraque" holding the "sacred bird Chopinois" whose "wonderful singing cures colic and corns" ("dont le chant merveilleux guérit la colique et les cors aux pieds")—thus a Siren with Orphic power.[31]

Chopin as a Siren is consonant with Sand's classical orientation. Indeed, in her *Histoire de ma vie*, in a paragraph devoted to the bird, which she identifies as "the superior being in creation," Sand proclaims the bird first as singer ("l'oiseau est chanteur") and last, because of what she sees as equality of the sexes in birds, as the "ideal of Hymen," the Greek god of marriage mentioned by Euripides and Virgil. Her paean to the bird is all a prelude to Sand proclaiming the *artist* as the "man-bird"—"L'homme-oiseau c'est l'artiste."[32] This classical inflection is what Sand intends in her rendering of Chopin as nightingale. For while "darkness, the rapt auditor and the invisible bird are basic elements of the convention that grew

Figure 1. Decorative fan from 1837. Bodies painted by Auguste Charpentier, heads by Paul Gavarni, and landscape by George Sand. An elaborate and fanciful legend permits us to identify the following people, from left to right: Luigi Calamatta, Maurice Sand-Dudevant, Charles Didier, Emmanuel Arago, Albert (Wojciech) Grzymała, Pierre Bocage, Franz Liszt, Eugène Delacroix, Fryderyk Chopin, George Sand, Felicien Mallefille, Enrico Marliani, Solange Clésinger, Michel de Bourges, Emile de Bonnechose, and Auguste Charpentier.

Figure 2. Detail from Charpentier's fan.

up about nightingale poems" in the Romantic era (elements all found in Sand's scene) and French nightingale poems abound (notably Alphonse de Lamartine's "Au rossignol" from *Harmonies poétiques et religieuses* of 1830), Sand is, with her personal knowledge of Chopin, getting at something tragic.[33] Since childhood, Sand adored the writings of the Roman poet Virgil. When her early supporter Henri de Latouche told her, as she was about to publish *Indiana*, to retain the name "Sand" yet find a new first name, the former Aurore Dudevant (née Dupin) seized on "George" as a tribute to Virgil's *Georgics*.[34] In the fourth book of this epic poem, the nightingale plays a central role—Orpheus's lament is compared to that of a nightingale lamenting the loss of her chicks:

> What could he do? Where go, his wife twice stolen from him?
> Could tears persuade ghosts, or pleading, Hell's numinous
>   powers?
> Death-cold, she now floated away in the hateful black boat.
> They say that for seven months uninterrupted,
> beneath a cliff towering over a desolate Thracian stream,
> he wept and, shivering under the stars, sang this song,
> gentling tigers and enticing the oaks to dances.
> He sang as the nightingale sings from the shade
> of a poplar lamenting her lost chicks that a hard-hearted
> ploughboy, spotting the nest, has taken before they fledged;
> she weeps all night and, perched on a branch, repeats her sad
> song, filling the night far and wide with her sorrowful plaint.[35]

For Sand, as for Virgil, the nightingale is associated with tragedy, with death, and with Orpheus.

Unlike the nightingale, the figure of Orpheus is an obvious allusion to death, both Eurydice's (twice over) and, eventually, his own. In her 1838 philosophical play, *Les sept cordes de la lyre* (*The Seven Strings of the Lyre*), an adaptation of the first part of Goethe's *Faust*, Sand, ever the ardent idealist, engages in the moral battleground over the purpose of art by rescuing Chopin from his own wordless art, which, in the aesthetic climate of the day, could be claimed (and soon was claimed) by the art-for-art's-sake crowd. In the play, Chopin becomes the character the Spirit of the Lyre and Sand the heroine Helen who arouses the love of this spirit, freeing him from his imprisonment in the physical instrument of the lyre and thus from the clutches of Mephistopheles. At once a correction to Goethe (whose materialism Sand publicly disdained in her essay on the fantastic drama), a rebuttal to Gautier (whose 1835 preface to *Mademoiselle de*

Maupin became the rallying cry for the art-for-art-sake's movement), and a defense of Chopin's art, *Les sept cordes* rendered Chopin's piano (turned on its side, as it were) as divine property. In Act 1, scene 8, Helen picks up the lyre, holds it up to the sky, and it resounds magnificently, on its own, without Helen touching its strings. The three onlookers respond euphorically:

> HANZ: O muse! O beauty inspired!
> CARL: What a celestial melody! What a marvelous hymn! My ears have never heard the like, and insensible as I usually am to music, I feel my eyes flooded with tears and my spirit transported to regions unknown before.
> ALBERTUS: Keep quiet, or at least speak softly. Watch the marvel. There is much to learn here. Don't you see that her hands are not touching the strings? Her left arm alone supports the instrument, leaning on her breast. As if the beating of her burning heart, as if a divine breath coming from her sufficed to make the strings vibrate, without the aid of any human art the lyre sings some strange song in an unknown mode.[36]

This ethereal music making anticipates the beginning of the second act of *Faust*, where Ariel sings accompanied by Aeolian harps (by definition, played only by the wind).

Such an interpretation downplays the obvious distinction in Sand's happy spin-off of the Orpheus tale: that the tubercular Chopin, as was common with tubercular sufferers of the day, was explicitly spiritualized, made only part of this world, hovering in a limbo between life and death. Indeed, the union of the Spirit of the Lyre and Helen is predicated on a kind of death, as they can only unite after both have ascended to heaven. The year in which Sand penned *Les sept cordes*, 1838, is the same year that Sand and Chopin traveled to Mallorca, where Sand quickly turned into the bedside nurse to a violently ill Chopin, caring for him as a mother would her sick child.

Chopin's feminization has received a fair amount of scholarly attention,[37] his infantilization less so. There is something apt in the idea of this very sick and diminutive man, miles from home, as an orphan child. Writing in her personal diary, Henriette Voigt qualifies her ecstatic response to Chopin by highlighting this childlike naturalness: "He has enraptured me—I cannot deny it—in a way which hitherto had been unknown to me. What delighted me was the childlike, natural manner which showed in his demeanor and in his playing."[38] Often in her letters and, significantly for us, in her dedication to *Les sept cordes de la lyre*, Sand employed the same infantilizing strategy as a way to cope with Chopin's sexual reluctance and/or abstinence. Sand's daughter, Solange Clésinger, a close friend of Chopin until his death, seems to have inherited this characterization of Chopin as a child, here asserting that Chopin's art was most suited to women, children, and angels:

> The woman, the child (young [Károly] Filtsch died so young!) brought a finer sense than the masculine talents did to this celestial music . . . Liszt played these adorable melodies badly. He botched them . . . Under the flexible and responsive fingers of Chopin's pale and frail hand, the piano became the voice of an archangel . . .[39]

Clésinger's claim is conveniently straightforward: Chopin transformed the piano into the voice of an angel. She touches upon the trope of extraterrestrial transport so common in descriptions of Chopin's playing, where the sound of Chopin's singing piano lifts both player and listener to an ethereal realm—to the place one goes when one has died.

Chopin as Orphic spirit, Chopin as orphan child. Though the precise origin of the name Orpheus is not known, French lexicographers have etymologically linked "Orphée" and "orphelin" through the Greek root *orbhao-*, meaning to be deprived, one of a spouse and the other of parents.[40] Thus another image, the Polish orphan, that is both generic and specific to Chopin—generic in that exiled Poles at this time, such as Chopin and poet Adam Mickiewicz, were deprived of their homeland, and specific to Chopin, in that the young man in Paris was far from his beloved French-born father and Polish mother. In *Dziady* and *The Books and Pilgrimage of the Polish Nation*, Mickiewicz presents Poland as Christ, an already crucified Christ taken down from the cross. The crucified Christ is thus given voice metonymically, through the wailing of his grieving mother. It is the metonym of the Polish Mother as Virgin Mother that testified to her dying children and embodied the vigil for Poland's resurrection.[41] Mickiewicz secures this image in his poem "To a Polish Mother," whose third stanza strikes the parallel between the Polish Mother and the Virgin Mary: "How your son is to be pitied, o unfortunate mother! Go, look instead at the Mother of the Savior, see the sorrowful features that surround her . . . for these same torments are going to reward your fervor."[42] And again in the seventh stanza: "Christ in Nazareth, during childhood, played with the cross, symbol of his death / Mother of the Pole! Have him learn early on to fight and brave the insults of his lot."[43] Years later, Mickiewicz would speak of this poem as a premonition, dating its composition as 27 November 1830, two days before the November Insurrection.[44] Chopin was at the time in Vienna, and news of the insurrection sealed his fate never to return to Poland.

Chopin was also a specifically *Polish* orphan, slowly dying away from home, missing his parents terribly, and for several years being cared for by Sand, who loved him but drew the line when it came to choosing between him and her actual children. What Sand perceived as Chopin's meddling in her biological children's affairs, behind Sand's back, was for her the last straw. The dying Polish orphan became an orphan twice over as his relationship with Sand ended.

Chopin as the child orphan of Polish Mother, as Orpheus, as a nightingale—all of these renderings of him index singing and death, a convergence that, in Chopin, amounts to a swan song: Chopin's tubercular song. Chopin's piano-singing thus announces his illness and, in its distinctive melancholy, laments not just Poland and his loved ones, but his own pending death. These death-inflected renderings—as nightingale, as Orpheus, as orphan—are likewise operatic. It was well known that Chopin adored the singer Laure Cinti-Damoreau, famous for her title role of the nightingale in Louis-Sebastien Lebrun's comic opera *Le rossignol*.[45] Chopin's dear friend and sometime collaborator Pauline Viardot went on to become the most famous operatic Orpheus of the century, in Berlioz's production of Gluck's opera.[46] And the heroine of Bellini's *La sonnambula*, Amina, is an orphan.[47] In this logic, Chopin's life constitutes an opera in the making.

The opera is a tragedy, with its central character, Chopin, dying of tuberculosis. It serves, as such, as an epistemological way station in the transit of wordless tubercular singing from the chests of Laënnec's patients to the voice of Violetta. But Chopin as a precursor to Violetta perhaps goes further. Consider the following: in 1844, Alexandre Dumas *fils* has a brief affair (less than a year) with the courtesan Marie Duplessis. She dies in 1847 of tuberculosis, and in 1848, Dumas releases his semi-autobiographical novel *La dame aux camélias*. Then, in 1851–52, Dumas, short of cash, decides to turn his novel into a play, and that play becomes a smashing success. While in Paris, Verdi and his then live-in lover (and future wife) Giuseppina Strepponi attend a performance of the play, and Verdi is deeply moved by it. He decides to use it for his next opera, resulting in the famous and beloved *La traviata* (1853). This story is well known.

But because the oft-cited reason for Dumas adapting his novel into a play is an economic one alone, neither Dumas scholars nor Verdi scholars have paid close attention to the changes Dumas made to the novel in adapting it to the stage. In the novel, Marguerite sings and plays the piano. In the play, she only sings, leaving the piano-playing to Varville and Gaston. In the novel, a scene between Marguerite and Gaston centers on Carl Maria von Weber's *L'invitation à la valse*. In the play, this piece becomes a polka. And, finally, Dumas adds to the play a scene that does not exist in the novel: Marguerite and the Count gossip about the affair of a "Polish prince" and a French woman, disagreeing over who fared better from the relationship.

These details would otherwise not command attention were it not for an extraordinary event that we know about thanks to the recently published correspondence between Dumas *père*, Dumas *fils*, and George Sand, which took place at the same time that Dumas *fils* was adapting his play and trying to get it on the stage. In a letter to his father dated 15 May 1851, Dumas *fils* relates how at the Polish border, in Myslowitz, he came into possession of the entire cache of George Sand's letters to Chopin, which Chopin's sister had been prevented from taking back to Poland and were now in the possession of the border police. Dumas *fils* begins his letter by noting an odd coincidence: that his father is in Berry visiting Sand and he is at the Polish border with the bundle of Sand's letters. He then relates his understanding of how the letters ended up there, and finally discusses the letters themselves, writing to his father, "I assure you that there is nothing sadder or more touching than all of these letters, whose ink has yellowed, and which were touched and received with *joy* by one now dead. That death, after all of the most intimate, gayest, liveliest details of a life—it is an impression impossible to render."[48] There ensue frank and warm letters between father and son, father and Sand, and son and Sand. For Dumas *fils*, the letters serve as a moving corrective to Sand's face-saving portrait of Chopin as "Prince Karol" in *Lucrezia Floriani* (1847), in which Floriani, based on Sand, is a noble and kind beauty who must nurse the sick and jealous Prince, who recently lost his fiancée and mother. The outcome of Dumas *fils* writing to his father and Sand about Sand's letters to Chopin is that these letters eventually make their way back to Sand, and she burns them all.

By relating this event I am suggesting that there are *two* love affairs between a writer and a tubercular sufferer that inform Dumas's adaptation of his novel to the stage. Indeed, as Julie Kavanagh shows in her recent biography of the famous courtesan, the real Duplessis was far from the Romantic portrait of her. She was "practical, willful, grasping, and manipulative."[49] If there is a real-life parallel for Marguerite's and Violetta's cry for freedom, it is Duplessis's response to Franz Liszt's rejection of her, "throwing herself into a frenzy of merrymaking that directly anticipates Marguerite's and Violetta's feverish *joie de vivre*."[50] In terms of singing as well, the Marguerite of the play approaches Chopin. In the novel and the play, Marguerite sings, but she *only* sings in the play (does not play the piano), putting her, in this vocal economy of tubercular singing in which Chopin's piano is the surrogate for his singing voice, at once closer to Violetta and to Chopin.

I thus am suggesting something more. Moved by Chopin's now-dead "joy," Dumas shapes his "second" Marguerite accordingly, and it is this Marguerite who serves as the model for Verdi's Violetta. In Violetta's ecstatic wordless singing on the word *gioir* we may, with reason, hear a faint trace of Chopin's joy, of his compositions and of the wordless chest-song that would have, to a diagnostic pathologist, announced his imminent death.

NOTES

1. Susan Sontag, *Illness as Metaphor* (New York: Farrar, Straus and Giroux: 1978), 32–33.

2. Whereas Leopold Auenbrugger's 1761 monograph on percussion—that is, tapping the body to determine its internal composition—is, in Jonathan Sterne's words, "short, vague, and incomplete" and thus found little favor in the medical community at the time, Laënnec's 700-page treatise puts forth a "systematic approach characteristic of the emergent scientific worldview." See Jonathan Sterne, *The Audible Past: Cultural Origins of Sound Reproduction* (Durham, NC, and London: Duke University Press, 2003), 119.

3. R. T. H. Laënnec, *De l'auscultation médiate, ou, Traité du diagnostic des maladies des poumons et du coeur: Fondé principalement sur ce nouveau moyen d'exploration* (Paris: J.-A. Brosson, et J.-S. Chaudé, 1819), 1:57. All translations not otherwise noted are mine.

4. Ibid., 1:17.

5. Ibid., 1:48.

6. R. T. H. Laënnec, "Auscultation of Sounds Not Necessarily Accompanying the Respiration and Voice," in *Classic Descriptions of Physical Signs in Medicine*, ed. Lawrence A. May (Oceanside, NY: Dabor Science Publications, 1977), 32.

7. David Kasunic, "Chopin's Musical Disease: Tuberculosis, Music, and Diagnostic Pathology in 1840s France," in *Chopin's Musical Worlds: The 1840s*, eds. Magdalena Chylińska and Artur Szklener (Warsaw: Narodowy Instytut Fryderyka Chopina, 2008), 118–20.

8. Cited in Jean-Jacques Eigeldinger, *Chopin: Pianist and Teacher, As Seen by His Pupils*, ed. Roy Howat, trans. Naomi Shohet, Krysia Osostowicz, and Roy Howat (Cambridge: Cambridge University Press, 1988), 279.

9. Cited in Robert S. Winter, "Orthodoxies, Paradoxes, and Contradictions: Performance Practices in Nineteenth-Century Piano Music," in *Nineteenth-Century Piano Music*, ed. R. Larry Todd (New York: Schirmer, 1990), 22–30.

10. Ibid., 239.

11. The two scholars who have engaged centrally with Laënnec but have not discussed the musical language of both editions of the treatise are Michel Foucault, *The Birth of the Clinic: An Archaeology of Medical Perception*, trans. A. M. Sheridan Smith (New York: Vintage Books, 1994); and Jonathan Sterne in *The Audible Past*, cited above. Friedrich Ludwig

Meissner's 1832 German translation of Laënnec's 1826 edition preserves Laënnec's notation and discussion *in toto* (2:327).

12. Jacalyn Duffin, *To See with a Better Eye: A Life of R. T. Laennec* (Princeton: Princeton University Press, 1998), 192.

13. For example, Sterne in his *Audible Past*.

14. R. T. H. Laënnec, *Treatise on the Diseases of the Chest and on Mediate Auscultation*, trans. John Forbes, 4th ed. (London: Henry Renshaw, 1834), 517.

15. Ibid.

16. R. T. H. Laënnec, *Traité de l'auscultation médiate et des maladies des poumons et du cœur* (Paris: J.-S. Chaudé, 1826), 423–24. These translations first appeared in David Kasunic, "Tubercular Singing," *Postmodern Culture* 24/3 (May 2014), http://muse.jhu.edu/ issue/32352, which examines the literary and operatic phenomenon of tubercular singing before and after Verdi's *La traviata*.

17. Ibid., 426.

18. Ibid.

19. Ibid.

20. Ibid., 427.

21. Ibid., 428.

22. See Jeffrey Kallberg's discussion of this attribution in note 72 of "Small Fairy Voices: Sex, History, and Meaning in Chopin," in *Chopin at the Boundaries: Sex, History, and Musical Genre* (Cambridge, MA: Harvard University Press, 1996), 261–62; and for a discussion of the effect of seeing Chopin play after only knowing his music in print, see David Kasunic, "Regarding Chopin: Visual Culture and Musical Genre in 1830s Paris," in *Chopin in Paris: The 1830s*, eds. Artur Szklener, John Comber, and Magdalena Chylińska (Warsaw: Narodowy Instytut Fryderyka Chopina, 2007), 271–285.

23. David Kasunic, "Chopin and the Singing Voice, from the Romantic to the Real" (PhD diss., Princeton University, 2004), 29–64.

24. Ibid., 52–63.

25. Kasunic, "Chopin's Musical Disease," 115–16.

26. Suspension points in the original.

27. From Sand's *Impressions et souvenirs* of 1873, translated in Eigeldinger, *Chopin: Pianist and Teacher*, 282–83.

28. Letter to J.-B. Pierret, dated 7 June 1842. Eugène Delacroix, *Lettres de Eugène Delacroix (1815 à 1863)*, ed. Philippe Burty (Paris: Quantin, 1878), 161–62. Suspension points in the original. Delacroix remained devoted to Chopin for rest of the composer's life, and as he wrote much about art, whereas Chopin avoided writing about it, Delacroix's writings are arguably our richest source for Chopin's aesthetic philosophy.

29. H. Berlioz, "De l'imitation musicale," *Revue et gazette musicale* (1 January 1837).

30. Reproduced in Ernst Burger, *Frédéric Chopin: Eine Lebenschronik in Bildern und Dokumenten* (Munich: Hirmer Verlag, 1990), 219.

31. See details about the fan, including a transcription of the legend, on the website for Les Musées de la Ville de Paris, http://parismuseescollections.paris.fr/fr/musee-de-la-vie-romantique/oeuvres/eventail-des-caricatures#infos-secondaires-detail.

32. George Sand, *Histoire de ma vie*, Book 1, 1st ed. (Leipzig: Chez Wolfgang Gerhard, 1855), http://www.gutenberg.org/cache/epub/39101/pg39101.txt.

33. Quotation from Frank Doggett, "Romanticism's Singing Bird," *Studies in English Literature, 1500–1900* 14/4 (1974): 554.

34. Belinda Jack, *George Sand: A Woman's Life Writ Large* (New York: Vintage Books, 2001), Kindle ed.

35. Virgil, *Virgil's Georgics: A New Verse Translation*, trans. Janet Lembke (New Haven: Yale University Press, 2005), 76–77.

36. George Sand, *The Seven Strings of the Lyre*, trans. George A. Kennedy (Chapel Hill: University of North Carolina Press, 1989), 86–87.

37. Jeffrey Kallberg paved the way for this scholarship with two essays: "The Harmony of the Tea Table: Gender and Ideology in the Piano Nocturne," *Representations* 39 (Summer 1992): 102–33; and "Small Fairy Voices: Sex, History, and Meaning in Chopin," in *Chopin Studies 2,* ed. John Rink and Jim Samson (Cambridge: Cambridge University Press, 1994), 50–71.

38. Cited in Eigeldinger, *Chopin, Pianist and Teacher*, 269.

39. Cited in ibid., 280–81. Suspension points in the original. Filtsch himself died of tuberculosis just shy of his fifteenth birthday. Suspension points in the original.

40. See, for example, "Raymond, Napoléon Landais" et al., *Dictionnaire des dictionnaires, ou vocabulaire universel et complet de la langue françaises*, 2nd ed. (Brussels: Société Belge de Librairie, 1839), 598.

41. For a consideration of Chopin as musical prophet in the context of Mickiewicz's poetry and the figure of the *Matka Polka*, see Halina Goldberg, "'Remembering That Tale of Grief': The Prophetic Voice in Chopin's Music," in *The Age of Chopin: Interdisciplinary Studies*, ed. Halina Goldberg (Bloomington: Indiana University Press, 2004), 54–94.

42. Instead of using the accepted English translation of the Polish, since my frame is Paris, I have translated directly from Christien Ostrowski's French version. Adam Mickiewicz, *Œuvres poétiques complètes de Adam Mickiewicz: Poésies diverses.—Les Aïeux.—Grajina*, vol. 1, ed. and trans. Christien Ostrowski (Paris: Firmin Didot Frères, 1859), vi.

43. Ibid., vii.

44. The confusion surrounding the dating of this poem and Mickiewicz's itinerary at the time is spelled out, with filial care, by Ladislas Mickiewicz in his *Adam Mickiewicz, sa vie et son œuvre* (Paris: Albert Savine, 1888), 127 and note.

45. Kasunic, "Chopin and the Singing Voice," 70–71.

46. Ibid., 195–203.

47. Ibid., 40–42.

48. Alexandre Dumas, *Lettres à mon fils*, ed. Claude Schopp (Paris: Mercure de France, 2008), 112–13. The emphasis on *joy* is mine.

49. Caroline Weber, "'My Favors Cost a Great Deal': The Life of 19th-Century Paris's Most Famous Kept Woman Belies the Legend," quoted in review of *The Girl Who Loved Camellias: The Life and Legend of Marie Duplessis* by Julie Kavanagh, *New York Times Book Review*, 21 July 2013, http://www.nytimes.com/2013/07/21/books/review/the-girl-who-loved-camellias-by-julie-kavanagh.html.

50. Ibid.

Chopin and Jews

JEFFREY KALLBERG

Chopin provokes puzzlement. Far more frequently than for most composers, the habitual response to a particular musical passage in Chopin is uncertainty over how to play it, how to hear it against similar moments, or even how to understand its basic significance. Sometimes the question is "What does this *mean*?" but often it is more like "What does *this* mean?"[1]

This "Chopin problem" is so well known that there might be a tendency to assume that uncertain responses arise only from his music. But a recurring trope in his letters provokes its own form of puzzlement: Chopin's invocation of the word *Jew,* in contexts that often go beyond the purely descriptive and instead verge into invective and abuse. In a correspondence that otherwise portrays a sympathetic and imaginative individual (albeit one decidedly less inspired in prose than in music), an overview of his use of "Jew" reveals something else entirely: something repulsive, something bitter, something distressing. For advocates of Chopin's music, the common reactions to these outbursts are to ignore them, to make excuses, to find ways to bracket off the invective from his sounding creations. Perfectly understandable—the words trouble our aesthetic sense, calling into question the positive emotions that his music instills in us. Yet it will not really do to avert our attention: not only do basic principles of biographical honesty compel us to think in a sustained way about Chopin's anti-Judaism, it is also possible that his tirades tell us something about his creative life.

But first we should look more closely at how Chopin used the word *Jew* and its related forms in his correspondence. We can discern a few basic categories of usage, not all of which are purely abusive. Sometimes the word appears in descriptions of Jewish performances, performers, and sounds. Most of the letters of this sort date from Chopin's Polish years; a few come during his period in Vienna; none come from his time in Paris. Though these letters readily draw on hoary caricatures and stereotypes, their intent is to provide amusement rather than to convey anger. Perhaps the most famous examples occur in the mock-newspaper reports that the fourteen-year-old Chopin sent back to his family from Szafarnia. Here are three passages from the plucky "reporter":

> *SZAFARNIA COURIER.* Domestic News on the 15th of August of the c[urrent] y[ear], at a musical gathering in Szafarnia consisting of a dozen or so personages and half-personages, His Lordship Pichon put on a display. He played a concerto by Kalkbrenner, which did not make so much of an impression, especially upon the small figures, as "The Little Jew" ["Żydek"] played by that same Mr. Pichon . . ., for he played so well, so well, as if he had been born a Jew.[2]

The autograph for this letter is not preserved; all editions of it derive from a fragment published by Kazimierz Władysław Wójcicki in 1856. At the ellipsis, Wójcicki describes what is probably another fragment of the *Courier*:

> We must explain here that shortly before this, when the Jews had arrived at the neighboring estate in Obrowo to buy grain, Fryderyk called them over and played a *majufes* for them. He played it with such enthusiasm and oblivion that it caused the tradesmen not only to jiggle and dance joyfully, but they insistently begged the squire to bring it about that this fiddler play for them at a wedding that was to occur shortly.[3]

Returning to an extant "issue" of young Chopin's *Courier*:

> *SZAFARNIA COURIER.* On the 1st of the m[onth] of the c[urrent] y[ear], His Lordship Pichon had just played "The Little Jew" when Mr. Dziewanowski, having summoned the Jewish leaseholder, asked his opinion about the Jewish virtuoso. The Jew approached the window, stuck his hooked-lofty nose into the room, and listened, saying that if Mr. Pichon should wish to play at a Jewish wedding, he would earn at least ten thalers. Such a declaration encouraged Mr. Pichon to *shtudeer* this sort of music to the best of his abilities, and who knows whether in time he will not devote himself entirely to such profitable harmony.[4]

In these instances, the young Pichon/Chopin himself passes for Jewish: "as if . . . born a Jew," "the Jewish virtuoso." He first plays a *majufes*—a stereotype of Jewish song, which Jews often had to perform for Gentiles as a degrading act—on the violin well enough to solicit an invitation from the Jewish tradesman to play at a wedding.[5] In the next rendition, at the piano, he again creates music suitable for a Jewish wedding, in the judgment of the (presumably actual) Jewish leaseholder, whose stereo-typical physiognomy Chopin mocks. Chopin jokes that pursuing these kinds of sounds might prove lucrative, engaging a common stereotype about Jews and money. Despite the many stereotypes, though, the overall impression is of a kind of proto-anthropological interest on the part of the young Chopin in Jewish sounds.

Sometimes, of course, Chopin used "Jew" as a simple ethnic/religious marker for people he encountered in his life. All of the letters containing such references date from after his immigration to Paris. Thus in a letter to his friend Wojciech Grzymała, written from Glasgow:

> I lived with the good Schwabe; you may have seen him once at Léo's? He's one of the leading manufacturers; he owns the tallest chimney in Manchester, which cost 5,000 pounds. He's a friend of Cobden's and himself a great *libre echanżysta*. A Jew, supposedly a Protestant, something like Léo.[6]

But his remarks about encounters with Jews were not always pleasant. In a letter to George Sand, confirming his return to Paris from Sand's country home in Nohant, Chopin noted:

> We arrived here as well as possible. There was a Jewess in the coach, thus all the misfortune.[7]

By far the most frequent invocations of "Jew" by Chopin occur in contexts that have to do with financial matters. The majority of these references—nearly all penned in anger—come in a set of letters from 1839 to 1841 in which Chopin instructed colleagues on how they should negotiate on his behalf with music publishers. Since some of the force of these invectives derives from the frequency with which Chopin writes them, we need to read several excerpts:

> Léo, the Jew! I can't send you the Preludes, because they aren't finished; I feel better, and I'll hurry and write a short

open letter in reply to the Jew with thanks; it will cut to the quick (and let it cut wherever you like).[8]

I didn't expect Jewishness on the part of Pleyel, but since it is so, I ask you to give him this letter. Unless he won't give you any troubles over the Ballade and the Polonaises. Otherwise, once you've received the 500 for the Ballade from Probst, take the Ballade to Schlesinger. If you have [to deal] with Jews, then make it at least with the Orthodox kind. Probst might swindle me even worse, because he's a sly bird you can't catch. Schlesinger has always swindled me: he's made enough on me, and he won't refuse new earnings; just be polite with him, because the Jew wants to be held in regard.[9]

Jews are always Jews, and Krauts are always Krauts, that's the truth, but what can you do—I have to deal with them.[10]

My God, must I really deal with scoundrels! That Pleyel, who said that Schlesinger was underpaying me, today 500 fr. per manuscript to each country seems too dear to him! Well, I prefer to deal with a real Jew. And Probst, the scoundrel, pays me 300 fr. for Mazurkas! Well, the last Mazurkas brought me a whopping 800. Probst 300, Schl[esinger] 400, and Wess[el] 100. I prefer to give my manuscripts for next to nothing, as I did in the old days, than to bow to such idiots. I prefer to be subservient to one Jew than to 3. So take them to Schlesinger. Unless you've come to an agreement with Pleyel.[11]

If they're going to be such Jews, hold up everything until my arrival. So the Preludes have been sold to Pleyel (I've received 500 fr.)—so he has the right to wipe the opposite side of his belly with them.[12]

If the Preludes have been printed, it was a prank played by Probst. But I shit on all that, and when I return, we won't be *pratsi-pratzu*. The Germans, the Jews—scoundrels, rascals, rogues, blackguards, etc., etc.—in a word, you finish off the litany, since you know them as well as I do by now.[13]

I am sending you a few lines from Schlesinger. I will not make philosophical comments about Jewishness, but I have to defend him a little, because, indeed, great works, such as your Oratorio, for example, cost a lot to publish, and they aren't bought, because, except for the Conservatory, no other établissement performs such things.[14]

Thank you for your good note—it's a pity that things can't be arranged. *Masset* surprises me, if he thinks that I'll get less than 300 fr. for a manuscript. And then, since I no longer want anything to do with London, why should it be *pour les 2 pays* 300 fr. more? —Cheats, *Yids*—but it's not important.[15]

From this compendium of curses, we learn that Chopin never used the epithet when writing directly to a publisher. Rather, the strong language was part of a rhetorical strategy meant to convince colleagues and friends of the financial injustices he has suffered, or will suffer, at the hands of publishers, a rhetoric meant at least in part to urge his colleagues to be as forceful as possible in their financial dealings. (Puzzlement again: Chopin's curses reveal something of his social graces: rare were the moments that he vented his anger directly to its object.) And Chopin applied the epithet equally to actual Jews (like his Parisian publisher Maurice Schlesinger) and to non-Jews (like the piano manufacturer and sometimes publisher Camille Pleyel). This is not to excuse Chopin's deployment of the term by claiming that he unreflectively drew on a common term of opprobrium for those who drove hard bargains. Rather, the point is just the opposite: Chopin knew the difference between naming as a Jew someone of the faith—hence the descriptor "the Orthodox kind" in reference to Schlesinger—and someone who was not, which plainly reveals the anti-Judaism in his usage.[16] Also, Chopin enlarges on the curses so as to engage with a number of ethnic stereotypes: circumcision (the joke about "cutting" in the first excerpt), moneylending, and human baseness, via two feculent references: Chopin shitting on a deal gone bad, and—in a particularly perplexing image—Pleyel wiping his shit with the Preludes he acquired from Chopin. Chopin, like many of his contemporaries, was apt to reckon people according to their "types," and this was as much the case when he reacted in anger as when he was trying to make wider sense of different kinds of people in the world.[17]

In reflecting on this verbal practice, we can note first that using "Jew" as an epithet was utterly common in Chopin's time. To mention just four examples from contemporaries known to Chopin: George Sand, Robert and Clara Schumann, and Franz Liszt all left behind invocations about Jews that required some explanatory scrambling on the parts of their biographers.[18] Writers often seize on the commonality of the epithet, on the one hand observing that, if one looks in the national dictionaries for most European languages of the nineteenth century, one of the definitions of *Jew* was "usurer."[19] On the other hand, biographers want to distance (by implication usually) Chopin's habits from, first, later nineteenth-century invocations of Jews (in which racial and religious hatred grows more acute), and second and most especially, from the horrors of the Holocaust in the twentieth century.[20] If we believe in the exercise of caution when judging figures from the past by ethical and moral standards of our time, this biographical stance makes good sense.

But it also leaves unexplained much about Chopin's attitudes toward Jews—and "Jews." If anti-Judaism could flow so easily from Chopin's pen in financial circumstances, how do we account for his many cordial and occasionally deeply personal relationships with Jews? Two of Chopin's closest musical friends were Jewish: Ferdinand Hiller and Charles-Valentin Alkan. Chopin most enjoyed Hiller's friendship during his first few years in Paris.[21] Chopin's relationship with Alkan started a few years after that with Hiller but lasted till the end of his life.[22] And Chopin enjoyed amicable relationships with plenty of other Jews: we saw a hint of this in one of the letters cited earlier, where Chopin referred to the "good Schwabe." Moreover, and focusing on just a partial list of Jewish composers in his realm, we can add Chopin's friendly interactions with Josef Dessauer, Fromental Halévy, Stephen Heller, Felix Mendelssohn, Giacomo Meyerbeer, Ignaz Moscheles, and Edward Wolff.

For writers on Chopin, that most Jews were not subjects of his broadsides serves to consign his curses to the realm of aberrant behavior (albeit behavior exhibited by many of his cultured contemporaries), and therefore as somehow separate from his core creativity. But perhaps it would be profitable to explore Chopin's anti-Judaism in a different way. Following the example of David Nirenberg, I would like to test the possibility that Chopin's negative attitudes toward Jews and Jewishness did important conceptual and aesthetic work for him.[23] Nirenberg's project examines the long history of anti-Judaism, from the ancient pharaohs to the twentieth century, and convincingly makes the argument that it has been a basic tool in the construction of Western thought. Over and over again, Nirenberg shows how fundamental negative tropes about Judaism—for example, its association with money and property, or Jews' supposed irrationality—worked as concepts against which all manner of systems of thought took shape.[24] Thus for the French philosophes Montesquieu, Voltaire, Rousseau, and Diderot—thinkers who, in the aggregate, were crucial to the formation of Chopin's own aesthetic tenets, as Jean-Jacques

Eigeldinger has shown—Jews served as the focus of debate about the new, globalized economy (worries entirely out of proportion to the demonstrable role of Jews in the actual circulation of goods), with Voltaire stigmatizing Jews for their roles in promoting credit, and Montesquieu reinforcing the sense that, wherever money was to be found, one would also find Jews.[25] Thus Chopin's contemporary Heinrich Heine, drawing on Hegel's dialectical philosophy, viewed the "Jew" and the "Greek" as abstract concepts, as categories that encompassed ways of thinking about the world: the "Jew" more ascetic and otherworldly, the "Greek" more life-loving and realistic. In this view, "Jewishness" could be a term of critique applied equally to "ethnic" Jews and to Christians.[26]

What kind of work did "Jews" and "Jewishness" do for Chopin? In his prose utterances, we can unsurprisingly perceive a basic sympathy with the attitudes expressed by both the philosophes and Heine. Working in a system of music publishing that codified international practices largely in the absence of formal treaties (and governed by case law in ways that must have seemed obscure to the financially untrained composer), Chopin struggled to make sense of the kinds of terms he could expect to command.[27] Drawing on the long Western tradition of attributing the cause of financial problems to Jews allowed Chopin a rationale (as dubious as it might look to an outside observer) to explain what was otherwise inexplicable. We have already noted examples of Chopin deploying "Jew" as an abstract critique of Christians.

Turning to his music, "Jews" and "Jewishness" certainly impinged on Chopin's musical world in the idiosyncratic moments of performance in Szafarnia, when the fourteen-year-old mimicked Jewish music on the violin and the piano. A great deal of scholarly ink has been spilled in pondering these performances, mostly in attempts to associate "The Little Jew" with a specific published work of Chopin's. There is a long tradition, dating to the second half of the nineteenth century, of assigning the "Żydek" label to the Mazurka in A Minor, Op. 17, No. 4, either in the form Chopin published it or in a presumably lost earlier version.[28] Occasionally, scholars consider other works, such as the Mazurka in A-flat Major, Op. 7, No. 4, or the A-minor contrasting theme (mm. 103ff.) from the Rondo in C Major, Op. 73.[29] Other writers think that "Żydek" was a preexisting tune of some kind (this is the argument that makes most intuitive sense to me).[30] Finally, some researchers focus on *The Little Jew* letters as a means of examining the question of Polish–Jewish relations in the nineteenth century.[31]

But "The Little Jew" letters hardly project the kinds of anti-Judaism that Chopin invoked when financial worries arose. So if we are to think about the possible aesthetic consequences of anti-Judaism in Chopin's musical life, we need to consider other evidence. One potential avenue has been suggested by Ruth HaCohen in her important book, *The Music Libel Against Jews*.[32] In its subject matter, extended historical scope, and breadth of critical analysis it is a fine companion to Nirenberg's *Anti-Judaism*. HaCohen explores the changing consequences within European musical cultures of the long tradition of non-Jewish listeners associating Jewish sound—including, but not limited to Jewish music—with "noise." The "noise libel" itself harkens back to the Middle Ages, when there circulated widely a story of a plot by Jews to murder a Christian boy in order to silence his singing of Marian antiphons (the most famous telling of the story is "The Prioress's Tale" from Chaucer's *Canterbury Tales*). By inversion—because it was the euphony of Christian chant that was squelched in this tale—and in a gesture meant to hold Jews at arm's length as "others," Jewish music (and sound more generally) was understood to embrace cacophony, dissonance, and incomprehensibility. In addition to the familiar physical stereotypes, then, Jews routinely submitted to aural typologies: their ghettos, scenes of nonstop clamor; their speech, disfluent; worshippers in synagogues, unruly; the music in their synagogues, discordant; the sound of the shofar, a form of wailing or barking.[33] These prejudices of course evolved in fluid ways, and were variously embraced, contested, and altered by successive generations of Jews and Christians.

HaCohen recounts in detail how aspects of the noise libel played out publicly in France during the July Monarchy, most prominently through Giacomo Meyerbeer and Fromental Halévy, with respect to both their operas and their persons.[34] Meyerbeer's operas, even those on explicitly Christian themes, could not escape the filter of the composer's Jewishness, and Halévy embraced the topic directly with his *La juive*, premiered in 1835. An opera of sufficient renown in Paris that we can safely assume Chopin knew it (even though we find no mention of it in his correspondence), *La juive* draws on the familiarity of Jewish "noise" at key moments of the staged drama. In the Introduction of Act 1, before we hear Eléazar (the father of the titular Rachel) sing, we hear him making noise, hammering in his jeweler's workshop, set near the cathedral of Constance. The noise is a provocation: it is a Catholic feast day, and the celebrants' ire is raised by the racket of someone laboring in defiance of the ceremony. The first verbal reaction to the sounds is Ruggiero's "What do I hear! and where does this strange noise come from!" (Qu'entends-je! et d'ou provient ce bruit étrange!). The noise is "real"—"heard" by the characters onstage—and chiefly projected by unpitched anvils in the orchestra, but Halévy emphasized its status as discordant sound by adding noumenal sounds (music we hear but the

Example 1. Fromental Halévy, *La juive*, Act 1, No. 1, mm. 366–67.
Example derived from Diana R. Hallman, *Opera, Liberalism,
and Antisemitism in Nineteenth-Century France.*

characters do not): valve horns playing the pitch G, which clash against the F♯s that Ruggiero sings to the words "strange noise" (*bruit* étrange).[35] (See Example 1.) In other moments, it is less noise that we hear than other aural stereotypes, especially orchestral effects meant to sound ungainly, or ugly (one good example is the opening of the "malediction scene" in the conclusion to Act 3). Halévy draws on these musical stereotypes not as novel effects, but rather as familiar gestures that his audience will recognize as part of the musical "color" of the opera. All of this is to say that representations of the noisiness of Jews were common coin in the first half of the nineteenth century.

But what might any of this noise libel have to do with Chopin? The very notion of "noise" of any kind would seem to be abhorrent to Chopin, whose entire musical aesthetic seemed predicated on the pursuit of elegance and eloquence. Especially so with respect to the sounds that he produced and his physical bearing at the piano. From testimony by his contemporaries as well as occasional comments emanating directly from him, we know that he strove to produce a beautiful, "singing" sound, by means of the simplest and most direct physical gestures. An ideal performance never overwhelmed the audience: indeed, if anything, Chopin was sometimes felt to err on the side of producing too little sound:

> His speciality was extreme delicacy, and his pianissimo extraordinary. Every little note was like a bell, so clear.

> Chopin played generally very quietly, and rarely, indeed hardly ever, *fortissimo*.

> According to Mikuli, Chopin played with a delicate touch, avoiding strong and shrill accents. He never dazzled by pure technique, nor overpowered by sheer sonorous power. He could not bear too loud a sound from the piano, and called it "a dog barking."[36]

The music that Chopin composed contributed profoundly to the overwhelming sense of his sensitivity and elegance, but so too did his physical bearing. He preferred any emotion—whether drama, tragedy, sadness, or joy—to emerge from the sounds produced, rather than conveyed by what he perceived to be excessive contortions of the body. We can recall his famous dictum, as recalled by Wilhelm von Lenz: "I indicate [*j'indique*], it is up to the listener to complete [*parachever*] the picture."[37] He variously kidded or mocked performers whose physical gestures or facial contortions drew attention to their bodies and away from the sounds they were producing.[38] His description of the Polish pianist Wojciech Sowiński captures these sentiments well:

> When I'm writing to you, I can't stand it when my bell goes into action, and in traipses something with great moustaches, large, overgrown, stout—he sits down to the piano, and not knowing himself what he is improvising, bangs, beats without any sense, hurls himself, crosses his hands, rattles for some five minutes on one key with one gigantic finger, which was destined somewhere out there in the Ukraine to wield a steward's whip and reins. Here you have a portrait of Sowiński, who has no other merit than a good figure and a good heart for himself.[39]

Pianists whose lack of self-control led them to produce "harsh" or "banging" sounds at the piano were repellent. But if Chopin loathed "noisy" pianists, why then consider the noise libel?

One of the curious features about Chopin's performing style is that, in the first sustained commentaries we have about it (dating from his last years in Warsaw), it was already well developed. We sense this clearly in an anonymous review of a concert Chopin gave during his first trip to Vienna in 1829:

> His touch, though clean and secure, has little of the brilliance of tone by which virtuosi proclaim themselves from the first bars; he accentuates only gently, like a person conversing in the company of cultured people, avoiding that rhetorical aplomb considered indispensable amongst virtuosos. He plays very calmly, without the fiery ardor which generally distinguishes artist from dilettante.[40]

But under what influences did the essence of his keyboard style emerge? Not from any piano teacher: he was essentially self-taught at the keyboard. Not, apparently, from any "Polish school" of pianists, though clearly he was aware of them and learned something from them. Not from any piano treatises, though he was aware of some of them. We know that he learned a great deal from singers, but this would have more to do with the how to mimic their production of melody than with how the body might be deployed in performance.

Chopin's autodidactic tendencies incline us to look inward for influences. And influences need not only be positive models; they can be negative, too. So the question is: given that we have Chopin's bemused reactions to the sounds of actual Jews, dating from when he was a teenager, and given that we have reason to suppose that his distaste for Jews was in place from a young age, is it possible that some element of his performing aesthetic derived from a desire to distance himself as a performer, as much as possible, from any associations with "noisy" Jews? Or said another way, could the very force with which Chopin dissociated his performing self from any suggestion of noise inform us, at least in part, about the origins of this aesthetic?

We have no direct testimony, one way or the other, that would help answer these questions, and arguments from silence should give us pause. Still, it is not hard to imagine that a repulsive factor might have propelled Chopin toward the development of his performing style. In the general realm of human behavior, decisions about who we want to be often reflect choices about who we do not want to be. Negative perceptions about the relationship between Jewish sound and noise might have pushed Chopin toward a sounding aesthetic that almost entirely distanced itself from associations with noise, which would be entirely in keeping with the kinds of cultural work that Jews and Jewishness did in Chopin's time, as Nirenberg and HaCohen have variously documented.

A few indirect slivers of evidence may give support to this supposition. The first comes from a letter where Chopin refers to an actual person as a Żydek. He reported to his family on a concert he was to hear in Vienna featuring the violinist Leo Herz and the pianist Theodor Döhler:

> We'll get to hear Herz, that little Jew, the violinist, who barely escaped being booed off the stage at Miss Sontag's concert at home in Warsaw, and the pianist Döhler, who'll be playing compositions by Czerny. And at the end of the concert, Herz is to play his own variations on Polish themes. You poor Polish themes! You have no idea what *majufeses* they'll lard you with, calling it Polish music for the sake of luring the public.[41]

That Chopin could react with such palpable distaste to the prospect of Herz interspersing Jewish tunes among his Polish themes demonstrates that he understood there was a clear line of demarcation between the two. To Chopin, Jewish tunes were suspect, certainly from the standpoint of his own sense of what counted as "authentically" national. Might there be a further implication that his own "Polish music" distanced itself from these inauthentic Jewish sounds?

The second piece of evidence emerges from an unusual choice of vocabulary that (as we saw above) Chopin occasionally used to characterize distasteful playing at the piano, namely that it resembled "barking."[42] Now, "barking" makes good sense as a term of derision applied to vocal production—humans making dog-like sounds from their throats.[43] But "barking" is not an intuitively obvious way to describe the tones that a pianist would produce at the keyboard, except to the extent that harshness or banging might interfere with the ability to make a melody "sing." But Chopin's term of approbation seems focused on the bad sounds themselves, not on their wider consequences. The chain of analogies seems clear: dogs bark, barking is subhuman, subhuman sounds do not inhabit the realm of human music, therefore barking is noise.

That this is an obscure way to characterize pianistic sounds raises the possibility that Chopin had some other association with "barking" that led him to use it, in effect as a metonym. "Barking" has a history as a term of denigration applied to Jewish sound. In the Catholic Church, papal texts from the Middle Ages through at least the nineteenth century likened the clamor of Jewish prayer to the braying of dogs (the Latin terms were most often *ululare* and *latrare*).[44] If Chopin through his Catholic upbringing had been exposed to this image, then the way that he used it when teaching students would have been characteristic of his handling of terms of Jewish abuse throughout his life. He did not use "Jew" as an invective in his public life, because this would violate norms of cultivated behavior. The most that he would allow himself were elliptical or allusive statements—into which category "barking" appears to fit, if it indeed connotes "Jewish" sound in some way.[45]

The third verbal clue, even more opaque, would also fit into the category of denigration via allusion. Chopin had another way to describe unpleasantly loud playing, and that was to call it "German":

> To play with great strength was German; as he told Mrs. Goddard in Paris, when she took her daughter Arabella Goddard, child of seven or eight, to play to him. "Why," said he, "she plays like a German," and when they left the house, as Mrs. Goddard told me lately, Chopin's last words were, "Never let the child play loud."[46]

This reminiscence of Alfred James Hipkins makes perfect sense when taken at face value, as an association of a more forceful mode of playing with a German school. Ignaz Moscheles made precisely this claim:

> Chopin's *piano* is so like a soft breath that he needs no vigorous *forte* to bring about the desired contrast; and one does not miss the orchestral effects that the German school demands of a pianist.[47]

Chopin would not have been alone associating German pianism with a greater forcefulness, so his comment to Arabella's mother is perfectly legible as a recommendation against playing like German pianists do.

Yet we know that Chopin sometimes substituted terms in discussions of music with amateurs. In an analysis of the famous entry from Eugène Delacroix's diary in which the painter recounts his conversation with Chopin about what constitutes "logic" in music, the answer being "fugue," Jean-Jacques Eigeldinger has convincingly argued that when Chopin cited Mozart as the composer who best epitomized "fugue," he did so using him as a stand-in for Bach, as a way to allude to formal counterpoint for a friend who knew little of Bach.[48] And so it is at least possible that Chopin's reaction to Arabella captures a similar allusive moment, for we saw in two of Chopin's rants a tendency to merge Germans with Jews:

Jews are always Jews, and Krauts are always Krauts, that's the truth, but what can you do—I have to deal with them.[49]

The Germans, the Jews—scoundrels, rascals, rogues, blackguards, etc., etc.—in a word, you finish off the litany, since you know them as well as I do by now.[50]

In both cases, the contexts included actual Germans, and of course Chopin knew the difference between Germans and Jews. But his words also allow for an easy elision of the two: the Germans in questions were also Jews, and, for Chopin in his anger, both Germans and Jews were rogues and scoundrels. If Chopin was hesitant in the presence of the mother of one of his pupils to give vent to an association tinged with anti-Judaism, he possibly could convey that sentiment by means of a substitute nationality.

This is perplexing terrain. If Chopin reckoned with the "noise libel," he did so by embracing something like its opposite, a performing aesthetic governed by delicacy and nuance. If he showed awareness of the noise libel in his own utterances, he did so with words whose evident, ordinary meanings have no apparent connection to Jews. "German" can refer to a person from Germany, but for Chopin it might also signify "Jew." "Barking" may refer allusively (and elusively) to "Jewish sound." As with his manifold musical variants, Chopin's words resist comfortable parsing; they frustrate certainty. What *does* this mean?

There is one last way we might consider the effect that anti-Judaism could have had on Chopin's art. One of the enduring stereotypes of Jews portrayed them as ugly, as physically grotesque.[51] This commonplace doubtless reared its head when Chopin, renowned in his day as a mimic, enacted the character type of a "squalid Jew."[52] Is it possible that the occasional instance of a grotesque work or passage in his music might reflect an aesthetic engagement with anti-Judaism? To mention ugliness in connection with Chopin might seem to verge on sacrilege: in the Chopin canon, the only thing as rare as ugly music are pieces meant to be funny. And there can be no thought that a reaction to Jewishness might have been the only impetus for Chopin on those rare occasions when he hazarded composing ungainly sounds: the ugly had been a rallying cry for progressive creative artists (especially those in France) from at least the time of Victor Hugo's Preface to *Cromwell* (1827), where the ugly emerges as an agent of dynamic development, in contrast to the more static possibilities of beauty.[53] While Chopin was intellectually at odds with much of the contemporary Romantic movement in the arts, he cannot have been entirely ignorant of its tenets and debates.

Two works by Chopin, composed roughly around the same time in the late 1830s, attracted attention from his contemporaries for their noisy inscrutability: the final movement of the Sonata in B-flat Minor, Op. 35 and the Prelude in A Minor, Op. 28, No. 2. Schumann, though fascinated with it, could not bring himself to recognize the finale of Opus 35 as music—"denn Musik ist das nicht"—and how better to consign a composition to the realm of "noise" than to brand it "not music"?[54] But there are proximate reasons (the preceding funereal March) to suppose that, if the rattling finale of the Sonata owes its unsettling noisiness to any external force, this would be something other than an association with Jews.

The A-Minor Prelude mystified Chopin's contemporaries, and this puzzlement has continued to the present. Schumann again led the way in proclaiming that the Opus 28 collection contains much that is "sickly, feverish, repellent," and though he did not specify where these qualities were to be found, we can safely assume that the A-Minor Prelude contributed to these impressions.[55] Writing specifically about the Prelude, James Huneker in 1900 asked, "Chopin seldom wrote ugly music, but is this not ugly, forlorn, despairing, almost grotesque and discordant?"[56] In 1990, Lawrence Kramer observed that "much of [the Prelude] is deliberately ugly by early nineteenth-century standards, and arguably by ours."[57]

The A-Minor Prelude is built out of overlapping, relentless processes (Example 2). A rocking, contrapuntally conceived accompaniment, the regularity of whose steady eighth-note motion stands in opposition to the dissociating effects of its increasing dissonance reaching a peak in mm. 11–14; a series of harmonic sequences thrown off course by deceptive, dissonant cadences; a downbeat, four-square rhythmic emphasis at the local level belied by rhythmic offsets at the beginnings of each phrase; fleeting allusions to the characteristic rhythms of a funeral march; first melodic and then accompanimental silences appearing unexpectedly. Nothing sounds normal in this prelude, even its utterly orthodox final cadence (so completely out of place with respect to the rest of the piece). Kramer's exemplary exploration perspicaciously details all these destabilizing effects in the historical context of what he calls the "impossible object," a body or body-substitute with three leading characteristics: "excessive in beauty or deformity"; arresting "an observer by its irrevocable strangeness"; and exerting "a fascination that arouses desire, repulsion, or both at once."[58] Kramer's analysis reads the abnormality of the Prelude—its status as an impossible object—in dialogue with a series of literary and pictorial examples that arouse similar anxieties for the reader/observer/listener (Wordsworth, Coleridge, Goethe, Géricault, and Manet figure prominently). In a speculative turn at the conclusion of the essay, Kramer

Example 2. Chopin, Prelude in A Minor, Op. 28, No. 2.

wonders if the composer's own ailing body might have served to stimulate this exercise in musical strangeness.[59] In this conjecture Kramer joins other scholars who, in supposing that an external force impinged on the composition of this compellingly ugly Prelude, locate it in Chopin's illness.[60]

And who would deny that this most enduring of filters might cast its pathological shadow over the perception of this prelude? Still, Chopin's relentless pursuit of ever more extreme dissonance seems so excessive as to suggest that more than frailty might have affected his thinking. Looking elsewhere, then, and remembering that Chopin himself left no evidence behind on this matter, it is intriguing that the terms that many listeners use to describe the A-Minor Prelude are also those stereotypically associated with Jews in Chopin's time. Might the noisiness of the prelude at least partially reflect Chopin's understanding of the musical nature of "Jews"? If there is any merit at all to this speculation, its point is not that Chopin made an attempt to write "Jewish music": the Prelude sounds nothing like any music by Jews he could have heard in Poland, nor does it resemble the quite-diatonic synagogal music that was composed during the July Monarchy.[61] Rather, Chopin may have been trying to evoke the sounding image of the "Jew" through music, and drew on the sonic distortions of the noise libel to do so.

Could the very tonality of the Prelude also have inclined Chopin and his listeners to locate musical imagery inflected by anti-Judaism in this piece? That one of the pieces and one of the passages claimed as published manifestations of "Żydek" are both in A minor might tell us something about general associations between this key and musical Jewishness. It would do so regardless of whether or not one supposes "Żydek" referred to a composition by Chopin. If one perceived some relationship between the dissonant prelude and the noise libel against Jews, and if one were furthermore inclined to find "Żydek" in a piece by Chopin, then perhaps the Prelude provided a tonal frame in which to identify possible candidates for "The Little Jew" among Chopin's published oeuvre. In this light, the persistence of piercing moments of dissonance across many (though certainly not all) of Chopin's mazurkas written in A minor (and this was one of his favorite keys in this genre) may hint further at some kind of vague and occasional connection between A minor and "noisy" Jewish sound.

The argument in this essay grows ever more speculative. Chopin's disquieting tendency to pivot between "Jew" as an ethnic and religious marker and "Jew" as a curse, while partly explicable by reference to commonplace discursive habits of the day, already pushes interpretative uncertainty to the forefront. Trying then to grasp if and how Chopin engaged the tropes of anti-Judaism thinking in his life and in his music leads us down a path of ever more faint hints and insinuations. The turn to the sounding reality of the renowned Prelude in A Minor does not provide an explanatory anchor. Instead, it stands as an aural synecdoche for our fundamental interpretative conundrum. What does this mean? Chopin's world is a place of allusion, oblique reference, and shaded meaning.

NOTES

1. A simple, characteristic example occurs in the first return of the principal theme of the Ballade in A-flat Major, Op. 47. The identical chord appears in mm. 2 and 38. In measure 2, Chopin directs the pianist to play the E♭ above middle C with the right thumb, but in measure 38, the notation calls for it to be played by the left thumb. The chord feels different in the hands of the pianist from one passage to the next, but this distinction will almost always escape audibility. What does this mean?

2. Chopin to his family, 19 August 1824, *Chopin's Polish Letters*, trans. David Frick (Warsaw: Fryderyk Chopin Institute, 2016), 42. "Pichon" is an anagram of "Chopin."

3. Kazimierz Władysław Wójcicki, *Cmentarz Powązkowski pod Warszawą* (Warsaw: S. Orgelbrand, 1856), 2:16; *Chopin's Polish Letters*, 42n7. That Wójcicki offered this fragment in indirect discourse makes it impossible to know how the term *majufes* relates to "Żydek" in the other "Couriers." In other words, we do not know whether Chopin wrote "Żydek," and Wójcicki interpreted it here as *majufes*, or whether he just wrote *majufes*.

4. Chopin to his family, 3 September 1824, *Chopin's Polish Letters*, 50. In the last sentence, as David Frick notes, Chopin makes a Polish verb out of the supposedly Yiddish (actually German) *studieren*.

5. On the *majufes*, see Bret Werb, "*Majufes*: A Vestige of Jewish Traditional Song in Polish Popular Entertainments," *Polish Music Journal* 6 (2003); available at http://pmc.usc.edu/PMJ/issue/6.1.03/Werb.html

6. Chopin to Wojciech Grzymała, 4–9 September 1848, *Chopin's Polish Letters*, 459. "Libre echanżysta" shows Chopin typically blending Polish and French, derived from "libre-échangiste," an advocate for free trade. Auguste Léo was a Parisian banker and acquaintance of Chopin's.

7. Chopin to George Sand, 29 October 1843, in George Sand, *Correspondance*, ed. Georges Lubin (Paris: Garnier, 1969): 6:258–59. A postscript from Maurice, Sand's son, suggests that the Jewish lady reeked of garlic. Sand refers to the incident with the Jews in a letter to Maurice, 1 November 1843, 6:261.

8. Chopin to Julian Fontana, 28 December 1838, *Chopin's Polish Letters*, 290.

9. Chopin to Julian Fontana, 12 March 1839, *Chopin's Polish Letters*, 295–96.

10. Chopin to Wojciech Grzymała, 12 March 1839, *Chopin's Polish Letters*, 295.

11. Chopin to Julian Fontana, 17 March 1839, *Chopin's Polish Letters*, 297–98.

12. Chopin to Julian Fontana, March 1839 (no day specified), *Chopin's Polish Letters*, 301.

13. Chopin to Julian Fontana, 25 April 1839, *Chopin's Polish Letters*, 304–5. Frick notes that "pratsi-pratzu" is a German Jewish pronunciation of the French *bras dessus, bras dessous*: "arm-in-arm."

14. Chopin to Józef Elsner, 30 July 1840, *Chopin's Polish Letters*, 323.

15. Chopin to Julian Fontana, 20 October 1841, *Chopin's Polish Letters*, 348.

16. A letter to Chopin's family, written from Vienna on 1 December 1830, may show an earlier example of Chopin's anti-Judaism applied to a banker named Geymüller, who initially declined to help Chopin until the composer revealed his high-born connections. Chopin then wrote: "Only then did he make a different face, but I, taking my leave, begged his pardon for distracting him from his business. Just you wait, h . . . ż . . . !" (*Chopin's Polish Letters*, 204.) The presumption is that Chopin's ellipses cloak the phrase *hycle żydy*—"scoundrel" or "good-for-nothing" Jews—but since this is only a presumption, this particular letter is best considered separately from the others. It is also worth noting that Geymüller was not Jewish, though as we will see, this did not necessarily matter to Chopin when he was angry about financial matters.

17. An abbreviated version of my investigation into the importance of "types" to Chopin is "*Con duolo*: On Chopin's Soul," in Artur Szklener, ed., *Chopin in Performance: History, Theory, Practice* (Warsaw: Narodowy Instytut Fryderyka Chopina, 2004), 79–96. On the prominence of "types" in Chopin's Paris, citing just two examples, neither the many *Physiologies* of Balzac nor the caricatures of Daumier would have been intelligible without a general societal understanding of "types." See Christopher Rivers, *Face Value: Physiognomical Thought and the Legible Body in Marivaux, Lavater, Balzac, Gautier, and Zola* (Madison: University of Wisconsin Press, 1994), 104–39; and Judith Wechsler, *A Human Comedy: Physiognomy and Caricature in 19th-Century Paris* (Chicago: University of Chicago Press, 1982), 91–95.

18. Thelma Jurgrau, "Antisemitism as Revealed in George Sand's Letters," in *Le Siècle de George Sand*, ed. David A. Powell and Shira Malkin (Amsterdam: Rodopi, 1998), 349–56. As Jurgrau notes, in response to a letter by Sand from 8 February 1848 in which she laments that France "is in the hands of Jews, and if Jesus returned, these people would put him back on the cross," the great Sand scholar Georges Lubin blamed Chopin: "This manifestation of antisemitism, rare in George Sand, appears to us due to the influence of Chopin" (Sand, *Correspondance*, 8:279). On the Schumanns' anti-Jewishness, see John Daverio, *Robert Schumann: Herald of a "New Poetic Age"* (New York and Oxford: Oxford University Press, 1997), 197; and on Liszt, see Serge Gut, "Liszt était-il antisémite?," chap. 15 in *Franz Liszt* (Paris: Fallois, 1989), 205–12.

19. An article from 1817 questioning the easy identity of "Jew" with "usurer" made the same point: "The word *juif* is used in French in the same way that *Giudeo, Judio, Jew* and *Jude* are used in Italian, Spanish, English and German with the same meaning, to which dictionaries add that of usurer, because Jews, it is said, are in the habit of practicing usury. Nevertheless, not all Israelites are usurers, and not all usurers are Israelites." *L'Israelite français* 1 (1817): 239, as cited and translated in Diana R. Hallman, *Opera, Liberalism, and Antisemitism in Nineteenth-Century France: The Politics of Halévy's "La Juive"* (Cambridge: Cambridge University Press, 2002), 258. To the list of languages mentioned in this article, we may add Polish: see Samuel Bogumił Linde, *Słownik języka polskiego* (Warsaw: Piiarów, 1807), under "Żyd: Żyd, lichwiarz, chciwiec, skąpiec, sknéra, zdzierca" (Jew, usurer, greedy person, miser, niggard, extortioner).

20. The key study of the post-1863 shifts in ethnic identities within concepts of Polish nationalism is by Brian Porter, *When Nationalism Began to Hate: Imagining Modern Politics in Nineteenth-Century Poland* (Oxford: Oxford University Press, 2000). Also helpful is Magdalena Opalski and Israel Bartal, *Poles and Jews: A Failed Brotherhood* (Hanover, NH: Brandeis University Press, 1992).

21. On the Hiller-Chopin relationship, see my "Hiller Recomposes Chopin," in *After Chopin: The Influence of Chopin's Music on European Composers Up to the First World War*, eds. Magdalena Chylińska, John Comber, and Jerzy Michniewicz (Warsaw: Narodowy Instytut Fryderyka Chopina, 2012), 355–70.

22. The recent discovery that two of Alkan's closest friends, the English composer Henry Field and the Spanish composer Santiago de Masarnau, referred to him by the

nickname "Abbé" complicates somewhat the view of Alkan as the archetypal Jewish composer of the mid-nineteenth century, even if Field (in whose correspondence I found the references) intended the term to be ironic. I discussed this issue in "Homosocial Exchange and the Trio of Chopin's Marche," a paper read at Washington University, St. Louis, MO; McGill University; and the annual meeting of the American Musicological Society in Louisville, KY (November 2015).

23. David Nirenberg, *Anti-Judaism: The Western Tradition* (New York: W. W. Norton, 2013).

24. Ibid., 6. Nirenberg takes care to distinguish his exploration of anti-Judaism from one that might treat anti-Semitism, "a word that captures only a small portion, historically and conceptually, of what [his] book is about" (3). The key notion is that anti-Judaism could thrive as much in reference to non-Jews as to Jews; it is more about an idea than an attitude toward a specific people. My reading of Nirenberg suggests that "anti-Judaism" is the relevant term with respect to Chopin's attitudes and behaviors.

25. Ibid., 344–47. On the eighteenth-century foundations of Chopin's creative sensibilities, see Jean-Jacques Eigeldinger, "Placing Chopin: Reflections on a Compositional Aesthetic," *Chopin Studies 2*, ed. John Rink and Jim Samson (Cambridge: Cambridge University Press, 1994), 102–39.

26. Ibid., 413–19. That Heine was himself a converted Jew makes his use of this particular set of abstractions all the more interesting.

27. For an excellent and concise summary of the legal contexts surrounding Chopin's publications, see Christophe Grabowski and John Rink, *Annotated Catalogue of Chopin's First Editions* (Cambridge: Cambridge University Press, 2010), xxi–xxiii. See also my "Chopin in the Marketplace," chap. 6 in *Chopin at the Boundaries: Sex, History, and Musical Genre* (Cambridge, MA: Harvard University Press, 1996), 161–214.

28. Barbara Milewski discusses some of this tradition in "Magical Returns and the Interior Landscape of Chopin's Mazurkas," in *The Sources of Chopin's Style: Inspirations and Contexts*, eds. Artur Szklener, John Comber, and Magdalena Chylińska (Warsaw: Narodowy Instytut Fryderyka Chopina, 2010), 71–80.

29. On Op. 7, No. 4, see Mieczysław Tomaszewski, "Wątek spotkań z muzyka żydowską: Zawirowania wokół Mazurka a-moll op. 17 no. 4," in his *Chopin fenomen i paradoks: Szkice i studia wybrane* (Lublin: Gaudium, 2009), 136–51, esp. 144. Tomaszewski ultimately rejects the possibility of Op. 7, No. 4 in favor of Op. 17, No. 4. On the Rondo Op. 73, see Tadeusz A. Zieliński, *Frédéric Chopin*, trans. Marie Bouvard, Laurence Dyèvre, Blaise and Krystyna de Obaldia (Paris: Fayard, 1995), 106.

30. See Milewski, "Magical Returns," 72.

31. On this topic, I particularly recommend James Loeffler, "Promising Harmonies: The Aural Politics of Polish–Jewish Relations in the Russian Empire," *Jewish Social Studies: History, Culture, Society* 20/3 (Spring–Summer 2014): 1–36. See also Graziella Di Mauro, "Chopin's Controversial Mazurka Op. 17, No. 4 'Little Jew,'" *Journal of Jewish Music and Liturgy* 11 (1988): 53–64.

On the general background to the question of Jewish contributions to Polish music, see Halina Goldberg, "Przynależność przez muzykę: Wkład Żydów w kształtowanie się muzycznej polskości," in *Topos narodowy: W muzyce Polskiej okresu postromantyzmu i młodej polski*, ed. Wojciech Nowik (Warsaw: Uniwersytet Muzyczny Fryderyka Chopina, 2008), 187–200. Also relevant is Goldberg's essay exploring Chopin's possible role as a kind of messianic prophet and bard for the Polish nation, and a possible model for Mickiewicz's Jewish-Polish Jankiel in *Pan Tadeusz*. See "'Remembering That Tale of Grief': The Prophetic Voice in Chopin's Music," in *The Age of Chopin: Interdisciplinary Inquiries*, ed. Halina Goldberg (Bloomington: Indiana University Press, 2004), 54–92. On Polish-Jewish relations in Chopin's time, an excellent recent study is Glenn Dynner, *Yankel's Tavern: Jews, Liquor, and Life in the Kingdom of Poland* (Oxford: Oxford University Press, 2014).

32. Ruth HaCohen, *The Music Libel Against Jews* (New Haven: Yale University Press, 2011).

33. Wagner notoriously summarized the state of these biases in Chopin's era when, in 1850, he referred to normal Jewish speech as "a creaking, squeaking, buzzing snuffle" ("Ein zischender, schrillender, summsender und murksender Lautausdruck") having "the character of an intolerably jumbled blabber" ("eines unerträglich verwirrten Geplappers"). See *Judaism in Music*, trans. William Ashton Ellis, in *Richard Wagner's Prose Works*, vol. 3: *The Theatre* (London: K. Paul, Trench, Trübner, 1894; repr. New York: Broude Brothers, 1966), 85.

34. Ruth HaCohen, "Jews (and Jewesses) Like You and Me: Vocal Imaginaries of Mendelssohn, Meyerbeer, Heine, and Halévy," chap. 4 in *The Music Libel Against Jews*, 179–238.

35. See the discussions of this scene in HaCohen, *The Music Libel Against Jews*, 202–3; and Hallman, *Opera, Liberalism, and Antisemitism in Nineteenth-Century France*, 154–58. For the distinction between "real" and "noumenal" sound in opera, I am of course indebted to the work of Carolyn Abbate.

36. Comments by Elise Peruzzi, Adolf Gutmann, and Karol Mikuli as related by Aleksander Michałowski, cited and translated in Jean-Jacques Eigeldinger, *Chopin: Pianist and Teacher, As Seen by His Pupils*, ed. Roy Howat, trans. Naomi Shohet, Krysia Osostowicz, and Roy Howat (Cambridge: Cambridge University Press, 1986), 56.

37. As cited and translated in Eigeldinger, *Chopin: Pianist and Teacher*, 278.

38. The category of friendly teasing fits Chopin's dedication on 6 June 1833 of a copy of the French first edition of his Etudes Op. 10: "*Au plus grimacieux et gracieux Franchomme./ le plus attaché FF. Chopin*" (To the most grimacing and gracious Franchomme from the most devoted FF. Chopin); see Grabowski and Rink, *Annotated Catalogue of Chopin's First Editions*, under "10-1-Sm" (67).

39. Chopin to Tytus Woyciechowski, 25 December 1831, *Chopin's Polish Letters*, 257.

40. Anonymous review from the *Wiener Theaterzeitung*, 20 August 1829, cited and translated in Eigeldinger, *Chopin: Pianist and Teacher*, 288.

41. Chopin to his family, 28 May 1831, *Chopin's Polish Letters*, 225–26.

42. In addition to the quotation from Mikuli cited above, there are also remarks by Chopin as related by Zofia Zaleska: "Play this note properly, don't let it bark," and again by Zaleska directly: "It was this arpeggio which brought upon one unfortunate student this somewhat too sharp rebuke from the master, who springing up on his chair, exclaimed, 'What was that? Was that a dog barking?'" Cited and translated in Eigeldinger, *Chopin: Pianist and Teacher*, 31, 60.

43. The one surviving instance of Chopin using "bark" in his correspondence fits into this category, with "bark" meaning "aggressively protest or complain." In March 1839, he wrote to Julian Fontana, "I'm asking Grzyma[ła] to pay for the moving costs. As far as the porter is concerned, he is certainly lying, but who will prove it? You'll have to give it to him, so that he doesn't bark." *Chopin's Polish Letters*, 301.

44. On the negative connotations of "barking" applied to Jews, see Kenneth Stow, *Jewish Dogs: An Image and Its Interpreters: Continuity in the Catholic-Jewish Encounter* (Stanford, CA: Stanford University Press, 2006), 29–32; and Stow, "The Bread, the Children, and the Dogs," in *Jew's Best Friend?: The Image of the Dog Throughout Jewish History*, ed. Phillip Ackerman-Lieberman and Rakefet Zalashik (Eastbourne: Sussex Academic Press, 2013), 113–34. HaCohen wishes to expand Stow's canine-inflected readings of *ululare* to include "wailing"—certainly a term applied often to Jewish religious practices (*The Music Libel Against Jews*, 22–23), but the weight of evidence adduced by Stow persuasively establishes the persistence of the association between Jewish sounds and those of dogs.

45. We earlier saw Chopin use an elliptical expression in a letter to his parents, writing the phrase "h . . . ż . . ." Might associations with "barking" been distantly associated with the presumed *hycle żydy* slur? One of the meanings of *hycel* is "dogcatcher" (Linde, *Słownik języka polskiego*, under "hycel, chycel"). I want to thank Barbara Milewski for enlightening

me about how Chopin's "proper" Polish bourgeois upbringing would have constrained him from uttering slurs in normal conversation.

46. Reminiscence of Alfred James Hipkins, as cited and translated in Eigeldinger, *Chopin: Pianist and Teacher*, 57.

47. Comment by Ignaz Moscheles, as cited and translated in ibid..

48. Eigeldinger, "Placing Chopin," 124–25.

49. Chopin to Wojciech Grzymała, 12 March 1839, *Chopin's Polish Letters*, 295.

50. Chopin to Fontana, 25 April 1839, *Chopin's Polish Letters*, 304–5.

51. The classic analysis of these associations is Sander L. Gilman, *The Jew's Body* (New York: Routledge, 1991).

52. See George Sand, *Histoire de ma vie*, in *Oeuvres autobiographiques*, ed. Georges Lubin (Paris: Gallimard, 1971), 2:442.

53. See Charles Rosen and Henri Zerner, *Romanticism and Realism: The Mythology of Nineteenth-Century Art* (New York: Viking Press, 1984), 18–19.

54. Robert Schumann, "Neue Sonaten für das Pianoforte," *Neue Zeitschrift für Musik* 14/10 (1 February 1841): 40. Schumann also found the third movement "repellent" (his word), and it is possible that part of his reaction derived from confronting more noise there, noise created by Chopin's struggle to find the right notation for the second left hand trill in the "march" section of the piece. Schumann would likely have known the Breitkopf & Härtel edition, and there he would have played the trill with a G♭ main note rather than the "correct" F—correct, that is, unless Chopin thought for a while of creating a contextually appropriate mixture of terror and awe by writing a dissonant trill.

55. Schumann, "Phantasien, Capricen, &c für Pianoforte, *Neue Zeitschrift für Musik* 11/41 (19 November 1839): 163.

56. James Huneker, *Chopin: The Man and His Music* (New York: Charles Scribner and Sons, 1900; repr. New York: Dover, 1966), 123.

57. Lawrence Kramer, "Impossible Objects: Apparitions, Reclining Nudes, and Chopin's Prelude in A Minor," chap. 3 in *Music as Cultural Practice, 1800–1900* (Berkeley: University of California Press, 1990), 72.

58. Ibid., 85.

59. Ibid., 100–101.

60. Hans von Bülow called the Prelude "Presentiment of Death." Rose Rosengard Subotnik draws attention to von Bülow's description at the end of her cogent exploration of contingencies of sense in this prelude. See Subotnik, "Romantic Music as Post-Kantian Critique: Classicism, Romanticism, and the Concept of the Semiotic Universe," chap. 7 in *Developing Variations: Style and Ideology in Western Music* (Minneapolis: University of Minnesota Press, 1991), 128–40. See also Anatole Leikin, "Chopin's A-Minor Prelude and Its Symbolic Language," *International Journal of Musicology* 6 (1997): 149–62: and Leikin, *The Mystery of Chopin's Préludes* (Farnham: Ashgate, 2015), 53–143.

61. On Parisian Jewish and synagogal music of this time, see the excellent study by Anny Kessous Dreyfuss, *Le passant du pont de l'Europe: Charles Valentin Alkan entre tradition et modernité* (Aix-en-Provence: Massoreth, 2013). There is also a fine book by David Conway, *Jewry in Music: Entry to the Profession from the Enlightenment to Richard Wagner* (Cambridge: Cambridge University Press, 2012), 231–37; as well as Tina Frühauf, "The Reform of Synagogue Music in the Nineteenth Century," in *The Cambridge Companion to Jewish Music*, ed. Joshua S. Walden (Cambridge: Cambridge University Press, 2015), 187–200.

For a first-rate complement to Kessous Dreyfuss's study of Alkan, one that looks closely at how being Jewish could affect the career and artistic production of another pianist-composer in Chopin's time, see Laure Schnapper, *Henri Herz, magnat du piano: La vie musicale en France au XIXe siècle (1815–1870)* (Paris: Editions de l'Ecole des hautes études en sciences sociales, 2011).

PART II

Musical and Pianistic Contexts

Middlebrow Becomes Transcendent: The Popular Roots of Chopin's Musical Language

JONATHAN D. BELLMAN

It is no exaggeration to say that much of the pianistic world is a Cult of Chopin, and it rapidly became so after his tenure (or reign) on the Parisian piano scene. Pianists and listeners the world over—from the most accomplished to the most unsophisticated—are drawn to his infectiously kinetic rhythmic vocabulary, melodic and decorative beauty, and ability to sustain a listener's focused attention. His famous Funeral March, the "Raindrop" Prelude, and the "Revolutionary" Etude (the familiar nicknames, the latter two of dubious provenance, are used here intentionally) are immediately recognized by millions. Taken all in all, his position of pianistic primacy has really never been in doubt.

Before the 1980s, the scholarly literature on Chopin was uneven: serious studies coexisted with hagiographies, sentimental effusions, biographical fantasies, interpretations based on nationalist agendas, and Soviet-era appropriations. More recently, scholars have addressed a variety of analytical, historical, cultural, and performance issues, producing studies that both illuminate and provide fertile ground for further inquiry. A question that has never been adequately answered, however, or even discussed beyond a kind of general acknowledgment, is *why* Chopin's music has always been so readily appreciated by listeners—far more even than that of still-popular contemporaries such as Robert Schumann and Franz Liszt. How to account for its immediate and continuing success? The answer, I believe, hinges on musical language: the gestures heard moment-to-moment on the musical surface rather than longer-term structural relationships. Chopin's music is disarmingly accessible, and his influences—the musics he most enjoyed—explain how his style evolved this way. These repertoires include far more than a familiar selection of revered masterworks, as we tend to conceive historical music today, or familiar pedagogical curricula, and it takes nothing from his music to ask which part of it was acquired outside the classroom.

One obvious point of departure is opera, because of Chopin's devotion to it. Józef Elsner, his composition teacher, was one of the foremost figures in Polish national opera, a genre in which many had hoped that Chopin would make his own mark, and Elsner was all too aware that his pupil—living in Paris and composing for the piano, not the stage—possessed a natural but untapped gift for evocative, characteristic music, required equipment for any opera composer. "You yourself transformed a few bars of an idea you once had for a 'Chorus of Devils' into an 'Angelic Chorus,'" he reminded Chopin in a letter of 13 November 1832. "However, you did it because a pair of beautiful eyes asked you to."[1] Theatrical music required a certain cleverness, a knack for immediate effect, and to successfully balance opera's varied (and somewhat contradictory) requirements of beautiful song, vocal virtuosity, engaging storytelling, compelling characters, and entertaining dancing is quite different from the counterpoint and thoroughbass studies that were an apprentice composer's daily bread. That Elsner, enlightened in this regard, cherished Chopin's potential for such work says much about his teaching and mentorship.

Like several other famous early Romantics, Chopin had not grown up in a family of professional musicians, and such opportunities as attending a cathedral choir school or securing a court apprenticeship were not open to him. He was drawn to vernacular musics; he made almost daily trips to Brzezina's, an important Varsovian music store that Halina Goldberg has called his "second school," where he could play through new publications.[2] In addition to whichever editions of the masters he encountered, such publications would have included piano-vocal scores of the latest operas (French, Italian, German, and Polish), dance publications for amateurs (polonaises, waltzes, mazurkas, etc.), and fantasias—both those based on popular tunes and narrative works that sought to depict storms and battles and the like. These genres were all deeply interwoven: dances often had melodic and ornamented sections, vocal pieces often had a dancelike character, and descriptive piano pieces could not have existed without the dance vocabulary and references to well-known songs and arias. Within the musical print culture, then, there was constant, intertextual conversation between dance, song, and story, both in the marketplace and—most important, for our purposes—under Chopin's fingers. More than merely "influencing" his own music, these popular elements form its very fabric.

Dance

Shortly after his arrival in Paris, Chopin proudly wrote his family that the elegant and fashionable pianist and teacher Frédéric Kalkbrenner liked his playing and had recommended that he sign on for three years of study. The transparently exploitative nature of such a plan alarmed friends and family in Warsaw (fortunately Chopin opted instead to follow his own star from that point forward), and it is to this odd historical moment that we owe Mikołaj Chopin's remonstrative letter to his son of 27 November 1831, which stated in part:

> You know I have done all that lay in my power to encourage your talents and develop them, and that I have never put an obstacle in your way: you know also that the mechanics of piano-playing occupied little of your time and that your mind was busier than your fingers. If others have spent whole days working at the keyboard you rarely spent an hour playing other men's music.[3]

Mikołaj's account makes for a pretty story, in that it aligns with later descriptions of the composer's preternatural ease at the piano, though it is not clear if by "playing" Mikołaj meant "practicing" or "learning" or just "playing through." (Further, the Bach preludes and fugues—more than a dozen of them—that Chopin remembered his whole life and found it impossible to forget had to get into his fingers at some point, and would hardly have been learned by desultory sight-reading.)[4] Regardless, it is clear that Chopin enjoyed a good deal of musical freedom throughout his developmental years; there is no record of parental pressure regarding what he should have been practicing or which influential people he should have been cultivating. A supportive and nonintrusive parenting style thus complemented his own natural musical inclination. Elsner and, when Chopin was younger, his organ teacher Wilhelm Würfel were key musical figures in Warsaw.[5] The boy practiced and played as much as he wanted and needed to, enjoyed opportunities for public performance, and in general became extremely well connected throughout the city's musical circles. He was not forced to go on tour or otherwise submit to a commercial strategy. His first published piece, which appeared when he was but seven, was a little polonaise.

Chopin's interest in Polish folk and national music is well known. Once, at fourteen, he gave a village girl a few coins to sing a mazurka for him, but this might have been an isolated occurrence; he was no Bartók, ranging out into the hinterlands to harvest musical finds from the collective memory of the rural classes. Rather, he availed himself of dance music publications, often intended for amateurs and featuring such Polish genres as the mazurka and polonaise.[6] Social dancing was a favorite pastime in the Warsaw of his childhood and youth; dancing masters were available to teach the younger members of the aspiring middle class, and there was a thriving market for publications of new music by professionals and amateurs alike—some even including dancing instructions.[7] After his early polonaises, mazurkas followed, and given the increasingly invasive Russian presence and resultant apprehension among the Poles, it is not at all surprising that national dances would be so central to his compositions—as genre, as musical influence, and as pervasive spirit.

Yet it was not just a matter of national sentiment, and it is important to understand how a dance could function as a topic, a subject for musical discourse, in a piece of music not specifically designated a dance.[8] Beginning in the seventeenth century, each dance of the Baroque suite had come to be associated with a different affect: the courante was noble and courtly, the sarabande expressive and pathetic, and other dances were conceived in similar terms. National dances signified in an even more obvious way. For example, Spain and Spaniards might be indicated by the fandango (which appears in Mozart's *Nozze di Figaro* and *Don Giovanni*), and whether indicating Count Almaviva or Don Giovanni, the dance implied a kind of grandee arrogance and seize-and-possess entitlement, a distant echo of the cold-blooded colonialism of "most Catholic Spain" (as Iberia had long styled herself), the feared and once unconquerable New World power.[9] An *ungherese* (that is, a "Hungarian Dance"—*ongherese* and *ongarese* were among the other common spellings), by contrast, could signify the pride of Hungarians and their equestrian heritage, or Hungarian Roma—that is, the Gypsies, Hungary's primary persecuted, pariah class, but also its primary musical subculture, with a wild but beloved style of music making. Thus a national dance evoked both a nation and all the stereotypes associated with it.

By the early nineteenth century, then, dance as extramusical signifier already had a long history. For Chopin, the meanings of the various Polish dances were multifaceted, inasmuch as they represented both his identity as a proud Pole and his predicament as an expatriate—his singing of the Lord's song, so to speak, in a strange land. Each of the dances accrued a cluster of affects, any and all of which might reflect something essential about Polishness. So the polonaise, a dance historically associated with the almost mythic nobility and courtliness traditionally associated with and located in the Poland of yore, evoked the proud posture and graceful carriage required of such a presentation step for couples. By Chopin's time, this dance could be an elegant Polish trifle dedicated to a member of the Russian royal family, or a battle piece—all martial rhythms and *ad astra per aspera* determination—like the famous polonaises in A (the so-called "Military," Op. 40, No. 1), and the A-flat, Op. 53, or a song, replete with Polish pride and melancholy (Op. 26, No. 1 in C-Sharp Minor is a good example), or even the apotheosized *poco più lento* polonaise-lullaby of the Op. 61 *Polonaise-Fantaisie*.[10] A wide variety of different Polish affects and cultural resonances, however varied or even contradictory, could be and were inherent in this dance.[11]

The situation with the *krakowiak* is somewhat different. Originating in the Kraków region, this was also known as Poland's "national dance," but the difference was that the krakowiak never had the same courtly associations as the polonaise, within Poland or outside it. Rather, it was a lively dance—in duple meter, with syncopation—that came to symbolize Polish national sentiment but without the wider cultural familiarity of the polonaise. Chopin did not avail himself of the dance all that often; the finale of the Op. 11 Piano Concerto No. 1 in E Minor, the Op. 14 *Rondo à la krakowiak*, and the furious closing section of the Op. 23 Ballade in G Minor are three examples. And though there was an operatic presence for the krakowiak in the Polish theater, it was never equal, in Chopin's works, to the other Polish dances.[12]

Clearly, the dance closest to Chopin's heart was the *mazur*, which he preferred to call by the diminutive form, *mazurka*. This indigenous dance from the Mazovian region (where Warsaw and environs are located) had a certain currency as a ballroom dance in Poland and beyond its borders—in France, for example. The related *oberek* and *kujawiak* dances are part of the mazurka family, but as those designations only came to be used in the 1840s (that is, after Chopin had departed Poland forever), fine distinctions between the subgenres do not seem very helpful here. For Chopin, this dance admitted of the widest possible range of moods and affective contrasts; his mazurkas range from the relatively rural, stamping, bagpipe-introduced Op. 24, No. 2 in C Major, to the sinuous, almost Orientalizing A-Minor without opus number ("A Emile Gaillard"), to the proud nobility of Op. 50, No. 1 in G Major, to the bel canto aria of Op. 17, No. 4 in A Minor—this last being an extraordinary reimagining of a mazurka as sung by an opera singer, full of *fioritura*, sighs, and regret.

The point about these Polish dances as heard in Chopin's music is that they were written in a fundamentally familiar idiom, evolving as they did out of the national musical vocabulary found not only in rural musical culture but also in amateur-level collections of dances, yet the symbolism was neither simple nor readily familiar. What non-Poles heard as a single national dance signifying Poland was for Chopin an entire world of Polish affective content to which such a dance might and did refer. Chopin's topical uses of the various Polish dances are deceptively simple in that the most naïve listener can appreciate their essential Polishness and relish the infectious rhythms and lovely melodies, whereas those with more experience are privy to the Polish national epic as viewed by the Poles themselves: nobility and elegance, tragedy and essential melancholy, rural good humor or even ballroom conviviality. The Polish dances could be topics themselves like other national dances, in other words, but for Chopin each could be a repository of the different affects of the Polish soul.

Finally, a ready national identification was not the only factor that made dance music accessible to listeners. Of course, it could be danced to—the young Chopin often played for dancers at parties—and even listeners' swaying or toe-tapping meant it could be enjoyed physically, with sympathetic reaction to the music. What such music does *not* require to be understood is musical training, or even much effort: the hard-won knowledge of how to follow the adventures of a fugue subject or the modulations and motivic developments of sonata form are irrelevant. Dance music was lovely and lively, beloved of audiences, and because dance is an elemental art form, fundamentally rooted in the body, the music that accompanies and evokes it is usually among the most popular. The essential dance underlying much of Chopin's music has always been one of its most salient characteristics, and it is one of the strongest reasons that his music has always been so widely loved and is so accessible to audiences of all kinds.

Song

Song is of course another elemental art form, and melody and vocality are likewise among the characteristics most often associated with Chopin's music. He urged his piano students to study singing, and the inherent lyricism of his piano works—the sheer beauty and vividness of expression—both set them apart and, paradoxically, enabled generations of commentators to overlook their real craft, and even to look down on Chopin's source material and his musical language. So, more important than the fact that one of Chopin's primary inspirations was song per se is that this song was of a very particular type—to wit, opera.

Opera—Polish, French, Italian, German—was a significant form of entertainment in Chopin's Warsaw. Chopin's letters testify to his frequent attendance, admiration of individual singers, and opinions of various works and productions. Some of his early pieces were based on operas: the B-flat-Minor Polonaise,[13] the middle section of which was based on the cavatina "Vieni fra queste braccia" from Rossini's *Gazza ladra*, and the Op. 2 Variations on Mozart's "La cì darem la mano" from *Don Giovanni* for piano and orchestra (the latter of which earned Schumann's famous "Hats off, Gentlemen! A genius!" comment). Chopin's 1830 arrival in Paris afforded him even deeper immersion in the Italian and French operatic repertories, and in 1833 he published two more opera-based compositions: the *Variations brillantes*, Op. 12 (on the air "Je vends des scapulaires," from the hugely successful *Ludovic* of Ferdinand Hérold and Fromental Halévy), and the *Grand duo concertante* for piano and cello on themes from Giacomo Meyerbeer's *Robert le diable* (jointly composed with his friend, the cellist Auguste Franchomme). These were from well-known operas, and there is no question that in composing pieces based upon them Chopin was hoping to benefit from the commercial interest the operas' popularity would generate.

The popularity of operatic music did not entirely depend on the theater-attending public. Piano-vocal scores disseminated this music far and wide, enabling amateur musicians to enjoy it in domestic circumstances. Operatic airs were the popular music of the day (much like musical theater favorites in the United States during the 1940s and 1950s) and provided the basis for numerous instrumental works like Chopin's. David Kasunic has demonstrated that the theme from the *Ludovic* Variations and elements of the piano part of the *Grand duo concertante* were based on the piano-vocal scores of the operas involved, not on actual performances, and that the arranger of the Meyerbeer piano-vocal score, Johann Peter Pixis, interceded on Chopin's behalf with the publisher, resulting in the contract for the *Grand duo concertante*.[14] So for all the popularity of opera productions, it was in large part the piano-vocal scores of those operas and the instrumental repertoire based on famous operatic melodies—the print culture and industry—that was responsible for the broad dissemination of opera music.

Operatic sources were not always identified. In at least one case, Chopin was understood to have quoted an operatic melody without acknowledgment: the melody of his Etude, Op. 25, No. 7 in C-sharp Minor, is an idealized version of "Teneri figli," from the second act of Vincenzo Bellini's *Norma*. Chopin and Bellini had been friends who met socially and had enjoyed discussing music, and this piece was composed shortly after Bellini's death. (Another example of Bellini's influence is the opening of the Ballade in G Minor, Op. 23, which recalls the introduction

of Bellini's song "L'abbandono.")[15] The connection between the opening siciliano of the Second Ballade, Op. 38 in F Major, and Raimbaud's
Ballade from Meyerbeer's opera *Robert le diable* was noted at the time;
besides several musical similarities, Meyerbeer's number was called a
"Pilgrim Ballade," and during the composition of Opus 38 a German
publisher's agent referred to it the same way.[16]

Still, the pervasive operatic character that has long been associated
with Chopin's music is based not only on melody and *fioriture*, but also
on dramatic posture and the kind of musical utterance best suited to that
effect. For example, when Chopin coached his student Adolf Gutmann
on the middle section of the Nocturne, Op. 48, No. 2 in F-sharp Minor,
it was in dramatic terms: "A tyrant commands, and the other asks for
mercy."[17] The passage (and Chopin's description; see Example 1) is redo-
lent of French grand opera: two different kinds of declamation, one
imperative and the other importuning and despairing, offer contrast to
the richly lyrical A section. The melodic and ornamental vocabulary of
Italian bel canto opera is more common in his music, though; the lush,
doomed love duet of the D-flat Major Nocturne, Op. 27, No. 2 or the
forlorn lament of the G-Minor Nocturne, Op. 37, No. 1 evoke Italianate
vocality on an idealized level.

In general, the nocturne genre reflects the character of the operatic
scene, not just aria. For example, Op. 15, No. 1 in F Major contrasts two
lovely, sunlit pastoral aria passages with an F-minor middle section that is
clearly a storm scene. The aforementioned Op. 37, No. 1 has a prayerful
chorus in its middle section; and the titanic Op. 27, No. 1 in C-sharp
Minor is as climactic a realization of fate—a crushing lament in the A
sections contrasted with a grand soliloquy in the B section culminating
in a *con anima* clarion call for Polish fidelity—as ever appeared onstage.
So Chopin's pitch-perfect evocations of opera include, in addition to aria
itself: chorus, duet, scene, recitative, and depictive instrumental interlude—all of which would exceed the powers of a mere melodist.

Still more of the operatic idiom may be discerned from a close and
contextual reading of Chopin's scores. His notation of the cantabile style
was more deliberate and painstaking than that of virtually any other composer. He was scrupulous in his phrasing, which often was asynchronous
between left and right hands; this seemingly minor point meant that even
when the note values were rhythmically aligned, the phrasing proscribed
perfect rhythmic simultaneity. This fundamental vocalism defined much of
what he considered to be good pianism: the lifting of the wrist functioned
as did a singer's pause for breath, for example;[18] and a variety of subtly
different articulations between the extremes of legato and *secco* staccato

Example 1. Chopin, Nocturne Op. 48, No. 2, Più lento, mm. 58–60.

were needed. The pianist was to aspire to the soloistic freedom of a singer accompanied by orchestra: the left-hand accompaniment was to be rhythmically stable while the melody was to be free, corresponding to and in constant awareness of the accompaniment, but not in absolute synchrony.

Today, such rhythmic play is often heard from jazz or pop vocalists— the exquisite sadness of a phrase might be prolonged past the cadential downbeat, or so unendurable that the singer has to finish her phrase early. Such personalized stylings were far more typical of operatic performance in the nineteenth century than today. That opera's compositional and performance conventions came to be integral to Chopin's musical language demonstrates the depth of his personal identification with the art form.

Yet among all the characteristic aspects of nineteenth-century vocal art, ornamentation is the most apparent. Embellishment of a preexistent tune or motive is a constant, on some level, in virtually all music; by the first part of the nineteenth century the practice had flourished for more than two centuries in Italian opera and was at its zenith. Famous singers kept notebooks (some of which still survive) of choice, effective passagework, including different versions of the same passage, and publications of famous arias "as sung by" operatic stars brought this ornamental vocabulary to the wider public.[19] Vocal ornamentation in performance had at least two important functions. First, in the highly competitive world of opera singing, it enabled each singer to distinguish her own performances from those of others, building a following and highlighting the aspects of her voice and technique that were most pleasing and noteworthy (the key elements of her brand, in other words). The second function was at least in some measure interpretive: the more notes, or the greater the difficulty of a passage, the deeper the implied emotion. Ornamentation tended to increase throughout an aria, and the final statement of farewell was expected to be the most devastating, the final utterance of (let us say) the word *morire* (to die) or *core* (heart, in the oft-used Neapolitan dialect) the most powerful.

Consider Chopin's comments about two singers in letters written to his friend Tytus Woyciechowski. From Paris, on 12 December 1831, he wrote that Laure Cinti-Damoreau "does chromatic scales better than Tulou, the famous flautist," but this pales in comparison with his earlier effusive praise of Henriette Sontag in a letter written in Warsaw on 5 June 1830:

> Her *diminuendi* are *non plus ultra*, her *portamenti* lovely and her scales, particularly the ascending chromatic ones, are sumptuous. . . . She has some ornamentations of an entirely new sort, with which she makes a huge impression, although not like Paganini. Perhaps it is because they are of a smaller sort. She seems to breathe into the stalls some sort of fragrance of the freshest flowers, and she caresses, delightfully, strokes the audience, but rarely does she move them to tears.[20]

At twenty, Chopin was already writing as a professional. When Bellini wrote in 1834 to Count Carlo Pepoli, the librettist of *I Puritani,* "Opera, through singing, must make one weep, shudder, die,"[21] he was speaking not of his own reactions, but rather of the creative responsibilities inherent in works for the theater, and the effect the composer produces in the audience. Although Chopin ultimately chose not to compose opera himself, that world was his world, and his understanding of the genre was profound.

What is more, his complete immersion in opera music and aesthetics meant that its influence on him extended beyond musical language. He even seemed to view his own life—indeed, reality in general—in terms of the dramatic conflicts of the historical operas he found so compelling, such as Auber's *Muette de Portici* or Rossini's *Guillaume Tell*. In a morbid meditation written in Stuttgart in September 1831, after he had received word that, in the aftermath of the November Uprising, Russia had taken Warsaw. Chopin's thoughts turned to his teenage sweetheart, Konstancja Gładkowska. His tormented images of love against the backdrop of a legitimately frightening opera-worthy political upheaval seem almost self-consciously theatrical:

> What is happening with her?—Where is she?—Poor thing!—
> Perhaps she is in the hands of the Muscovite!—The Muscovite
> pushes her—strangles—murders, kills her!—Oh, my Life, I
> am here alone—come to me—I'll dry your tears, I'll heal
> the wounds of the present—recalling the past to you. Then,
> when the Muscovites weren't there yet. Then, when only a
> few Muscovites wanted most ardently to please you, but you
> mocked them.[22]

"I will heal your wounds by recalling the past"? Such a conceit might be effective onstage, but not in the world of flesh and blood. That he would fall back on that in an unguarded and vulnerable moment illustrates much about his relationship to the medium, and perhaps the way he was performing, on some level, even for himself.

To summarize: Chopin loved singing, and its natural rhythm and phraseology were integral both to his playing and his composition. He was immersed in opera's print culture as both producer and consumer, and the operatic vocabularies—of form, of melodic style, and of interpretive performance inflection, of dramatic conception—are fundamental to his style. The clearest demonstration of his affinity for both Italian and French grand opera is found in the nocturnes: Italianate melodies, more dramatic formulas of French grand opera, airs for solo and duet, recitatives, dramatic scenes of the kind that would have been well placed in the works of either school. Ornamentation is realized at a level well beyond an actual vocalist's capability, of course, with melody itself being transformed into a higher kind of elaboration via Chopin's unique and mesmerizing *fioriture*. His decorative vocabulary was far richer than those of his contemporaries in piano circles, perhaps inspired by particular opera singers (his youthful reference to Sontag's "ornamentation of an entirely new sort" is especially suggestive in this regard). The operatic art—its singable and dramatic aspects, its essential need to reach audiences on their level—was, for his music, definitive.

Story

Opera remains the best remembered narrative form of the early nineteenth century, but it was not the only one. The new publications that Chopin played through at Brzezina's music store would certainly have included descriptive piano fantasies, which since Franz Kotzwara's (in)famous *Battle of Prague* (ca. 1788) had been a flourishing genre of musical ephemera. Kotzwara's piece was probably the only one that ever had any real staying power (it appears, as a cultural phenomenon, in novels by both Mark Twain and William Makepeace Thackeray), but myriad pieces that followed sought to capitalize on it with ever newer effects and approaches.

Formally, such pieces were arranged in episodes, either in separate sections or with transitions between them. Captions, which could be read aloud, appeared at the beginning of each section to describe the action, with such phrases as "Attack with Swords" and "Horses Galloping" (Kotzwara, *Battle of Prague*), "The Tower of a Mosque Destroy'd" (Benjamin Carr, *The Siege of Tripoli*, 1804–5), or "The British Assail the Enemy, and Drive Them from the Heights" (Neville Challoner, *Waterloo*, 1815). A large percentage of these programmatic fantasias were battle pieces, with depictions of the giving of orders, reveilles and fanfares, cannons, flying bullets, and other kinds of ordnance. There were also memorial pieces, such as those after the French Revolution about the death of Louis XVI and his family. Later, other kinds of disasters—both natural and man-made—began to serve as subjects. What works in this genre had in common was basic storytelling targeted to the taste and pianistic ability of the amateur market: captions explained the dramatic content, so the significance of the musical gestures could be readily understood.

Three approaches to musical expression were used most frequently in these compositions, and they are all found in Chopin's works. The first of these, the use of mimetic musical gestures, functioned something like onomatopoeia, when the sound of a thing becomes the basis of the word for it, like *splash* or *sizzle*; so a low open octave in the midst of military pandemonium could signify "cannons," and short notes in the upper register labeled "bullets flying," and so on. Combining such cannons and bullets with stern commands, trumpet calls, and the hurly-burly of battle resulted in a panoramic battle-scene in tones, the centerpiece of many of these fantasies. Chopin's applications of this kind of tone-painting tended to be subtle: in addition to the aforementioned storm scene from Op. 15, No. 1, the virtuosic closing sections of all four of his ballades imitate—on the highest artistic level—violent pandemonium in a way few if any other composers were able to manage. On a more local level, the flamenco guitar flourishes in the Bolero, Op. 19, and the stylized water droplets heard throughout the Barcarolle, Op. 60 certainly belong in this depictive category as well. Chopin never labeled his effects, though, so identifications require careful comparisons with cognate passages by other composers.

The second expressive strategy is that of musical topics, discussed above in connection with dances, where the accepted symbolism of a particular dance type retains its significance across a variety of repertories. In fact, the topical vocabulary and operative principles went far beyond dance type; throughout the Common Practice Period, extending roughly from 1650 to 1900, a single figure, rhythm, or texture, dance-related or otherwise, could stand for a cluster of associations. The imitation of a horn call, for example, might suggest the hunt and everything associated with it: the outdoors, virile action, pursuit, nobility—indeed, via the old symbolism of the Great Huntsman, memory and even death. Similarly, a slow march in minor mode called up images of everything relating to death: funerals, memorials of tragic loss, grief.

Chopin's use of topical gestures to signify, to Poles, his own multi-faceted identity and, to non-Poles, the image of Poland Unbowed draw upon this tradition and at the same time move far beyond it. Beside the Polish dances mentioned above and their vocal and narrative associations, we find in Chopin's music marches of various kinds that may signify patriotism, resolve, noble grief, or other national sentiments. He also makes use of chorales to suggest prayer, supplication, and shared communal emotion. When used in tandem with instrumental imitations—horns, Polish bagpipes, drums—these gestures evoke an idealized, almost mythological *Polonia*.

The third strategy found in the descriptive fantasias is that of literal musical quotation, or at least of melodic figures so close as to be a recognizable reference to a famous song. Around the turn of the nineteenth century, for example, Daniel Steibelt produced fantasias that depended on quotations for their expressive vocabulary; one of these, *Britannia* (1797), was an "allegorical overture" about a successful sea battle against the Dutch (probably the Battle of Camperdown). Holland was at the time called the Batavian Republic and was under French control, so Steibelt indicates the enemy forces with a French song, "Marlborough s'en va-t-en guerre" (Anglophones know the tune as "For He's a Jolly Good Fellow"). The British are triumphantly represented not only with "God Save the King"—which is also found in several other fantasias, including Beethoven's *Wellington's Victory*—but also two songs by Thomas Augustine Arne, "Britain's Best Bulwarks" and "Rule, Britannia!" and

Henry Purcell's "Britons Strike Home!" On a more sophisticated level, the same composer's *Journée d'Ulm* (The Battle of Ulm, ca. 1805) used a wide variety of quotations, mostly from famous operas of the previous decades (by Grétry, Gluck, and Piccinni), to recount a Napoleonic victory over the Austrians. This work depended upon recognition of the operatic tunes quoted and on their contexts in the various original plots, which would inform the listeners' understanding of their deployment in this new story. What looked like a typical commercial pastiche, then, instead was really a sophisticated intertextual narrative in which well-known tunes took on rather subtle functions.

Karol Kurpiński, a Polish opera director and composer Chopin would come to know during his years of study at the Warsaw Conservatory, discussed the function of melodic reminiscence, whether quotation or a more indirect allusion, in an 1821 article: "Music . . . finds efficient expression in reminiscences of songs that have a certain significance; though mere recollections, they thereby speak all the more forcefully to the heart. Arias that have become ingrained in the memories of everyone through frequent repetition may serve as allusions, particularly during public solemnities."[23] The reference to "arias"—numbers from operas—would prove to be especially relevant to Chopin, given the near-reminiscences of Meyerbeer and Rossini used in his Second Ballade and such cases as the etude-reminiscence of Bellini's "Tenere figli" mentioned above. From the reference to "public solemnities," though, it seems that Kurpiński was also thinking about national and patriotic airs, and Chopin made use of these also.

The clearest proof of Chopin's use of these strategies is found in descriptions of his improvisations. One of the best known accounts is from 1844, by the Polish poet Józef Bohdan Zaleski, who describes how Chopin played the Polish national anthem "in a whole gamut of different forms and voices, from that of the warrior to those of children and angels."[24] Chopin, apparently, had a series of figurations and treatments through which any melody might effectively be put: a lesser-known account from 1837 by Chopin's friend and admirer, the Marquis de Custine, though no less laudatory, suggests just how formulaic such a display might have been:

> Yet again I came to be enchanted by the magician, the sylphe of Saint-Gratien. For themes, I gave him the *ranz des vaches* and the Marseillaise. It is entirely impossible to describe for you what he made of this musical epic. One saw rustics fleeing before the conquerors. It was sublime.[25]

The *ranz des vaches* or *Kuhreihen* was a well-known melodic figure (or a loosely related family of figures; the soft arpeggiated melody that opens the third section of Rossini's overture to the opera *Guillaume Tell* is the best known example) that is characteristic of the horn calls of Swiss cowherds, reputed to produce morbid homesickness in their countrymen. While the image of herdsmen fleeing before French revolutionaries may indeed have been sublime, it does not make much historical sense. Another description of a Chopin improvisation, by the novelist Henri de Latouche, does not mention a specific melody but offers a series of similar images:

> The Pole found, on the wisest of pianos, the rustic songs of Berry, now the final, plaintive phrase of a plowman on the hill, now the beginning of melody the spinner brings with her into the wood. Here is a wedding bourrée, there the mower's bagpipe. Could one paint a country with more beautiful harmonies? But soft! Now we are on the battlefield of Ostrolenka. Do you hear the prayers of the Polish army before the battle? How could God refuse victory to those who had implored thus? Their tears obtained His noble and pious assistance.[26]

Perhaps the most detailed account is from Solange Clésinger, George Sand's daughter:

> Under the flexible and responsive fingers of Chopin's pale and frail hand the piano became the voice of an archangel, an orchestra, an army, a raging ocean, a creation of the universe, the end of the world. What divine majesty! What elemental forces, what cries of despair! What triumphant hymns! What suave grace, what angelical tenderness, what infinite sorrows! What funeral marches and triumphal processions! What rays of sunlight on flowers in full bloom, on the glittering river, on the valley of scented lemon trees! What tears from the depths of the damp cloister! What impatient whinnyings of the war-horse, what duels of knights, what village or courtly dances (what minuets) interrupted by the jingling of arms or the cannon of the citadel! And what melancholy raindrops falling one by one on the tiles in the cell garden![27]

The images described in these accounts divide themselves neatly into the three expressive strategies described above: imitations of a bagpipe, cannons, battle, cries of despair, and weeping; topics of funeral march, courtly and country dance, and choruses of children and angels; and quotations of the Polish anthem, the *Marseillaise*, and the *ranz de vaches*. Such images are very much the stuff of the descriptive fantasias, though undoubtedly realized with far more artistic sophistication. Given Chopin's familiarity with these strategies, how do they present in his own published works? That is, how did he transform well-understood, if often crude, musical ideas from the ephemeral, even forgettable music he sight-read in his youth into his own demonstrably unforgettable compositions? A family of figures (see Examples 2a–2f) found in virtually all of the battle piece fantasias will illustrate: the Laments of the Wounded. Such passages of woeful grief often served as a pause between musical depictions of the battle itself and a triumphant finale.

The passage in Kotzwara's *Battle of Prague* labeled "Cries of the Wounded" features sighing, supplicating pairs of broken thirds followed by languishing two-note slurs, the intervals giving way to solo grief, all in a dark F-minor tonality (Example 2a). Four years later, strikingly similar materials are found in the third section, "They Separate Her from Her Children," of *The Sufferings of the Queen of France*, a 1793 fantasia by Jan Ladislav Dussek chronicling the final days of Marie Antoinette. This section closes with a seven-bar passage labeled "The Farewell of her Children" (Example 2b), which juxtaposes paired thirds à la Kotzwara and languishing two-note slurs of various intervals. The vocabulary of lament expands with Daniel Steibelt's 1797 *Britannia*, which has two separate sections labeled "The Cries of the Wounded," found in Examples 2c and 2d. The first of these consists of grim melodic fragments and two-note slurs, now more chromatic than in Kotzwara and Dussek (a trend that would continue to develop), set against a mid-range Alberti accompaniment. A few bars later, the second of the two sections intensifies the crying-thirds idea by inverting them into chromatic sixths, lending an intensified poignance. The "Cries of the Wounded" section from the same composer's *Journée d'Ulm* places the thirds within the context of a $\frac{2}{4}$ *opera seria* accompaniment over a quasi-Baroque, tragically descending bass line, while further expanding—with gasping grace notes and plaintive ornaments—the vocabulary of cries and wails (Example 2e).

And there are other fantasia passages of similar pathos as well: Neville Challoner's 1815 *Battle of Waterloo* and Sor's 1826 piece on the death of Tsar Alexander both use analogous lamentation figures. The real connection to Chopin, though, is probably an 1818 piece by Wilhelm Würfel, who

2a. Kotzwara, *Battle of Prague* (1788), "Cries of the Wounded."

2b. Dussek, *The Sufferings of the Queen of France* (1793), "The Farewell of her Childern"

later became his organ teacher. Würfel's *Grande fantaisie lugubre au souvenir des trois héros Prince Joseph Poniatowski, Kościuszko et Dąbrowski,* Op. 18 is a commemorative work on the deaths of three national heroes (which actually took place over a span of four years). The work features a large section titled "Deep Sadness of the Nation," which Würfel fashions out of the entire tragic vocabulary: paired thirds and other intervals embedded in the accompaniment, a variety of melodic two-note slurs (especially beginning off the beat, a centuries-old "sobbing" gesture), affective grace notes, and inexorably rising and falling, often-chromatic bass lines (Example 2f). This passage is an extended and concentrated treatment of the lament topic

The Cries of the wounded.

2c. Steibelt, *Britannia* (1797), "The Cries of the wounded." (i)

The cries of the wounded.

2d. Steibelt, *Britannia* (1797), "The cries of the wounded." (ii)

2e. Steibelt, *Le journée d'Ulm* (ca. 1805), "The cries of the wounded."

from one of the more mature examples of the programmatic repertoire; as it was by a major musical figure in Warsaw and one close to Chopin, I suspect that it would have been impossible for him not to have known it.

Cognate musical depictions of grief and complaint are also to be found in Chopin's own works, if not quite as literally. Consider the descending sequence of sighs in the coda of the Nocturne in D-flat Major, Op. 27, No. 2 (1837; Example 3): it is not quite as obvious as the examples already cited, but—particularly when repeated with the sobbing, gasping grace-note additions that we know to have been an intensification of the stock vocabulary of lament—this pattern suggests a grief of Aristotelian signifi-cance, a god or hero brought low. The unbearably beautiful F-minor melody that begins in measure 7 of the Ballade No. 4 in F Minor, Op. 52 (1843; Example 4) is long-breathed but composed primarily of keen-ing two-note pairs (C–D♭–B♮ –C, F–E♮, and following a kind of B♭ pickup back to D♭–C), but so displaced that the diminished third and augmented fourth separating them catch the ear first. In the accompaniment, the sighing paired thirds seen in earlier pieces are now paired triads that

2f. Würfel, *Grande fantaisie lugubre* (1818), "Deep Sadness of the Nation."

Example 3. Chopin, Nocturne Op. 27, No. 2, in D-flat Major, mm. 62–70.

work the very same way. (Compare the left-hand part of Example 4 with the Kotzwara passage in Example 2a.)

Now we can begin to formulate an explanation for our original point of departure—the open-armed reception that Chopin's music has consistently received from pianists, professional and amateur alike, and by listeners of all levels of experience and sophistication. Melodism, irresistible dance rhythms, a characteristic inflection—however celebrated these aspects of his compositional language are in and of themselves, they are an incomplete explanation because a great deal of music with those characteristics has nonetheless disappeared without a trace. Rather, it is a matter of style and idiom: the Nocturne and Ballade examples in Examples 3 and 4 demonstrate the direct line between some of Chopin's most sublime music and the humble and ephemeral music of the consumer market—Chopin effected imaginative and sophisticated transformations, certainly, but the inheritance is clear. Understanding these musical signs enables us to hear more than just the notes; we immediately perceive the

Example 4. Chopin, Ballade No. 4 in F Minor, Op. 52, mm. 8–12.

long-standing cultural associations, and thus his music can reach us on a deeper level so that we understand something more specific, such as the gestural vocabulary of tragic lamentation rather than merely a bland melancholy. And this is but one example of a family of such figures: the "word of command" gestures from the battle pieces find a higher incarnation as Chopin's written-out recitatives, heavenly and angelic voices are apotheosized as the *vox angelica* trio of the famous Funeral March, Op. 35, III, and so on. Further examples are legion.

It is not that Chopin was limited to that which would please middlebrow tastes and thus does not belong in the first rank of artists himself; that long-discredited view was based on senselessly restricted views of what worthwhile art is. Rather, it is that Chopin's intimate familiarity, since childhood, with the most popular repertories of the time, coupled with a musical education that was in certain ways conservative, meant that his art could achieve the eighteenth-century aesthetic of music *für Kenner und Liebhaber*, music that would be appreciated equally by musical cognoscenti, educated professionals and connoisseurs, as well as by people of much less musical sophistication. Chopin wore his learning lightly; for all the real craft, formal sophistication, and artistic command, his music—which was indeed made up of the most infectious dance rhythms, the loveliest melodies, the most attractive piano figuration and "hooks"—required no musical equivalent of a literary language with which a listener must struggle before attaining even an imperfect understanding of it. He composed his masterpieces in the pianistic home dialect or common speech, the language of opera, dance, and consumer music—the music people avidly heard and played, in other words, not that which needed to be studied and mastered for purposes of artistic or cultural self-improvement.

Chopin's visionary pieces—ballades that defined a new musical form (but one that originated in the descriptive piano fantasias), nocturnes that evoked opera scenes while surpassing their models in beauty and eloquence, etudes (whatever their technical difficulties) that were ultimately essays in *la chopinisme* more than they were mechanical exercises—whether Polish, Italianate, or Gallic in inflection, were musical essays in the vernacular language of the piano, accessible to everyone. Although there will always be a certain critical suspicion of music this popular and pleasing, Chopin's accomplishment recalls that of Dante Alighieri, a comparison already suggested in the pen-and-ink sketch, by Eugène Delacroix, of Chopin clothed as a late-medieval Tuscan. Dante was the first artist to produce masterpieces in Tuscan Italian rather than Latin, and thereby the first to elevate that vernacular to a cultivated language, thereafter to be studied, cherished, and preserved. Similarly, from the constituent vernaculars of his time, Chopin fashioned a cultivated pianistic language that is similarly revered and imitated. And thus, his music is able to communicate directly to listeners of all kinds, and his unique position among piano composers remains unchallenged.

NOTES

1. Arthur Hedley, ed., *Selected Correspondence of Fryderyk Chopin* (London: Heinemann, 1962), 114.

2. Halina Goldberg, "Musical Life in Warsaw During Chopin's Youth" (PhD diss., City University of New York, 1997), 80.

3. Quoted in Hedley, *Selected Correspondence of Fryderyk Chopin*, 94.

4. Jean-Jacques Eigeldinger, *Chopin: Pianist and Teacher, As Seen by His Pupils*, ed. Roy Howat, trans. Naomi Shohet, Krysia Osostowicz, and Roy Howat (Cambridge: Cambridge University Press, 1986), 135–36n137.

5. Chopin seems always to have been grateful for the guidance of his piano teacher Wojciech Żywny, though Żywny enjoyed nothing like Elsner's reputation.

6. See Goldberg, "Musical Life in Warsaw," 87–102; and Barbara Milewski, "Chopin's Mazurkas and the Myth of the Folk," *19th-Century Music* 23 (1999): 113–35.

7. A fine summary of this cultural preoccupation may be found in Goldberg, *Music in Chopin's Warsaw* (New York: Oxford University Press, 2008), 62–85.

8. The subdiscipline of topic theory is devoted to understanding the musical vocabulary of the Common Practice from precisely this perspective: how such individual gestures were used and understood, and thus what they meant to contemporary audiences. The subject is given its clearest and most pithy explanation in Leonard G. Ratner, *Classic Music: Expression, Form, and Style* (New York: Schirmer Books, 1980), 9. A more

recent comprehensive treatment of the subject is found in Danuta Mirka, ed., *The Oxford Handbook of Topic Theory* (Oxford and New York: Oxford University Press, 2014).

9. Mozart's Count and Don feel entitled to women, for the most part, and by the nineteenth century the hard edges of the Spanish cultural stereotype were fading. Chopin's own Bolero, Op. 19 has a much lighter touch; there is a good-humored combination of sun-bathed Spanish character music, specifically guitaristic virtuosity, with a polonaise middle section (as if to say, "Admit it; you expected this from me anyway").

10. For an in-depth discussion of the polonaise, see Eric McKee's essay in this volume.

11. Background on the polonaise may be found in Maja Trochimczyk, "Polonaise," in the Polish Dances section of the website of the Polish Music Center at the University of Southern California, http://pmc.usc.edu/dance/polonaise.html.

12. Background on the krakowiak may be found in Maja Trochimczyk, "Krakowiak," http://pmc.usc.edu/dance/krakowiak.html.

13. KKp 1188 and 1189; composed in 1826.

14. David Kasunic, "Chopin and the Singing Voice: From the Romantic to the Real" (PhD diss., Princeton University, 2004), 204–20.

15. The correspondence between Bellini's song and Chopin's First Ballade is discussed in more detail in Jonathan D. Bellman, *Chopin's Polish Ballade: Op. 38 as Narrative of National Martyrdom* (Oxford and New York: Oxford University Press, 2010), 78–79.

16. Ibid., 111–12.

17. Eigeldinger, *Chopin: Pianist and Teacher,* 81.

18. Ibid., 44–45.

19. A good selection of singers' ornamental versions are collected in Austin B. Caswell, *Embellished Opera Arias* (Madison, WI: A-R Editions, 1989), which uses these notebooks as source material.

20. Chopin to Tytus Woyciechowski, 5 June 1830, *Chopin's Polish Letters*, trans. David Frick (Warsaw: Fryderyk Chopin Institute, 2016), 249, 164.

21. Quoted in Friedrich Lippmann, "Vincenzo Bellini," in *New Grove Dictionary of Music and Musicians* (1980), 2:449.

22. This passage is from the so-called Stuttgart Diary, a fearful and morbid series of entries Chopin wrote in his album in the second half of September, 1831, after he left Warsaw but before he arrived in Paris. *Chopin's Polish Letters*, 233.

23. Karol Kurpiński, "O expresji muzycznej i naśladowaniu" (On Musical Expression and Mimesis), *Tygodnik muzyczny i dramatyczny* 6 (9 May 1821), trans. John Comber. This article is reproduced in its entirety in this volume. The passage in question is discussed in Halina Goldberg, "'Remembering That Tale of Grief': The Prophetic Voice in Chopin's Music," in *The Age of Chopin: Interdisciplinary Inquiries*, ed. Halina Goldberg (Bloomington: Indiana University Press, 2004), 64–65; and in more detail in Goldberg, "Descriptive Instrumental Music in Nineteenth-Century Poland," *Journal of Musicological Research* 34/3 (Summer 2015): 224–48.

24. The complete passage may be found in John Rink's essay "Chopin and Improvisation" in this volume.

25. Astolphe de Custine to Sophie Gay, early June 1837, in J.-F. Tarn, *Le Marquis de Custine* (Paris: Fayard, 1985), 245 (my translation). Also quoted in Irena Poniatowska, ed., *Chopin and His Critics: An Anthology* (Warsaw: Fryderyk Chopin Institute, 2011), 384.

26. Henri de Latouche, "Monthly Almanac," April 1844, in Henri de Latouche, *La journée d'un fou*, quoted in Henri de Latouche, *La vallée aux loups* (Paris: Michel Lévy, 1875), 249–51 (my translation). Also quoted in Poniatowska, *Chopin and His Critics*, 385.

27. Quoted in Eigeldinger, *Chopin: Pianist and Teacher,* 281.

Karol Kurpiński on the Musical Expression
of Polish National Sentiment

TRANSLATED BY JOHN COMBER
INTRODUCED AND ANNOTATED BY HALINA GOLDBERG

As one of Poland's leading opera composers, Karol Kurpiński (1785–1857) devoted a good deal of thought to the relationship between text and music. Kurpiński, who arrived in Warsaw in 1810, and Chopin's composition teacher Józef Elsner, who came to the Polish capital about a decade earlier, composed their dramatic works during the politically charged period when the expression of Polish nationality in music was the most important and pressing creative challenge faced by composers. While Elsner's published theoretical writings focused mostly on effective use of Polish prosody in musical settings, Kurpiński's observations often concerned broader questions of mimesis and expression, especially as they relate to music's ability to convey national sentiments.

Chopin enthusiasts remember Kurpiński mostly as the man who led the orchestra during young Fryderyk's official debut at the National Theater on 17 March 1830, when the young pianist premiered his F-Minor Concerto, Op. 21, and the *Fantasia on Polish Themes*, Op. 13; overtures from Kurpiński's and Elsner's operas were on the same program. But Kurpiński was involved with many facets of Warsaw's musical life. Shortly after he arrived in Warsaw he became the second conductor for the orchestra of the National Theater, with support from Elsner; later, starting in 1824, he became the sole director of the opera and a rival of Elsner. Kurpiński was a prolific composer of some two dozen operas and numerous instrumental and sacred works, and he was also active as a teacher at the Warsaw Conservatory and an organizer of the capital's musical life. In May of 1820, Kurpiński launched the publication of a weekly journal devoted exclusively to music, *Tygodnik Muzyczny* (The Music Weekly). The periodical had a rather difficult existence, and after a two-month hiatus in November–December 1820, it resumed as *Tygodnik Muzyczny i Dramatyczny* (The Music and Drama Weekly). In total, it survived only slightly over a year, but during this period its readers were exposed to timely aesthetic and theoretical topics, and so the foundations were laid for professional music criticism in Poland.

Kurpiński wanted to understand how music can portray a specific character or narrative whether text is present or absent. For example, in one article he addressed the expressive role of music in conveying dramatic action in pantomime ballet.[1] Another example is found in his fantasia for violin and piano, "Dumanie nad mogiłą Wandy " (Musings at the Tomb of Wanda), the title of which references the legendary Polish princess who purportedly lived in the eighth century and bravely protected the welfare of her country.[2] The piece contains no text, but its character derives from the legend. In his writings, Kurpiński advocated the use of familiar musical gestures and topics, as well as musical quotations to create such musical narratives, but he warned that they needed to be used in a manner that results in a "continuous, flowing speech."[3]

The essay "O historycznych pieśniach ludu Polskiego" (On the Historical Songs of the Polish People) was published in no. 26 of *Tygodnik muzyczny* (25 October 1820) as the last segment of the series "O pieśniach w ogólności" (On Songs in General).[4] The title of the series aside, only the first of the articles discussed the idea of national identity in songs coming from diverse countries. In later installments Kurpiński focused on Polish music—sacred songs, regional and dance genres (including the polonaise and mazurka), and historical songs, which emerge in response to "sudden traumas experienced by the whole nation."[5] The significance of the essay "On the Historical Songs of the Polish People" is twofold: first, Kurpiński offers a compendium of patriotic songs, listed chronologically to mirror the sequence of historical events that took place in Poland between 1791 and 1814. Many of these songs are no longer remembered—even in Poland—but they would have been known to every Polish patriot of Chopin's generation. Second, Kurpiński discusses compositional strategies that are relevant to Chopin's oeuvre: the use of topics and familiar tunes that "trigger certain recollections" to create a musical narrative. To demonstrate this strategy, he offers his own composition, "Elegia na śmierć Tadeusza Kościuszki" (Elegy on the Death of Tadeusz Kościuszko) for elocutionist and orchestra (in piano transcription), in which he uses topical gestures as well as quotations from and allusions to Polish and foreign songs to narrate, in tones, the life of the hero. We include musical excerpts from the "Elegy" to illustrate Kurpiński's discussion of this piece.

In the spring of the following year, in a series of six installments titled "O expressyi muzyczney i naśladowaniu" (On Musical Expression and

Mimesis), Kurpiński revisited the subject of music's capacity for convey-ing meaning.[6] In this essay, he notes that instrumental music lacks the specificity and perfection of expression that is possible when music works with a text (a familiar idea in eighteenth-century criticism), and accord-ingly, he devotes most of his discussion to opera and sacred music. Of particular interest are the last two segments of the series, in which the author attempts to refine the distinction between *depictive* imitation, of which he disapproves, and "passionate and dramatic music, which is also imitative."[7] (Despite the aesthetic stickiness of Kurpiński's attempt to privi-lege some kinds of imitative music over others, it is nonetheless a rare nineteenth-century example of imitative music of any kind being taken seriously.) He also reconsiders the role of mimesis in characteristic instru-mental compositions, such as symphonies and concerti, and in ballet and pantomime. Most significant is Kurpiński's discussion of the potential for national feeling to be aroused by vague recollection or subtle allusion to familiar patriotic tunes. He calls this a "suggestive expression" in music, pointing to the dream music passage from Elsner's opera *King Łokietek* as a melodrama in which topical gestures and patriotic tunes are laced together to create a powerful historical narrative.

Kurpiński thus challenges today's narrow understanding of Polish musical nationality in Chopin's era as being dependent upon the use of folkloric national dances. Instead, he notes the importance of patriotic songs and of specific compositional strategies that can be employed to narrate Polish history through music. These concepts were adopted and refined by Chopin in his narrative works, especially the ballades, Fantasy, Op. 49, and the *Polonaise-Fantaisie*, Op. 61.[8]

On the Historical Songs of the Polish People
Karol Kurpiński
Tygodnik muzyczny 26 (25 October 1820)

To this very day, Polish people have certain worldly and sacred songs that commemorate the more noteworthy events in the country: for example, songs of Our Lady of Częstochowa[9] mention the Tatars, the Swedes, the plague and various afflictions that have beset our nation; worldly [songs mention] the Cossacks, illustrious Polish leaders, John III [Sobieski] at Vienna, the good Saxon times, the Confederates, etc.[10] Such songs should be collected together, set in chronological order and, if not published, then at least painstakingly preserved; they should stand among the most precious national keepsakes. In a word, an ancient little song from any country that sings of the famous history of its nation—be it Scottish, Swiss, Slavonic, American—stirs us to dream; what then about the songs relating the famous history of our own fatherland? How dear they will be to our future generations! From the passing of the Constitution of the Third of May 1791 to the present, we have a collection of songs that clearly mark out the sequence of events that our fatherland has experienced. Among the most significant are the following:

Polonaise played and sung on the Third of May:
It was through the Sejm's accord
That our freedom was restored;
Hail! all the estates will sing,
Long live our beloved king, etc.

The Kościuszko Polonaise:
We sigh with woe when you depart, etc.

Mazurka:
A navy coat with collar red.

Mazurka:
Come on lads, look lively now,
The harvest time's upon us, etc.

March:
Kościuszko, our father, will defend us.

Sonata and polonaise: "The Battle of Racławice."[11]

Polonaise *triste* to be played:[12] "Kościuszko's capture, 1794."

Song:
The homeland's waning, crashing down,
Farewell you darling children now.

Mazurka:

> *O such woe as ne'er before*
> *Is now our lot, Mazovians.*

Legionnaires' Mazurka [Dąbrowski Mazurka
("Poland Has Not Yet Perished")]:

> *Poland has not yet perished*
> *While there's life within us,*
>
> .   .   .   .   .
>
> *March, march Dąbrowski,*
> *From the Italian lands to Poland.*

March of 1806:

> *What eagles these, what visions?*

March of Prince Józef [Poniatowski March].

Grand triumphal march on the return of the Polish
army from its victory over Austria in 1809.

March:

> *Mount up, brothers, mount up,* from 1812.

Finally, Hymn to Alexander I, Emperor of All Russia,
from 1814.

Not only would such a collection be a valuable memento for posterity,
but it would also be of great assistance for the future to composers in
pieces in which the music is to trigger certain recollections ([Fr.] *reminis-cence*). Allow me, dear readers, to back this assertion with an analysis of
my own music to Kantorbery Tymowski's "Elegy on the Death of Tadeusz
Kościuszko" (which we purposely append here, even though it was already
given by the publishers of the *Tygodnik Warszawski* [Warsaw Weekly]). Our
sensible readers will no doubt not take the above evidence as an indica-tion of vainglory.

Example 1a. The Kościuszko Polonaise, mm. 1–6 (poet and composer unknown).

We sigh with woe when you depart
Goodbye to the friendship of the hearth,

Example 1b. The Kościuszko Polonaise, mm. 11–14.

More than life itself we loved,
respected you as it behooved.

Example 1c. The Kościuszko Polonaise, mm. 19–22.

And as you leave, then fare you well.
And good things of our friendship tell.

Example 2. Kurpiński, "Elegy on the Death of Tadeusz Kościuszko," mm. 1–18.

The opening bars of the introduction strike up the motive of the "Kościuszko Polonaise," but in a sad key and in the serious rhythm of a four-quarter beat; that draws attention to the subject of the poetry [See Examples 1a and 2]; in the fifth bar, the monotonous striking of the bass with the use of the pedal expresses the gloomy sound of the bell, during the course of which one can hear a familiar Swiss melody, "Ah, only there, where we are born"[13]—transporting the listeners for a moment to the place where our hero's life came to an end. In the subsequent lines, which are merely a preface to the work, the initial motive is repeated with variation up to the words "Time avenges the suffering of nations . . ." Here the music audibly intones the English song "Rule Britannia," and in the fourth bar one immediately hears—*piano*, as if from distant America—the song of freedom "Let's go, sons of the fatherland."[14] At its end one hears a snatch of the "Kościuszko Polonaise" in four beats to the measure, while the bass expresses the movement of billows on the ocean during the line: "The knight was borne on the ocean's waves." [See Example 1b and 3.]

Example 3. Kurpiński, "Elegy on the Death of Tadeusz Kościuszko," mm. 35–57.

The next three *tremolando* unisons express the three clouds threatening our nation and Kościuszko's secret return. The pastoral tones of the Cracovians transport the listener to the area of our ancient capital, where

"Kościuszko comes
to make heroes of the farming folk."

Example 4. Kurpiński, "Elegy on the Death of Tadeusz Kościuszko," mm. 78–83.

These last two lines, with the subsequent four, gave me plenty to think about, since they contain the essence of our entire revolution: in the two bars it was necessary to depict the farming folk, in the next two the folk already as valiant knights, in the fifth their victory, in the sixth the demise of the country—that is, the final, heavy sigh of the fatherland. The music could not be stretched any further, because the music should not break the unity of these lines. [See Example 4.] Moving on, the sounding and stopping of the music corresponds to the poem's structure; but when [the recounting of Kościuszko's past] resumes, the music also returns to the historical realm, with that sad polonaise titled *Kościuszko's Capture*. [See Example 5.] Again, in accordance with the structure, the lyre falls silent; it only awakens on the words "America! Kościuszko's returning to you," and

Example 5. Kurpiński, "Elegy on the Death of Tadeusz Kościuszko," mm. 114–21.

Example 6. Kurpiński, "Elegy on the Death of Tadeusz Kościuszko," mm. 145–50.

it repeats again what was previously heard on the words "The knight was borne on the ocean's waves," ending appropriately for the line "Where the same hand fights and plows." Again the music plays a snatch of the "Kościuszko Polonaise," in the minor key and at a slow tempo in four beats to the measure, to enhance the strength of the words "Kościuszko bowed by Father Time," etc. [See Examples 1c and 6.], and again pauses until the line "Companion to Kościuszko's fame" (Prince Józef [Poniatowski]), where the music plays the motive of the "[Poniatowski] March" led through various keys in a tumultuous sound and ends sadly with the words "And with the knight, all hope was dashed." [See Example 7.] Then funereal tones can be heard amid the declamation, like a mother's prayers on the death of her darling son. The end is not important.

Example 7. Kurpiński, "Elegy on the Death of Tadeusz Kościuszko," mm. 151–59.

Example 7. continued, mm. 160–74.

On Musical Expression and Mimesis

Karol Kurpiński

Tygodnik muzyczny i dramatyczny 5 (9 May 1821)

The composer who—after conferring with his heart—finds a suitable idea for expressing a poet's thoughts does not remain content with that. He must still bring to bear his creative gift of combining refined taste, sensitivity, and honest aspirations in his choice of the song's key and tempo and in his selection of voices and instruments to perform it.

Although one obtains the greatest force of musical expression from the combining of tones [i.e., harmony], the quality of their sound ([Fr.] *tymbre*) is not immaterial. An energetic and grandiloquent *bass voice* is suited to strong emotions, sacred songs; it has too much solemnity and even harshness for expressing tender feelings. A *tenor*, on the contrary, commends itself with its sweetness and suppleness: its noble and keen accent lends the silkiest expression to words of love. A *woman's voice* combines strength and lightness; tender and graceful in the middle tones, in the top range it displays the splendor and firmness necessary for grand effects.

Religious hymns could not make do without horns and flutes. The bassoon is a good accompaniment for a *dumka* ([Fr.] *une romance*). The oboe is graceful in a pastorale; the clarinet is both melancholy and martial; the violin is universal, it is the principle and the master of the orchestra.

Lowering the third gives a *minor* tone, a sad and gloomy hue.

A triple meter in rapid motion has little refinement; its common liveliness should be offset by a slowing of the *tempo*.

The choice of key is likewise a very important thing, since each has its distinctive coloring: F major, E major, and D major are magnificent; E-flat minor and C minor are serious, sad and sacred; A major and E major express tenderness; B minor is harsh and wild; G major is rustic, C major martial, and F minor funereal. A composer, while not wishing to take these remarks as inviolable law, ought to use the various means provided by his art, without departing unduly from the prescribed character of these keys. Let him seek out overtures, arias, duets, choruses, and even dance pieces from the oeuvre of the great masters, and he may realize that such remarks are not irrelevant.

Though all feelings may be characterized by certain keys, which the composer uses to express them, music is nevertheless the art of imitation, limited as it may be, since nature provides its models and the means to awaken the truth. Aristotle, Cicero, Rousseau, Batteux, and many others have confirmed this principle.

The term *imitative music* is commonly used for music that faithfully represents certain sounds heard in passing, such as the clanking of hammers in a forge, the singing of birds, the whistling of the wind and the clattering of horses.[i] I would rather call such music *depictive* (picturesque), to distinguish it from passionate and dramatic music, which is also imitative.

The critics have aimed their barbs particularly at such *depictive* imitation and, by blaming the art itself for the artists' mistakes, the critics themselves have fallen into an incurable error. Corelli in his concerto titled *Christmas Night* wished to depict the adoration of the angels and the shepherds;[15] Handel endeavored to convey the gushing of a waterfall in one of his symphonies;[ii] and in his oratorio *Israel in Egypt* Handel presumed to imitate with *pizzicato* the leaping of the locusts with which Moses plagued the Land of the Pharaohs; finally, Raimondi, in Amsterdam, rendered his *The Adventures of Telemachus*[16] in [the form of] a symphony.[iii] Although the music of these masters is excellent, in this respect they missed the mark.

However, when the listener is enlightened by some signs, words, or pantomime, such *depictive imitation* acquires delightful charms, and its faithfulness is perhaps the foremost virtue of the work. For example, the ritornello of the duet in *Nowy dziedzic*[17] that depicts the uncorking, pouring, and tasting of a bottle of Chambertin, gives the listener a pleasant satisfaction: play it without pantomime to a consummate expert for the first time, and I vouch that he will call this fine idea poor. Beyond this lovely trifle I could cite many serious sections from oratorios by Haydn and Jommelli where imitation is used with good judgment and taste and the effect is certain because the words or action admit of no false explanation. Yet such imitation should be used *only when relating some action or during the action itself,* and secondary details, be they of the utmost congeniality, should be drowned out by the stream of the principal features.

If some composers are reproved for images that are occasionally inaccurate, we would reply that every proficient artist, when imitating, ought to beautify nature.[iv] A shooter imitates the speech of birds to the point of deceiving them. What would be thought of a musician who used the same method? The *truth* would be perfect, but the *image* would be wretched.

---

i. See *Tyg. Muz.* no. 1, section I.

ii. *Water Music.*

iii. It is not worth speaking of various battles, elegies, and the titles of concertos, sonatas, fantasias, etc.

iv. In Paris, at a rehearsal of the opera *Zemire et Azor,* when the echo aria had been repeated, a certain amateur asked Grétry why he had not used female voices instead of the flutes and horns answering Zemire's words. He replied: "There would be too much truth and little illusion" (*Essai sur la musique,* vol. 3).

At the first performance of *Orphée,* the leading actor, wishing to imitate nature entirely, used, in accordance with the words, an ear-splitting cry; he then realized that he could not find art in straightforward imitation (Michel-Paul Guy de Chabanon, *Observation sur la musique, et principalement sur la métaphysique,* vol. 1, 66).

One can imitate the song of the nightingale and the lark, but that is not what we seek; rather we demand a delightful blending of diverse melodies.

At the end of spring, go to Bielany [near Warsaw], for example, or even to Bielany near Kraków, and take pleasure in the early morn at sunrise; I will not describe the beautiful view, as it is not the setting that is at issue here. Hark, and you will hear the fluent tones, marvelous roulades, and pearly cadences of the nightingale joining with the tender accents of the lesser whitethroat, the twittering of the goldfinch, and the thirds of the cuckoo. The continuous trills of the larks embellish the intermittent cooing of the turtledoves and the bold rhythm of the quail. The crowing of the cocks, the lowing of the cattle, and a bell from a hermits' tower afford you pleasant distraction; across the neighborhood their cleansed and weakened sounds will join that charming concert from time to time. Should the murmuring of water, the rustling of lightly swaying leaves, and the humming of bees serve as a bass complement to these distinct melodies; and should the monotonous pounding of a watermill from afar, or the even patter of a floating oar lend them a regular beat, you will have the most perfect musical union bestowed by the harmony of nature.

This a musician should paint. So, can he succeed? I refer this question to those who are familiar with Armide's scenes, the duet "Qui dove scherza l'aura" in *Axur*, Griselda's duet with her father, the women's chorus "Like Drops of the Morning Dew" from [Kurpiński's opera] *Zbigniew*, and Haydn's *The Creation* and *The Seasons*.[18]

Music also finds efficient expression in reminiscences of songs that have a certain significance; though mere recollections, they thereby speak all the more forcefully to the heart. Arias that have become ingrained in the memories of everyone through frequent repetition may serve as allusions, particularly during public solemnities: barely has the clarinet played the theme than the words fly from mouth to mouth. The use of these speaking songs, these musical sayings, is most helpful in ballets, pantomimes, and comic operas. There are also wordless pieces of music to which fortuitous assimilation has lent suggestive expression. For instance, through the tones of a specific march, you see before you the national troops: you see the Commander [*Naczelnik*, an affectionate sobriquet for Tadeusz Kościuszko], the retinue of knights around him, the movement of the whole army, the banners of the more illustrious sons of the fatherland; a few bars . . .[19] represent to you in a single moment a great picture with its smallest details. —Do you know this polonaise? —"I had the pleasure of dancing it with the Emperor at the duchess's ball: it was the very first dance; it reminds me of how each of the ladies was dressed, and it is as if I were still gazing at the entire dancing company." Anyone finding himself in a foreign land hums songs from home, and in that fond illusion sees himself among his acquaintances, amid the beloved family for which he longs.

Why are older people so attached to old music? Because the pleasantest moments of their lives, the keenest emotions they have experienced, are imperceptibly linked to certain melodies heard or repeated in their youth.

Who better than we Poles can judge the power of patriotic songs upon the minds of the people, especially soldiers? They have been more effective than any oratory: tones that like electrical sparks strike all ears and resound in every heart in a single moment, so that even the timorous become heroes.

May any Pole who seeks evidence of the effects of suggestive expression listen to the dream music from the opera *Łokietek*.[20] There are no words, because there are no earthly words that could say so much so powerfully in a brief moment. After two bars, you already understand everything; your heart quivers, you are transported despite yourself; and if you can break free from the distraction for a moment to behold the entire assembly, you will marvel that all share a single emotion.

May at least this last proof of the expressive power of music convince all who regard the art as mere idle amusement.

[Editors' note: Arabic superscripts refer to editorial endnotes; the footnotes denoted by lower-case roman numerals are part of Kurpiński's original.]

NOTES

1. *Tygodnik Muzyczny* 13 (26 July 1820).
2. Published in *Tygodnik Muzyczny* 7 (14 June 1820).
3. *Tygodnik Muzyczny* 13.
4. The five earlier installments, nos. 6, 7, 8, 9, 11, were published during the summer, starting with the 7 June issue.
5. *Tygodnik muzyczny* 8 (21 June 1820).
6. *Tygodnik muzyczny i dramatyczny*, nos. 1–6, published between 11 April and 6 May 1821.
7. *Tygodnik muzyczny i dramatyczny* 5 (9 May 1821).
8. The literature devoted to this aspect of Chopin's work and its presence in nineteenth-century music in general continues to grow. Representative examples include Mieczysław Tomaszewski, "Fantasie F-Moll op. 49: Genese, Struktur, Rezeption," *Chopin Studies* 5 (1995): 210–23; Halina Goldberg, "'Remembering That Tale of Grief': The Prophetic Voice in Chopin's Music," in Goldberg, ed., *The Age of Chopin* (Bloomington and Indianapolis: Indiana University Press, 2004), 54–92; and Goldberg, "Descriptive Instrumental Music in Nineteenth-Century Poland: Context, Genre, and Performance," *Journal of Musicological Research* 34/3 (Summer 2015): 224–48; Jonathan D. Bellman, *Chopin's Polish Ballade: Op. 38 as Narrative of National Martyrdom* (New York: Oxford University Press, 2010); and Bellman, "Expressive and Narrative Strategies in the Descriptive Piano Fantasia," *Journal of Musicological Research* 34/3 (Summer 2015): 182–203.

9. This revered icon, also known as the Black Madonna of Częstochowa, as well as the Pauline monastery in Jasna Góra where it is housed are woven into Polish history as symbols of nationhood. Since the Black Madonna is credited with many miracles, the monastery is the most important pilgrimage destination in Poland. There is a substantial body of music associated with Jasna Góra.

10. The Bar Confederation (sometimes viewed as Poland's first national uprising) was formed in 1768 by Polish magnates for the purpose of military resistance to reforms spearheaded by Catherine the Great of Russia, which they viewed as setting limits to their power and threatening Poland's sovereignty.

11. The Battle of Racławice, which took place in 1794 at the start of the Kościuszko Insurrection, was a spectacular victory of the Polish troops (led by Kościuszko) over the Russian forces.

12. At the time, the concept of a dance for listening was new and not always understood by audiences. This is underscored in a letter from Chopin's sister to the composer, in which she comments on the discomfort of the Polish listeners with Chopin's mazurkas that are "not for dancing." Therefore, the "contemplative" function of such dances had to be somehow indicated. The term *triste* was often used as a cue.

13. "Nur in dem Land, wo wir geboren, Lacht uns die Ruh, blüht uns das Glück." A duet from the opera *Die Schweizer-Familie* by Joseph Weigl.

14. The tune here is "La Marseillaise," which, of course, is anachronistic, as the events referenced in this passage took place during the years 1776–84, when Kościuszko traveled to America to fight in the Revolutionary War. "The Marseillaise" was not composed until 1792, but Kurpiński clearly chose it not for its specific association with America's Revolutionary War, but as a tune that would be easily recognized by his listeners as a "song of freedom." Today the incipit of "The Marseillaise" is typically translated as "Arise, children of the fatherland." In the nineteenth century, other versions circulated. For instance, in "The Marseilles [*sic*] March: Sung by the Marseillois Going to Battle" (published in London by J. Bland, ca. 1792, and later by Rt. Birchall, ca. 1802) the first line is translated as "Ye sons of France awake to glory."

15. Arcangelo Corelli, Concerto Grosso in G Minor, Op. 6, No. 8, the "Christmas" Concerto, inscribed by the composer "Fatto per la notte di Natale."

16. The symphony *Les aventures de Télémaque dans l'isle de Calypso* by the Italian violinist and composer Ignazio Raimondi premiered in Amsterdam in 1777.

17. The Polish staging of François-Adrien Boieldieu's opera *Le nouveau seigneur de village.*

18. Kurpiński is likely referencing the following works: the setting of *Armide* is probably the one by Christoph Willibald Gluck, as Rossini's works were only beginning to gain the interest of Polish audiences and his *Armida* of 1817 was probably not known there (Gluck's operas were not performed in Warsaw at the time, but his music was known and held in high esteem); "Qui dove scherza l'aura" is the opening duet from Antonio Salieri's *Axur, re d'Ormus*, which was immensely popular in Warsaw (as it was in Vienna) having been shown 120 times between 1793 (Polish premiere) and 1820; the duet of Griselda and her father is probably from Ferdinando Paër's opera *Griselda, ossia La virtù al cimento* (1798) on a well-known libretto, a work that made the composer's reputation in Vienna and was performed in Warsaw in 1818; and the bucolic scene "Like drops of the morning dew" is from Act 1 of Kurpiński's own *Zbigniew* (1819), a lyric tragedy about events from the reign of the twelfth-century Polish King Bolesław III Wrymouth, set to a text by Julian Ursyn Niemcewicz, which was conceived in the manner of ancient tragedy with choruses.

19. Suspension points in original.

20. The opera *Król Łokietek* (King Ladislaus the Elbow-High) by Józef Elsner (1818).

Dance and the Music of Chopin: The Polonaise

ERIC MCKEE

> Could any other dance . . . truly surpass the polonaise as an
> example of noble pride and grandeur? It would be the minuet,
> itself and alone, that could challenge its position with regard
> to majesty. If you simply consider greatness and the effect
> of its noble pride, the polonaise will certainly have the first
> place alone.
>
> —C. J. von Feldtenstein,
> *Erweiterung der Kunst nach der Chorographie zu Tanzen*

During the first three quarters of the eighteenth century the minuet
reigned supreme on ballroom dance floors as "the universal dance that
all nations in Europe prefer over their national dances" (see Figure 1).[1]
Having made its ascendency within the opulent court balls of Louis XIV,
the minuet quickly became recognized as the premiere dance of the ruling class. Not only did it symbolize social position, but it also captured
in artful motion (at least in intent) noble character, complaisant attitude,
and stylized habits of social life. By mastering the minuet one learned not
only how to behave on the dance floor but off as well. The English nobleman Philip Dormer Stanhope (1694–1773), in a series of letters to his son,
repeatedly promoted the benefits of mastering the minuet: "The greatest
advantage of dancing well is that it necessarily teaches you to present
yourself, to sit, stand, and walk, genteelly; all of which are of real importance to a man of fashion."[2] In another letter Stanhope drives his point
home: "Do everything in minuet-time; speak, think, and move always in
that measure—equally free from the dullness of slow, or the hurry and
huddle of quick time."[3]

Considering the "universal" popularity of the minuet, it is remarkable that Poland in the eighteenth century was the only country in all of

Figure 1. *La menuet de la Cour*, 1775, attributed to Le Couteur.

Western and Central Europe that did not use the minuet as an emblem of its ruling class or as a template for genteel behavior. The polonaise served these functions; it also represented the nation of Poland, its people, customs, and history.

As can be seen in Figure 2 by Jean Pierre Norblin, not only did the Poles spurn the minuet from their ballroom dance floors, they also rejected the prevailing French taste in fashion, preferring their own national garments and coiffures, which had a distinctly Eastern flair.[4] In the Norblin painting the nobleman wears a buttoned-up *żupan*, with a collar and long, tight-fitting sleeves, over which a *kontusz*, a long robe, is worn with a silk sash tied around the waist. A characteristic feature of the *kontusz* are sleeves cut open from the armpit to elbow, hanging loosely or thrown over the shoulder. From a strap fastened to the sash hangs a saber. The noblewoman wears a pink European-cut gown with a *kontusz* over it and a cap with feathers.

The Polish gentry's embrace of Eastern culture is rooted in the ideology of Sarmatism. Based on legend and historical misreading, Polish nobles during the seventeenth and eighteenth centuries adopted the belief, based on legend and historical misreading, that they were descendants of an ancient race of mounted hunter-warriors, the Sarmatians, who

Figure 2. Dancing a polonaise, painting by Jean Pierre Norblin (ca. 1790).

originated in Asia, north of the Black Sea. "Polish nobles," according to Halina Goldberg, "in their attempt to define themselves in contrast to the Western European milieu, cultivated this exotic image in manner and in costume."[5] Among the core values of Sarmatism were military prowess, liberty, piety, respect for antiquity, gallantry and chivalry (with its references to the Middle Ages).[6] To Western sensibilities, "Sarmatian" culture was an odd mixture of warrior masculinity combined with exuberant displays of hospitality and reverence toward other nobles. Reviled by progressive Poles during the Enlightenment as a form of obscurantism, Sarmatism was revived by nineteenth-century Polish Romantics, most notably in Adam Mickiewicz's epic poem *Pan Tadeusz* (1834). In the excerpt from this work found in the introduction to this volume, Mickiewicz apotheosizes the polonaise as the Sarmatian dance par excellence (and indeed, Chopin's understanding of the dance changed profoundly thereafter).

In the face of such exotic otherness, the polonaise and the minuet have much in common beyond their noble associations. Both employ a metrical organization of three beats per measure ($\frac{3}{4}$), both employ a single repeating dance step throughout (with variation), both are moderate in tempo (the minuet slightly faster), both served as the ceremonial opening dance of the ball, and both defined the social order of the participants with the highest-ranking leading the others.

Well aware of their shared noble associations, Polish dance commentators often began their discussion of the polonaise by comparing it to the minuet. Their endgame was to show how native Polish elements made the polonaise far superior, in their view, to the more theatrical and artificial minuet. In an article on Polish dance types, poet Kazimierz Brodziński (1791–1835) writes:

> As far as Polish dance, the polonaise can be called a serious knightly dance; the French minuet is a dance of an elegant court and educated society. It does not express any emotions; sincere gaiety is as far from it as simple naïveté. It is a reflection of higher taste of Parisian society under Louis XIV. It is formal and contractual; every movement is carefully calculated. . . . The polonaise is equal to the minuet as a noble dance, but has more freedom and less theater. . . . It is a dance of monarchs, of heroes, and even of old men; it is the only dance that fits a knight's dress. It does not express any sentiment of passion, but seems to be a triumphant procession, and the expression of serene noble sentiments.[7]

Later in the article Brodziński observes that the minuet acquired an effeminate nature due to its overly civilized refinement. In contrast, he notes that the freer and less-refined polonaise is, above all else, a showcase of the Polish nobleman.

I offer a study of the polonaise from several vantage points. First, I develop this historical introduction further and discuss the polonaise's choreography. In the second section, I return to the minuet as a point of reference and identify key musical characteristics of the Polish ballroom polonaise during the second half of the eighteenth century. In the third section I explore several of the polonaise's expressive and cultural associations in currency during the last quarter of the eighteenth century and beyond: national identity, otherness, and the Polish nobleman. During the 1790s new styles of polonaise music emerged apart from the standard ballroom style: melancholy polonaises, heroic polonaises, brilliant polonaises, and polonaise adaptations of popular stage music. In the fourth section I explore musical features of two of these: the melancholy polonaise and the heroic polonaise. In the final section, this historical and stylistic background is brought to bear on an expressive reading of Chopin's two Op. 40 polonaises.

Historical Overview and Choreography

Polish written accounts of a walking dance begin to appear in the sixteenth century.[8] As an act of communal celebration polonaises were common fare at peasant weddings and other village festivals. The dance was known under a variety of names: *chodzony* (pacer), *chmielowy* (hoppy), *wolny* (slow), *powolny* (leisurely), *taniec wielki* (great dance), *pieszy* (walker), and *taniec polski* (Polish dance). Upon entering the Polish court in the late seventeenth century, *taniec polski* and *taniec wielki* were the preferred names. In the eighteenth century Western European sources adopted the French term polonaise, which was then adopted by Polish composers in the eighteenth and nineteenth centuries (or its Polish translation, *polonez*).

In its early history the polonaise was often accompanied with singing, but as it developed into a court dance it became chiefly instrumental. By the mid-seventeenth century it entered the highest Polish courts and served as the opening and closing dance at all royal functions. Warsaw's two leading newspapers in the eighteenth century, *Gazeta Polska* and *Kuryer Polski*, routinely covered royal balls and made special note of who led the opening polonaise. The 4 August 1735 issue of the *Gazeta Polska* reports that on the previous day, during the name-day celebration of King Augustus III, "The ball began with the King and Queen in the *taniec polski*; the dance was accompanied by the orchestra, trumpets, winds, and cannon salvos." The 13 June 1747 issue of the *Kuryer Polski* reports that King Augustus III, perhaps in a ploy of terpsichorean diplomacy, required guest dignitaries from foreign countries to participate in the dance:

> The *taniec polski staroświecki* [ancient Polish dance] began with the sound of trumpets. His Majesty the King danced first with his newly betrothed, and they were preceded by pairs of the Polish gentlemen and ministers, each with a torch, and in front of them four Saxon marshals with scepters. After his Majesty the King danced, then her Majesty the Queen continued and *per consequens* the entire family with her Highness the Prince, as well as the French and Bavarian envoys.

The popularity of the polonaise in Poland continued beyond the eighteenth century, finding its way from the dance floor to the parlor keyboard. In the opening years of the nineteenth century it accounted for 96 percent of the published dance works for piano.[9] As for the dance floor, as late as 1829 the *Kuryer Warszawski* reports that "at every ball the polonaise is danced first, followed by the mazur, cotillion, waltz, and gallop. To be fashionable it is necessary to have one's handkerchiefs and gloves embroidered in colored silk or even gold thread."[10]

Choreography

The choreography of the polonaise is as follows: couples, arranged in order of their social rank, proceed arm-in-arm through and around a designated space (interior and/or exterior). The step most often prescribed by Saxon dancing masters was the *pas de bourrée*, a flexible walking step that can accommodate duple-, triple-, or quadruple-metered dances. As performed in the polonaise, which is in triple meter, dancers begin with a long, sweeping first step, followed by two shorter steps on the balls of the feet with a straighter, higher position of the body.[11] It was left to the pleasure and imagination of the lead male dancer to cut a pathway and introduce along the way various gestures and figures that the other dancers were required to imitate (e.g., circling round each other while holding the partner's hand, forming group circles, passing under the elevated hands of all the couples behind them). The duration of the dance was determined by the lead couple. In recalling balls he attended as a young man, Polish diarist Jan Duklan Ochocki (1766–1848) observes that the opening polonaise "could last up to two hours."[12]

Polish nobility were known for their effusive gestures of reverence, which were largely based on a Sarmatian code of conduct.[13] According to the 1791 travel diary of Johann Joseph Kausch, "men and women express their pleasantness or pleasure in the same way: both bow the entire body forward, with their hands hugging the other person's knees or even lower if they want to show greater reverence. No other civilized country can perform as low a bow as the Poles do."[14] To show adulation of high nobility, not only would noblemen kiss the other person's hand but also the chest, stomach, knees, and feet.

In the polonaise the woman was the object of reverence. Kazimierz Władysław Wójcicki, an acquaintance of Chopin, writes:

> Once the music began, a nobleman of the most distinguished age would approach a respected noblewoman, bow, lay a kiss on her hand, and form the first couple in the center of the room. . . . He would then take off his hat, put it on his right hand, and the lady would lay her hand upon its soft surface. On the next downbeat, he would lower his head as a sign of respect for his partner, throw the sleeves of his *kontusz* over his shoulders, stamp his feet . . . and lead the dance.[15]

Gołębiowski recounts "at times he would kneel down before her as she walked around him, or would even raise a toast to her health by taking off her shoe and placing a chalice in it—and everybody else had to follow his lead, no excuses given or accepted."[16] In an 1814 review of polonaises composed by Michał Ogiński, E. T. A. Hoffmann writes: "The polonaise returns to the expression of chivalry, of which the romantic veneration of women is an integral part, that one can still find in Poland more than anywhere else."[17] In less flattering terms Johann Friederich Reichardt observes that at certain points during the dance the Polish nobleman "momentarily grovels like a servant."[18]

Extravagance was exhibited not only in local gestures, but also in the overall course of the dance. Gołębiowski observes that "sometimes, bored with an ordinary circle, the leader walked his partner and the chain of dancers that followed through other rooms and chambers."[19] Later in the night, after many drinks, Gołębiowski reports that it was not unusual for "someone intentionally and in jest to place an obstacle in the path of the dancers, such as a stool, so the dancers would have to jump over it in the process."[20] Liszt's 1852 book on Chopin, an idealized misreading of the past—brimming with factual errors, gaping holes, and wild stretches of the imagination—nonetheless contains a vivid description of the polonaise that resonates with earlier Polish accounts:

> The host's task was to lead the formation in a thousand capricious meanderings through apartments thronged with guests who were later to join the brilliant procession. Although the dancers liked to be conducted through the most distant galleries, gardens and groves, where only distant echoes of the music reached the ear, they welcomed the return to the ballroom where they were always greeted with redoubled fanfares. . . . Guided by the host on the first circuit, the dancers were led through long detours, where they encountered architectural and decorative surprises in keeping with the pleasures of the day and which the host would display with pride. The more imaginative and unexpected the artifice, the more the younger guests applauded.[21]

Musical Characteristics of the Polish Ballroom Polonaise

In this section I identify musical features of the Polish ballroom polonaise in the second half of the eighteenth century. My observations are based on a study of seventy-one polonaises drawn from the four sources that follow:[22]

1. A musical dice game by Johann Philipp Kirnberger, *Der allezeit fertige Polonoisen- und Menuettencomponist* (The Ever-ready Polonaise and Minuet Composer) (Berlin: G. L. Winter, 1757).

Kirnberger spent ten years in Poland (1741–51) working as a musician in the service of three courts and a Benedictine cloister. Upon returning to Berlin in 1751, he became an important source of information and proponent of Polish music.[23] Six years after his return, Kirnberger published what is thought to be the first musical dice game.

Polish composers seldom wrote minuets, nor were they part of the ballroom dance repertoire. Prussian composers, however, often wrote minuets and polonaises. Kirnberger's project affords an opportunity to study how one composer, performer, and theorist, intimately familiar with both Polish and Austro-German dance practices, defined the musical characteristics of the two leading ceremonial dances of the upper class.

2. Nine polonaises and seven minuets by Carl Philipp Emanuel Bach contained in *Carl Philipp Emanuel Bach: Miscellaneous Keyboard Works*, vols. 1 and 2, ed. Peter Wollny (Los Altos, CA: Packard Humanities Institute, 2005).

Bach's polonaises and minuets provide another source for comparison. He often paired minuets and polonaises together in the same publication.

3. A polonaise attributed to Józef Grabowiecki, reproduced in Johann Friedrich Reichardt, "Nazionaltänze Polnisch," *Musikalisches Kunstmagazin* 2 (1782): 95–98.

In 1782, Johann Friedrich Reichardt published a short article, "Nazionaltänze Polnisch," in the Berlin journal *Musikalisches Kunstmagazin*. Reichardt's intent was to educate his readership on the characteristic features of a "true national" polonaise from Poland. He illustrates his discussion with a polonaise by Józef Grabowiecki, which he claims was a favorite in Polish ballrooms.[24] He also provides an annotated violin part "in order to append the very characteristic bowings that the Polish musicians generally use."

4. Six manuscript collections of instrumental Polish polonaises (ca. 1775–1800), comprising sixty polonaises in all. Published in *Polonezy z XVIII wieku na zespoły instrumentalne* (Polonaises from the 18th Century for Instrumental Ensembles), transcribed and edited by Karol Hławiczka (Warsaw: Polskie Wydawn, 1967).

According to Hławiczka, all the manuscripts are most likely of Polish origin, written during the last quarter of the eighteenth century.[25] Although the collections are composed by different (mostly unknown) composers in different locations, they are remarkably similar in style, which attests to the stability and homogeneity of the polonaise during this time period.

Melody

Examples 1 and 2 provide a minuet and polonaise composed by C. P. E. Bach in 1765. Bach's minuet melody is conjunct in style and reserved and graceful in character as befits the choreography of the dance (see Example 1). The music reflects the ideal physical and mental attitude of self-assured nonchalance—what was often referred to in dance manuals as "complaisance."[26] Complaisance entails an "artful carelessness, as if [dancing] were a natural emotion, without a too curious and painful practicing. . . . To

Example 1. Carl Philipp Emanuel Bach, Minuet, Wq 112/3.

dance too exquisitely is, I must own, too laborious a vanity."[27] For the aristocracy of Western Europe, attitudes, postures, and gestures of constraint were morally based and motivated by the highly valued virtues of modesty, forbearance, self-control, and a disdain for revealing one's inner feelings. When mastered, the attitude of complaisance created an aura of genteel refinement and unflappable inner calm. In the physical realm complaisance is characterized by suave and relaxed body motions, the look of floating weightlessness, and controlled vitality. Dancing masters sharply criticized any signs of exuberance, excess of body motions, and gestures of strength. The tranquil center of all movement was the torso, which was at all times to remain relatively still and upright.

Example 2. Carl Philipp Emanuel Bach, Polonaise, Wq 112/5.

In sharp contrast, polonaise melodies of all four sources offer sweeping melodic gestures, often involving large ranges and athletic leaps of tenths and twelfths, as found in the opening measures of Bach's polonaise (see Example 2). As I discuss later, such expansive musical gestures provide a corollary to the mental and physical attitudes of the Polish nobleman and are in flagrant violation of Western European social codes. Polonaise melodies also inhabit higher metrical levels—eighth-note and sixteenth-note levels, whereas the less active minuet rarely goes beyond the triplet level (with the exception of ornamental turns and trills).

Four- and eight-bar phrases are the norm for European ballroom dances of this time period. David Neumeyer refers to such dances as possessing quadratic syntax.[28] An unusual feature of Kirnberger's, Bach's, and Grabowiecki's polonaises is the presence of six-bar phrases (see, for example, the opening phrase of Bach's polonaise in Example 2). The sixty instrumental polonaises contained in the manuscript collections confirm that non-quadratic phrase lengths are a defining feature of Polish ballroom polonaises. Out of sixty polonaises, 66 percent have at least one six-bar phrase and 30 percent contain phrases of either three, five, or seven bars.[29] As Koch observes, "Because of the indeterminate figures of the dance, it need not consist of any specific number of bars; the two parts of which it is composed [polonaise + trio] may therefore comprise an arbitrary number of measures, as long as the rhythm remains steady."[30]

Dynamics and Articulation

Although Kirnberger does not provide dynamic markings, the other three sources do, and these indications are extraordinary in their abundance, range, and rapid alternation. Bach marks his minuet "*p sempre*," but in contrast, his polonaise includes ten dynamic markings, and the opening three measures of each reprise contain five changes between *forte* and *piano*.[31] In his article Reichardt identifies as typical for Polish polonaises "frequent strong accents" and "frequently alternating *fortes* and *pianos*"—performative gestures requiring sudden physical assertion on the part of the performer.[32] The dynamic markings he provides for Grabowiecki's polonaise are even more extreme than Bach's: 46 dynamic markings for 35 measures of music (see Figure 3).

Reichardt also includes two articulation markings: a stroke (') and a backslash (\). "The backslash marking means a strong pressure with the bow. . . . The preceding short staccato notes marked with a stroke should be played with a down bow, detaché, and the following accented notes down bow again."[33] Reichardt's backslash likely corresponds to *sf* or *sfz*, common markings in Polish manuscripts of this period. The double down bow requires of the violinist a quick retracting motion of the bow arm and the accented second note a physical assertion of the bow against the violin string. When used together this pair of articulation markings is not only the most energetic performative gesture in the piece but also marks, together with the dynamic markings *p-f*, the most characteristic rhythm of the polonaise—the syncopation (see measures 1 and 2), which I discuss below.

Because of the arbitrary nature of the phrase lengths, the phrase organization of Polish ballroom polonaises is rather unpredictable. The

Figure 3. Polonaise attributed to Józef Grabowiecki. Johann Friedrich Reichardt, "Nazionaltänze Polnisch," *Musikalisches Kunstmagazin* 2 (Berlin, 1782): 99.

sudden and, on occasion, extreme shifts in dynamic level heightens the sense of unexpectedness.[34] These dynamic changes are often coordinated with non-quadratic phrase organization, and also, as in the Grabowiecki polonaise, occur within phrases and within measures. Sudden dynamic changes are also found in the minuets and contredanses of Haydn, Mozart, and other Viennese composers, but they are not as prevalent and, when they do occur, serve to underscore a quadratic phrase organization.

Syncopations occur when a duration initiated on a weak beat is held over into a strong beat, as is found in the opening two measures of Figure 3. Twenty-three out of 154 measures (15 percent) of Kirnberger's polonaise music contain syncopations, but only one out of 96 measures of his minuet music does. Syncopations are the signal rhythmic marker of polonaises during this period.[35] What is commonly thought of as the *sine qua non* of polonaises—the accompanimental pattern (♪♫ ♫♫)—is entirely absent from this repertoire (I refer to this rhythm as the "standard polonaise accompaniment"). Although this rhythmic pattern is occasionally found in melodies, it is not used as a standard feature of Polish polonaise accompaniments until the opening decade of the nineteenth century. Indeed, several eighteenth-century German sources claim that this rhythm is a feature of German polonaises, not Polish. According to Marpurg:

> The original polonaise in the good taste that prevails in current-day Poland does not accept the rhythm of the eighth-note with two appended sixteenth notes. . . . This rhythm belongs to the German polonaise. The original prefers syncopations between the first and second—or the second and third—quarter.[36]

Form

All sixty polonaises contained in the Polish manuscript collections are paired with second polonaises, titled trios. All but four end with the trio rather than returning to the first polonaise. Possibly under the influence of the German minuet, polonaises composed after 1800 include a *da capo* return of the polonaise after the completion of the trio. Typically, the two individual dances are organized in a three-part *da capo* layout. A little over half of the polonaises begin with a two-, four-, or—most commonly— six-bar introduction, often in unison texture with martial rhythms and fanfare flourishes. Assertive in character—a call to arms of sorts—this segment typically ends on a dominant half cadence, which prepares the entrance of the main theme. The keys range from E-flat major (three flats) to A major (three sharps). Major mode prevails; only four polonaises are set in minor keys.

The national hallmark of polonaise genre is its cadence. In her book *Metrical Manipulations in Haydn and Mozart*, Danuta Mirka observes that

Example 3. Cadence from C. P. E. Bach's minuets, Wq 114/4.

Example 4. Polonaise cadence from MS 628, no. 2.
Published in *Polonezy z XVIII wieku na zespoły instrumentalne*, transcribed and
edited by Karol Hławiczka (Warsaw: Polskie Wydawn, 1967), 33.

the placement of the tonic of a V–I cadence on the metrical downbeat
"was considered obligatory throughout the eighteenth century."[37]
Following musical convention, Kirnberger's and Bach's minuet cadences
are well behaved—their tonics all fall on downbeats. Example 3 provides
an example drawn from Bach's minuets of a perfect authentic cadence:
the melodic arrival of scale-degree 1 on the downbeat is coordinated
with the harmonic arrival of the tonic in the accompaniment. Polonaise
cadences of all sources consulted in this study, however, follow standard
Polish practice: the melody of the cadential measure begins with four
sixteenth notes on the first beat, leading to scale-degree 7 or 2 on the second
beat (notated as a quarter note or a grace note), which resolves to scale-
degree 1 on the third beat; in performance practice, the grace note
receives a quarter-note duration (see Example 4).[38] In the accompaniment
the tonic harmony arrives on the second or third beat of the measure.

As a violation of the downbeat rule, German commentators cite Polish
cadences as "thoroughly distinctive," "peculiar," "unprepared," and
"very odd."[39] Reichardt attempts to describe the cadence's odd qualities:
"The closing pitch of the melody arrives on the last and thus the weakest
beat, and is only very faintly heard, since the beat before the last note is

accented, and the last note itself is so quickly cut off that one can scarcely hear it."[40] To put it another way, the duration of the cadential tonic is not commensurate with its tonal significance within the phrase. Just as soon as it arrives, the next phrase begins, leaving no opportunity to mentally linger on the tonal goal of the phrase. Thus another aspect of the music contributes to a sense of abruptness.

Tempo

All sources agree that the tempo of the polonaise is slower than the minuet, but just how much slower is open to debate. Christian Gottlieb Hänsel, the earliest source consulted, recommends a tempo twice as slow as the minuet.[41] Based on his experience in Poland, Kirnberger is the most trusted of the non-Polish sources: the polonaise is "faster than the sarabande, but one-third slower than the minuet, so that eight measures of a polonaise equals twelve of a minuet."[42] Marpurg, who may have obtained his information from Kirnberger, provides the most detailed description:

> In forty-eight seconds, or in a minute minus twelve seconds, a Polish dance with sixteen bars will have completely ended. There are therefore two quarters per second, or two bars in three seconds. A polonaise of twenty bars, properly repeated, is completely carried out in a minute. Seldom will a Pole ask for a slower tempo, otherwise he must have been compelled to do so by old age.[43]

Vieth in 1792 said the Polish polonaise is "somewhat slower than the minuet, but quicker than the German polonaise."[44] Koch, at the beginning of the eighteenth century, places the tempo of the polonaise between andante and allegro.[45]

Some Cultural Associations of the Polonaise

Across Europe writers uniformly identified the polonaise as the national dance of Poland and as a rendering of Poland itself—its people, character, and customs. "Perhaps no other dance is as much a picture and expression of national character as the Polonaise," observes Reichardt.[46] Polish commentators were even more explicit in relating how the polonaise reflected Polish society. Brodziński, in a stretch of imagination, drew comparisons of the choreography to Poland's Sejm (national parliament) and *liberum veto*. For example, he mentions that any nobleman "can, according to his liking, pride, or jealousy, declare *odbijany* [change of partners], and the leader and all the others are required to obey his request. This privilege is . . . similar to the unfortunate *nie pozwalam* [*liberum veto*]."[47]

After Poland lost its sovereignty in the final partition of 1795, a theme emerges in both German and Polish sources: the polonaise as the historical consciousness of Poland, representing both the glories of the past and the sorrows and struggles of the present. Commentators, both Polish and non-Polish alike, routinely narrativized the polonaise dance as evoking memories and emotions associated with those memories. Hoffmann muses that "one clearly observes that inner romantic mood which resonates even now as from the purple glow of a golden, long-past age."[48] Princess Hélène de Ligne in 1815 observes that "when the elderly people wish to join in the dance they ask for a polonaise . . . and then the good people perform the figures and move around with a contented smile on their faces as they recollect the good old times, and the way they used to smile."[49] During the opening decades of the nineteenth century, Wójcicki reports, "one could only find the traditional polonaise danced in the homes of established families, where men wore the *kontusz* and *żupan* and where the ancient tradition was allowed to warm itself merrily by the heat of the fireplace."[50] As I discuss below, the act of memory and the sentiments of nostalgia, melancholy, and frustration brought about by the loss of Poland's sovereignty found full realization in Ogiński's "melancholy" polonaises, which were conceived for listening sans dancing.[51]

Otherness

"The German polonaise is as different from the true polonaise as the gravedigger is from the priest, although both are dressed in black," writes Johann Kirnberger.[52] Kirnberger ought to have known, given the time he spent working in Poland. Such was the polonaise's Sarmatic exoticism that it was widely believed that only Poles could compose or perform the dance correctly. "If you don't have Polish blood be careful—even when you master the steps you should not consider yourself a good Polish dancer," warns C. J. von Feldtenstein.[53] In more drastic terms, Hoffmann writes: "German composers who are not in the least adequately nationalized in Poland in order to become fully acquainted with the private spirit of Poland's main dance will definitely not succeed in composing a Polonaise. . . . Such efforts will result in a half-breed [*Zwittergeschlecht*]."[54]

In a remarkable 1803 article published in a Berlin journal, Józef Elsner, Chopin's composition teacher, calls into question the very definition of the polonaise and its generic boundaries:

> It cannot escape the notice of the thoughtful composer—particularly one who has spent a long time in Poland—that the polonaise, which itself is regarded only as a piece for dancing, does not belong to any particular genre of music, in consideration of the many possible variations of the melody as well as the harmony. That it can be just as happily applied to concertos, symphonies, or even opera numbers is demonstrated by the many examples in this essay, and by the enthusiasm with which it is received, though the authentic Polish style seldom prevails. This [style] can be very difficult to realize, even for a composer who comes from Poland and is well acquainted with the actual character of the polonaise. Since the style is something that lends itself better to discovery than description, and performance is the soul of music, the statement appears to be justified that only in Poland can one be fortunate to be inspired to create this genre of music; ... what is most important to address about the Polish dances is a sentiment very much bordering on melancholy, and that what is happy must be associated with effusive sentimentality—or rather, the mood must certainly be changeable in order to establish a musical poetry that might win the overall approval of the Poles.[55]

For Elsner, the essence of a polonaise cannot be rendered into musical notation; rather, it is a specifically Polish performance practice, one that can be applied to any genre. Furthermore, it is not enough to be a Pole to compose a polonaise. The Polish musician must also be able to render the stirrings of his Polish soul through musical motion. Elsner invites us to ponder how we can discern a true Polish polonaise if Poles in his time could not.

Although the historical veil can never be lifted, one cultural association in particular may have influenced polonaise performance practice and composition to a degree greater than others: the Sarmatic gestures of the Polish nobleman. As we have seen, the Polish ballroom polonaise showcases the Polish nobleman—his peculiar mannerisms, his proud and noble attitude, and his veneration of women. Elsner does not assign gender to his description, but within the context of his time it is likely that his descriptors of "effusive sentimentality" and changeable moods can be read as markers of Polish masculinity.

The Polish Nobleman

The polonaise was the only ballroom dance of the upper classes to show-case the nobleman. With the minuet, the couple is the center of attention. Traversing intricate movements in opposition to each other while everyone else watches, the male and female receive equal attention as they attempt to display "everything beautiful and charming in nature which a body is capable of employing."[56] The contredanse, the most popular dance of the second half of the eighteenth century, was a group dance for couples—three, four, or "as many will."[57] It provided an opportunity for shared pleasure in a community of dancers where all were equal in status to the other. As Nicolas Framéry observed in 1791, "They dance to breathe out a feeling of joy which grows constantly in proportion to the number of danc-ers, and thus has no need for spectators."[58] For the waltz the (male) gaze is fixed upon the woman—her beauty, her sexual vulnerability—so much so that in many literary accounts, both fictive and nonfictive, the presence of the male partner is either marginalized or completely expunged.[59]

In 1756 dancing master Charles Pauli characterized the polonaise as "serious, grave, and masculine. It is danced by a large company at the same time, in couples, with the men leading their ladies."[60] In recounting its history, Brodziński asserts that the polonaise was originally danced by men alone,[61] a claim repeated by Karol Czerniawski in his influential 1847 dance treatise.[62] Gołębiowski provides a description of various mas-culine mannerisms found at the opening of the dance:

> The polonaise . . . cultivates the man's seriousness and kind-ness, as befits a knight. . . . At the beginning of the dance he places his hat under his arm or on his hand, which is extended to the woman for her to lay her hand upon. When she does he kisses her hand, twists his mustache, and then rests his hand on his saber's hilt, showing off his manhood, pride, and ele-gance, and giving the woman the respect due to her.[63]

As for the woman, Brodziński notes:

> It is not the place for the lady to display grand coquetry or dazzling gestures of her figure, but for her to express only

modest dignity. And with her wonderful gown proper for this dance, with her height and beautiful figure, and with her long, easy strides while leading the silent procession she represents the ideal of some higher being.[64]

Liszt, in his book on Chopin, provides a summary account of the mannerisms of the Polish nobleman. The description testifies to the currency of the Sarmatic topoi in Liszt's time, although from a romanticized and nostalgic perspective:

> With the Poles of former times the blend of masculine resolve with devotion to the women they loved could become strangely compulsive, noble to the point of pomposity. . . . Most unusually, the polonaise was intended to draw attention to men, to emphasize their looks, courtly manner, and military bearing.[65]

As for the man's garments and physical gestures, Liszt notes:

> Those who have never worn the *kontusz* . . . would find it difficult to imagine the mannerisms, slow bows, sudden straightening, and subtleties of silent pantomime which the Poles of times past displayed as they paraded military-fashion in the polonaise. As they did so, the men fingered their long mustaches or their sword-hilts, both integral parts of the costume and objects of vanity.[66]

Whereas gestures of minuet dancers involve small graceful movements of the head, arms, and hands while the torso remains relatively still, in the polonaise the Polish nobleman utilizes the full range of his gestural space—both small stylized motions of the hands as well as large sweeping gestures involving the entire body. The boxed summary provides a list of the physical gestures, attitudes, and associations of the polonaise as described by writers from Charles Pauli, in 1756, to Franz Liszt, in 1852. Another boxed summary—of the musical characteristics of the Polish ballroom polonaise (ca. 1775–1800)—is provided on the next page.

Having looked at the dance and the music separately, we are now in a position to consider dance/music relations. Music, musical performance, and dance share a conceptual basis: they may be conceived as dynamic processes (either literally or metaphorically) involving motion, velocity,

---

Summary of the Ballroom Polonaise as Danced

Physical gestures of the Polish nobleman
- extravagant gestures of reverence involving large body motions
- smaller gestures involving the mustache, hat, and sword
- foot stomping
- sudden changes in movement

Attitude of the Polish nobleman
- noble and chivalrous
- proud
- pompous
- sentimental
- mood changes

Cultural associations of the ballroom polonaise
- Poland: history, character, customs
- Otherness
- Polish nobleman

---

weight, height, depth, and gravity. To the degree that dance composers are able to render the physical gestures of the dance into correlated musical gestures, music is able to provide a "sonic analogue" of the dance, thereby evoking associations of movement, but also of character, attitude, and cultural context.[67] The dynamic musical processes found in polonaises—abrupt changes in dynamics, texture, and phrase lengths; sweeping melodic gestures involving large ranges and leaps; active and aggressive dynamics and articulation markings—correlate to the pompous attitude and extravagant physical gestures of the Polish nobleman, such as deep bows with outstretched arms, stomping of the feet, and sudden changes of movement and attitude. And as I have noted, performers who provided music for the dancers also execute similar patterns of physical exertion.

A small detail worth mentioning: polonaise melodies, without exception, begin on the downbeat. Such unprepared openings suggest an air of confidence. In operatic melodies, strong-willed (typically male) characters typically begin squarely on the beat. Characters of weaker constitution (typically female) often begin their melodies with an anacrusis. In Mozart's *Don Giovanni* the title character opens the majority of his melodies on the downbeat. In moments of uncertainty, the characters Zerlina and Donna Elvira enter with anacruses. (Consider the seduction aria "Là ci

---

Musical Characteristics of the Polonaise

Melody, rhythm, dynamics, articulation
- sweeping melodic gestures involving a wide range
- wide leaps
- syncopations
- aggressive articulation markings
- sudden and, at times, extreme changes in dynamics

Tempo
- moderate tempo, somewhat slower than the minuet

Form
- fanfare introduction
- non-quadratic phrase lengths
- weak beat cadences
- polonaise/trio

---

darem la mano." Confident in his powers of persuasion, Don Giovanni begins on the downbeat without introduction; unsure how to react, Zerlina opens her reply with an eight-note anacrusis.) Returning to the realm of dance, a characteristic feature of waltzes—the dance type most closely associated with femininity—is a one-bar anacrusis. Such themes are characterized by cantabile melodies (often supported by another voice in parallel thirds or sixths), soft dynamics, and a *dolce* or *delicatissimo* expression marking; in other words, the melodies are strongly feminine. Thus the lack of anacruses in polonaise melodies, together with other gender markers, supports a masculine reading.

Though the music may be heard as providing a sonic analogue of the Polish nobleman, there is no evidence to suggest that dancers attempted to coordinate their movements to the music beyond keeping time to the beat. The result is two media in counterpoint simultaneously communicating the same topic—the Polish nobleman. One can only imagine the expressive effect that occasional points of synchronicity between the two media had on its participants and observers.

Heroic and Melancholy Polonaises

Power shifts in the political arenas of Poland, Russia, Prussia, and Austria during the latter part of the eighteenth century resulted in the emergence of two distinct types of polonaises: the Russian heroic polonaises of Józef Kozłowski (1757–1831) and the Polish melancholy polonaises of Prince Michał Kleofas Ogiński (1765–1833). These two types existed side by side with other polonaise types: ballroom polonaises, keyboard polonaises for dilettantes, Polish patriotic polonaises, brilliant polonaises, polonaises within operas, and polonaise adaptations of popular stage music.

Warsaw-born Kozłowski began his music career in 1775 as a teacher at the court of Prince Andrzej Ignacy Ogiński, where he taught Andrzej's two children, Prince Michał Kleofas and Princess Józefa.[68] In the early 1780s Kozłowski moved to St. Petersburg and became music master in the service of Prince Grigory Potemkin, commander of the Russian army. On 28 April 1791, Potemkin organized and hosted a gala to celebrate the defeat of the Turks at the fortress of Izmail, a decisive victory that brought a quick end to the Russian-Turkish war. Kozłowski, who was responsible for the musical entertainment, composed four choral polonaises for the evening ball. The opening polonaise, "Grom Pobedï razdavaisya!" ("Thunder of Victory, Resound!"), which announced the ceremonial arrival of Empress Catherine II, was an instant success and shortly thereafter assumed the position as Russia's first national anthem.[69]

Example 5 shows the opening section of Kozłowski's polonaise. It preserves some musical features of the Polish ballroom polonaise—major mode, martial rhythms, weak-beat cadences (not shown in the excerpt), and an expression of majestic grandeur. Noticeably absent are syncopated rhythms as well as sudden changes in dynamics, articulation, phrase lengths, and expression. Nor are there sweeping melodic gestures involving expansive ranges and large leaps. Instead consistency and continuity of musical materials prevail. A repeated two-bar melodic segment, which invites vocal participation, calls forth the rhythms of the march. Also woven into the fabric is the rhythmic pattern ♩ ♫ ♩ ♬ and variations thereof. As mentioned previously, this accompaniment pattern did not become a standard feature of Polish polonaises until the opening decade of the nineteenth century. Thus what is commonly thought of as quintessential Polish rhythm probably originates from non-Polish sources.[70] Contributing to the musical consistency is predictable phrase organization and a harmonic rhythm based on repeated patterns of duration. Finally, the passage leads to a metrically stable half cadence (the work concludes with a standard metrically weak cadence).

Kozłowski's music centers not on the individual mannerisms of a nobleman as found in the Polish ballroom polonaise, but represents the unification and rejoicing of an entire nation in a moment of celebration.

Example 5. Opening of "Grom Pobedï razdavaisya!" by Józef Kozłowski, text by Gavrila Derzhavin (1791). Translation: "Triumph's thunder louder, higher! / Russian pride is running high! / Russia's glory sparkles brighter!"

This is bombastic military music—a musical victory lap in ¾ time—that evokes a mythic sense of time and space appropriate to the occasion. The music and its social function preserve three associations of the Polish ballroom polonaise: high ceremony, military bearing, and the veneration of women—namely, Empress Catherine II.[71] It expunges two: Polish national identity and with it the Polish nobleman.

The Russian heroic polonaise in the style of Kozłowski's "Grom Pobedï razdavaisya!" did not take root in Polish soil. The Poles had little to celebrate, certainly nothing on the scale of the Russian victory over the Turks. In the partitions of 1793 and 1795 Russia, Prussia, and Austria erased Poland from the political map of Europe and divided the land among themselves. Russia claimed the largest portion of land and population. As Richard Taruskin notes:

> The victory that thundered through Kozłowski's martial strains now included victory over Poland, and the old Polish aristocratic dance now symbolized Russia's ascendancy. This "Occidentalist" irony helped spawn a host of imitations that made Kozłowski's polonaise the prototype of an indigenous Russian genre, and tied the parade-ceremonial polonaise "irrevocably to the theme of [Russian] patriotism."[72]

Although a gifted musician, Kozłowski's student Prince Michał Kleofas Ogiński was groomed, following in his father's footsteps, as a diplomat. As a young man he served as an envoy in Holland and England, and as a member of the Sejm. When the Polish uprising against Russian occupation began in spring of 1794, Ogiński fought under the command of General Tadeusz Kościuszko (a distinguished veteran of the American Revolutionary War), leading his own regiment. Although Poland claimed a few early victories, it stood little chance against a numerically superior Russian army. Five months after Poland expelled Russian forces from Warsaw, Russia returned and retook the city in the Battle of Praga. In the aftermath Russian troops pillaged Warsaw and massacred an estimated 20,000 Warsaw residents.[73] Composer Karol Kurpiński wrote in 1820:

> Soon after our country lost its sovereignty, Ogiński began writing melancholic polonaises. In a short time the power of his expressive melody saw a proliferation of many imitators. So many in fact that up to this day almost no one writes

happy polonaises fit for dancing; nearly all are sad, or concert ones intended for listening only.[74]

During the period 1795–1820 composers of polonaises, such as Ogiński, Elsner, Stefani, and Kurpiński, retooled their polonaises with plaintive lyrical melodies that leaned heavily toward the minor mode. In a letter to a friend written in 1828, Ogiński recollects his state of mind when he composed his polonaises in the 1790s:

> With the tragic end of our insurrection, which resulted in the annihilation of my Fatherland, all of my concepts were paralyzed. Forced to leave my homeland, brought to poverty, deep in darkest thoughts and often succumbing to misery, I did not have time nor desire to play music. If, during my travels after leaving the country, I accidentally stumbled upon a piano, I sat down and mindlessly extracted sounds that were sad, agonizing, and sometimes violent, as if inspired by a delirium. After a few hours of my fingers wandering on a keyboard (usually of a low quality) I noticed in surprise that I was improvising themes, fantasies, and melodies that were deeply melancholic, which would bring tears to the eyes of the least sensitive beings.[75]

According to Brodziński, Ogiński's polonaises did indeed bring listeners to tears. Brodziński's writes about a party he attended as a young man (ca. 1810s):

> During an evening party the young people (half of them German) danced waltzes and fashionable foreign polonaises. In disgust, the gray-headed men in *kontusz* left the room, one of them—with a violin in hand—wanted to remind them of the old polonaises. They invited me to join their company and we went down into a lower room. A glass of wine, poured straight from the barrel, was passed around while we listened to polonaises by Ogiński, which exuded national expression and plaintive sadness. The sight of these old men, tapping their feet to the rhythm, vigorously moving their hands in enthusiasm, shedding maudlin tears . . . and in a place dimly lit by a lamp was a scene truly worth painting and which was even more touching with wine—the

only solace the old men had among the memories of past traditions and lost youth.[76]

Ogiński's Polonaise in F Minor is provided in Example 6. Although Ogiński studied violin under Giovanni Maria Giornovicchi and Giovanni Battista Viotti, his polonaises are conceived for the pianoforte.[77] Furthermore, they are intended to be performed in the intimacy of the salon (or basement) as listening music sans dancing. Abrupt changes in textures and mood, as we have seen, are features of Polish ballroom polonaises. Untethering the polonaise from the ballroom allowed Ogiński to explore an even wider range of musical contrasts—registrally high and delicate passages, passages without a steady underlying beat, cadenzas, fermatas—all without needing to pay heed to the feet of the dancers. As Hoffmann notes, the volley of contrasting emotions are sometimes extreme in their range of expression: Ogiński's music "creates that certain grandeur exactly like that of chivalry itself; but within it play—in all sorts of dark and bright colors—hot, passionate longing; hopeless sorrow; the rapture, the exultations of love."[78] As suggested earlier, such expressive variability in the minor mode encourages narrative responses from listeners; thus several of Ogiński's polonaises received descriptive titles: "The Partition of Poland," "Les Adieux," and "Polonaise funèbre." As Elsner notes, "The mood must certainly be changeable in order to establish a musical poetry that might win the overall approval of the Poles."[79]

Just as the Polish ballroom polonaise of the 1770s and early 1790s represented Poland at that time, the melancholy polonaise reflected Poland after 1795, under vastly different political circumstances. The leading narrative found in contemporary literature of the 1790s and opening decades of the nineteenth century centers on Poland's loss of nationhood and memories of its former glories. According to Halina Goldberg, the "purpose [of Ogiński's music] is not to accompany dance, but to invoke the past through listening."[80]

After the Napoleonic Wars, the Congress of Vienna (1814–15) established the "Polish Kingdom," a small semi-autonomous state under Russian rule with its own liberal constitution, currency, and Polish administration. In practice, however, Emperor Alexander I and especially his successor Nicholas I disregarded any restriction of their power, leaving the Kingdom of Poland little more than a puppet state of the Russian Empire. Nonetheless, Warsaw regained a sense of political optimism bootstrapped by a cultural renaissance and economic boom.[81] Karol Kurpiński, who played a vital part in Warsaw's musical life during this time, expresses

Example 6. Michał Ogiński, Polonaise in F Minor.

his hope in restoring the polonaise to its former glory: "But now—with the rebirth of our Kingdom—the style of this dance, which is beloved in Europe, will again be characterized by its serious procession and *staropolską* [ancient Polish] noble pride."[82]

In another case of "Occidentalist" irony, Kurpiński dedicated thirteen out of twenty-one of his polonaises published in Warsaw from 1820 to 1831 to Emperor Alexander I and his successor Nicholas I. His most well known, "Witaj Królu" (Welcome King), was written in 1825 for the Warsaw coronation ceremony of Russian Emperor Nicholas I as King of Poland (see Example 7). Five years later the armies of Nicholas I crushed the Poles after the November Uprising of 1830.[83] Appropriately for the occasion, Kurpiński's polonaise follows the model of the Russian heroic polonaise established by Kozłowski. The music is celebratory and majestic throughout—multimedia designed for the ceremonial entrance of Nicholas I. The only substantial change in expression and musical materials occurs between the polonaise and the trio. After a *fortissimo* arrival at the end of the polonaise the trio accompaniment begins quietly with a two-bar introduction stating the standard polonaise accompaniment pattern. All other changes—dynamics, texture, motivic material—support a largely quadratic phrase organization. And to a degree greater than Kozłowski, Kurpiński's melodic gestures avoid large leaps.

Chopin's Polonaises Op. 40, Nos. 1 and 2 (1838–39)

"Since the conquest of Warsaw, whenever I dance a polonaise I half expect a Cossack to come bursting in and put an end to it—alas, the poor Poles!"[84] It seemed everyone had a personal reaction to the plight of the Poles, and as a symbol of the Polish nation, its people, culture, and customs the polonaise served as a conduit for the expression of the Polish story. This narrative impulse is found both in listeners' predisposition to narratize the music and dance, and in composers' attempts to render the Polish story into music. Thus it is not surprising that Chopin, in polonaises composed after he left Warsaw, increasingly draws on elements of the fantasy, culminating with his final essay, the *Polonaise-Fantaisie*, Op. 61 (1846).[85] The polonaise as a narrative vehicle was also appropriated as a topic in art (for example, see Kwiatkowski's painting *Chopin's Polonaise—Ball in Hôtel Lambert in Paris*, reproduced in this volume) and in literature. By far the most important poetic rendering of the polonaise is found in the final book of Mickiewicz's epic poem *Pan Tadeusz*, which was published in Paris in 1834, about four years before Chopin composed the two polonaises of Opus 40. As Goldberg and Bellman have argued, *Pan Tadeusz* had a profound impact on the Polish emigre community living in Paris and the character Jankiel, a prophet-bard, provided a hermeneutical context for the interpretation of Chopin as a performer and composer.[86]

In this final section I interpret Chopin's Polonaises Op. 40, Nos. 1 and 2 within the context of the preceding discussion. The analyses are in no sense complete or definitive. My only intent is to offer a few observations that demonstrate how viewing Chopin's polonaises in light of the social dance practices upon which they are based can open new modes of musical meaning.

Example 7. Karol Kurpiński, "Witaj Królu." Polonaise for
the coronation ceremony of Russian Emperor Nicholas I as King of Poland.
Text by Ludwik Osiński and Franciszek Grzymała.

Example 7 continued. Translation: "Hail, King of the Polish land, /
Father among Your children, / You returned the name [and] laws to us. /
[For this you get] eternal gratitude and glory."

If Chopin's mazurkas were viewed as "guns buried in flowers" aimed at "the mighty autocrat of the north," as Schumann quipped in 1836, the Polonaise in A Major, Op. 40, No. 1 is a loaded canon in full view of the gates of St. Petersburg (see Example 8a).[87] Surely the purest expression of Polish majesty in all of Chopin's works, Op. 40, No. 1 nonetheless falls within the category of the Russian heroic polonaise. Following Kozłowski's "Grom Pobedï razdavaisya!" and Kurpiński's "Witaj Królu," Chopin's music is a model of motivic consistency and rhythmic continuity. The phrase organization is quadratic, largely built out of the varied repetition of an opening fanfare motive. Absent are abrupt changes in phrase lengths, dynamics, and musical expression.

Although Op. 40, No. 1 lacks the sudden dynamic jolts of earlier Polish polonaises, it is in its notation Chopin's loudest work: the music never drops below *f* and reaches the level of *fff* four times. Jean-Jacques Eigeldinger identifies twenty works that contain the dynamic level of *fff* or the marking *il più forte possible,* in all 36 times.[88] Not only does Op. 40, No. 1 have the longest sustained *fff,* but it is only one of two works in which *fff* is used to amplify an entire theme (Nocturne in C-sharp Minor, Op. 27, No. 1 being the other). The remaining 34 appearances of *fff* highlight the climactic arrival of the final cadence of the piece (12 times) or an important sectional cadence (22 times). The massive sound of Op. 40, No. 1 is not only a result of its extreme dynamics but also of a chordal texture based on an underlying five-voice framework.[89]

But Chopin's real achievement is that he infuses the Russian model (which includes Kurpiński's Polish polonaises for Russian monarchs) with key sensibilities of the Polish nobleman—extravagance and exuberance of attitude and body, thereby returning the heroic polonaise to its native soil. Most important, the music's sweeping melodies and swaggering leaps invoke the large bodily gestures peculiar to the Sarmatic nobleman. Although Chopin's melody, like Kozłowski's and Kurpiński's, is built out of two-bar groups and vocal in nature, it ascends beyond the limits of a normal human voice by means of a rising sequence, climaxing two octaves higher on E♯ which, as a temporary leading tone, yearns to reach even higher (see Example 8a). Connecting the two-bar groups together, descending arpeggiations in the bass provide motion and continuity, avoiding what would otherwise be an overly rigid two-bar grouping (the bass arpeggiations also forecast the main motive of the trio).

Example 8a. Chopin, Polonaise, Op. 40, No.1, mm. 1–8.

Placing the music within the context of the ballroom, whether for dance or high ceremony, does not mean to suggest that this is music designed for social function. Rather, the music provides a mythified imaginary space in which the ballroom polonaise and all of its cultural associations provides a narrative context for the listener.[90] And nowhere else is a sense of mythification of nobility more apparent than in the trio (see Example 8b). Chopin follows Kurpiński's model: a melody, more flowing and legato in nature, is supported by the standard polonaise accompaniment. While the homorhythmic texture of the opening polonaise coheres all voices together in a sense of collective agency, the melody and accompaniment texture of the trio is more subjective in nature: the accompaniment supports a single voice, the persona of a single narrative character, which I interpret as the Polish nobleman.

Typically trios employ a reduced texture with melodies that are softer, shorter, less prominent, or by some other means subservient to the

Example 8b. Chopin, Polonaise, Op. 40, No. 1, mm. 25–40.

opening polonaise melody.[91] In Op. 40, No. 1 Chopin reverses this power relationship by several means: the accompaniment maintains the deep register established in the opening polonaise; Chopin underscores the melody with *ff*—the loudest dynamic level in the piece thus far; though the melody is rhythmically more restrained than the opening it is nonetheless assertive in character, descending an octave and a half in giant arpeggiated steps, first over a tonic harmony in mm. 25–26, then in mm. 27–28 over a dominant harmony, and finally the second half of the melody (mm. 29–33) initiates an ascent in contrary motion to the bass that leads to a sustained *fff* return of the melody, towering seven half steps over the highest registral peak of the opening polonaise.

At the head of the melody Chopin affixes the unusual marking *energico*, rather than the more common *dolce* or *con espressivo* markings, as found in many of his other polonaise trios. The performer is asked to foreground patterns of musical exertion that result in a more energetic shaping of the musical material. The first half of the melody correlates to large bodily motions, and the second half contains bursts of energy, especially palpable on the downbeats of measures 29 and 30. Both hands unite in repeated statements of the standard polonaise rhythm. Instead of two sixteenth notes on the second half of the first beat, Chopin notates a sixteenth-note triplet with the last note tied over to the second beat. The perception, however, is not a triplet but slightly rushed third and fourth notes of the polonaise pattern, which provides a sense of urgency and forward propulsion. Overall the trio's melody marks the elongated stride, physical gestures, and attitude not of mortal man but of a mythic Polish nobleman. As the Polish renaissance writer Mikołaj Rej describes, the Polish nobleman "is like an eagle which without any fear looks straight into the sun, or like a commander-in-chief who by his noble posture and proud bearing inspires his soldiers and subordinates to courageous acts."[92]

No. 2

Although the minor mode is an indicator of the melancholy polonaise, I interpret both Op. 40 polonaises as heroic. The A-Major Polonaise presents the quintessential expression of the Polish heroic polonaise: compact in form, forceful in persuasion, and brimming with martial rhythms and extravagant melodic gestures. In the C Minor, Op. 40, No. 2, Chopin introduces tragic elements and distorts basic features of the heroic polonaise to the point of failure (see Examples 9a and 9b).

Example 9a. Chopin, Polonaise, Op. 40, No. 2, mm. 1–18.

Melancholy polonaises tend to be slower in tempo, more reflective and lyrical in nature, and more prone to sudden shifts in phrase lengths, dynamics, and mood.[93] In support of a heroic reading of Op. 40, No. 2, note that Chopin provides the tempo and expression marking *Allegro maestoso*. The term *maestoso*, Italian for majestic, indicates the presence of a high style closely associated with nobility. Although the accompaniment certainly lacks any sense of power and majesty, the melody features martial rhythms, bounding leaps, and an extraordinarily large range of over two octaves, all gestural traits that correlate to the Polish nobleman. Recast the melody in the major mode, transpose it up two octaves, and play it over a standard polonaise accompaniment and you have the power and majestic resonance of the A-Major Polonaise. Following a heroic reading, Zdzisław Jachimecki hears the opening two bars of Chopin's melody as an

Example 9b. Chopin, Polonaise, Op. 40, No. 2, mm. 35–40.

ironic reference to Kurpiński's coronation polonaise "Witaj Królu."[94] In another interpretation the Polish historian Ferdynand Hoesick views the opening theme as a funeral procession for a war hero.[95] To a point I think Hoesick's interpretation has merit. German and Polish sources, beginning with Pauli in 1756, often referred to the polonaise as a type of march.[96]

Several other factors support a funereal reading. The key of C minor has a long association with funeral music.[97] Second, rather than positioning the majestic melody in an elevated place of honor, Chopin submerges it into the depths of the piano and veils it with a softly pulsating accompaniment. Third, Chopin deemphasizes bodily engagement with the term *sotto voce* (very softly, as in a hushed voice). Lastly, he imbues the music with sonic symbols of darkness and death: the tonality lurches into the flat side—from three sharps (A major) to three flats (C minor), a distance of a tritone on the circle of fifths.[98] In addition the Phrygian mode, inflected by flat scale-degree 2, is deeply woven into the tonal fabric.[99]

However, despite being buried in the catacombs of the piano's register, the melody is quite alive, unmatched even by the A-Major Polonaise in the extravagance of its gestures and expansiveness of range. And its presence grows. Organized as a repeated two-phrase period (8+8/8+8), on its repetition Chopin increases the dynamic level from *p* to *f*. As in Op. 40, No. 1, which progresses from *f* to *ff* to *fff*, the technique of gradually ratcheting up dynamics establishes a trajectory and intensification toward some goal. For Op. 40, No. 1, the goal is the second statement of the trio's striding majestic theme at the level of *fff* (see Example 9b). For the C-Minor Polonaise, measure 35 has all the markings of not only an arrival point but also as an expressive reversal from heroic tragedy to heroic victory. Both hands unite in chordal texture thundering out a D-flat major triad at the level of *ff*, which completes the dynamic trajectory *p* to *f* to *ff*. But most important, the music emphatically initiates the opening of the standard polonaise rhythm, a generic marker found in all of Chopin's published polonaises—except this one. The polonaise rhythm is abruptly cut off on the fourth note and left incomplete. Up to this point the accompaniment has provided a nearly constant stream of pulsing eighth notes. The absence of an underlying pulse on the fourth note of measure 35 lays bare its deformity. A feeble response ensues: the dynamic level drops to *p* and a short, syncopated melodic fragment is repeated three times over a dominant harmony. Though the gestural and rhythmic contents of this passage are marked by incompleteness and ambiguity, the harmonic progression is clear: $\flat\mathrm{II}^6$–V^9 twice repeated. Not only does $\flat\mathrm{II}^6$–V^9 inflect the Phrygian mode but it also involves root motion by a tritone, another sonic symbol of death. Indeed, the V^9 contains two tritones, which are prominently voiced in measures 36 and 38.

The gestural incompleteness and rhythmic discontinuity of this passage sever the body from the procession and along with it any hope of restoring to the music its rightful glory. Only brokenness, failure, and death remain. This is nineteenth-century Poland rendered in musical terms: an opening majestic theme speaks *sotto voce* deep at the bottom of the musical texture as from a tomb; although it fails in its attempts to emerge, it continues to live. The polonaise ends with a culminating statement of the theme at the dynamic level of *ff* but still submerged in the bass register. Such a narrative brings to mind Poland as Christ of Europe, a doctrine popularized by the Romantic poet Adam Mickiewicz in his *Books and the Pilgrimage of the Polish Nation* (1832).

> And Poland said, "Whosoever will come to me shall be free and equal for I am FREEDOM." But the Kings, when they heard it, were frightened in their hearts, and they crucified the Polish nation and laid it in its grave, crying out, "We have slain and buried Freedom." But they cried out foolishly . . . For the Polish Nation did not die. Its body lieth in the grave; but its spirit has descended into the abyss, that is, into the private lives of people who suffer slavery in their own

country . . . For on the Third Day, the Soul shall return to the Body; and the Nation shall arise and free all the peoples of Europe from Slavery.[100]

Chopin provides two views of Poland. Opus 40, No. 1 speaks of the power, supremacy, and glory of Poland as exemplified in the mythified gestures of the Polish nobleman. Stripped of nationhood and under the oppressive rule of Russia, the music does not represent the Poland of Chopin's time. Instead, the music may be heard to reflect the Polish dynasty prior to the partitions as well as an imagined Poland of the future. Surrounded by sonic symbols of failure and death, the maestoso theme of Op. 40, No. 2—the spirit of the Polish nation—has "descended into the abyss," awaiting resurrection.

NOTES

1. The epigraph from Feldtenstein's *Erweiterung der Kunst*, which was published in 1772 by Schröder in Braunschweig (Brunswick), is on pages 83–84. I am indebted to Laura Hedden for her assistance with this and other translations from the German. "Universal dance" quotation from Charles Pauli, *Elemens de la danse* (Leipzig: 1756), 64.

2. Philip Dormer Stanhope Chesterfield, *Letters Written by the Late Right Honourable Philip Dormer Stanhope, Earl of Chesterfield*, vol. 2 (London: T. Barrois, 1815), 83.

3. Philip Dormer Stanhope, *The Letters of Philip Dormer Stanhope, Earl of Chesterfield*, vol. 2 (London: Richard Bentley, 1845), 405.

4. Jan Norblin, *Polonaise*, http//:commons.wikimedia.org/wiki/File:Jan_Norblin_Polonais.jpg.

5. Halina Goldberg, "Descriptive Instrumental Music in Nineteenth-Century Poland," *Journal of Musicological Research* 34/3 (Summer 2015): 243.

6. Andrzej Waśko, "Sarmatism or the Enlightenment: The Dilemma of Polish Culture," *Sarmatian Review* 17/2 (1997).

7. Kazimierz Brodziński, "Wyjątek z pisma o tańcach," in *Melitele*, ed. Antoni Edward Odyniec (Warsaw: A. E. Odyniec, 1829), 85–86. For a similar discussion, see Łukasz Gołębiowski, *Gry i zabawy różnych stanów* (1831; Warsaw: Wydawnictwa Artystyczne i Filmowe, 1983), 10–11. I am grateful to Thom Johnson Zawadzki for his assistance with the English translations from Polish.

8. For a comprehensive history of the polonaise, see Karol Hławiczka, "Grundriss einer Geschichte der Polonaise bis zum Anfang des 19. Jahrhundert," *Svensk tidskrift för musikforskning* 1 (1968): 51–124.

9. Wojciech Tomaszewski, *Warszawskie edytorstwo muzyczne w latach 1772–1865* (Warsaw: Biblioteka Narodowa, 1992), 167. Only two minuets were published in Warsaw between the years 1801 and 1850.

10. *Kuryer Warszawski*, 3 March 1829.

11. No Polish dance manuals published in Poland during the eighteenth century or the opening decades of the nineteenth century survive. The first two Polish dance treatises known to exist were published in 1846 and 1847. Jan and Ignacy Staczyński, *Zasady tańców*

salonowych (Warsaw: J. Tomaszewski, 1846); and Karol Czerniawski, *Charakterystyka tańców* (Warsaw: St. Strabski, 1847). For detailed descriptions of the polonaise's choreography I rely on dance treatises published in Saxony. From 1698 to 1763 Poland was under the rule of two Saxon kings (Augustus II and his son Augustus III); as a result Saxony experienced an influx of Polish culture, including its music and dances.

12. Quoted in Jan Bystroń, *Dzieje obyczajów w dawnej Polsce*, vol. 2 (Warsaw: Państwowy Instytut Wydawniczy, 1976), 215–16.

13. See Maria Bogucka, "Gesture, Ritual, and Social Order in Sixteenth- to Eighteenth-Century Poland," in *A Cultural History of Gesture*, ed. Jan Bremmer and Herman Rodenburg (Cambridge: Polity Press, 1991), 190–209.

14. Quoted in Wacław Zawadzki, *Polska stanisławowska w oczach cudzoziemców*, vol. 2 (Warsaw: Państwowy Instytut Wydawniczy, 1963), 294.

15. Kazimierz Władysław Wójcicki, "Społeczność Warszawy w początkach naszego stulecia," in *Biblioteka Warszawska*, vol. 4 (Warsaw: Gebethner i Wolff, 1876), 100–101.

16. Gołębiowski, *Gry i zabawy różnych stanów*, 312.

17. E. T. A. Hoffmann, "Zwölf Polonoisen für das Pianoforte vom Grafen Oginsky," in *Allgemeine musikalische Zeitung* 47 (Leipzig: 1814): 792. Hoffman lived in Warsaw from 1804 to 1807 serving as a Prussian government councillor. He was a friend of Józef Elsner, Chopin's theory and composition teacher. Together they founded the Harmonie-Gesellschaft, a Warsaw music society that organized lectures and concerts. See Halina Goldberg, *Music in Chopin's Warsaw* (New York: Oxford University Press, 2008), 257–59.

18. Johann Friedrich Reichardt, "Nazionaltänze Polnisch," *Musikalisches Kunstmagazin* 2 (Berlin: 1782): 95–98.

19. Gołębiowski, *Gry i zabawy różnych stanów*, 313.

20. Ibid.

21. Franz Liszt, *Liszt's Chopin*, trans. and ed. Meirion Hughes (Manchester, UK: Manchester University Press, 2010), 68–69. This excerpt, along with other descriptions of Polish customs contained in Liszt's book, was likely provided by Carolyne zu Sayn-Wittgenstein, Polish noblewoman and romantic partner of Liszt.

22. Other repertoire I consider includes 349 polonaises from the collection of Anna Maria, Princess of Saxony, daughter of King Augustus III of Poland, *Polonezy ze zbiorów Anny Marii Saskiej*, ed. Karol Hławiczka, in *Źródła do historii muzyki polskiej*, vols. 13, 17, and 21 (Kraków, 1967–1971); and eight polonaises by Józef Elsner published in the Polish journal *Wybór pięknych dzieł muzycznych i pieśni polskich* (A Selection of Fine Musical Works and Polish Songs) (Warsaw, 1803–5).

23. Szymon Paczkowski, "Bach and Poland in the Eighteenth Century," *Understanding Bach* 10 (2015): 132. An example of Kirnberger's influence can be found in Friedrich Wilhelm Marpurg's discussion of the polonaise, "according to the observations of Herr Kirnberger," in *Kritische Briefe*, vol. 2 (Berlin: Friedrich Wilhelm Birnstiel, 1761), 43.

24. Grabowiecki's polonaise also appeared anonymously in a 1773 Polish manuscript. See the critical notes of Karol Hławiczka, *Z polonezów polskich na fortepian* (Kraków: Polskie Wydawnictwo Muzyczne, 1975). A portion of Reichardt's article is reprinted in the Hamburg journal *Magazin der Musik* 1 (1783): 54–55.

25. Hławiczka, *Polonezy z XVIII wieku na zespoły instrumentalne*, xiii.

26. For a discussion of the concept of complaisance in dance, see Shirley Wynne, "Complaisance: An Eighteenth-Century Cool," *Dance Scope* 5/1 (1970): 22–35.

27. John Weaver, *An Essay Towards a History of Dancing* (London: Printed for Jacob Tonson, 1712), 65; quoted in Wynne, "Complaisance," 31.

28. David Neumeyer, "The Contredanse, Classical Finales, and Caplin's Formal Functions," *Music Theory Online* 12/4 (2006). See also Eric McKee, "Social Dances of the

Late Eighteenth Century," in *Oxford Handbook of Topic Theory*, ed. Danuta Mirka (Oxford and New York: Oxford University Press, 2014), 164–93.

29. Both Poźniak and Hławiczka cite six-bar phrases as a characteristic feature of Polish polonaises; Stefan Burhardt and Piotr Poźniak, *Polonezy, kozaki, mazury z przełomu XVIII na XIX w.: Rękopis nr. 164, Bibliotheque municipal w Wersalu* (Kraków, 1973), xvii; Hławiczka, *Polonezy z XVIII wieku*, xxi. Adrian Thomas also notes the irregular phrase organization. See "Beyond the Dance" in *The Cambridge Companion to Chopin*, ed. Jim Samson (Cambridge: Cambridge University Press, 1992), 146.

30. Heinrich Christoph Koch, *Musikalische Lexicon* (Frankfurt: August Hermann der Jüngere, 1802), 690.

31. A change of dynamics—*f* to *p*—is implied by the piano marking on the second beat.

32. Reichardt, "Nazionaltänze Polnisch," 95.

33. Ibid.

34. Several of the polonaises in the five manuscript collections contain dynamic shifts from *ff* to *pp*. Similar extreme contrasts of dynamics are also found in the polonaises of Józef Elsner and other Warsaw composers in the opening decades of the nineteenth century.

35. Hławiczka, "Grundriss einer Geschichte der Polonaise," 104. According to Hławiczka syncopated rhythms fell out of fashion in Polish polonaises composed after 1830.

36. Marpurg, *Kritische Briefe*, 43. See also Koch, *Musikalische Lexicon*, 690; and Johann Georg Sulzer, *Allgemeine Theorie des schönen Künste*, vol. 3 (Leipzig: Weidemann, 1771–74), 716–17.

37. Danuta Mirka, *Metrical Manipulations in Haydn and Mozart* (New York and Oxford: Oxford University Press, 2009), 74.

38. For Polish performance practice of cadential grace notes, see Hławiczka, *Polonezy z XVIII wieku na zespoły instrumentalne*, iv.

39. Heinrich Christoph Koch, *Introductory Essay on Composition* (1787; New Haven: Yale University Press, 1983), 79; Koch, *Musikalische Lexicon*, 690; Reichardt, "Nazionaltänze Polnisch," 95; and Gerhard Ulrich Vieth, *Versuch einer Encyklopädie der Leibesübungen* (Berlin: Carl Ludwig Hartmann, 1794), 442.

40. Reichardt, "Nazionaltänze Polnisch," 95.

41. Christian Gottlieb Hänsel, *Allerneueste Anweisung zur aeusserlichen Moral* (Leipzig: Auf Kosten des Autoris, 1755), 109.

42. Kirnberger, *Die Kunst des reinen Satzes in der Musik*, vol. 1 (Berlin and Königsberg: G. J. Decker und G. L. Hartung, 1774), 202.

43. Marpurg, *Kritische Briefe*, 45. In other words, Marpurg's tempo equals the metronome marking of 120 beats per minute.

44. Vieth, *Versuch einer Encyklopädie der Leibesübungen*, 442.

45. Koch, *Musikalisches Lexicon*, 1158.

46. Reichardt, "Nazionaltänze Polnisch," 95.

47. Brodziński, "Wyjątek z pisma o tańcach," 89–90. The *liberum veto* (Latin for "free veto") allowed any individual member of the parliament to nullify any legislation under consideration by shouting *Sisto activitatem!* (Latin for "I stop the activity!") or *Nie pozwalam!* (Polish for "I do not allow!").

48. Hoffmann, "Zwölf Polonoisen," 793.

49. Princess Hélène de Ligne, *Memoirs of the Princess de Ligne*, vol. 2 (London: R. Bentley & Son, 1887), 112–13.

50. Wójcicki, "Społeczność Warszawy w początkach naszego stulecia," 100.

51. Concerning nostalgia and the mazurkas of Chopin, see Halina Goldberg, "Nationalizing the *Kujawiak* and Constructions of Nostalgia in Chopin's Mazurkas," *Nineteenth-*

Century Music 39/3 (2016): 223–47. In this article Goldberg identifies the polonaises of Ogiński as "musically the earliest representation of nostalgia for lost Poland."

52. Johann Kirnberger, introduction, *Oden mit Melodien* (Danzig: 1773).

53. Feldtenstein, *Erweiterung der Kunst*, 84.

54. Hoffmann, "Zwölf Polonoisen," 793.

55. Józef Elsner, "Inwieweit ist die polnische Sprache zur Musik geeignet?" *Der Freimüthige* 122 (1803): 487. Republished in the Leipzig journal *Allgemeine musikalische Zeitung* 40 (1821): 682–83.

56. Feldtenstein, *Erweiterung der Kunst*, 37.

57. John Playford uses this phrase repeatedly in *The Dancing-Master*, 5th ed. (London: W. Godbid, 1675).

58. Quoted in Wye Jamison Allanbrook, *Rhythmic Gesture in Mozart* (Chicago and London: University of Chicago Press, 1983), 62; Nicolas Framery, *Encyclopédie Méthodique* (Paris: Chez Pankoucke, 1791), under "Contredanse," 316.

59. Concerning the waltz and its feminine associations, see Eric McKee, *The Decorum of the Minuet, Delirium of the Waltz* (Bloomington: Indiana University Press, 2012), 95–106.

60. Charles Pauli, *Elemens de la danse* (Leipzig: Saalbach, 1756), 64.

61. Brodziński, "Wyjątek z pisma o tańcach," 88.

62. Czerniawski, *Charakterystyka tańców*, 42. Czerniawski used Brodziński's 1829 article "Wyjątek z pisma o tańcach" as a starting point, "endeavoring to finish the work which Brodziński began" (see preface to the 1860 edition of *Charakterystyka tańców*). This suggests that, at least for Czerniawski, there were no significant dance publications in the intervening years.

63. Gołębiowski, *Gry i zabawy różnych stanów*, 311–12.

64. Brodziński, "Wyjątek z pisma o tańcach," 91.

65. Liszt, *Liszt's Chopin*, 67–68. Likewise, Michel Paul Guy de Chabanon characterizes the Polish nobleman's attitude as "grave and majestic . . . turning to pomposity," in *De la musique considerée en elle-même et dans ses rapports avec la parole*, 2nd ed. (Paris: Chez Pissot, 1785), 93.

66. Liszt, *Liszt's Chopin*, 68.

67. Lawrence M. Zbikowski, "Dance Topoi, Sonic Analogues, and Musical Grammar: Communicating with Music in the Eighteenth Century," in *Communication in Eighteenth-Century Music*, ed. Danuta Mirka (Cambridge: Cambridge University Press, 2008), 283–309.

68. Nickolai Findeizen, *History of Music in Russia from Antiquity to 1800*, vol. 2 (Bloomington: Indiana University Press, 2008), 211.

69. Kozłowski did not confine himself to heroic polonaises, but composed polonaises in a variety of styles, including ballroom, pastoral, fantasy, and polonaises based on popular operatic tunes.

70. Warsaw composer Karol Kurpiński pondered: "Who knows if [the polonaise] did not sprout from the Spanish *fandango* during the reign of Zygmunt I?" Kurpiński, "O tańcu Polskim czyli tak przezwanym *Polonezie*" (About the Polish Dance also Known as the Polonaise), *Tygodnik Muzyczny* 11 (1820): 11. Although the accompaniment rhythm is a defining feature of the fandango, Kurpiński is clearly wrong. Zygmunt I reigned as King of Poland from 1506 until 1548. The fandango emerged as a popular Spanish dance during the eighteenth century. During the latter half of the century it appeared as an exotic topic in stage works of Gluck, Paisiello, and Mozart. See Jonathan D. Bellman, "Ongherese, Fandango, and Polonaise: National Dance as Classical-Era Topic," *Journal of Musicological Research* 31/2–3 (2012): 70–96. The bolero, which became popular at the end of the eighteenth century, is another Spanish dance that uses this accompaniment rhythm. Hławiczka, following Hugo Riemann, believes "it is quite possible that the emergence of the bolero in

the 1780s may have contributed to the adaptation of this rhythm in the polonaise accompaniment." Hławiczka, "Grundriss einer Geschichte der Polonaise," 101; Hugo Riemann, *Grundriss der Kompositionslehre*, vol. 2 (Leipzig: Max Hesse Verlag, 1897), 39.

71. The chorus sings panegyric verses by Gavrila Derzhavin in honor of both the Russian victory over the Turks and the person of Empress Catherine II: "Brilliant Empress, gaze at visions / And behold, a woman great:/In your thoughts and your decisions / As one soul we all partake."

72. Richard Taruskin, *Defining Russia Musically: Historical and Hermeneutical Essays* (Princeton: Princeton University Press, 1997), 284. Taruskin quotes A. M. Sokolova, "O. A. Kozlovskiy," *Istoriya russkoy muziki v desyati tomakh*, vol. 4 (Moscow: Muzïka, 1986), 98. At least one dancing master took notice of Russia's appropriation of foreign dances: "The Russians afford nothing remarkable in their dances, which they now chiefly take from other countries." Giovanni-Andrea Gallini, *A Treatise on the Art of Dancing* (London: 1772), 194.

73. Adam Zamoyski, *The Last King of Poland* (London: Jonathan Cape, 1992), 429.

74. Kurpiński, "O tańcu Polskim czyli tak przezwanym *Polonezie*," 12. Kurpiński exaggerates. Though melancholy polonaises dominated the market, the repertoire of the last decade of the eighteenth century and opening two decades of the nineteenth century included a wide variety of polonaise styles, including ones "fit for dancing." It is also important to recognize a body of Polish patriotic polonaises that were either performed individually (for example, a polonaise by General Kościuszko "composed for the patriotic army of Poland") (the Kościuszko Polonaise) or used within operas (sung and instrumental). Beyond their patriotic overtones, this repertoire does not constitute a distinct category of polonaises but draws on a wide variety of styles. Also, this repertoire lacks the consistency and continuity of musical materials and the monumental grandeur of the Russian heroic polonaise. On the subject of patriotic polonaises, see Halina Goldberg, "Descriptive Instrumental Music in Nineteenth-Century Poland: Context, Genre, and Performance," *Journal of Musicological Research* 34/3 (Summer 2015): 224–48; and Alina Nowak-Romanowicz, *The History of Music in Poland: The Classical Era, 1750–1830*, trans. John Comber (Warsaw: Sutkowski, 2004), 191–273.

75. Michal Kleofas Ogiński, *Listy o muzyce*, eds. Tadeusz Strumiłło and Anna Papierzowa (Kraków: Polskie Wydawnictwo Muzyczne, 1956), 37–38.

76. Brodziński, "Wyjątek z pisma o tańcach," 93.

77. While conceived for the pianoforte, Ogiński's polonaises were transcribed for a variety of instrumental ensembles. See Hoffmann, "Zwölf Polonoisen," 793.

78. Ibid., 794.

79. Elsner, "Inwieweit ist die polnische Sprache zur Musik geeignet?," 682–83.

80. Goldberg, "Nationalizing the *Kujawiak* and Constructions of Nostalgia in Chopin's Mazurkas," 238.

81. Goldberg, *Music in Chopin's Warsaw*, 16–17.

82. Kurpiński, "O tańcu Polskim czyli tak przezwanym *Polonezie*," 12.

83. For the record, as principal conductor of Warsaw's National Theater Kurpiński was most likely responsible for providing music for state occasions. Soon after the beginning of the November Uprising Kurpiński composed a rousing insurrectionary song, "Warszawianka." On 5 April 1831 Kurpiński conducted its premiere at the National Theater.

84. Quoted from a review written by Robert Schumann of *Grand Dramatic Polonaise* by I. Nowakowski. Henry Pleasants, *The Musical World of Robert Schumann* (New York: St. Martins Press, 1965), 129.

85. In a letter to his friend Julian Fontana (24 August 1841), Chopin describes his Polonaise, Op. 44, as "a sort of Polonaise, but more of a fantasy." *Chopin's Polish Letters*, trans. David Frick (Warsaw: Fryderyk Chopin Institute, 2016), 335.

86. Halina Goldberg, "'Remembering That Tale of Grief': The Prophetic Voice in Chopin's Music," in *The Age of Chopin: Interdisciplinary Inquiries*, ed. Halina Goldberg (Bloomington: Indiana University Press, 2004), 54–92; Bellman, *Chopin's Polish Ballade: Op. 38 as Narrative of National Martyrdom* (Oxford and New York: Oxford University Press, 2010), 114–44.

87. Robert Schumann, *On Music and Musicians*, trans. Paul Rosenfeld (Berkeley: University of California Press, 1983), 132. Schumann never reviewed Opus 40. He includes Chopin's Op. 26 Polonaise in a review of an imaginary ball attended by Florestan and Eusebius, but provides no discussion of the music. Pleasants, *The Musical World of Robert Schumann*, 128–33.

88. Jean-Jacques Eigeldinger, *Chopin: Pianist and Teacher, As Seen by His Pupils*, ed. Roy Howat, trans. Naomi Shohet, Krysia Osostowicz, and Roy Howat (Cambridge: Cambridge University Press, 1986), 126.

89. A foundational part of a composer's early training was counterpoint. Starting just with two voices composers learned the proper handling of consonances and dissonances within different rhythmic contexts. The goal was to have complete mastery of four voices. A texture of four independent voices (SATB) is the basis of not only choral music but also of instrumental music.

90. My approach aligns with Schumann's imaginary engagement with Chopin's waltzes Op. 18, Op. 34, Op. 42. Although these works were not designed for the ballroom floor, Schumann nonetheless provides a ballroom context for his interpretations. For example: "His three waltzes [Op. 34] will delight above all—so different in type are they from the ordinary ones, and of a kind as could occur only to Chopin—perhaps he was inspired to new creations while he gazed, great artist that he is, among the dancers whom he has just roused by playing. So throbbing a life flows in them that they seem to have been actually improvised in the ballroom." Pleasants, *The Musical World of Robert Schumann*, 139.

91. For example, see the trio of Chopin's Polonaise, Op. 71, No. 3.

92. Quoted in Bogucka, "Gesture, Ritual, and Social Order," 191.

93. Chopin's first two commercially published polonaises, Op. 26, Nos. 1–2 (in C-sharp minor and E-flat minor, respectively), provide examples of his approach to the melancholy polonaise.

94. Zdzisław Jachimecki, *Frédéric Chopin et son œuvre* (Paris: Delagrave, 1930), 62–63.

95. Ferdynand Hoesick, *Chopin: Życie i twórczość*, vol. 4 (1910–11; Kraków: Polskie Wydawnictwo Muzyczne, 1967), 201.

96. Pauli, *Elemens de la danse*, 64.

97. Some examples include Henry Purcell, "Funeral March for Queen Mary"; Mozart, "Marche funèbre del Sigr. Maestro Contrapunto," K. 453a; and Beethoven, Symphony No. 3, Op. 55, *Marcia funebre*.

98. See Rita Steblin for a discussion of the sharp/flat principle in key associations. Simply stated, the sharp/flat principle holds that the sharp side of the circle of fifths correlates to brightness and positive aspects in human experience; the flat side to darkness and negative aspects in human experience. Steblin, *A History of Key Associations in the Eighteenth and Early Nineteenth Centuries*, 2nd ed. (Rochester, NY: University of Rochester Press, 2002), 96–128.

99. On the association of death with the Phrygian mode, see William Kimmel, "The Phrygian Inflections and the Appearances of Death in Music," *College Music Symposium* 20 (1980): 42–76.

100. Quoted in Norman Davies, *God's Playground: A History of Poland*, vol. 2 (New York: Columbia University Press, 1982), 9. Suspension points in the original. The topos of "the grave" permeates the contemporary writings devoted to the fall of Poland. "Every abundant and suddenly emergent literature is like a cypress decorating the grave of the nation, or at least the grave of the political order within which the nation's existence was unfolded until that time." —Henryk Rzewuski, 1840.

The Barcarolle and the *Barcarolle*: Topic and Genre in Chopin

JAMES PARAKILAS

Chopin's Barcarolle, Op. 60, announces its topic in its title; the opening theme realizes that topic unproblematically, and the rest of the work barely departs from it. This hardly seems like the kind of music for which topic theory is needed. That theory in its modern, self-conscious form (as opposed to the informal way in which music criticism has always involved the naming of topics) was developed in the 1970s by Leonard Ratner and his then student Wye Jamison Allanbrook for the study of late eighteenth-century music, in particular for detecting and explicating musical topics in genres that do not betray topics in their titles: sonatas, symphonies, arias, ensembles, and the like.[1] In a Mozart aria, for example, even when Figaro tells us that he'll play the music if his master wants to dance, we still need Allanbrook to tell us that his music is alternating between a minuet and a contredanse and to explain the social distinction encoded in that choice of dances.

Since the 1980s, other scholars have extended the study of musical topics, mostly continuing Ratner's and Allanbrook's concentration on late eighteenth-century music, but recently stretching to include nineteenth-century works as well.[2] Strikingly, the nineteenth-century works they discuss continue to be largely sonatas, symphonies, and the like, rather than programmatic works or character pieces.[3] When a composition is titled *The Hebrides* or *Mazeppa*, we evidently don't need anyone to tell us what its topical content is, any more than if it is titled *Barcarolle*. Chopin used generic titles almost exclusively, and certain of them—sonata, concerto, prelude, etude—denote function or medium or musical process without suggesting the musical content and social associations of a topic (in that sense, they are like "aria" for Mozart). But the majority of his works have generic titles that do specify a topic. They associate the work with a particular dance (waltz, mazurka) or kind of song (nocturne, ballade), or they announce a definite pianistic character (scherzo, impromptu).

To think that Chopin has given his topical game away when he employs one of these topic-specifying generic titles would be to miss a strategy that is central to his art: those titles in fact cover an endless fluidity with topics. And no topic shows that fluidity more dramatically than the barcarolle, one of the most pervasive topics in his music, even though only Opus 60, among all his works, actually bears the title. It is the leading or exclusive topic in almost half of his nocturnes and a variably strong presence in his four ballades. It also turns up unexpectedly to provide contrast or transformation in works of still other genres. In the first part of this study, these uses of the barcarolle topic provide examples for cataloging Chopin's methods of infiltrating topics within genres that specify other topics. That process of cataloging facilitates an examination, in the second part of the study, of how rich the play of topicality can be when the topic and the genre are the same, as they are in the Barcarolle, Op. 60.

Barcarolle as a Topic in Other Genres

In the safety of its own genre, a topic can play with its conventions and still make itself believable; in the context of another genre it can make itself known only when the music insists on the conventions of that topic. For the barcarolle topic to assert itself in a nocturne, we need our attention drawn to barcarolle features beyond those that the barcarolle and the nocturne have in common. Both genres, after all, are types of piano solos designed to remind us of a type of salon song, usually a vocal duet with piano, sung to love lyrics. What distinguishes the barcarolle from the nocturne is that the salon song we are imagining behind the piano piece is understood as a boatman's song—specifically one sung by a Venetian gondolier, or perhaps by a pair of his passengers, as would be the case in Offenbach's famous Barcarolle. But transported from being sung on a canal to being sung in a salon, the song needs to have a rhythm and accompaniment suggesting the waves rocking the boatman's boat as he sings. That rhythm is conventionally a gentle $^6_8$ (or a multiple of it), the duple meter suggesting the leisurely oscillation of the boat and the triple division of the beats allowing the accompaniment under the vocal lines to embody the smooth rise and fall of waves within that oscillation.

So many of Chopin's nocturnes have the wavelike, swaying rhythms of the barcarolle that it would be easy to take the features of the barcarolle topic as the defining features of his nocturnes. But some very different topics, such as the march, also have their place in the nocturnes, requiring us to take a topically expansive view of the genre overall. Even the "barcarolle" nocturnes, though they may all announce that topic by their straightforward use of barcarolle rhythm and accompaniments, make such diverse uses of the topic that no one example can adequately illustrate what Chopin is up to when he infiltrates the barcarolle topic into a nocturne.

For one thing, though wavelike bass lines are characteristic of the barcarolle topic, the waves in these nocturnes are all distinctive in shape and character, and the character of each is a key to the individuality of the whole work. In an early (1827) case, for instance, the posthumously published Nocturne in E Minor, Op. 72, No. 1, the bass line, which as in many barcarolles serves as introduction to the melody, is a restless figure, surging and coiling back twice, peaking on a dissonant sixth before retreating to the fifth of the chord. Not only is the rise and fall of this bass twice per measure (the piece is notated in triplet $^4_4$) conventional for a barcarolle in that it creates the effect of an endless succession of waves, but the line is conventionally expressive: this wave embodies emotional turmoil.

The unbroken sequence of waves through the entire Nocturne in E Minor lulls the listener into what feels like a dream. Nocturnes or love songs of any sort tend to the dreamy, but barcarolle waves are especially apt at lulling us into dreams. In this work the two long stanzas carry us through the same narration twice, as if our unconscious mind needed to work through a disturbing issue twice before we could let go of it. In the first stanza the singer enacts the song's emotional turmoil, moving to the key of the minor dominant; the turmoil resolves to tranquility right at the cadence, where the key turns to the major mode just as the restless wave accompaniment resolves to a smooth rise and fall, which is sustained for nine measures (mm. 22–30). In the second stanza the music returns to the opening key, wave-form, and song for another fifteen measures, even stormier than before (mm. 31–45), remaining in the tonic minor before resolving, this time for good, with the same major cadence and tranquil waves.

The Nocturne in G, Op. 37, No. 2, by contrast, opens with comparatively nondescript waves in the bass, but those waves prove capable of leading the melody at will. The bass is only halfway through its first wave before the melody enters: a fluid duet of thirds and sixths. Jean-Jacques Eigeldinger writes that these intervals "don't adhere to the model of the vocal duo, but participate in a strictly pianistic play of colors,"[4] a judgment hard to credit since these deliciously chromatic duet lines offer as convincing a pastiche of the vocal nocturnes heard in Parisian salons as any passage in the Chopin nocturnes.[5] What particularly marks these phrases as vocalistic is their billowing phrasing: in effect, the singing answers the watery waves in the bass with waves of breath. This feels like a boat ride in full sunlight with a light breeze, and before long the sun induces daydreaming. Nicholas Temperley credits Chopin with inventing what he calls "harmonic daydreaming" in passages of static or repetitive harmony,[6] but here the daydreaming manifests itself in thematic stasis while the harmonies drift—aimlessly, it seems—from key to key, as often as once a measure, and sometimes back again. The vehicle for this drifting is the bass line, initially so conventional in its waves, but soon developing a penchant for chromatic sidestepping, at breaks in the melody, that takes the melodic duet along wherever it goes.

In the middle of a passage where the harmony drifts downward by a step at every measure, the music tumbles into a new thought (measure 28). The waves in the bass are replaced by a single deep note on the downbeat of each measure, the billowing duet by a mostly chordal melody in a steady long–short rhythm. Now it is the melody that embodies the rocking of the boat, and the rolling of the waves is not represented at all. This is a second theme that will alternate three times with the first, giving this nocturne two equal modes of expression, two variants of the barcarolle topic alternating with each other. This contrasts with Chopin's more usual practice in barcarolle nocturnes, which is to set off the barcarolle topic in the outer sections by a more rhetorical topic, sometimes agitated in expression (Op. 9, No. 3; Op. 27, No. 1; Op. 48, No. 2). As this melody begins, the bass keeps stepping down, one note on each downbeat, until it reaches the low C that was the lowest note on most of the pianos Chopin and his public played. The attention of a listener who is imagining being on that rocking boat is being directed into the depths of the water. Memories are rising up from those depths. In the dialogue between the initial daydreaming in the sunlight and what wells up from the depths, the story of this nocturne is launched.

Chopin's ballades and scherzos are longer works than his nocturnes, closer in scale to his Barcarolle. But the scherzo, typically fast and light-footed, does not seem a likely place to look for the barcarolle topic. Chopin's four are all marked *presto*, are all in ³⁄₄, beginning and ending with wild energy. But in each case the sound and fury clears away in the middle, allowing a stiller, more reflective voice to be heard, like a memory or a dream emerging into consciousness. In the Scherzo No. 4 in E Major, Op. 54, he gives that moment of stillness over to the barcarolle topic.

Breaking off at the height of a *stretto*, he slows the *presto* tempo so that its $^3_4$ meter can accommodate a wave in the bass that rises and falls every two measures, as if in a barcarollish $^6_8$ (measure 393). A single voice delivers one stanza of the new melody, joined by a second voice in eloquent counterpoint on the next stanza, making the barcarolle texture complete. Before the third stanza comes a break in which we hear only a mysterious presence rising in diminished harmony from the depths, and in the third stanza a pause in the wave rhythm of the bass leads to an extension of the wave interval to four measures. At this sign the reverie is finished, and the scherzo returns.

Chopin evidently loved the effect of an escape into dreaming at the heart of a ternary work (and indeed many other places—see Halina Goldberg's chapter in this volume). The barcarolle topic was no doubt an obvious means to that effect, and the one he used in the posthumously published *Fantaisie-Impromptu*, Op. 66, though he also turned to less obvious topics, such as the dream mazurka in the middle of the Polonaise in F-sharp Minor, Op. 44. But it is still arresting to come upon this dream barcarolle in the middle of a scherzo at full flight. The experience challenges our capacity to integrate the two disparate sound-worlds, more than the inverse effect does: the intrusion of a nightmare *agitato* in the midst of a dream barcarolle in the Nocturne in B Major, Op. 9, No. 3, or the lurid eruption at the heart of the whispered barcarolle that is the Nocturne in C-sharp Minor, Op. 27, No. 1.

The ballades open themselves to the barcarolle topic in a very different way. They are piano works that suggest the complexity of narrative voices and dialogue, the richness of changing scenes and action of the folktales in song that give them their name. And they do it all in the framework of a $^6_8$ meter in moderate tempo, with the result that the barcarolle topic can enter the picture at any time. But so can many other topics, some of which are not easy to tease apart from it. Thus the Second Ballade, Op. 38 in F Major, opens with melody and accompaniment moving together in the endlessly repeating long–short rhythm that was identified above as an alternative way of rendering the barcarolle topic. But does it signify that topic here? Jonathan Bellman associates this music instead with the siciliano topic and cites good evidence for doing so (one piece of which is an operatic barcarolle).[7] A lot depends, it seems, on the context. And how about the similar rhythm of the B-flat theme (mm. 80–99) of the Fourth Ballade, Op. 52 in F Minor? Is there more barcarolle than siciliano, more boat ride than dance, in its swaying? The Third Ballade, Op. 47 in A-flat Major, has every imaginable kind of lilt in its rhythms, one giving way effortlessly to another. At one point, we even hear the "standard" bar-carolle texture of melody over a wavelike bass, but that is such a short passage (mm. 136–43) that if we call it a boat song passage, can we imagine it as a whole scene in the story?

The most extensive passage in all the ballades that can be ascribed to the barcarolle topic comes well into the Fourth Ballade, and that shows the wavelike bass of the barcarolle washing over themes that had been introduced earlier without that marker. This happens when the narrating theme of this ballade is heard for the third time, emerging in its original form (at measure 146) from a dreamy canonic mist. As the theme reaches its second stanza (measure 152), its melody breaks into elaborate can-tilena, and its formerly plodding accompaniment turns into high-swelling waves. The impassive narrating voice of a ballade has been transformed, in the middle of delivering its lines, into the luxuriantly expressive voice of a nocturne—a nocturne of the barcarolle topic. And Chopin is not done with that topic; the theme dissolves into swirls, from which the B-flat theme (that siciliano or alternative-barcarolle theme) emerges (now in D-flat), riding its own long, smoothly cresting waves (measure 169). As this theme proceeds, the singing and waves rise together in excitement until the song disappears completely into the exuberance of the waves (mm. 191–95). The barcarolle topic has taken on a life of its own, trans-forming everything in its path: first a theme with which it previously had no association and then one with which its connections were question-able, until the wave accompaniment that was the sign of that intruding topic overpowers both themes and itself becomes the theme of the story.

A related case of topical transformation occurs in the Largo of Chopin's Piano Sonata No. 3 in B Minor, Op. 58. The movement opens with no hint of the barcarolle; we hear four measures in a stately march rhythm, a rhythm that is maintained in both the melody and the accompaniment of the ensuing theme. But in this theme there is a rather stiff sway to the march step, due to Chopin's arrangement of the da-dum beats of the bass, alternating low da-dums on the strong beats with high da-dums on the weak beats. With that delicate oscillating effect he prepares an opening for the barcarolle topic later. The theme, meanwhile, is closed out by a march phrase that balances the opening, followed by a passage of dream music marked by endless undulations in the treble—still not "barcarolle" waves in the bass, but introducing the triplet rhythm. The passage is notable for its sheer length; it lasts three times as long as the theme it drew us away from, long enough to make us forget we ever heard that theme. And when we emerge from the dream, thanks to a passage of marching chords derived from the close of the march theme, we return to the reality we had forgotten we left behind: the march theme comes back, now with its da-dum bass smoothed into a barcarolle wave accompaniment. This is a remarkable transformation, combining the pitches of the original da-dum bass with the undulations of the dream sequence so that we feel we have not quite shaken off the dream. This may seem too subtle a variation to count as a "thematic transformation," yet it accomplishes in the most powerful way exactly what that term really refers to: the transferral of a theme into a new topic.

The Barcarolle Topic in the Barcarolle, Op. 60

The analysis offered so far has relied on the stated principle that a topic in a foreign genre has to announce itself plainly, by insisting on the conventions of the topic, in order to be recognized. In the one work Chopin named *barcarolle* he could conversely be freer with the conventions of the topic, since performers and listeners would still work to interpret the music as a barcarolle. The extent to which and the ways in which he exercised that freedom make a fascinating study.

If we skip over the introductory first three measures of the Barcarolle, Op. 60, we can say that the first theme of the work opens by invoking the barcarolle topic in the most conventional way possible: with two alternating versions of a wavelike bass line in double $^6_8$ meter that repeat until, after more than two measures, a songful duet melody enters, mostly in thirds, unfolding in its own long, wavelike phrases. But the introductory phrase, though it feels like part of the same boat ride, is less observant of the conventions of the topic and more particular in its evocation of sights, sounds, and movement. It starts with a booming octave in the bass, followed immediately by a triad in the treble that rings out overtones of that bass note. What sonic event do we imagine hearing? A peal from one of the great bells of the Campanile di San Marco, heard across the water from a gondola at some distance, the separation of the fundamental and overtones suggesting the distance the sound has traveled? Or perhaps the sound of the bell answered by the splash of a wave against our gondola? In any case this unforgettable pair of sounds gives us a sense of space and movement, high and low, far and near, sound answering sound, in a scene that is brought abruptly to life.

The composite sound then continues in a more fluid movement, in which the two upper voices, converging in three-note groups, seem to circle above and in sync with the bass, which undulates from its offbeat dominant-pedal notes. From the gondola we feel and see and hear the water eddying around us. Chopin's pedal indications cut off the resonance of the booming opening chord just as the eddying motion begins, revealing that motion exactly when the dominant pedal is in its highest octave (three octaves above the opening boom) and thereby exposing it to a glint of sunlight for just two beats before the damper pedal and a lower register restore a darker shade. Here, as throughout the Barcarolle, Chopin's pedal indications partner miraculously with the notes to suggest the evanescent colors of waves dancing in the sunlight. Most pianists ignore those and many of Chopin's pedal indications in this work, denying us the chance to hear that late-Delacroix or proto-Impressionist side of the work.[8]

Even the otherwise conventional barcarolle bass that introduces and underlies the main theme (measure 4ff) gets its glint of *plein-air* color from the lifting of the pedal whenever the ninth of the harmony, G♯, rubs against the tonic F♯, or in comparable places where leaving the pedal down would result in a dissonant smear. The pattern of the bass remains essentially unchanged for the first six measures of the theme, through changes from a duet in thirds to one in sixths and from F-sharp major to D-sharp minor, but then begins a signifying set of evolutions. First the wave motion gets simpler and faster, one wave per beat rather than the original one per two beats (measure 12). As this happens, the duet melody moves forward, mostly in thirds and sixths, toward a cadence, but in the excitement of that approach, the arpeggiated bass suddenly rises to a greater stretch than before (measure 14) and the duet melody meets the cap of that wave with an offbeat splash and a tumble of sixths (marked *leggiero*). This is a moment that exposes the ambiguity of the barcarolle topic. The duet writing in sixths here may be as true to the salon tradition of vocal nocturnes as the comparable writing in the G-Major Nocturne, Op. 37, No. 1, and yet at this very moment our sense that we are listening to a vocal duet threatens to dissolve into imagining that we are simply listening to the splashing of waves. Evidently we are in a state of daydreaming, where the two kinds of imagining can infiltrate each other.

From this point, Chopin tilts for a while toward letting us daydream about the motion of splashing waves and rocking boats, while the singing of the song fades from our consciousness. It is a surprisingly long while (mm. 15–23) for us to surrender to the feeling of being in a boat that is simply swaying in the waves, going nowhere—a pleasurable effect that Carlo Caballero has aptly described by the Italian term *indugio* (lingering).[9]

This lasts long enough for us to consider that the dreamy aftermath of the duet stanza we have just heard is as important to Chopin's conception of the barcarolle genre as the singing of the duet itself. At the start of this aftermath the bass and treble collaborate for five measures (mm. 15–19) in a passage that, as it gently rocks, slips from C-sharp major to B major and then to the dominant of D-sharp minor. This brings us to a new singing voice, presented in a way that contradicts the conventions of the barcarolle: a melody—a sequence of short but urgent phrases—appears in the tenor range, harmonized by two voices below it, while the treble parts (once again a duo, partly in sixths) produce a pair of phrases that are considerably splashier, whether we imagine them as a competing set of voices, engaged in virtuosic salon singing, or as the sound of a boat caught in the crashing of waves. In effect, the traditional roles of the barcarolle topic have been inverted in these two measures (20–21): what is most clearly a set of singing voices is heard in the lower range and the depiction of waves in the upper. The result is that a half-realized, or perhaps half-remembered, trio of voices seems to emerge for just a moment to sing their plea and then disappear into the waves.

Almost immediately, the trilling of the duet voices is restored in the treble register, leading into a second stanza of their song, their barcarolle. This stanza is both more elaborate vocally—as we might expect if we thought of this as representing a duet by prestigious singers at a Paris salon—and less adventurous harmonically, the lack of modulation allowing a full close after two stanzas. And the post-cadential swaying in the waves that was heard at the end of the first stanza lasts for just two measures this time (mm. 33–34) before being interrupted. The interruption comes as a single line (mm. 35–38), the first time we have not heard a melody and accompaniment together since the wavelike bass that introduced the main theme of the work. This new single line, which has a different wavelike rhythm and course, leads the music into new territory, the tale into a new stage.

The Barcarolle as a Genre

This move raises the question of the barcarolle as a genre. What kind of piano work are we embarked on, and what does our sense of that genre suggest we should expect at this moment of transition? We can't look to other Chopin barcarolles for guidance, since this is his only work under that title. We can look to earlier works in the genre, especially by composers of his acquaintance whose works he is likely to have known. These would include the Venetian Gondola Songs from Mendelssohn's collections of *Songs Without Words* from the 1830s and early '40s,[10] which seem to have established the barcarolle topic in the piano repertory— the swaying bass accompaniment in $^6_8$ meter, the dreamy melody in duet texture above it. But those are real miniatures; each is formally a single stanza of a song, with a simple frame. We are already far enough along in the Chopin Barcarolle to know that that work is far more ambitious in conception and elaborate in form.

A closer model can be found in Sigismond Thalberg's Barcarolle in A Minor, Op. 60, of 1839.[11] This is a large-scale work in which an idea of virtuosic singing lurks behind the challenging melodic figuration and in which the accompaniment figuration in the bass changes regularly, usually suggesting a different kind of wave motion. The formal stages also bear a resemblance to what we have found already in the Chopin: an introduction that breaks off on the dominant, a complex song stanza, followed by a passage of music more concerned with wavelike motion than with presenting a second song theme. In both works, then, the barcarolle genre seems defined by the interweaving of the idea of a romance sung in a boat with the idea of the boat ride as an experience that absorbs the imagination of anyone listening to the song, transporting that listener into a daydream, disconnected from the here and now and thus from the barcarolle the listener has been hearing. But the challenge is that the feeling of being transported on the boat needs to be sustained or the dream will be shattered.

In both barcarolles, then, that absorbing, dream-inducing wave music (at the end of one song verse in the Thalberg, two in the Chopin) leads to a change of song and a change of wave motion, but this new material still belongs to the barcarolle topic. In fact, it was not unprecedented for Chopin to lead from one kind of barcarolle to another, as we found he did in the G-Major Nocturne, Op. 37, No. 2. Here, as in the Thalberg, the new barcarolle song will turn out to be the dreamy center of a large-scale ternary work. But whereas in Chopin's E-Major Scherzo, Op. 54, the dreamy central barcarolle marks an escape from the character of the work as a whole, this dream barcarolle is launched from and returns to music that is itself dream-inducing.

The launch is effected by that startling single line (mm. 35–39) that sets off at the moment when the post-cadential rocking in F-sharp major abruptly settles on F-sharp minor. The sense that this line is taking us somewhere new is awakened not only by the stripped-down texture, but also by a slightly faster tempo. The tonal ambiguity of the line allows Chopin then to pull us from F-sharp minor to A major without letting us feel any modulation. And the winding motion of the line allows us to feel that we are drifting into the recesses of our memories, awaiting a new impression.

We are met with a new wavelike accompaniment, it seems, over which we might expect a new song to be sung. This is a lapping bass figure, which will underlie the music for a considerable stretch (mm. 39–49), only to be succeeded by a more continuous version of the same for an even longer stretch. Though there is nothing remarkable about this figure as a barcarolle bass, it is remarkable how it generates what is heard over it: not a distinct melody, but more layers of lapping motion. After one measure of lapping in the bass, a second lapping figure begins in the alto range, and half a measure later a sustained note that entered with that alto line begins a third lapping motion in the soprano range. The only progression here is the modulation in the next two measures from A major to G-sharp major, and that feels more like a surge in the motion of the boat (met by a musical splash in measure 43) than like an expressive modulation in a song. The motion continues through a modulation from G-sharp major to F-sharp major (mm. 45–46), through a passage that laps on an augmented-sixth chord for a whole long measure (measure 49) before modulating to A major; this entire passage then repeats, only with that more continuous version of the lapping bass and a louder, richer version of the upper lines (mm. 51–61).

If we think of this stretch (mm. 39–61) as the barcarolle waves preparing the arrival of the new barcarolle song, that song does arrive (mm. 62–71), and it is a pretty tune in duet thirds and sixths, with its own, slightly new wavelike accompaniment. But how do we account for the strange temporal proportions? There are twenty-three measures of preparation for a ten-measure song. In fact, that "preparation" is the longest unified stretch of music in the Barcarolle and the passage in which the work most fully reveals its secret agenda. This agenda also shows itself in the wave music heard following both stanzas of the song in the opening section and in the coda of the Barcarolle (mm. 103–16): a passage of absorption in the waves frees us from absorption in someone else's song to lose ourselves in our own imaginations. The present passage is not only the longest, but the most sensually indulgent of these: once we have heard that augmented-sixth chord resolve to its dominant chord within one measure (48), the only reason to hear it again, in an *indugio* that lasts twice as long (in measure 49) before it resolves a second time, is to enjoy losing ourselves in it, not wanting ever to hear it resolve. Then, in the repetition of the entire passage in richer, stronger form (mm. 51–61), passion is added to sensuality. And all of this human feeling emanates from the most impressionist musical scene-painting of the early nineteenth century, a wavescape without figures, a barcarolle awaiting its song.

From this prolonged pleasure-taking in the sensuality of the waves emerges the pretty duet (mm. 62–71) that is the sunniest melody of the Barcarolle as well as the breeziest, its syncopations against the steady waves suggesting a boat buffeted by irregular gusts of wind. But this duet is not brought to completion; it is interrupted at the crest of a phrase by a solitary trill that diverts us to another theme (mm. 72–77) and then a third (mm. 78–83), which serves as the retransition to the main theme of the Barcarolle. The sunny duet, then, after so long a preparation, does not establish itself as the principal theme of this middle section; it serves instead as the first item in a thematic sampler in which each item connects to the barcarolle topic in a different way. The sunny duet provides an example of the barcarolle topic in its classic form: the double $^6_8$ meter, the wavelike bass, the songful duet melody. If in fact we heard it as the principal theme of the middle section, it might disappoint us in that it has so much in common with the principal theme of the first section. How would that enrich the generic conception of the work as a whole?

Enrichment comes instead from hearing that classic version of the barcarolle topic followed by the two that succeed it. The first of these, marked *meno mosso*, might be assigned to the "ballade" barcarolle topic: no continuous wave motion in the bass, but an accompaniment of chords in the steady, swaying siciliano rhythm found in one theme of each of the last three Chopin ballades. This gives way (measure 78) to a passage in what might be called the "nocturne" barcarolle topic: a leisurely wave bass line of considerable range, supporting a florid solo melody, also of considerable range. Chopin marks this melody *sfogato* (poured forth), evoking the singing of a *soprano sfogato*, an operatic diva like Maria Malibran or Giuditta Pasta who had an enormous range and distinct timbres in each register of that range. The melody Chopin writes here exceeds any human singing range, but that makes it all the more clear that he is pushing the limits of the barcarolle topic, which in its classic form offers melodies that do not require an opera singer's range or agility (even if we might like to imagine opera singers performing them). In terms of the barcarolle topic, the bass line in this passage is even more remarkable than the melody. Twice a measure that bass line starts a wave motion from the deep, but then it drops out. These are waves that rise to a crest and stop there, wait and rise again, leaving it to the *soprano sfogato* melody to create the only sustained sequence of rising and falling waves in the passage. Here too Chopin seems to be pushing the boundaries of the barcarolle topic (in a direction that Gabriel Fauré would pursue in his piano barcarolles decades later).

But if this passage points to future developments in the genre, in another sense it completes Chopin's survey of his own creative range with the barcarolle topic. In three brief passages he takes us from a simple example of the topic at its most readily recognizable to a more ambiguous, siciliano-like model and from there to a passage in which the two elements of the topic—the wave and the song—take problematic forms. At the same time this survey reminds us of the range of genres in which he has implanted the barcarolle topic. It is as if in treating the barcarolle as a genre of its own in this work, he could allow himself to reflect musically on his whole practice with the barcarolle as a topic. And in placing this reflection at the end of the middle section of the Barcarolle, in the wake of that long, dreamy passage of staring into the waves, it is as if Chopin has created this whole composition around the figure of the artist, giving himself over to a state of mind that will allow him to contemplate his own work. We can decide, as performers and listeners, whether to consider this sequence as a time-out, in which Chopin capriciously displays the topical versatility he has withheld from the rest of the Barcarolle, or as a moment of widened perspective that places the Barcarolle within the frame of Chopin's previous and potential treatments of the topic.

Sorting the Themes by Topical Element

As the *sfogato* melody heads, amid trills, toward its cadence, that soloistic voice is joined by a second voice, creating a double trill that we have heard before. As before, it leads to the principal theme of the Barcarolle, that is—depending on how you look at it—to the reprise of the first section of the work or the third stanza of the song, returning after the long hiatus of the middle section. Looking at it as the third stanza of the song draws our attention to the fact that it follows the course of the second stanza, not the first. Comparing it to the second stanza draws our attention to the differences. This time, instead of starting at *forte* and growing softer and louder by turns, the stanza starts at *forte* and grows louder, reaching *fortissimo* at its cadence. The difference is magnified by the doubling of the wavelike bass line at the octave this time, while the melodic part is the same as before, except for two measures with a new octave doubling (mm. 86–87). It is hard to know what term to use to describe this revision. There is not enough change to describe it as a variation or a thematic transformation. The doubling of the bass line, without any balancing in the upper voices, makes the wave motion more prominent, at the expense of the song. But the same joyous effect of sunlight dancing on the waves is provided by the same on-again, off-again damper-pedal instructions— or near-enough the same, allowing for the greater challenge of playing the bass line in octaves. We are on the same boat ride, hearing the same song as before, but taking in that experience with more immediacy and intensity, perhaps, after our daydreaming and contemplating interlude. The climbing sequence of chords that brought the second stanza to such an exquisite cadence, diminishing into a haze of pedaling (measure 32), turns into its opposite, a bright, surging breaker of a wave, at the end of the third stanza (measure 92), through the simple expediency of reversing the dynamics (and a slight thickening of the chords).

After this third stanza there is no aftermath of lapping waves, as there is after each of the previous stanzas. Instead, Chopin moves right into his alternative song, the sunny duet in A major from the middle section, now transposed into the tonic key of F-sharp major (mm. 93–102). What began as a reprise of the first section of the work, in other words, has turned into a resorting of the material of both earlier sections. The material is sorted according to whether it contributed to the song element of the barcarolle topic or the wave element. First we hear those two duets that defined the song element of the Barcarolle (mm. 84–102), one now flowing into the other so that they seem like the large stanza of a single song. Then, in a coda, over a tonic pedal, we hear new versions of three passages that evoked the motion of waves and boats in the absence of song: first (mm. 103–10) the upper line from the opening of the middle section (mm. 41–42ff); next (mm. 111–12) the lulling motion that succeeded each of the song stanzas in the first section (measure 15ff); and finally (mm. 113–15) the tenor phrases that emerged, after the first stanza only, from that lulling motion (mm. 20–21).

What sense does this reordering make? To reduce it to a demonstration of how the composer analyzed his own material would be to miss the way this part of the Barcarolle builds on the momentum and experiential narration of the whole work. To assess that, let us return to the moment of reprise, the third stanza of the principal duet. By presenting a third stanza that replicates the second, except with its bass line doubled at the octave and growing in volume, Chopin suggests that this return is a continuation of the original song and that our experience of listening to this song is opening onto a wider horizon. Something of the same happens when that stanza leads directly into the second stanza of the duet from the middle section. The full volume continues, the full texture continues (with octave doublings in both the duet lines and the wavelike bass line), and it is easy not even to notice that our singers have slipped from one song to the other. But there are also subtle changes: the tempo picks up slightly, and the octave texture of the bass line has filled in with chords (as it actually began to do a few measures earlier). The pedaling is also more continuous now than it has been before, which with the thicker texture in both hands produces a gaudy, dissonant blurring of overlapping chords that Chopin's fastidious pedaling has largely avoided until now. Gone is the daydreaming that the alternation of song stanzas with mere lapping waves has invited the listener to fall into. In its place has come an experience in which continuous, full-throated singing while riding the waves energizes the listener's focus on the here and now.

What becomes of that directed energy when the music of lapping waves and daydreaming returns in the coda? Even though Chopin is crossing his own line here (measure 103) from song material to wave material, he now transforms his wave material so that it too sounds like a continuation of the previous song. The melody here, derived from phrases of three or three-and-a-half measures that emerged out of the layers of waves in the middle section, is here rationalized into one-measure phrases in a more songlike sequence. Their accompaniment, meanwhile, is not a new and distinctive wave pattern this time, but one continuous with what we have just been hearing. The feeling of directed energy is also sustained by the continuing high volume (*sempre forte*) and bright coloring of dissonances blurred by continuous pedaling. In fact, as the melody goes through its sequence, the tonic pedal that underlies the passage creates stronger and stronger dissonances against notes struck at the same time: a G-major triad against F♯s (on the downbeat of m. 105), E-minor and B-flat-major triads against F♯s (on the downbeats of mm. 108 and 109), and most strikingly an E♯ and G♮ against F♯s (downbeat of measure 110: another augmented-sixth sonority, but this time struck right over the F♯ into which both notes are going to resolve). If we consider this passage a thematic transformation, it is a transformation that restores the premise of the barcarolle topic, since a passage that offered only the wave element of that topic has been transformed to embody both the song and the wave.

All this transforming does not drive daydreaming out of the picture. With its insistent melodic motive and its dissonant blur of overrich chords, this passage has a nostalgic power worthy of Ravel. But it is a phantasmagoric nostalgia, a far cry from the sweet images and feelings induced by the rocking of the boat on sun-glinting waves in the first and middle sections of the Barcarolle. How far a cry, how far we have come on this boat ride of impressions, daydreams, and contemplation, Chopin is about to remind us. At that most dissonant collision of sounds (the E♯and G♮ against the low F♯s, measure 110), the melodic sequence—and with it our sense of a sustained song uniting all parts of the work—dissolves. After an airy spray of a wave we return (mm. 111–12) to the simple rocking music that succeeded both the first two stanzas of the opening song (mm. 15, 18, 33), exactly as before.

This is a crucial moment, signaling that we are still where we were then, staring into the waves; signaling perhaps that everything we have dreamed since then—songs, scenes, visions, thoughts—was a mirage; signaling perhaps that we are now done dreaming. But we are not quite done. We have still to hear the second utterance (mm. 113–15) by the trio of male voices that emerged at an earlier moment of staring into the waves (mm. 20–21). This utterance, a new melody appearing at the very end of the work, sounds more contented than that earlier one, and the wave that rises above it is less splashy than its predecessor. It is the second airy spray of a wave within a few measures, this one gathering strength as it tumbles through seven octaves into the depths of the water to bring on the two rousing signals that really do foreclose further dreaming by ending the piece.

What kind of work is the Barcarolle? It might be tempting to call it a discourse in tones on the barcarolle topic, if its progression did not defy discursive, let alone narrative, logic. It is more of a fantasy on the barcarolle topic, the way Chopin's *Polonaise-Fantaisie* is a fantasy on the polonaise topic, the F-Minor Fantaisie a fantasy on the march topic, certain of the mazurkas fantasies on the mazurka topic. Here, as in those fantasies, he treats the topic freely. Not only does he not need to make the topic identifiable in a work that he calls Barcarolle, but he goes beyond the humble idea of the barcarolle topic as a convention-bound language used to create a dreamy and amorous atmosphere. He does use the conventions of the topic—those of duet singing in the treble register over wavelike motion in the bass—but he then sets those elements free of one another, creating a dazzling new pianistic sound world of *plein-air* impressions that launch the listener's imagination into a dreamlike train of thought. It is dreamlike in that it takes customary ideas—especially the conventional association of song and wave—apart and recombines them; in that it serves up memories of the composer's own earlier repertory of barcarolle styles for us to contemplate even while it is moving past them; and in that it takes its own realistic sequence of actions—especially the sequence of song stanzas with pauses between them—apart and reorders them. Because Chopin's barcarolle genre creates a dream structure around a topic that is itself dream-inducing, he makes us feel that we are not simply along for the boat ride, but are partners with him in the experiment of discovering new potential of imagining, associating, and feeling within the barcarolle topic.

In the Wake of the Barcarolle

The Barcarolle was one of Chopin's last compositions, and he did not turn to the genre or even the topic again. Later composers produced enormous numbers of piano barcarolles, and insofar as Chopin's music was among the influences on them, they imitated Chopin's treatment of the barcarolle topic more than his concept of the genre. (What would it mean, after all, to imitate the concept of this exceptionally idiosyncratic work?) In some cases, later composers followed his example by evoking the topic unconventionally. Tchaikovsky, for instance, in his Barcarolle "June," No. 6 in the piano suite *The Seasons*, Op. 37, defied the $^6_8$ convention by casting the work in common time. But given how frequently he demonstrated his ability to establish a musical topic convincingly while in the "wrong" meter, he clearly didn't need the example of Chopin's Barcarolle to inspire that venture in his own barcarolle.

A much closer approach to Chopin's attitude toward the barcarolle topic can be found in the thirteen piano barcarolles of Gabriel Fauré. In the opening measures of his Barcarolle No. 7 in D Minor, Op. 90, for instance, we find him conflating the wave and song functions, though by different means from those Chopin used in the middle section of his Barcarolle: Fauré uses the notes of his melody to fill in when the middle and bass parts are not sounding new notes, so that it takes all the parts together to create the continuous motion of a wave. Even then the wave motion is cut short at the end of each measure, creating a pattern of incomplete waves, such as Chopin created in the bass line of the *sfogato* section of his Barcarolle. This passage nevertheless sounds not the least bit like Chopin.

In his barcarolles Fauré pursued what intrigued him about the barcarolle topic—in particular the relationship of song to waves—from one work to another over the course of his whole career, just the way Chopin pursued his interest in the nocturne or ballade or mazurka topic. With the barcarolle topic, Chopin over the course of his career explored ways of refining and varying its conventional expressiveness, and he expanded its expressive effect by situating it in other genres. Only at the end of that process did he turn to the barcarolle as a genre, and by then what apparently intrigued him were the new sonic and conceptual possibilities he could explore by deconstructing the topic.

NOTES

1. Leonard Ratner, *Classic Music: Expression, Form, and Style* (New York: Schirmer Books and London: Collier Macmillan, 1980); Wye Jamison Allanbrook, *Rhythmic Gesture in Mozart*: *"Le nozze di Figaro" and "Don Giovanni"* (Chicago: University of Chicago Press, 1983).

2. A representative selection of essays, written by many of the leading scholars who have worked in this area, is found in Danuta Mirka, ed., *Oxford Handbook of Topic Theory* (Oxford and New York: Oxford University Press, 2014).

3. See for instance Julian Horton's "Listening to Topics in the Nineteenth Century," in Mirka, *Oxford Handbook*.

4. Jean-Jacques Eigeldinger, "Venezie Immaginarie: Appunti sulle Barcarole di Chopin," in *Chopin e l'Italia*, ed. Jerzy Miziołek (Rome: L'Erma di Bretschneider and Warsaw: Narodowy Instytut Fryderyka Chopina, 2015), 156.

5. See James Parakilas, "'Nuit plus belle qu'un beau jour': Poetry, Song, and the Voice in the Piano Nocturne," in *The Age of Chopin: Interdisciplinary Inquiries*, ed. Halina Goldberg (Bloomington: Indiana University Press, 2004), 203–23.

6. Nicholas Temperley, "Fryderyk Chopin," in *New Grove Early Romantic Masters 1: Chopin, Schumann, Liszt* (New York and London: W. W. Norton, 1985), 50.

7. Jonathan D. Bellman, *Chopin's Polish Ballade: Op. 38 as Narrative of National Martyrdom* (Oxford and New York: Oxford University Press, 2010), 145–51.

8. Until the Barcarolle appears in the Peters *New Critical Edition* of Chopin, the composer's pedal indications are best studied in the reproductions of the first editions in Chopin's First Editions Online (www.chopinonline.ac.uk/cfeo). Autograph and other sources are due to appear in the Online Chopin Variorum Edition (www.chopinonline. ac.uk/ocve).

9. Carlo Caballero, "Strange Gondolas: Oneiric Turns in Fauré's Barcarolles," keynote address read at Focus on Piano Literature 2012: Gabriel Fauré, 2 June 2012, University of North Carolina, Greensboro.

10. Felix Mendelssohn, *Songs Without Words*, Op. 19b, No. 6, in G Minor; Op. 30, No. 6, in F-sharp Minor; Op. 62, No. 5, in A Minor.

11. Sigismond Thalberg, Barcarolle, Op. 60 (Paris: J. Meissonier, [1839]), is reproduced at International Music Score Library Project/Petrucci Music Library (http://imslp.org/).

Chopin and Improvisation

JOHN RINK

Themes

The conventional practices and values of classical performance today differ radically from those of Chopin's musical world. Perhaps the most fundamental difference concerns the significant role played by improvisation in public and private musical circles during the first few decades of the nineteenth century.[1] Whereas modern performers tend to ascribe authority to the inferred intentions of composers and to the notational artifacts that have been handed down over successive generations, musicians some two hundred years ago approached written texts with much greater flexibility and freedom. Moreover, the "here and now" was prized by performers and listeners alike, hence the "*stagione* principle" referred to by Carl Dahlhaus,[2] along with the prevalence of "Rossinian aesthetics" versus the "Beethovenian aesthetics" that eventually would prevail.[3] During Chopin's lifetime, professional performers—especially pianists—sought to dazzle their audiences with daring improvisations on themes proposed by individual listeners and on familiar melodies drawn from folk traditions or the latest operas. Singers and instrumentalists indulged in spontaneous ornaments of all kinds, and composers themselves often tried to capture the spirit of improvisation in their published works, especially those in the popular "brilliant style."[4] In addition, musicians regularly improvised in more domestic settings, including *salons* of greater or lesser social ambition.

Chopin engaged in each of these practices at different stages of his life. Eyewitness accounts, annotations in the scores used by his pupils, and features of his compositional style reveal that all facets of his musical activity—performing, teaching, and composing—were profoundly influenced by improvisation.[5] The discussion that follows will consider the role of improvisation in respect of each of these activities. We will discover that Chopin's characteristically singular approach to improvisation was marked by a dramatic change midway through his career in accordance with his evolving aspirations.

Variant 1: Chopin as Improviser

Chopin's remarkable skills as an improviser made a mark on those fortunate enough to hear him in action. For example, his friend and amanuensis Julian Fontana commented in the preface to his 1855 posthumous edition of Chopin:

> From his earliest youth, the richness of [Chopin's] improvisation was astonishing. But he took good care not to parade it; and the few lucky ones who have heard him improvising for hours on end, in the most wonderful manner, never lifting a single phrase from any other composer, never even touching on any of his own works—those people will agree with us in saying that Chopin's most beautiful finished compositions are merely reflections and echoes of his improvisations.[6]

Another friend, the banker Wojciech Grzymała, similarly observed the differences between Chopin's improvisatory playing and his published music, as Eugène Delacroix reported in a journal entry of 20 April 1853:

> [Grzymała] told me that Chopin's improvisations were far bolder than his finished compositions. They would doubtless stand in the position of the sketch for the picture as compared with the picture when finished.[7]

The qualitative differences cited in both accounts are hardly surprising, not least because formal and expressive norms tend to be stretched if not transcended in the act of improvisation, hence the "far bolder" music that typically results.[8] Moreover, one of the defining features of improvisation is its immediacy: the overriding goal is usually the *effect* of the sounding music rather than the cohesion and durability of an underlying musical conception. Although improvisation is often thought of as composition in real time, such an understanding is misguided: despite apparent similarities, not to mention those between improvisation and the performance of composed music, improvisation is distinctive in terms of what it is and what it does, not least because it conditions and invites a heightened level of engagement on the part of those who observe it as it happens.

Chopin is known to have improvised on many dozens of occasions, whether in public concerts or before assembled listeners in comparatively private contexts. A survey published by Krystyna Kobylańska in 1990 enumerates thirty-seven occasions when Chopin improvised "on known themes," whether in whole or in part, as well as twenty-nine "on unknown themes."[9] The former included improvisations on Polish songs such as "Chmiel" (Hops), Spanish melodies, religious themes, dance tunes, and, in keeping with contemporary fashion, operatic arias—for instance, from Auber's *La muette de Portici*, Albert Grisar's *La folle*, and Rossini's *Il barbiere di Siviglia*. Some improvisations on unknown themes were performed on newly invented instruments.[10] Many of Chopin's documented improvisations took place in salons and the homes of friends and associates in Warsaw, Paris, Dresden, and elsewhere.

Despite their typical lack of detail, the abundant surviving descriptions of Chopin's improvisations contain fascinating insights, as does his own correspondence. For example, soon after a concert in Warsaw on 22 March 1830, when he performed his Concerto in F Minor along with an improvisation on two Polish songs—"Świat srogi" (A World That's Harsh) and "W mieście dziwne obyczaje" (Strange Customs in the City)—Chopin wrote to his friend Tytus Woyciechowski: "I improvised, which pleased the first-tier boxes very much. To tell you the truth, I improvised not as I had wished, because it was not for that world."[11] This confession speaks volumes not only about Chopin's willingness to adapt his performance approach to suit the occasion, but also, more importantly, about his ability to improvise in different styles, namely "public" and "private." That in itself was not unusual: other noted improvisers such as the composer-pianist Johann Nepomuk Hummel referred explicitly in their writings to disparate styles of improvisation, such as "galant" versus "strict and fugal."[12] What is more striking is Chopin's almost complete renunciation of improvisation in public concerts not long after establishing himself in the French capital in late 1831; there is only one known reference to this type of improvisation in the Paris reviews published thereafter, namely, an allusion in Léon Escudier's critique to Chopin "preluding" on the piano during a public performance in 1841.[13] In contrast, his improvisatory playing in more intimate circles continued unabated.

Despite the apparent gulf between Chopin's public and private improvisations and his growing disenchantment with the former from the early 1830s onward, two testimonies point to certain commonalities.

The earlier account concerns the only known occasion when Chopin improvised in public in France, during a concert at the Hôtel-de-Ville in Tours on 3 September 1833. According to a review released several days later, the concert ended with an improvisation on three themes in succession: the "air écossais" from Boieldieu's *La dame blanche*, "L'or n'est qu'une chimère" from Meyerbeer's *Robert le diable*, and a Polish "air patri-otique." The reviewer observed furthermore that

> after treating [these themes] separately and lengthily with great care [*inquiétude*], after taking them through all the keys suggested by his imagination, and after having plucked all the petals from the flowers, [Chopin] introduced two mazur-kas of his own composition; having then modulated these while indulging in ever stranger contrasts, he returned to the first three themes, which he successively reproduced in playing the finale of this improvisation, where he achieved the greatest heights.[14]

Compare this to an account from some thirteen years later, on 9 July 1846, when Chopin improvised in George Sand's salon at Nohant before a number of friends and associates. An ecstatic letter written the following day by one of them—the young Elisa Fournier, from La Rochelle—pro-vides extraordinary detail about the music they heard:

> He played a parody of a Bellini opera that made us dou-ble up in laughter . . . then a prayer of the Polish people in distress, which made us cry; then a rendition of a tolling bell, which gave us shivers; then a funeral march so grave, so sombre, so sad that it broke our hearts. . . . Eventually emerging from this unhappy mood, and after a moment's rest, brought back to his senses by a few notes sung by Mme George, he played . . . a bourrée . . . carefully working out the musical ideas, [and then] a *tour de force* the likes of which I could never have imagined. He imitated on the piano a lit-tle music box. . . . His sparkling touch, finesse, and dexterity . . . were of unrivaled delicacy. Then, suddenly, a cadenza, endless and so faint one could hardly hear it, interrupted by the music box which . . . seemed to be breaking down. He [then] played a melody—I think one from the Tirol—with

a missing note in the music box so that each time it should have been played there was a hiccup.[15]

The defining structural feature of both of these improvisations seems to have been a succession of generic types which in turn evoked a series of moods and emotions. Although such an approach might have resulted in a musical hodgepodge—a true potpourri—the effect in Chopin's hands appears to have been captivating and convincing. As we will see, the fact that some of his works are similarly constructed points to the influence that improvisation had on his compositional approach and aesthetic, and it also reveals one of the potential sources of meaning in his music.[16]

Consider in this respect the following description of the poet Józef Bohdan Zaleski, whose diary records an improvisation in which Chopin

> evoked all the sweet and sorrowful voices of the past. He sang the tears of the dumkas and finished with the national anthem, "Poland Has Not Yet Perished" (the Dąbrowski Mazurka), in a whole gamut of different forms and voices, from that of the warrior to those of children and angels. I could have written a whole book about this improvisation.[17]

Another Polish émigré moved by Chopin's improvising was the doctor Ferdynand Dworzaczek, who in 1835 heard Chopin "give free rein to his imagination":

> All of a sudden his music rang out with a song which went to the heart of my soul . . . a well-known song . . . a song from the homeland . . . beloved . . . from the family home . . . from childhood years . . . My heart throbbed with yearning, tears sprang to my eyes—I leapt up: "Fryderyczku!" I cried, "I know that song from the cradle . . . my mother used to sing it . . . I have it in my soul, and you just played it!" He looked around with a strange expression. His eyes shone; his fingers were moving delicately over the keys. "You never heard this tune before!" he declared. "But I have it here, here, in my soul!" I cried, pressing my hand to my breast. "Oh!"—he rose and embraced me—"you have just made me indescribably happy, there are no words for it. You never knew this

song . . . only its spirit: the spirit of the Polish melody! And I am so happy to have been able to grasp it and reveal it."[18]

That Chopin was capable of capturing the spirit of Poland as suggested here is borne out by many testimonies. One of his surviving songs—an "immense national threnody"[19] titled "Śpiew z mogiły" (Hymn from the Tomb), which was based on a poem of Wincenty Pol—might have originated as an improvisation on 3 May 1836; it was later reconstructed by Julian Fontana and published as Op. 74, No. 17, in 1874, twenty-five years after Chopin's death in 1849. Other works that seem to have begun life as improvisations include the early mazurkas in G major, B-flat major, and D major, which Chopin ostensibly improvised at a dance evening in Warsaw in the mid-1820s, and the drinking song "Hulanka" (with text by Stefan Witwicki), which appeared posthumously in 1859 but seems to date from 1830.

Variant 2: Chopin as Performer

Although Chopin apparently ceased to improvise complete "works" in public after settling in Paris, innumerable accounts confirm that an improvisatory quality characterized his performances of composed music, including his own. Indeed, two hallmarks of his playing were spontaneity and variety. Alfred James Hipkins, who tuned Chopin's pianos during his stay in Britain in 1848, observed that he "*never* played his own compositions twice alike, but varied each according to the mood of the moment, a mood that charmed by its very waywardness."[20] In his memoirs, Charles Hallé similarly recalled how Chopin intentionally defied his own dynamic indications in a given performance of the Barcarolle, Op. 60, thereby heightening the music's expressive effect:

> In spite of his declining physical strength, the charm of his playing remained as great as ever, some of the new readings he was compelled to adopt having a peculiar interest. Thus at the last public concert he gave in Paris, at the . . . beginning of 1848, he played the latter part of his "Barcarolle," from the point where it demands the utmost energy, in the most opposite style, *pianissimo*, but with such wonderful nuances, that one remained in doubt if this reading were not preferable to the accustomed one. Nobody but Chopin could have accomplished such a feat.[21]

The improvisatory approach to rhythm that also distinguished Chopin's playing was noted by other witnesses, among them his pupil and associate Wilhelm von Lenz:

> In the fluctuations of speed, the holding back and pushing on [*Hangen und Bangen*], in rubato as he understood it, Chopin was charm itself; each note was rendered in the most perfect taste, in the noblest sense of the word. If he happened to improvise a *fioritura*—a rare occurrence—it was always somehow a miracle of good taste.[22]

It is interesting to compare this account of Chopin's improvised ornamentation with those of other witnesses. For example, Carl Mikuli—a prized student of Chopin—reported that the latter "took particular pleasure in playing . . . Field's Nocturnes, to which he would improvise the most beautiful *fiorituras*."[23] According to Mikuli's own pupil, Raoul Koczalski, "Chopin liked here and there to add ornamental variants [*Verzierungen*]" when playing his own compositions; furthermore, "Mikuli told me he had a particular predilection for doing this in the mazurkas."[24] These testimonies suggest that Chopin was inclined to add improvised ornaments especially when playing his nocturnes and mazurkas, no doubt because the rhythmic flexibility characteristic of each genre afforded variation of this kind.[25]

Ornamental variants that either are attributable to improvisatory playing or convey the "feel" of improvisation survive both in the annotated scores of Chopin's students and associates (among them, Jane Stirling, Camille Dubois, and Ludwika Jędrzejewicz) and in his own manuscripts. The Nocturne in E-flat Major, Op. 9, No. 2, is an especially interesting case, with some twenty known variants emanating from Chopin himself. These serve a number of functions: for instance, simulating vocal *portamento* by connecting discrete pitches with diatonic or chromatic slides (e.g., in mm. 4–5; see Example 1), replacing notated figuration with more ambitious *fioriture* (e.g., in mm. 14, 16, 22, and 24; see Example 2), and substituting altogether new material for the cadenza and the coda as published (Example 3).[26] Chopin certainly did not intend all such ornaments to be played in a single performance, which would be impossible in any case because multiple versions exist of some of them. Nevertheless, some pianists today include so many when performing the Nocturne that the effect can be overpowering. An altogether more convincing approach can be heard in the recordings by Raoul Koczalski, whose elegant playing

Example 1a

Example 1b

Example 1. Chopin, Nocturne in E-flat Major, Op. 9, No. 2, mm. 4–5.
a) As published in the French first edition (Paris: Schlesinger, 1833).
b) With variant reproduced in Mikuli's separate edition (Leipzig: Kistner, 1885).

of this nocturne accords with firsthand descriptions of Chopin's own performance style. Not only is Koczalski's choice of variants judicious and tasteful, but his execution is extremely subtle—especially the ravishing cascade in thirds at measure 24, which ends the main body of the work.[27]

Variant 3: Chopin as Composer

Like the variants that Chopin pencilled into the scores of students and associates, the printed ornamentation in his music as published often derives from an improvisando style—for instance, the many *fioriture* in works as stylistically disparate as concertos, nocturnes, and ballades; embellishments of cadences and fermatas (e.g., measure 132 of the *Grande Polonaise*, Op. 22, and measure 134 of the Ballade in F Minor, Op. 52; see Example 4); and cadenzas (e.g., in the introduction to the Variations on "Là ci darem la mano," Op. 2, and the Prelude in C-sharp Minor, Op. 45). Chopin clearly wanted the performance of these ornamental

Example 2a

Example 2b

Example 2. Chopin, Nocturne in E-flat Major, Op. 9, No. 2, mm. 14–15.
a) French first edition. b) Mikuli's 1885 edition.

passages to be improvisatory in character, as confirmed by markings like
senza tempo, used for the cadenza in the Nocturne in B Major, Op. 9, No.
3, and *sfogato* (poured out, unrestrained) in measure 77 of the Barcarolle,
Op. 60. Referring to the *delicatissimo* turning figure in measure 65 of the
Fantasy on Polish Airs, Op. 13 (see Example 5), Lenz commented: "It looks
so simple! Chopin used to say of these ornaments that 'they should sound
as though improvised, the result not of studying exercises but of your
sheer mastery of the instrument.'"[28]

Other "improvisatory" features of Chopin's compositions include *portamento* and *parlando* effects, which result from the composer's pianistic
reinterpretation of bel canto principles (see the second movements of
the two piano concertos); characteristic melodic and accompanimental
figuration, such as the left-hand chord-outlining pattern found in many

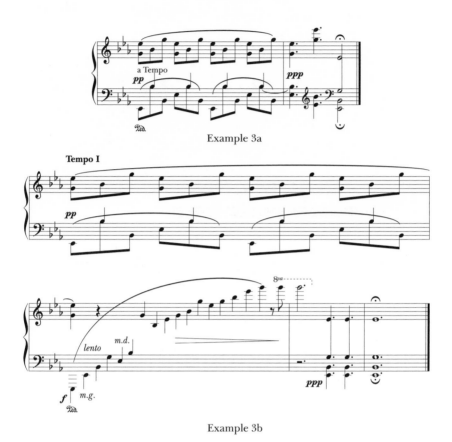

Example 3a

Example 3b

Example 3. Chopin, Nocturne in E-flat Major, Op. 9, No. 2, ending.
a) French first edition. b) Mikuli's 1885 edition.

of the nocturnes, which was designed to support a freely intoned melody above; and cross-rhythms, for example, "playing twos [and fives] against threes, each in a separate hand, which requires perfect independence of the hands for the parts to fall harmoniously into place," which Jean-Jacques Eigeldinger describes as an innovation involving both technical control and improvisatory flexibility to avoid the stiffness that a mathematically exact execution would convey.[29]

The influence of improvisation on Chopin's music extends beyond these surface features to the genres he used and to recurrent features of the music's large-scale organization.[30] The musicologist Ernst Oster alluded to this when stating that "some of [Chopin's] compositions, the Ballades or

Example 4a

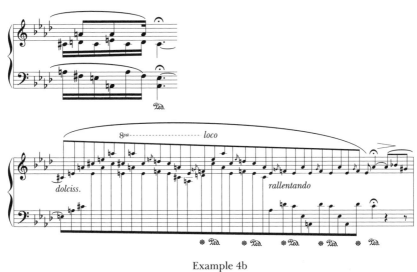

Example 4b

Example 4. "Improvisando" ornamentation.
a) Chopin, *Grande Polonaise*, Op. 22, measure 132.
b) Chopin, Ballade in F Minor, Op. 52, measure 134.

Example 5. Chopin, *Fantasy on Polish Airs*, Op. 13, measure 65.

the F-sharp Major Impromptu [Op. 36], are fantasies of the freest kind."[31] The successive genres invoked in the Impromptu recall the descriptions of Chopin's own improvisations cited above. As I have written elsewhere:

> One can hear a melodic "narration" at the opening, then a prayer, then a triumphal march, then a return of the narrative melody but in a succession of increasingly virtuosic variations; finally a return of the prayer and then a last, summarizing grand gesture which reminds one of the march, thus drawing together the principal ideas of an extraordinary composition.[32]

Similarly, Jim Samson refers to the thematic treatment in Chopin's Ballade Op. 52 as "a characteristic succession of contemporary improvisation, where the theme (on occasion supplied by an audience) would be played 'straight,' then processed in various ways, including canonic-fugal and cantabile-decorative styles." He notes moreover that "Cortot goes so far as to describe the work as a kind of 'stylized improvisation.'"[33] Other genres used by Chopin with a direct or indirect link to improvisation include preludes (Op. 28 and Op. 45) and fantasies (Fantasy, Op. 49, and *Polonaise-Fantaisie*, Op. 61).

References to the influence of improvisation on Chopin's compositional *process* can be found in primary and secondary sources alike. For instance, Gerald Abraham comments that in comparison with composers such as Beethoven, for whom "the printed notes" embodied a "practically immutable" ideal,

> Chopin's contact with his sound-medium was more immediate; the printed forms of his works were often, as his own numerous variants and changes of mind show, the records of music that, however finely polished and worked out, was originally and essentially keyboard improvisation; the record remained but the improviser's own moods constantly changed.[34]

This observation accords well with the accounts of (among others) George Sand and Chopin himself, who in several letters revealed that he composed at the piano, and that without an instrument he was unable to work. Writing from Palma in 1838 while he awaited shipment of a piano from France, Chopin complained to Camille Pleyel of his inability to compose: "I dream of music but I can't write any because there are no pianos to be had here—in that respect it is a barbarous country."[35] To Julian

Fontana he wrote: "Meanwhile, my manuscripts sleep, but I cannot sleep, only cough."[36]

George Sand's description of Chopin at work is particularly illuminating:

> His invention [*création*] was spontaneous, miraculous. He found it without seeking it, without anticipating it. It came at his piano, sudden, complete, sublime; or it sang in his head during a walk, and he grew anxious to hear it aloud by trying it out on the instrument. And thus began the most distressing labour I have ever witnessed. It was a series of efforts, of indecisions, of impatience to recapture certain details of the theme he had heard: what he had conceived all of a piece he then overanalyzed in trying to write it down, and his regret at not finding it in the form he considered just right threw him into despair. He shut himself in his room for days on end, weeping, pacing, breaking his pens, repeating and altering a single bar a hundred times, notating and then cancelling it no less often, and then starting again the next day with meticulous, desperate perseverance. He would spend six weeks on a page before coming back to what he had written on the first attempt.[37]

From this it appears that Chopin's compositional method amounted to a process of improvisatory trial and error, whereby an entire work would evolve from a single idea through experimentation and gradual refinement at the keyboard. Hence Jim Samson's assertion that

> Chopin's total involvement with the piano was right at the heart of his creativity. A composition would begin life at the piano, its overall conception already formed and its melodic and harmonic details often already realised before he set pen to paper. He drew much of his inspiration directly from his exploration of novel keyboard textures and sonorities and he allowed the limitations of the instrument to define the boundaries of an enclosed musical world which could "contain" the expressive extremes of a widely ranging language.[38]

One of the most distinctive stylistic elements resulting from Chopin's "improvisatory" compositional technique and from his close contact with the piano while composing is his use of harmony at both local and structural levels. Referring to specific passages in the composer's works, Abraham comments:

> There can be little doubt, I think, that Chopin's harmony—the most important, most individual, and most fascinating of all aspects of his music—was . . . largely inspired, or at any rate discovered . . . by improvisation at the keyboard. There may have been precedents for some of his harmonic exploits, notably in Spohr, but it is obvious that many of them were directly inspired by the timbre of the instrument or brought to light by the improviser's delicate fingers. And this is all the more important since even Chopin's basic ideas are frequently harmonic rather than melodic.[39]

Features arising from the music's origins at the piano keyboard include chains of parallel harmonies, both chromatic and diatonic, which would have been programmed into Chopin's "delicate fingers," as would some of the sequential progressions used by the composer (e.g., patterns based on fifths, thirds, and stepwise motion).[40] Especially striking cases can be found in the mazurkas, for example, Op. 6, No. 1, mm. 5–8; Op. 30, No. 4, mm. 128–32; and Op. 59, No. 2, mm. 81–88, respectively shown in Examples 6a, 6b, and 6c. The appearance of harmonic sequences in the introductions in certain early and late works alike (for instance the Rondo in E-flat Major, Op. 16, and the *Polonaise-Fantaisie*, Op. 61) also stems from improvisatory practices. This was a well-known device dating from the eighteenth century that helped improvisers "get the ball rolling" thanks to the momentum generated by the sequential models.[41] The use of ostinato in the left hand to support varied figuration in the right (for example, introduction in the *Fantasy on Polish Airs*, Op. 13, with a pedal point on the dominant supporting right-hand filigree, and the Berceuse, Op. 57, referred to by Chopin himself as "mes variantes" because of the successive melodic elaborations over a simple harmonic progression heard repeatedly in the lower part) also had a practical origin. Some of the figuration in question is archetypally improvisatory, as is the preluding figuration embellishing the harmonic sequences in the introduction of the *Polonaise-Fantaisie* and in the Fantasy, Op. 49. In the latter, prelude-inspired arpeggiations also have a significant "punctuating" role throughout the work.

The Fantasy, Op. 49, has other features that were typical of improvisatory practice, including both the recitative-like passage at the end

Example 6a

Example 6b

Example 6c

Example 6. "Improvisatory" harmonic progressions.
a) Chopin, Mazurka in F-sharp Minor, Op. 6, No. 1, mm. 5–8.
b) Chopin, Mazurka in C-sharp Minor, Op. 30, No. 4, mm. 128–32.
c) Chopin, Mazurka in A-flat Major, Op. 59, No. 2, mm. 81–88.

(compare the recitative-inspired conclusion to the Nocturne in B Major, Op. 32, No. 1) and a telltale succession of genres—among them different types of march—to which reference has already been made. In view of the work's title, one might expect Opus 49 to constitute an especially compelling example of Chopin's improvisatory playing, but the formal and harmonic structure underpinning the work is more complex and sophisticated than one would expect to find in improvised music, even that of an acknowledged master like Chopin.[42] The same holds for other compositions with an avowedly improvisatory character that realistically could not have been improvised in the form in which they were published, among them the Impromptu in F-sharp Major, Op. 36, and the Ballade in F Minor, Op. 52, discussed above. Here it is instructive to consider alongside Grzymała's claim that Chopin's improvisations were bolder than his finished pieces the converse observation that Chopin's compositions were undoubtedly more "worked out" than his improvisations ever could have been.

Coda: Recapturing the Art of Improvisation

However deep the gulf between music as improvised and music as published, it is possible for modern pianists to capture the feel of improvisation when performing works by Chopin. In this final section I offer comments and make recommendations toward that end.[43] The first issue to raise concerns the variety and spontaneity of Chopin's playing. Nothing would be more inimical to these qualities in one's own playing than a sense of inevitability, which unfortunately is what emerges in modern performances all too often. Even if the music is well known and thoroughly rehearsed by the performers in question, it must sound as if it is being discovered for the first time—as if it is being improvised. There are specific ways to create such an effect, and one of them is to avoid a foursquare tempo that ends up imposing metronomic rigidity. This does not mean that an excess of rubato is warranted: on the contrary, there is evidence that Chopin's playing was characterized not only by surface freedom but also by an underlying temporal logic. One of the best ways for modern pianists to achieve this essential synergy is to apply principles of breathing learned through collaboration with singers or wind players to their own work as solo pianists. This in itself will not make music sound improvised, but at the very least it will help avoid the formulaic regularity that blights some Chopin playing today.[44]

Linked to this is the possibility of embellishing one's performances with the variants that flowed from Chopin's pen. We know from the accounts cited above that no two performances of his were alike, and the modern pianist can engage in a similar flight of imagination by making judicious use of the variants now included in editions such as the *Wydanie Narodowe* (Polish National Edition) and *The Complete Chopin—A New Critical Edition* (published by Edition Peters). As a member of the jury of the Seventeenth International Fryderyk Chopin Piano Competition held in Warsaw in October 2015, I was struck by the fact that very few contestants ventured away from the printed score by introducing variants of the type that colored Chopin's own playing. Admittedly, this sort of "improvisation" poses challenges of all kinds, including the need to avoid the overpowering effect to which I previously referred, as well as the corresponding need to ensure that whatever material is added fits within the prevailing expressive context. Unfortunately, commercial recordings offer relatively few exemplars of "good practice" along these lines.[45]

Of course, the modern pianist could go further by improvising altogether new variants in the style of Chopin, even though this could invite accusations of "tampering" with the texts handed down to us by Chopin. On the other hand, one is most at risk of violating the spirit of Chopin by adhering too slavishly to the letter of the score. Clearly it is necessary to strike a balance between fidelity and innovation—though where that balance should fall is a matter of personal choice on the parts of performers and listeners alike.

As a pianist, I take liberties of this kind when playing certain works by Chopin but not others; for example, I would be reluctant to "tamper" with the texts of the sonatas, ballades, and scherzos, which do not lend themselves to such intervention. In contrast, I regard the Waltz in F Minor as ripe for this sort of improvisatory approach. For this attractive piece, which was composed in 1842 but never published during Chopin's lifetime, five distinct autograph manuscripts survive, along with a Polish edition dating from 1852 which was based on a sixth manuscript prepared by Chopin himself.[46] Each of these sources is unique in terms of both compositional details and, in one case, musical form. For this reason among others, it is impossible to regard one single source as necessarily definitive, just as it would be unjustifiable to conflate elements in a single consolidated edition as this would give a false impression of Chopin's variable intentions. That is why the *Waltzes* volume in *The Complete Chopin* contains three different versions: one based on the manuscript dedicated to Elise Gavard (MS 3 in Table 1); a second with multiple variants drawn from the other four surviving manuscripts (MS 1/2/4/5); and a third based on the Polish first edition (PFE) from 1852, which itself was prepared from the manuscript that Chopin inscribed in the album of Countess Plater (now lost). In the five surviving manuscript sources, the Waltz consists of a first section A,

Table 1. Waltz in F Minor: formal outlines in Chopin's manuscripts,
the Polish first edition, and the author's performance.

MSS 1–5:	A	A	B			
PFE:	A	A	B	*da capo*	A	B
Rink:	A1	A2	B1	*da capo*	A3	B2
	MS 3	MSS 1/2/4/5	MS 3	PFE	PFE	MSS 1/2/4/5

which is repeated, followed by a B section in the mediant key, A-flat major.
Only in the Polish edition is *da capo* indicated at the end of Section B, such
that one plays the A section a third time, followed by a repeat of the B section. As it happens, I was inclined to repeat the A and B sections in a *da capo*
of my own instigation long before I encountered the Polish edition, and
when I did discover it, I was reassured that an authoritative source backed
up my musical instincts. I then gained the courage to engage in a process
of improvisation along the lines of Chopin's own. Thus, rather than play all
of the sections identically on each of their appearances, I initially perform
Section A according to the Gavard manuscript; then, when repeating the
opening section, I freely intermix variants drawn on the spot from the
other four manuscripts,[47] thereby achieving the spontaneous variety for
which Chopin was noted. I proceed to play Section B in the Gavard version, which in essence serves as my "base text," with the *da capo* to follow.
On its third hearing, Section A is modeled upon the Polish edition, in which
the texture is fuller, thus justifying its use in the third and last appearance
of the section, while the ensuing repeat of Section B is flexibly embellished
with variants from the four manuscripts to which I have referred. Table
1 presents the formal pattern in the five manuscripts, the more elaborate
counterpart in the Polish first edition, and the basis of the "improvised"
version in my own performance. Example 7 shows an excerpt from Section
A in the three successive statements that I described above.

It must be emphasized that the aim of this "improvisation" is not
unbridled eclecticism or variety for the sake thereof: on the contrary,
what emerges is a "narrative" of sorts, progressing from simpler to more
embellished versions of the music in what ideally comes across like a natural flow of ideas. It goes without saying, however, that the extent to which
such an approach can be regarded as successful depends not only on the

Example 7a

Example 7b

Example 7c

Example 7. Chopin, Waltz in F Minor, mm. 17–20.
a) First statement: based on the Gavard manuscript.
b) Second statement: hypothetical, "improvised" version incorporating
variants from the other four surviving manuscripts.
c) Third statement: based on the Polish first edition (1852).
(Examples 7a and 7c from Chopin, *Waltzes*, ed. Grabowski; Example 7b
compiled by the author from disparate sources reproduced in the former).

nature of the flow and the combination of ideas, but also on the attitude
of listeners to such freedom and flexibility. Without wishing to justify
my approach or any spontaneous decisions I make as necessarily "right,"
I would nevertheless claim that only when modern musicians cease to
regard the composer's texts as sacrosanct and instead engage in the sorts
of practices for which Chopin himself was known can they begin to capture the sense of his music as it sounded two hundred years ago and as he
breathed life into it, in improvisation after improvisation.

NOTES

1. For a useful introduction to improvisation in the early nineteenth century, see Robert Wangermée, "L'improvisation pianistique au début du XIXe siècle," in *Miscellanea Musicologica: Floris van der Mueren* (Ghent: L. van Melle, 1950), 227–53.

2. Carl Dahlhaus, *Nineteenth-Century Music*, trans. J. Bradford Robinson (Berkeley: University of California Press, 1989), 140.

3. For further discussion, see *The Invention of Beethoven and Rossini: Historiography, Analysis, Criticism*, ed. Nicholas Mathew and Benjamin Walton (Cambridge: Cambridge University Press, 2013).

4. For further information, see Jim Samson, *The Music of Chopin* (London: Routledge and Kegan Paul, 1985).

5. See Jean-Jacques Eigeldinger, *Chopin: Ame des salons parisiens 1830–1848* (Paris: Fayard, 2013); John Rink, "The Legacy of Improvisation in Chopin," in *Muzyka w kontekście kultury*, eds. Małgorzata Janicka-Słysz, Teresa Malecka, and Krzysztof Szwajgier (Kraków: Akademia Muzyczna, 2001), 79–89; and Krystyna Kobylańska, "Les improvisations de Frédéric Chopin," *Chopin Studies* 3 (1990): 77–104.

6. Julian Fontana, preface to *Oeuvres posthumes pour piano de Fréd. Chopin* (Paris: J. Meissonnier fils, 1855), 1–2; translation from Jean-Jacques Eigeldinger, *Chopin: Pianist and Teacher, As Seen by His Pupils*, ed. Roy Howat, trans. Naomi Shohet with Krysia Osostowicz and Roy Howat (Cambridge: Cambridge University Press, 1986), 282.

7. Eugène Delacroix, *The Journal of Eugene Delacroix*, trans. Walter Pach (New York: Crown, 1948), 294.

8. For further discussion, see John Rink, "The Evolution of Chopin's 'Structural Style' and Its Relation to Improvisation" (PhD diss., University of Cambridge, 1989).

9. Kobylańska, "Les improvisations."

10. Two such instruments were the choralion and the eolipantalion, which were similar to the organ. See Halina Goldberg, *Music in Chopin's Warsaw* (New York: Oxford University Press, 2008), esp. 37–40.

11. Chopin to Woyciechowski, 27 March 1830, in *Chopin's Polish Letters*, trans. David Frick (Warsaw: Fryderyk Chopin Institute, 2016), 148.

12. J. N. Hummel, *Ausführliche theoretisch-practische Anweisung zum Piano-Forte-Spiel* (Vienna: Tobias Haslinger, 1827), 461; my translation.

13. Léon Escudier, "Concert de M. Chopin," *La France musicale* (2 May 1841), 156. See also Eigeldinger, *Chopin: Ame des salons parisiens*, 57.

14. H.-T. Poisson, "Concert," *Journal politique et littéraire d'Indre et Loire* (8 September 1833): 2–3, quoted in Eigeldinger, *Chopin: Ame des salons parisiens*, 60; my translation.

15. Elisa Fournier to her mother, dated 9–10 July 1846, quoted in Georges Lubin, *George Sand en Berry* (Paris: Hachette, 1967), 28–29; my translation.

16. See Halina Goldberg's account, in "Descriptive Instrumental Music in Nineteenth-Century Poland: Content, Genre, and Performance," *Journal of Musicological Research* 34/3 (Summer 2015): 226, of the "Concert of Concerts" of the innkeeper Jankiel in Adam Mickiewicz's 1834 epic poem *Pan Tadeusz*. Goldberg observes that "the 'Concert of Concerts' and the immensely popular descriptive instrumental compositions related to it, both Polish and foreign," provide a "backdrop against which the narrative works of Chopin and their reception can be better understood" (225). I would argue that the improvisations of Chopin as characterized both by the review of the 1833 Tours concert and by Elisa Fournier should similarly be understood against that backdrop, likewise the accounts of others who heard Chopin improvise.

17. Józef Bohdan Zaleski, personal diary (2 February 1844); translation adapted from Eigeldinger, *Chopin: Pianist and Teacher*, 283–84.

18. Ferdynand Dworzaczek, quoted in Paulina Wilkońska, *Moje wspomnienia o życiu towarzyskim w Warszawie* (Warsaw: PIW, 1959), 154; translation from Eigeldinger, *Chopin: Pianist and Teacher*, 284 (suspension points as in the original).

19. Eigeldinger, *Chopin: Âme des salons parisiens*, 66; my translation.

20. Alfred Hipkins, quoted in Edith J. Hipkins, *How Chopin Played: From Contemporary Impressions Collected from the Diaries and Notebooks of the Late A. J. Hipkins* (London: Dent, 1937), 7.

21. Charles Hallé, quoted in C. E. and Marie Hallé, *Life and Letters of Sir Charles Hallé* (London: Smith & Elder, 1896), 36.

22. Wilhelm von Lenz, *Die grossen Pianoforte-Virtuosen unserer Zeit aus persönlicher Bekanntschaft* (Berlin: Behr, 1872), 47; translation from Eigeldinger, *Chopin: Pianist and Teacher*, 52.

23. Carl Mikuli, Foreword to *Fr. Chopin's Pianoforte-Werke*, 17 vols. (Leipzig: Kistner, 1879–80), 1:3; translation from Eigeldinger, *Chopin: Pianist and Teacher*, 52.

24. Raoul Koczalski, *Frédéric Chopin: Betrachtungen, Skizzen, Analysen* (Cologne: Tischer & Jagenberg, 1936), 203; translation from Eigeldinger, *Chopin: Pianist and Teacher*, 52.

25. For further discussion, see Eigeldinger, *Chopin: Pianist and Teacher*, 120–22, nn. 98–99.

26. These variants have been compiled in the Nocturnes volume of the *Wydanie Narodowe* (Polish National Edition), ed. Jan Ekier and Paweł Kamiński (Kraków: Polskie Wydawnictwo Muzyczne, 1995), 22–25; see also the corresponding volume in the Wiener Urtext series. One of the most valuable sources of Chopin's variants is Carl Mikuli's separate edition of the Nocturnes, *Fr. Chopin's Es dur-Nocturne, Op. 9, No. 2*, published by Kistner in Leipzig in 1885; this can be viewed at http://www.chopinonline.ac.uk/ocve/.

27. Koczalski's recordings of Op. 9, No. 2, were released as Polydor 65786 (1925); Polydor 67246 (1938); and Mewa 33 (1948). There have been several reissues: Polydor 65786 was reissued in fragmentary form on *Raoul Koczalski Plays Chopin*, Pearl/Gemm 9472 (1991) and complete on *The Complete Raoul von Koczalski*, vol. 1, Marston 520632-3 (2010). Polydor 67246 appears on *Raoul Koczalski: Chopin, 4 Ballades*, Dante HPC042 (1996).

28. Wilhelm von Lenz, "Übersichtliche Beurtheilung der Pianoforte-Kompositionen von Chopin," *Neue Berliner Musikzeitung* 26/36 (1872): 283; translation from Eigeldinger, *Chopin: Pianist and Teacher*, 52.

29. Eigeldinger, *Chopin: Pianist and Teacher*, 19.

30. See Rink, "The Legacy of Improvisation in Chopin," 79–82, on which some of the ensuing discussion is based.

31. Ernst Oster, "The *Fantaisie-Impromptu*: A Tribute to Beethoven," in *Aspects of Schenkerian Theory*, ed. David Beach (New Haven: Yale University Press, 1983), 197–98.

32. Rink, "The Legacy of Improvisation in Chopin," 83. The intriguingly awkward transition in mm. 59–60 of the Impromptu hints at actual improvisatory practice: it is as if the fingers are stopping to "think" how to proceed from one passage to the next, without a clear goal having been identified. Although this reference to "thinking" may seem frivolous, it is precisely the characterization of improvisatory process put forward in David Sudnow, *Ways of the Hand* (Boston: MIT Press, 1978).

33. Jim Samson, *Chopin: The Four Ballades* (Cambridge: Cambridge University Press, 1992), 19.

34. Gerald Abraham, *Chopin's Musical Style* (London: Oxford University Press, 1939), 51.

35. Chopin to Camille Pleyel, 21 November 1838; translation from Fryderyk Chopin, *Selected Correspondence of Fryderyk Chopin*, trans. and ed. Arthur Hedley (London: Heinemann, 1962), 163.

36. Chopin to Julian Fontana, 14 December 1838; translation from *Chopin's Polish Letters*, 289.

37. George Sand, *Histoire de ma vie*, repr. in *Oeuvres autobiographiques*, ed. Georges Lubin, 2 vols. (Paris: Gallimard, 1971), 2:446; my translation.

38. Samson, *The Music of Chopin*, 4.

39. Abraham, *Chopin's Musical Style*, 77.

40. This sort of "programming" is essential in learning the art of improvisation. For discussion, see Jeff Pressing, "Improvisation: Methods and Models," in *Generative Processes in Music: The Psychology of Performance, Improvisation, and Composition*, ed. John A. Sloboda (Oxford: Clarendon Press, 1988), 129–78.

41. By way of example, compare the opening sequential progression in Mozart's Fantasy in C Minor, K. 475 with those in Chopin's Fantasy, Op. 49, and *Polonaise-Fantaisie*, Op. 61. See also John Rink, "Schenker and Improvisation," *Journal of Music Theory* 37/1 (1993): 1–54.

42. See Carl Schachter, "Chopin's Fantasy Op. 49: The Two-Key Scheme," in *Chopin Studies*, ed. Jim Samson (Cambridge: Cambridge University Press, 1988), 221–53.

43. See also Jonathan Bellman, "Improvisation in Chopin's Nocturnes: Some Suggested Parameters" (DMA diss., Stanford University, 1990), for discussion and examples of how the modern pianist might improvise ornaments in the Nocturnes, based on principles defined by the author.

44. See Jean-Jacques Eigeldinger, ed., *Frédéric Chopin: Esquisses pour une méthode de piano* (Paris: Flammarion, 1993), concerning Chopin's frequent references in his unfinished piano method to music's language-like properties, including the use of temporal and dynamic inflection to reflect as well as to engender a sense of musical meaning.

45. One exception is the 21-CD set of Chopin's complete works played on period instruments produced by the Narodowy Instytut Fryderyka Chopina (Fryderyk Chopin Institute): *The Real Chopin—Complete Works*, NIFCCD 000-020 (2010).

46. The sources are as follows: MS 1: autograph manuscript, dedicated and dated "à Mademoiselle Marie de Krudner, Paris le 8 Juin 1842," Bibliothèque nationale de France, Paris, W.20 (1); MS 2: autograph manuscript, dedicated and dated "à Madame Oury, Paris 10 Décembre 1842," private collection, United States; MS 3: autograph manuscript, dedicated "à Mlle Elise Gavard," Bibliothèque nationale de France, Paris, Ms. 117; MS 4: autograph manuscript, dedicated "à Mme la Csse Eszterhazy," Abbaye de Royaumont, Asnières-sur-Oise, F. Lang's collection; MS 5: autograph manuscript, bequeathed by the Rothschild family, Bibliothèque nationale de France, Paris, Ms. 110; PFE: Polish first edition (Kraków: I. Wildt, 1852), plate no. 3, based on autograph manuscript in album of Countess Plater (now lost). For further details, see Fryderyk Chopin, *Waltzes*, in *The Complete Chopin—A New Critical Edition*, ed. Christophe Grabowski (London: Edition Peters, 2006).

47. The "second statement" in Example 7b—which represents only one possible permutation—is based on MS 5, with material drawn from MS 1 and MS 4 in measure 18 (right-hand part) and from MS 1 and MS 2 in measure 19 (left-hand part).

Chopin Among the Pianists in Paris

SANDRA P. ROSENBLUM

When Chopin appeared on the scene there were no longer any truly original great pianists. Chopin introduced into piano music an element of which it had long been devoid: sensibility. He transformed the piano and gave it a soul. One would need to have heard him to know how the instrument was transfigured under his fingers. It had such an unparalleled charm, a kind of magnetism that was impossible to escape. Chopin has made of the piano a *solo* instrument.

In this respect he has had a great influence on the modern school. Some of us understood that a pianist had a more worthy purpose to fulfill than to astonish his listeners with wonders of a transcendent athleticism.

—Hippolyte Barbedette (1861)

In September 1831, after an eight-month stay in Vienna, followed by two months of traveling, Fryderyk Chopin arrived in Paris.[1] A virtual unknown, he had come to a city bubbling with artistic creativity. Among the multitude of pianists active there, Friedrich Kalkbrenner was generally regarded as the best, known especially for what Chopin called his "magical touch—an incredible smoothness and a mastery that is apparent in his every note."[2] The many others, although not all present simultaneously, included Ferdinand Hiller, Mme Marie Pleyel, Ignaz Moscheles, Franz Liszt, Sigismond Thalberg, and Henri Herz. Jan Ladislav Dussek and Felix Mendelssohn had appeared on the Paris stage earlier. While in the French capital, Chopin immersed himself in the world of opera and developed friendships with numerous opera stars. The French *grand opéra* influenced his harmonic and dramatic language, but it was the Italianate bel canto style that nourished his predilection for the singing tone. Yet, however French his disposition, the seeds for all these elements of his musical aesthetic and pianism were sown in Warsaw, long before he ever sought the wider world.

The Pianistic Environment in Chopin's Warsaw

Several musicians residing in and passing through Warsaw left their imprint on young Chopin's pianism. Wojciech (Adalbert) Żywny—born in Bohemia where he studied violin, piano, harmony, and counterpoint with Jan Kuchar, "from the [J. S.] Bach tradition"—was Chopin's piano teacher from 1816 to 1822, during which time he introduced his young pupil to Bach's *Well-Tempered Keyboard* and works from the classical repertoire.[3] Although Żywny was primarily a violinist, he gave piano lessons (of questionable quality) to many students. When Żywny decided that there was nothing more he could teach his talented twelve-year-old student, Chopin was left to his own devices.

Given the limited guidance from Żywny, Chopin might have turned for pianistic advice to Václav Vilém Würfel, a highly respected pianist and organist, with whom Chopin probably studied thoroughbass and the organ.[4] Adrienne Simpson observed that Würfel "often worked with young Fryderyk, on whom he had a strong influence."[5] This influence has not received much attention, but the older man's polonaises and *Grande fantaisie lugubre* strongly suggest that Chopin gleaned compositional ideas from him in addition to instrumental mastery.

Chopin's composition teacher at the Warsaw Conservatory was Józef Elsner, a leader in developing higher music education in Warsaw. He recognized Chopin's unique talent and predilection for the piano, allowing him to compose in the virtuoso genres then popular. Chopin's Variations Op. 2 on Mozart's "La ci darem la mano," the *Fantasia on Polish Airs*, Op. 13, *Rondo à la krakowiak* Op. 14, and the two concertos all represent particular styles of the day. But even in this repertoire there are glimpses of Chopin's innate predilection toward a refined legato cantabile—as opposed to the Viennese pearled style or *jeu perlé* preferred in Warsaw. Elsner corresponded with Chopin for some time after he arrived in Paris, trying to goad him into composing a Polish national opera, but Chopin had decided to concentrate his efforts in the pianistic realm. In a letter of 27 November 1831 to Chopin, Elsner explains his instructional principles: "To teach composition does not consist of setting down rules, above all when one is in the presence of students whose talents are obvious. Let them find out for themselves so that finally one day they may surpass themselves."[6]

The results of this philosophy were not long in appearing. The composition of Chopin's Etudes Op. 10, widely recognized as blazing the direction for Chopin's expansion of keyboard technique and artistry that led to that of the later Romantic period, had begun in Warsaw and continued in Vienna and Paris, where the etudes were published in 1833.

Following rapidly on their publication, the French journal *Le Pianiste* printed an extensive review. The anonymous author commented on their difficulty and innovative pianistic challenges. He noted, for instance, that the first etude "facilitates with intensity the extensions in the right hand and this in a completely new way." More significantly, he drew attention to their artistic merits, a quality unexpected from pieces in a genre that heretofore served purely pedagogical purposes:

> But beware! Do not judge them at the first or even second reading. Behave as you do with Lamartine's odes that you love so much. Look for the real meaning; discover the song, always graceful, but often enveloped in such a way as to make it difficult to find.
>
> From the outset this young author takes his place at the level of the great masters. . . . It was professed that he deserved the epithet enigmatic; I do not share this point of view. . . . Let us perhaps only say that Fr. Chopin's compositions belong to a separate order of things, but are always deserving of the trouble one will take to execute them well.[7]

The imaginative pianistic writing and unexpected profundity of the Opus 10 etudes could not have stemmed from Chopin's teachers; instead, Nicolò Paganini's Warsaw performances have traditionally been credited with providing the initial impulse toward their composition.

In his early years Chopin would also have had the opportunity to learn from performances by other first-rate artists, a host of opera stars, and several pianists in Warsaw whose performance styles he is known to have admired. These included Maria Szymanowska, Caroline de Belleville-Oury, Johann Nepomuk Hummel, and Aleksander Rembieliński. Among the earliest such performances was a private one by Rembieliński, who had arrived in Warsaw after six years in Paris and whom Chopin first described in a letter of 30 October 1825 to his friend Jan Białobłocki.

> Mr. Rembieliński . . . plays the piano as I have never heard anyone play before. You can imagine what a delight it was for us, who have never heard anything so excellent here. . . . I won't expand on my description of his quick, smooth, rounded manner of playing, but . . . his left hand is as strong as his right, which is an unusual thing in one person.[8]

This emphasis on truly equal hands resonates with the remark from Louis Adam, in his 1804 *Méthode de piano du Conservatoire*, that the left hand "should be trained in the same way as the right," avoiding a weak part near a brilliant one, and it would become a critical aspect of Chopin's unique pianism.[9] Writing again to Białobłocki, probably in June 1826, Chopin mentioned that he had been seeing Rembieliński fairly often. "You wouldn't believe how splendidly he plays."[10] No doubt the teenage Chopin and his pianist friend from Paris exchanged many ideas on pianism. To have equally well-developed technique in both hands would become a *sine qua non* for Chopin's oeuvre.

Chopin also held in high esteem the pianism of Maria Szymanowska, twenty-one years his senior. Before her first concert in Warsaw in March 1827, he wrote Białobłocki: "I will definitely be there and send you a report about the reception and the playing."[11] Unfortunately, no record of Chopin's further comments seems to exist. However, Maurycy Mochnacki, Chopin's friend and a leading Polish critic, described her playing in 1827 with words that resonate with later descriptions of Chopin's pianism:

> Beautiful and full touch, charming simplicity, and [a] high level of musical understanding, plus the avoidance of elaborate or forced ornamentation that destroys the serious flow of a harmonic progression. . . . By imitating the sound of the violin, Madame Szymanowska successfully improved the nature of her instrument. . . . In the *Adagio* [she] advanced the imitation of the human voice to the highest degree.[12]

Further in this article Mochnacki writes of the two schools of "forte-piano" playing, differentiated primarily by their touch. The first is exemplified by Clementi and Field, both of whom are associated with the sonorous English pianos that were conducive to a singing legato; the second by Moscheles and Hummel, who played the drier Viennese instruments. After further describing Szymanowska's playing, Mochnacki placed her in the English school.[13]

From Warsaw Szymanowska proceeded to St. Petersburg, where a review of her playing in the *Journal de St.-Petersbourg* included the following observations:

> Madame Szymanowska achieved a rare ability to induce the instrument to sing. . . . She was apparently able to benefit greatly from her study of the singing techniques of the best European singers. . . . Applying the imitation of human singing to an instrument that is not at all suited to that purpose

certainly required, besides hard work, a lot of thinking and an ability to plan ahead. . . . Following their [best singers'] example, she sometimes reaches a real *ad libitum*, not paying attention to the tempo and the meter of the musical work that she performs.[14]

Was this a somewhat vague description of Szymanowska's rubato? The vocalistic rubato Chopin realized at the piano held a steady tempo and meter in the accompaniment while allowing the melody to be performed *ad libitum*—of all types of rubato employed by Chopin, this was the most written about and most *mis*understood. Or was the reviewer describing a truly agogic rhythmic freedom, the lengthening or shortening of certain beats, which Chopin used as well, but in a disciplined way?

Chopin was also attentive to the pianism of Anna Caroline de Belleville(-Oury) who, although of French descent, had studied with Carl Czerny in Vienna between 1816 and 1820. She played in Warsaw in June 1830, when she and Chopin met. He wrote to his dear friend Tytus Woyciechowski that she plays "with an extraordinarily light touch, and very elegantly," traits consistent with his own pianism.[15] In 1842 he had occasion to present Belleville with the Waltz in F Minor, Op. 70, No. 2, and reminded her that the sound of Hummel's *Adagio* that he had heard her play some years ago at Erard's still sounded in his ears. "In spite of the grand concerts here, few piano performances can make me forget the pleasure of having heard you that evening."[16]

The critic William Gardiner adds another perspective on Belleville's playing:

> In the hands of Mademoiselle de Belleville, the piano-forte becomes another instrument. Her mode of treating it is strikingly new. . . . The fingers range not in the accustomed track, but strike, and rest upon the keys in every part; often sliding from back to front, as in the act of wiping them. This singular motion imparts to her adagios unspeakable richness.[17]

It is not unlikely that Chopin noted with approval her "sliding" on the keys, and the way this contributed to the effectiveness of her light touch and elegant aesthetic. This quality in Chopin's playing, much remarked upon over the years, came to be associated mostly with the French school: in addition to Kalkbrenner's advocacy of the caressing touch in his piano method, Chopin's fellow Paris-dwelling Pole, Antoine de Kontski, went into much greater detail in his own treatise.[18] However, this touch had earlier, non-French origins: Johann Joachim Quantz, referring specifically to the pianoforte, had noted its bene-fits in his mid-eighteenth-century flute treatise, and Johann Nicolaus Forkel had associated it with the key-board playing of J. S. Bach.[19] In this last case it seems to have come from clavichord playing, and naturally would have been most effective on eighteenth- and early nineteenth-century instruments, with their lighter touch and shallower key-depth, as well as on French instruments, in which that aesthetic survived longer than elsewhere.

Such a subtle approach to touch and articulation would have been particularly beneficial in evoking the different ways a singer might inter-pret an aria, realizing the syllables in different ways. The need for diverse kinds of articulation was acknowledged by Louis Adam, essentially the founder of the French school of pianism, in his 1804 treatise, and virtu-ally by all the important French pedagogues throughout the nineteenth century. Chopin's love of the opera and especially of the human voice were strong and pervasive influences on his compositional and perfor-mance styles. In a letter of 5 June 1830 to Tytus Woyciechowski he wrote about the singer Henriette Sontag, "a messenger from God, as some of her enthusiasts have rightly called her."[20] Chopin had already heard her several times and his remarks in this letter strongly reflect traits of his own music and playing: "Her voice is very well trained; her diminuendos are *non plus ultra*; her portamentos lovely and her rising chromatic scales especially are superb." Further on in this letter he says: "She has some ornamentations of an entirely new sort, with which she makes a huge impression, although not like Paganini. Perhaps it's because they are of a smaller sort. She seems to breathe into the stalls some sort of fragrance of the freshest flowers, and she caresses, delightfully, strokes the audience, but rarely does she move them to tears."[21]

Later in 1830 Chopin and Tytus left for Vienna, on the journey that ultimately brought Chopin to Paris. In a letter of 9 November 1830 he informed his family that in Wrocław (Breslau) he played the Rondo-Finale of the Concerto in E Minor and improvised on a theme from Auber's *La muette de Portici*:

> One of the local connoisseurs approached me and praised the novelty of the form, saying that he never had the oppor-tunity to hear anything in this form. I don't know who it was, but perhaps he was the one who understood me best.[22]

It is generally agreed that this "connoisseur" was August Kahlert, music critic for the local newspaper and friend of Robert Schumann.

Kahlert described Chopin as "almost frail with a pale face," then assessed his "peculiar way of handling the instrument" and his "exceptionally fully developed technique. . . . His playing eschews all heaviness, all shrill and glaring sounds that occur in usual piano technique. [His] melodiousness in the most difficult staccatos and arpeggios . . . is gained only after a full acquaintance with the new fingering." This he specifies as Chopin's use of the third, fourth, and fifth fingers of the right hand. Kahlert also observes that "Chopin adds an admirable melodiousness which is often lacking at the piano." He concludes that Chopin must have been trained in Clementi's manner of playing although he added considerable new difficulties.[23]

Thus Chopin's pianism was well formed by the time he arrived in Paris.

Chopin's Performances in France

While in Vienna Chopin had procured from Dr. Johann Baptist Malfatti—remembered mainly as Beethoven's physician—a letter of introduction to the opera composer Ferdinand Paër. This provided him entrée into the circle of musicians residing in Paris, including Friedrich Kalkbrenner. Although he was so impressed with Kalkbrenner's playing that he compared him to the illustrious Paganini, whom he had heard in Warsaw, Chopin wisely resisted a proposal from the virtuoso to study with him for three years; instead he began the arduous task of planning a concert to introduce himself to the public. The reviews of his playing at this early stage demonstrate that his pianism was immediately understood to be quite unlike any other and in particular unlike that of Liszt and Thalberg.

Chopin's first public concert in Paris took place on 26 February 1832. The centerpiece of the program was his own Concerto in E Minor, Op. 11, which—according to a review in *La Revue musicale*—was received with "as much astonishment as pleasure."[24] As in the Barbedette quotation that opened this essay, the reviewer (probably François-Joseph Fétis) emphasized Chopin's contribution to revitalizing piano music: "Here we have a young man who, giving himself over to his natural inclinations and following no models whatsoever, has effected, if not a total resuscitation of piano music, at least a part of what we have so long been searching for in vain. . . . There is vitality in his melody, fantasy in his passage-work, and originality in everything." Its faults, however, included "too many colorful modulations, so much confusion in the linking phrases that it sometimes seems as though one were hearing an improvisation rather than a finished composition." The playing of this young artist was "elegant, relaxed, and graceful; it is marked by both brilliance and clarity." The perceptive critic also noted that whereas Beethoven wrote "music for the piano," Chopin's music was "for pianists."[25]

Although the concert was an artistic success, it did not meet financial expectations. The hall was half empty and many in the audience were Polish émigrés. The concert also failed to generate the much-desired teaching engagements. In a letter of 25 April 1832 to Józef Nowakowski in Warsaw, Chopin wrote of the difficulty of finding students to teach in Paris and the even greater difficulty of arranging concerts. At the same time there was an epidemic of cholera that kept people disinclined to socialize.[26]

Three years later, by June 1835, Chopin had made his mark in this city so rich in pianists that it was occasionally referred to as Pianopolis. After discussing the abuses of the piano by others, a lengthy, anonymous article in *Le Pianiste* proclaimed:

> Without doubt, the group of pianists offers some exceptions; we cite in particular M. Chopin, who prefers *thought* to the tour de force, and whose compositions as well as manner of performing are distinguished by a correctness of design that has nothing shabby, confined, or too foreseeable; by an originality without pretension, a daring without indiscretion, a luster without showiness, an energy without punches, and an expression always clear, always felt, and deeply moving. M. Chopin has succeeded in singing on the piano, which is the most exceptional quality in this genre; above all he has succeeded in softening the tone of the instrument, removing a little of its characteristic dryness and disconnectedness. . . . The notes that he plays are ripe, while those of most of his colleagues are green. Beyond this, the characteristic in which M. Chopin demonstrates the most unquestionable superiority is the expression of gentle feelings that he creates with grace, simplicity, delicacy, and a freshness of unmatched imagery.[27]

This elegant summation of Chopin's attributes as a pianist emphasizes the highly cultivated vocalism that was favored by Parisians and for which French piano builders designed their instruments. His legato cantabile touch mitigated a little of the piano's dryness; "notes that are ripe" may refer to a richness of tone arrived at by his individual style of technique. Carl Mikuli, one of Chopin's most successful professional students, wrote later, "He treated the various styles of touch very thoroughly, more especially the full-toned legato."[28] The "full-toned legato" may refer to passages that Chopin marked *sostenuto*, especially when the texture changes from many short notes to longer ones. Examples include the A-major passage (measure 53) of the Waltz in A Minor, Op. 34, No. 2; the secondary theme (measure 41) of the opening movement of the Sonata in B Minor, Op. 58; and the secondary theme (measure 35) in the Impromptu in A-flat Major, Op. 29.[29]

The anonymous author then returns to his original theme that pianists of Chopin's style of playing are truly exceptional. For the great majority of others he uses adjectives such as disorderly (*désordonné*), vague, strange, unintelligible, or describes their performances as a tour de force—in sum, criticizes what we would call the "acrobaticism" or athleticism of most artists. He points out that "the majority have adopted Listz [!] as their leader." This theme is restated many decades later by Alfred James Hipkins, who traveled with Chopin during his stay in England and Scotland in 1848. He calls the performance style of Chopin's music in the late nineteenth century "pseudo Chopin," pointing out that "it comes filtered through the school and traditions of quite another piano genius, the pyrotechnic virtuoso Liszt."[30] Unfortunately, Liszt's widespread concertizing and the public admiration for his style of pianism led many other pianists to adopt his manner of playing for pieces well beyond Liszt's own repertoire.

Hipkins and many others positioned Chopin and Liszt as opposites: one spoke his most personal thoughts to the piano, the other made the piano into an orchestra. They were "as different from each other as Racine was different from Corneille," as Józef Brzowski put it.[31] While Liszt reveled in the adulation of public performances, Chopin tried to avoid them, telling his student Emilie von Gretsch that "concerts are never real music, that one must give up the idea of hearing in them the beauty of art." Emilie, however, "could not agree with him but rather ascribed the unnatural willfulness to his sorrow not to possess the strength anymore for performing."[32]

Between 1832, his first public appearance in Paris, and 1838 Chopin participated in only seventeen concerts, all but one announced in the press.[33] But not until March 1838 was he prevailed upon to offer a concert outside of Paris. It was his only one, in Rouen, given for the benefit of a compatriot in need, the violinist Antoni Orłowski, who had been Chopin's classmate at the Warsaw Conservatory. Interest in this concert was great enough for a French review of it to have been adapted into English—with some British restraint—and printed in the London journal *The Musical World*:

CHOPIN'S CONCERT AT ROUEN. — This is an event of great interest to the musical world. Chopin, who has for so many years withdrawn himself from the public, and permitted only a few friends to witness his extraordinary powers, might have been compared to the fabulous island on which only single travelers were permitted to land. But this musician, whom once to have heard was never to forget, has at length given a large public concert in behalf of a Polish countryman, and played before an audience of five hundred persons. Thus there only needed some call of benevolence, some recollection of the land of his fathers, to overcome his aversion to a public performance, and the effect was beyond everything. Every captivating melody, every delicacy of execution, every melancholy fantasy, the whole poetry of the art, penetrated and enraptured each individual of this large assembly, as heretofore the chosen few, who with a sort of devotion hung upon his strains. The whole room was as if electrified, and resounded with bursts of admiration. . . . When the question is asked, who is the first pianoforte player in Europe, Thalberg or Liszt? All may be able to say, as everyone who hears him does say, it is Chopin.[34]

This reviewer, like others, clearly focused on the sheer musicality, the originality of Chopin's conceptions, and the power of the performer's delicate execution. Thalberg's pianism was akin to Liszt's in its desire to please large audiences with virtuosic antics. Thalberg was also characterized as "cold and even glacial . . . the *imperator* of notes."[35]

Later, in a self-serving article about Chopin's concert of 1841, Liszt created a distinction between concert and salon:

In Monday's concert, Chopin had preferred to select from his works those furthest from classical forms. He did not perform any concerto, sonata, or variations, but preludes, studies, nocturnes, and mazurkas. Speaking to a circle [*une société*] rather than a public, he could show with impunity the melancholy, deep, chaste and dreamy poet that he is. . . . He was seeking delicate sentiments rather than noisy enthusiasm.[36]

Escudier wrote of the same concert: "Chopin is a pianist of conviction. He composes for himself, he plays for himself."[37]

Rather than the public concert, Chopin's preferred venue was the salon; here the intelligentsia gathered to discuss politics, the arts, and listen to him play his latest, sometimes unpublished pieces, followed by improvisation.[38] Berlioz opined that in the salons Chopin "gave the best of himself."[39] Among those he frequented most was that of the Marquis Astolphe de Custine, known for his spirit of independence and liberalism. A letter from Custine to Chopin of early July 1836 offered just such an invitation: "Play for us what you have recently composed and improvise whatever strikes you."[40] By 1840, in a letter to his friend Varnhagen d'Ense, Custine described Chopin as "the first pianist of the world, not excepting Liszt and Thalberg."[41]

Here is Elise Fournier's (née Giraud) letter of 10 July 1846 to her mother, reporting the preceding evening at George Sand's estate in Nohant:

> What an evening we have spent, dear Mama! . . . You would have been so happy, as we were, to hear Chopin's admirable talent. He was infinitely compliant . . . and only around midnight ceased taking us, as he pleased, through all the happy and sad, cheerful or serious emotions, following what he himself was feeling. In all my life I have never heard such a talent, prodigious in its simplicity, sweetness, kindness, and humor. In this last mood he played a caricature of one of Bellini's operas that made us roar with laughter, such was his acuity of observation and his spiritual mockery of Bellini's style and musical habits; then a prayer of Poles in their distress that brought us to tears; then an etude on the sound of alarm that brought us to shivering; then a funeral march so somber, so grave, so painful that our hearts were swelling, our chests tightening. . . . We could hear only the sound of a few sighs ill-contained by an emotion too deep to be controlled. . . . After a moment of rest . . . he made us listen to pretty airs of a dance called *la bourrée* . . . [and then] ended this long . . . exhibition by a tour de force. . . . He imitated on the piano the little pieces of music we lock up in snuff boxes, key racks, etc., with such truthfulness . . . that we could never have believed it was a piano sounding. . . . All this pearling, this refinement, this speed of little steel tongues that make an imperceptible cylinder vibrate, was rendered with unrivalled delicacy that was barely heard. . . . [Suddenly it was] interrupted by the machine, which probably had something wrong with it. Chopin played one of those airs for us . . . for

which the cylinder was missing a note, and [as he played] this note always "clicked" every time it should have played.[42]

Georges Mathias, who taught advanced piano classes at the Paris Conservatory and was one of Chopin's most successful former students, wrote an extended preface for a volume of exercises taken from Chopin's works, compiled by the Conservatory professor and his former student Isidor Philipp. Here Mathias tried to describe the range of emotions encompassed in Chopin's performances of his compositions. In the nocturnes, one of the genres received with most approbation by the French, he found tenderness, charm, and terror:

> Expressions of intimate grief; some measures . . . that throw you into the abyss . . . terrible oppression bordering on death (first nocturne, Op. 27); ecstasies broken by sobs; delicious caresses. . . . The genius has inspired him and has consumed him. . . . [A] singular thing, this divine poet in music was also a technician of the first order: perhaps no one has contributed to the extension of the capacities of the piano as much as he.[43]

The descriptions of Chopin's playing in France indicate that he was instantly recognized as being highly original. In addition, his expressivity in many different moods, as well as the elegance and delicacy of his execution, pierced the souls of his listeners, winning plaudits from most critics and the general public alike.

Touch, Articulation, and Pedagogy in the French School of Pianism

The piano was developing rapidly during the first half of the nineteenth century, and nowhere more so than in France. Erard and Pleyel were the chief competitors in Paris, where the musical environment focused on vocal music, especially opera, so their principal goal was to create an instrument that could sing.[44] The aesthetic issues of particular importance to the authors of French piano methods—articulation and touch, especially in relation to singing legato tone, and approaches to tempo rubato—were the same in which Chopin distinguished himself.

The importance of legato was highlighted in the first French piano method written expressly for the instruction of the students at the newly founded Paris Conservatoire, the *Méthode de piano du Conservatoire* by

Louis Adam (1804). Although larger and more inclusive than Muzio Clementi's *Introduction to the Art of Playing on the Piano Forte*,[45] the *Méthode* of Adam is closely related to the earlier tutor. Among other adoptions, Adam showed Clementi's three manners of detaching notes, but quantified his rather vague descriptions. According to Adam, a note under a vertical dash loses three-fourths of its value; under a dot one-half its value; dots on several notes under a slur lose one-quarter of their value. This last he called *notes portées* (*portato* in today's parlance).[46] Adam also followed Clementi in stating that when the choice of "the *legato* or of the *staccato* is left to the taste of the executant, it is best to adhere to the *legato* and reserve the *staccato* to throw certain passages into relief" and by contrast to perceive the advantages of the legato.[47]

Not surprisingly, then, much of the attention in the three-volume *Cours complet pour l'enseignement du forte-piano*, published ca. 1820 by the pianist and teacher Madame Hélène de Montgeroult, is focused on making the piano sing. "The art of singing well is the same on any instrument," writes Montgeroult. She points out that one ought not make concessions or sacrifices because of the mechanism of interpretation, but asks how one can attain this singing tone on an instrument whose means are so limited? Illusion ought to come to the rescue, she concludes, and so she describes the Italian school of operatic singing, which the pianist ought to emulate: "The breath can take a little more or a little less time in every measure, yet the orchestra keeps a steady beat; but the singer unfolds the course of the phrase freely and it is only at the end [of the phrase] that he has to find himself in time again with the orchestra. . . . When applying this procedure to the Piano, one finds that the right hand, which plays the melody, can be compared to the singer, and the left hand to the orchestra which accompanies it."[48]

Throughout her volumes Montgeroult applied this vocalistic rubato to the piano as a means of sustaining the sound or "singing on the piano," with instruction on the appropriate embellishment of melodies to enhance the legato lines. It is a type of rubato first described by the castrato singer Pier Francesco Tosi in 1723 and clarified by his translator, Johann Ernst Galliard, in 1742.[49] Its tradition was carried on by C. P. E. Bach, Louis Adam, and many others, and its notated usage appears sporadically in the music of Mozart, Haydn, and Beethoven. Its application became a prominent issue in the performance of Chopin's music. In fact, it was so often *mis*understood that one of his best students and sometime assistant Camille O'Meara Dubois took the opportunity to emphasize its correct use in her very brief invited "letter" for the introduction to *Frédéric Chopin: De l'interpretation de ses oeuvres*,[50] by Jan Kleczyński, a Pole who studied piano with Antoine Marmontel and was mentored on the interpretation of Chopin's works by Dubois and another Chopin pupil, Princess Marcelina Czartoryska. In approving Kleczyński's criticism of amateurs who use an exaggerated rubato in Chopin's music, she wrote, "Let me recall a counsel of my beloved master: 'That your left hand be your choir master and always guard the beat.'"[51] Indeed, today this rubato is usually called "contrametric."

Shortly after he arrived in Paris, Chopin wrote to Tytus that Herz, Liszt, and Hiller "are all zeroes compared with Kalkbrenner."[52] In 1831 the reigning virtuoso was greatly admired for his smooth, sustained, harmonious playing, a marvelous sonority, a faultless neatness in the most difficult passages, and a left-hand bravura without equal. Tranquility of the arms and body allowed his audience to listen without being distracted by gymnastics, however, "Kalkbrenner's phrasing lacked somewhat in expression and communicative warmth, but the style was always noble, true, and of the grand school."[53] Many considered him a product of Clementi's pianistic style.

Kalkbrenner's *Méthode pour apprendre le pianoforte*, published ca. 1830, like the methods of Alexis de Garaudé (1820) and Henry Lemoine (1827), also includes the four types of touch described by Adam, whose student he had been. However, Kalkbrenner adds that the notes under dots and a slur "should be played [*porter*] as if with one finger."[54]

Six pages later the term "caressing" appears: "The manner of attacking a note ought to be infinitely varied, according to the different feelings one wants to express; sometimes through caressing the key, sometimes through hurling oneself on it as the lion who seizes its prey."[55] The original English translation of 1837 is less colorful, forgoing the lion and instructing that "a gentle caressing pressure of the keys will draw forth a mellow soothing quality of tone, while in *forte* passages the utmost decision and energy is required to produce the desired effect."[56] Kalkbrenner never described what he meant by "caressing" the keys, but Charles Timbrell opined that it is "sliding the finger from the middle to the edge of the key with a gentle pressure."[57] To me, Kalkbrenner's statement about the "manner of attacking a note" implies that in addition to the movement of the finger on a key, the sound is also affected by the manner in which the muscles are prepared. Chopin's approach emphasized a supple hand and relaxed wrist.

In 1840 Pierre Zimmerman, the most influential professor of piano at the Paris Conservatoire from 1816 to 1848, published his own three-volume *Encyclopédie du pianiste compositeur*. He also emphasized finger-based technique, pointing out that "the arm is a bad assistant that one ought to learn to pass over. . . . If one strikes the piano it gives in exchange a dry and shrill sound."[58] Several points of interest in this tutor stand out. Zimmerman's description of the much-discussed *portato*, indicated by staccato dots under a legato slur, seems to imply a sliding withdrawal from the key as well as a unique reference to the voice. Such notes "are played heavily; the finger seems to withdraw from the keys with effort. There should be no separation at all. Often these sorts of notes are played with a single finger. In that way it is the imitation of a voice having difficulty breathing."[59] See Examples 1a and 1b for Zimmerman's illustration and a cognate figure in Chopin's Nocturne in G Minor, Op. 37, No. 1.

The numerous descriptions of the realization of *portato* passages are but one indication that during the first half of the nineteenth century there must have been multiple nuances of touch that could scarcely have been notated or described. Using Chopin's music as his example, Zimmerman also emphasized the importance of the pianist recognizing the individual style of each composer:

> Accuracy is . . . so strictly necessary for the good execution of a piece of music that I consider it a duty that one must absolutely achieve; but it is not enough for the artist to limit himself to accuracy. It is the spirit of the author that one must reproduce.
>
> [Chopin's] music has a character that permits one to relax the rigorous observance of the beat a bit. . . . But it is a question for certain pieces of this master, of only a certain ease [*abandon*] filled with the indescribable charm under the fingers of the author. Chopin, like any original talent, cannot be imitated; however, one must try to enter into the spirit of his compositions in order not to do the opposite.[60]

Relaxing the rigorous observance of the beat was another type of rubato practiced by Chopin. According to his former student Karol Mikuli, this consisted of "accelerating or slowing down this or that theme. . . . It always justified itself by a strengthening or weakening of the melodic line, by harmonic details, by the figurative structure."[61] This may be termed agogic rubato, in contrast to the contrametric rubato described above.[62]

Georges Mathias offers these amusing thoughts on the abuse of rubato:

> Very often when one hears the music of Chopin one is exasperated by use of the *rubato*, used at every opportunity, used to the utmost, at random without rhyme or reason. It is

Example 1a. Zimmerman, *portato* example in *Encyclopédie du pianiste compositeur,* 1:41.

Example 1b. Chopin, Nocturne in G Minor, Op. 37, No. 1,
measure 6 (transcribed from the French first edition).

the fault of many amateurs, and it is also necessary to say:—it is the fault of many artists.

Do you know those mirrors that reflect your image all distorted, that make you burst out laughing?—Exaggerated *rubato* is exactly that.[63]

The year 1840 also saw the publication of the *Méthode des méthodes de piano,* whose authors were François Fétis (editor of *La Revue et gazette musicale*) and Ignaz Moscheles.[64] Fétis wrote the lengthy text; Moscheles provided the simple exercises and some etudes, and commissioned the remaining etudes from among the better-known pianists of the day, including Chopin, some of whose aesthetic innovations left him with decidedly mixed feelings.[65] The text reflected a conservative bent: fingering should be symmetrical; wrists remain quiet; large leaps of the hand (a tenth or more) are a difficult characteristic of "modern music"; instructions for using the damper pedal are elementary; and heavy use of exercises is advocated to achieve each goal. The authors also rely on frequent references to the playing of Clementi and Kalkbrenner as paragons of a pure style.

In his influential earlier set of *Studies for the Piano Forte,* Op. 70, published in 1825, Moscheles also presented the commonly described three ways of shortening notes, adding that if staccatos under a slur were in slow movement, "the notes must be held nearly their full length, so as to leave betwixt each notes but a very slight break."[66] This is the traditional *portato*. According to Mathias, Moscheles expressed himself "with chagrin on the subject of stretches of a tenth, so frequent in the music of Chopin: they annoyed Moscheles who found that it was an unnecessary difficulty."[67] Moscheles—who was born in 1794 and had been friendly with Beethoven—was thus a link between the Classical and Romantic schools of pianism.

Additional descriptions of how to render the notes with dots under a slur emphasize again the variety of touch that was expected in fine performance. In 1845 Antoine Kontski (Antoni Kątski), a compatriot of Chopin, published his tutor, *L'indispensable du pianiste*. Without showing notes under a slur, he described a *"carezzando"* touch that he indicated by the sign (o) over each note. It meant that after striking the key very delicately, the forearm "must draw backward, and from that the finger will slide to the end of the key" (which is strikingly similar to Timbrell's surmise about Kalkbrenner's "caressing" touch quoted above). In Kontski's example those notes lose about a quarter of their value as normally described for the *portato* touch; however, along with caressing the key, he advises use of the pedal to sustain the sound and make the piano sing.[68] This so-called *carezzando portato* with pedal legato was a new turn. Not everybody responded favorably to the idea, however. Some years later a critic in *Neue Zeitschrift für Musik* wrote that "the touch will never become clear to anyone from Kontski's description."[69]

Chopin's "Projet de Méthode"

In this environment, with many shades of opinion on technique, performance, and aesthetics, Chopin was perceived as unique. Toward the end of his life he began a piano method, which would remain unfinished—it is now usually called the "Sketch for a Method"—in which many of his observations show him to be the "thinking" virtuoso: "I suggest some practical and *simple* ideas which I know from experience to be really useful. As art is infinite within the limits of its means, so its teaching should be governed by the same limits in order to give it boundless potential."[70] Music, he said, was "the art of expressing one's thoughts through sounds."[71]

Chopin's difference from his colleagues as pianist and teacher is already discernable on the first page of the "Sketch" where he introduces the scale of B major, fingered for two octaves. He preferred starting students with the B scale rather than C, which has no natural pivot point for the hand. Later, he offers the instruction to place the fingers on the keys from E to B in the B scale. This puts the three long fingers on the short black notes and is the most congenial position for the hand as a starting point. Unsurprisingly, he wrote a number of exercises in his sister Ludwika's copy of the manuscript specifically using this position.

Chopin did not believe in a plethora of exercises and taught technique only as it would serve interpretation: "A well-formed technique is . . . [one] that can control and vary a beautiful sound quality."[72] Clearly, touch and tone were at the core of Chopin's playing and teaching. Jan Kleczyński described Chopin's five-finger exercises using different touches on E, F♯, G♯, A♯, B. First exercise: staccato "effected by a free movement of the wrist"; second, a "legato staccato . . . in which the finger rests somewhat longer on the key" (usually termed *portato*); third, an "accented legato" in which the dots under the slur are replaced with accents; fourth, slurred notes.[73]

Could Kleczyński's account of Chopin's accented legato be related to Thalberg's description of notes with dots under a slur, which "are to be neither slurred nor detached, but produced as they are by the human voice, the first ones a little more forcibly sounded than the rest"?[74]

Chopin's idea of finger independence also differed from that of his contemporaries, who, he wrote, mistakenly trained all fingers to be equally powerful. He relied on the shape of the hand to develop the strength of each finger for its best use: "A supple hand; the wrist, the forearm, the arm, everything will follow the hand *in the right order.*"[75] He stressed that "one cannot try to play everything from the wrist, as Kalkbrenner claims."[76] However, Chopin's free, relaxed wrist was certainly novel compared with Fétis's limitations on the use of the wrist. Emilie von Gretsch was instructed that where a singer would breathe in a bel canto line, an accomplished pianist should raise the wrist, then let it fall on "the singing note with the greatest suppleness imaginable."[77]

Henry F. Chorley, a music critic for the London *Athenaeum*, left other noteworthy observations of Chopin's playing. One was quoted in an otherwise unpublished article that Hipkins contributed to Joseph Bennett's serialized biography of Chopin: "M. Chopin's notation is, by fits, needlessly teasing—his harmonies, from time to time, are such as require his own sliding, smooth, delicate finger[s] to 'carry off.'"[78] Was this sliding a stroking of the key from back to front, about which much has been written, or merely sliding from black to white note or sideways from white to white?

Chorley offers particularly insightful observations on Chopin's playing in his review of a later matinée:

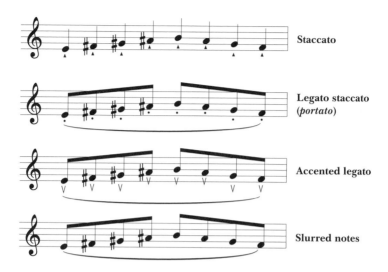

Example 2. Kleczyński's description of the varieties of Chopin's touch.

His treatment of the pianoforte is peculiar, and though we know that a system is not to be "explained in one word," we will mention a point or two entirely novel. . . . Whereas other pianists have proceeded on the intention of equalizing the power of the fingers, M. Chopin's plans are arranged so as to utilize their natural inequality of power, and, if carried out, provide varieties of expression not to be attained by those with whom evenness is the first excellence. Allied with this fancy are M. Chopin's . . . manner of sliding with one and the same finger from note to note, by way of producing a peculiar *legato*, and of passing the third over the fourth finger. . . . After the "hammer and tongs" work . . . to which we have of late years been accustomed, the delicacy of M. Chopin's tone and the elasticity of his passages are delicious to the ear. He makes a free use of *tempo rubato*, leaning about within his bars more than any player we recollect, but still subject to a pre-siding sentiment of measure such as presently habituates the ear to the liberties taken. In music not his own we happen to know he can be as staid as a metronome, while his mazurkas, &c., lose half their characteristic wildness if played without a certain freak and license—impossible to imitate, irresistible if the player at all feels the music.[79]

Chorley's reports concur with much that we know about Chopin's teaching and the information in his "Sketch." For example, Chopin tells us that there are "as many sounds as there are fingers." The rhythmic license Chopin used in playing the mazurkas was often termed a Polish or nationalist rubato, distinct from the contrametric and agogic rhythmic freedoms already described, though in all probability his playing was characterized by a free and shifting mix of all three.[80] Yet, whatever he discovered while still in Poland, his varieties of articulation, touch, and understated aesthetic also clearly resonated alike with the aesthetic of the Parisian virtuosi and with their audience.

Conclusion

All who heard Chopin play agreed that he was a unicum who could not be classed in any school. As early as 1834, shortly after the publication of the Etudes Op. 10, A. Guémer wrote that "terms of comparison are absolutely lacking. . . . With him thought, style, conception, even to the fingering, everything shows him to be an individual."[81] He was indeed unique, even if in the early years Chopin's Parisian listeners associated him with Field or Kalkbrenner. What all three pianists had in common were elegance and restraint that did not disappear with Chopin but faded out gradually toward the end of the nineteenth century. As pianos grew more powerful and concert halls became larger, Chopin—the most persuasive exponent of the intimate pianistic aesthetic—came to be interpreted in ways alien to his own distinctive style. Today some scholars and pianists are striving to rediscover a manner of playing more attuned to his personal idiom.

In his own time, however, music connoisseurs understood Chopin's intimate style as the pinnacle of art. Marmontel, who heard Chopin play numerous times, summed this up eloquently:

> If we look for a point of comparison between Chopin's effects of sonority and certain procedures of painting, we can say that that great virtuoso inflected sound as the skillful painters handle light and the surrounding air. To wrap melodic phrases, ingenious arabesques of ornaments, in a mezzotint that floats [tient] between dream and reality, that is the summit of art, and it was the art of Chopin.[82]

And from a societal viewpoint, Chopin's impact on his listeners is well drawn in the prescient letter Custine sent to him in February of 1848, before the ailing genius fled to London to escape the uprising in Paris. Much about it rings true in the present day:

> You have gained in suffering and poetry. The melancholy of your compositions penetrates still further into our hearts; one is alone with you in the middle of a crowd. It is not a piano, but a soul [that plays], and what a soul! Preserve yourself for your friends; it is a comfort to be able to hear you sometimes. In the difficult days that threaten us, only art as you feel it can reunite men who are divided by the reality of life. One may love and understand each other through Chopin. You have turned the public into a circle of friends; finally, you are equal to [the demands of] yourself. That says it all.[83]

NOTES

1. The epigraph is from Barbedette's *Essai de critique musicale* (Paris: Leiber, 1861); original French in *Chopin and His Critics: An Anthology*, ed. Irena Poniatowska et al. (Warsaw: Fryderyk Chopin Institute, 2011), 362 (trans. Nicole Bernstein).

2. Chopin to Tytus Woyciechowski, 12 December 1831, in *Chopin's Polish Letters*, trans. David Frick (Warsaw: Fryderyk Chopin Institute, 2016), 245.

3. On Żywny and the Bach tradition, see Jim Samson, *Chopin* (New York: Schirmer Books, 1996), 13. At this time Bach was not widely known in Poland but this early exposure to his music left an indelible mark on the style and texture, especially regarding counterpoint, of Chopin's music.

4. Halina Goldberg, *Music in Chopin's Warsaw* (New York: Oxford University Press, 2008), 111–15.

5. Adrienne Simpson, "Václav Vilém Würfel," *Grove Music Online, Oxford Music Online*. Oxford University Press, accessed August 7, 2016, http://www.oxfordmusiconline.com. proxyiub.uits.iu.edu/subscriber/article/grove/music/30621.

6. Józef Elsner to Chopin, in *Correspondance de Frédéric Chopin*, ed. Bronislas Edouard Sydow, 3 vols. (Paris: Richard Masse, 1981), 2:35 (trans. Nicole Bernstein).

7. Anonymous, *Le Pianiste* 1 (November 1833): 6 (trans. Nicole Bernstein).

8. Chopin to Białobłocki, *Chopin's Polish Letters*, 66.

9. Louis Adam, *Méthode de piano du Conservatoire* (Paris: Au Magasin de Musique du Conservatoire Royale, 1804), 66.

10. Chopin to Białobłocki, *Chopin's Polish Letters*, 74–75.

11. Ibid., 85.

12. Quoted in Sławomir Dobrzański, *Maria Szymanowska: Pianist and Composer* (Los Angeles: Figueroa Press, 2006), 47; originally from *Antologia polskiej krytyki muzycznej XIX i XX wieku* (Anthology of Polish Music Criticism), ed. Stefan Jarociński (Kraków: Polskie Wydawnictwo Muzyczne, 1955), 45, 44. Translation slightly amended.

13. For more about this article by Mochnacki, the two types of pianos and the playing that each fostered, as well as Chopin's change from one type to the other in his last two Warsaw concerts, see Halina Goldberg's unique volume, *Music in Chopin's Warsaw*, esp. 43–53.

14. Quoted in Dobrzański, *Maria Szymanowska: Pianist and Composer*, 48; originally from Igor Belza, *Maria Szymanowska* (Kraków: Polskie Wydawnictwo Muzyczne, 1958), 89.

15. Chopin to Tytus Woyciechowski, 5 June 1830, *Chopin's Polish Letters*, 164.

16. Chopin to Mme. Anna Caroline de Belleville-Oury, 10 December 1842, *Correspondence de Frédéric Chopin*, ed. Sydow, 3:125 (trans. Nicole Bernstein).

17. William Gardiner, *The Music of Nature* (Boston: Sanborn, Carter, and Bazin, 1856), 185–86, in the London printing of 1837, cited by Jonathan Bellman in "Frédéric Chopin, Antoine de Kontski and the *Carezzando* Touch," *Early Music* 29/3 (August 2001): 240, 245.

18. Frédéric Kalkbrenner, *Méthode pour apprendre le piano-forte à l'aide du guide-mains* (Paris: 1831, repr. 1850), 12; Antoine de Kontski, *Indispensable du pianiste* (Paris: 1845), 15–17 in the 1851 edition.

19. J. J. Quantz, *Essay of a Method for Playing the Transverse Flute*, trans. and ed. E. Reilly (London: Faber and Faber, 1966), chap. 17, 259. For Forkel's thoughts on Bach's touch see J. N. Forkel, *On Johann Sebastian Bach's Life, Genius, and Works*, 1802, trans. A. C. F. Kollmann (1820?), in Hans T. David and Arthur Mendel, eds. *The New Bach Reader*, rev. and enl. Christoph Wolff (New York: W. W. Norton, 1998), Part 6, 432–33.

20. Chopin to Woyciechowski, *Chopin's Polish Letters*, 162.

21. Ibid., 164.

22. Chopin to his family, 9 November 1830, ibid., 195–96.

23. Karol Musioł, "Echoes of Chopin's Wrocław Concert in Musical Criticism and in Literature," from *Chopin in Silesia*, trans. and slightly amended by C. Boniakowski (Katowice: PWSM, 1974), 6–8. Kahlert's perceptive critique was originally published in a supplement to the Berlin periodical *Der Gesellschafter* of 1834 titled "Über Chopin's Klavier–Kompositionen." See further excerpts in Jean-Jacques Eigeldinger, *Chopin: Pianist and Teacher, As Seen by His Pupils*, ed. Roy Howat, trans. Naomi Shohet, Krysia Osostowicz, and Roy Howat (Cambridge: Cambridge University Press, 1986), 289–90.

24. The confusion regarding which of his two concertos Chopin played on this occasion is elegantly discussed by Jean-Jacques Eigeldinger in "Chopin's First Concerts in Paris (1832–1838): A Clarification," in *Music in Paris in the 1830s*, ed. Peter Bloom (Stuyvesant, NY: Pendragon Press, 1987), 296–97.

25. *La Revue musicale*, 3 March 1832, 38–39. Translated by Peter Bloom in *Source Readings in Music History*, ed. Oliver Strunk and Ruth Solie (New York: W. W. Norton, 1998), 82.

26. Chopin to Józef Nowakowski, *Chopin's Polish Letters*, 259.

27. *Le Pianiste* 2/15 (5 June 1835): 119. Although many of this journal's articles were published anonymously, the writers were very often Henri Lemoine or Charles Chaulieu, both products of Louis Adam at the Conservatoire. See Shaena B. Weitz, "*Le Pianiste* and Its History of Pianism in Paris," in *Piano Culture in 19th-Century Paris*, ed. Massimiliano Sala (Turnhout, Bel.: Brepols, 2015), 332–33.

28. Carl Mikuli, Foreword to *Fr. Chopin's Pianoforte-Werke*, ed. Mikuli (Leipzig: Kistner, 1879–1880), iii.

29. When a sostenuto marking may also imply slowing the tempo is a complex topic best discussed elsewhere. However, often the change from many short notes to fewer long notes creates the need for a full tone and effects a slowing down without changing the beat.

30. Extracted from a lengthy biography of Chopin by Joseph Bennett in *The Musical Times* (1 June 1882): 315. The section quoted is from a paper on the topic of Chopin in England written for Bennett's biography by Alfred James Hipkins, who was by that time working for the piano manufacturer John Broadwood & Sons.

31. Józef Brzowski, "Słowko o smaku w muzyce" (A Word on Taste in Music), in *Pielgrzym*, 1845, 4:97–98. Quoted here from *Chopin and His Critics*, 59.

32. Maria von Grewingk, *Eine Tochter Alt-Rigas, Schülerin Chopins* (Riga: Löffler, 1928), 19 (trans. Susan Adams). Emilie von Gretsch passed this information, and much more, to von Grewingk, who had the volume published.

33. A list of these is collated by Eigeldinger, "Les Premieres Concerts de Chopin à Paris (1832–1838)," in *Music in Paris in the 1830s*, 251–97.

34. The original article appeared in *Revue et gazette musicale*, 25 March 1838; and was adapted into English in *The Musical World* 9/31 (May 1838): 85.

35. The pianist-composer Émile Prudent, quoted in Jean-Jacques Eigeldinger, *Chopin: Âme des salons Parisiens* (Paris: Fayard, 2013), 232.

36. "Concert de Chopin," *Revue et gazette musicale*, 2 May 1841, 245–46 (trans. Nicole Bernstein).

37. Escudier, *La France musicale*, 2 May 1841, 156–57. This article also contains an enlightening comparison between Schubert and Chopin.

38. Marie-Paule Rambeau, "Chopin et le salon du Marquis de Custine (1836–1848)," in *Chopin's Musical Worlds: The 1840s*, eds. Magdalena Chylińska, John Comber, and Artur Szklener (Warsaw: Narodowy Instytut Fryderyka Chopina, 2008), 59.

39. Hector Berlioz, obituary in *Le Journal des débats*, 27 October, 1849; quoted in Rambeau, "Chopin et le salon du Marquis de Custine," 56n2.

40. Marquis de Custine to Chopin, *Correspondance de Frédéric Chopin*, 2:194 (trans. by the author).

41. Custine to Varnhagen d'Ense, 10 December 1840, *Lettres à Varnhagen d'Ense*, éd. Roger Pierrot (Paris: Slatkine, 1979), 388; quoted in Rambeau, "Chopin et le salon du marquis de Custine," 59.

42. Quoted in Georges Lubin's *George Sand en Berry* (Paris: Hachette, 1967), 28–29 (trans. Nicole Bernstein). Jeffrey Kallberg places this description in the context of Chopin's wider interest in mechanical things in "Chopin's Music Box," in *Chopin's Musical Worlds*, 189–202.

43. Georges Mathias, Preface to Isidor Philipp's *Exercices quotidiens tirés des oeuvres de Chopin* (Paris: J. Hamelle, [ca. 1897]), vii. Trans. by Sandra Rosenblum and Ronald Richardson. The Preface is dated 12 February 1897.

44. Additionally, the relative absence of the clavichord in France increased the desire to have an expressive keyboard instrument. Maria van Epenhuysen Rose, "Un clavecin piano et forte, d'une harmonie ronde et moëlleuse: Aesthetic features of the early French piano," in *Le Pianoforte en France 1789–1820*, ed. Florence Getreau (Paris: CNRS Editions, 2009), 166. See also Sephanie Frakes, "*Cantabile* in French Methods for Piano, 1797–1840," in Sala, *Piano Culture in 19th-Century Paris*, 284–90.

45. Muzio Clementi, *Introduction to the Art of Playing on the Piano Forte*, 1801 facs., introduction by Sandra P. Rosenblum (New York: Da Capo Press, 1974), 8–9.

46. Louis Adam, *Méthode de piano du Conservatoire* (Paris: Au Magasin de Musique du Conservatoire Royal, 1804), 154–55.

47. Ibid., 151; Muzio Clementi, *Introduction to the Art of Playing*, 9.

48. Hélène de Montgeroult (1764–1836), *Cours complet pour l'enseignement du forte piano*, 3 vols. (Paris: Janet et Cotelle, 1820), 1:1; trans. Maria van Epenhuysen Rose in "L'Art de Bien Chanter: French Pianos and Their Music Before 1820" (PhD diss., New York University, 2006), 379. Montgeroult had been a student of Jan Ladislav Dussek. In an article published in August 1834 in *Le Pianiste*, Charles Chaulieu compared Dussek's playing style to that of an unnamed contemporary pianist, most likely Chopin: "The particular grace with which he sang on his instrument has never been equaled by anyone. A single pianist . . . whom we hear too seldom, reminds us of him a great deal" (151).

49. Pier Francesco Tosi, *Opinioni de' cantori antichi* . . . (Bologna: dalla Volpe, 1723); [Johann Ernst] Galliard, trans. and ed., *Observations on the Florid Song* . . . (London: Wilcox, 1742), 2nd. ed., 1743 (repr., London: Reeves, 1926) 129.

50. Jean Kleczyński [Jan Kleczyński], *Frédéric Chopin: De l'interpretation de ses oeuvres* (Paris: Mackar, 1880). Original Polish text was published in 1879. Kleczyński was one of the most important writers on Chopin's music in the second half of the nineteenth century.

51. Camille O'Meara Dubois to publisher Mackar, in prefatory material to Kleczyński, *Frédéric Chopin*, n.p.

52. Chopin to Woyciechowski, 12 December 1831, *Chopin's Polish Letters*, 245.

53. My translation and condensation of Antoine Marmontel, *Les Pianistes cèlébres* (Paris: A. Chaix, 1878), 100–101. Marmontel won a first prize in piano at the Paris Conservatoire where later he was professor of the advanced class.

54. The tutors mentioned are Alexis de Garaudé, *Méthode complète de piano* (Paris: de Garaudé, 1820) 28–29; Henri Lemoine, *Méthode pratique pour le forte-piano* (Paris: L'Auteur, 1827), xvi, viii; and Frédéric Kalkbrenner, *Méthode pour apprendre le pianoforte*, 2nd ed. (Paris: Pleyel, ca.1830), 8.

55. Kalkbrenner, *Méthode pour apprendre*, 14.

56. F. Kalkbrenner, *Method of Learning the Pianoforte*, trans. anon., 3rd ed. (London: D'Almaine, [1837]), 11–12.

57. Charles Timbrell, *French Pianism: A Historical Perspective*, 2nd ed. (Portland, OR: Amadeus Press, 1999), 37.

58. Pierre-Joseph-Guillaume Zimmerman, *Encyclopédie du pianiste compositeur* (Paris: L'Auteur, 1840), Part 1, 28.

59. Ibid., Part 1, 41.

60. Ibid., Part 2, 59.

61. Quoted from Eigeldinger, *Chopin: Pianist and Teacher*, 50. This information from Mikuli was passed on by Aleksander Michałowski in "Jak grał Fryderyk Szopen?" (How Did Frederick Chopin Play?), *Muzyka* 9/7–9 (1932): 72–77. See also Mikuli's Foreword to *Fr. Chopin's Pianoforte-Werke*, iii.

62. Further discussion of the types and uses of rubato can be found in Sandra P. Rosenblum, *Performance Practices in Classic Piano Music: Their Principles and Applications* (Bloomington: Indiana University Press, 1991); and Richard Hudson, *Stolen Time: The History of Tempo Rubato* (Oxford: Oxford University Press, 1994).

63. Georges Mathias, Preface to *Exercices quotidiens*, v.

64. François Fétis and Ignaz Moscheles, *Méthode des méthodes de piano* (Paris: M. Schlesinger, 1840).

65. This division of responsibility is confirmed in *François-Joseph Fétis et la vie musicale de son temps, 1784–1871*, a volume published by the Royal Library of Brussels in 1872 for an exhibit celebrating Fétis's accomplishments.

66. Ignaz Moscheles, *Studies for the Piano Forte*, Op. 70, Bk. 1 (London: S. Chappell and J. B. Cramer, Addison & Beale, 1825), 6.

67. Mathias, Preface to *Exercices quotidiens*, vi. Moscheles had delivered himself of these opinions in London in 1839.

68. Antoine de Kontski, *L'indispensable du pianiste* (Paris, 1845; 2nd ed., Paris: 1851), 16–17. See also Bellman, "Frédéric Chopin, Antoine de Kontski and the *Carezzando* Touch," 398–407.

69. This critic considered Kontski's compositions "in the middle between charlatanry and more genuine artistry." Anonymous, "Werke für Pianoforte von Antoine de Kontski," *Neue Zeitschrift für Musik* 53 (1860): 114.

70. Chopin's "Sketch for a Method," quoted in Eigeldinger, *Chopin: Pianist and Teacher*, 193. Compare this with Elsner's comment on teaching cited earlier. For a complete

discussion of Chopin's *Méthode*, see Eigeldinger, *Esquisses pour une méthode de piano* (Paris: Flammarion, 1993).

71. Chopin, "Sketch for a Method," in *Esquisses*, 195. Other incipient thoughts appear on the same page.

72. Ibid.

73. Jean Kleczynski, *The Works of Frederic Chopin and Their Proper Interpretation*, trans. Alfred Whittingham (London: Wm. Reeves, 1882), 27–30. Original Polish text published in 1879.

74. Sigismund Thalberg, *The Art of Singing Applied to the Piano-Forte* (Boston: O. Ditson [1859]), 3. Interestingly, Thalberg opened this volume with a direct quotation without naming the writer: "A celebrated woman [Montgeroult] has said that the art of singing well is the same with any instrument." Chopin regarded Thalberg with some disdain.

75. Chopin, "Sketch for a Method," 194. Italics in the original.

76. Ibid., 195.

77. Grewingk, *Eine Tochter Alt-Rigas, Schülerin Chopins,* 10.

78. A. J. Hipkins, contribution to Joseph Bennett, "Chopin," *The Musical Times* (6 May 1882): 315; Chorley's original article from *Athenaeum*, 6 May 1848.

79. Bennett, "Chopin," 315–16. Hipkins again quotes Chorley from the *Athenaeum* of 1 July 1848.

80. See Eigeldinger's detailed discussion in *Chopin: Pianist and Teacher*, 120–22, notes 98–100.

81. A. Guémer, "Exécution musicale: Liszt, Ferd. Hiller, Chopin et Bertini," *Gazette musicale de Paris* (5 January 1834): 6.

82. Marmontel, *Les pianistes célèbres,* 5.

83. Custine to Chopin, February 1848, *Correspondance de Frédéric Chopin*, 3:325 (trans. Nicole Bernstein).

The Hand of Chopin:
Documents and Commentary

JEAN-JACQUES EIGELDINGER
TRANSLATED BY VIRGINIA E. WHEALTON

The mind makes the hand; the hand makes the mind.
—Henri Focillon

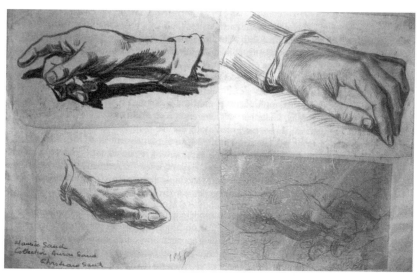

Figures 1a–1d (clockwise from top left). Maurice Sand-Dudevant,
sketches of left hand, charcoal and red chalk, 1845. Private collection (France).

This essay contains reproductions of four studies of hands that have been attributed to Maurice Sand-Dudevant. If these drawings—or even a single one of them—indeed portray the hand of Chopin, at present they are the only ones known to have been made during the pianist's lifetime. Astonishingly, Eugène Delacroix left no mold of Chopin's hands.

Held in a private collection, this group of drawings came from the estate of Aurore Lauth-Sand, the daughter of Maurice, as specified in the handwritten will of Christiane Sand, the wife of Aurore's adopted son.[1] The four sketches have been pasted together on a single sheet of paper. The date "1845," found at the bottom of one of the drawings, was probably written by Maurice, and failing that, by Aurore Lauth-Sand.[2] Whatever the case, these drawings were done early in Maurice's artistic career, when he studied with Delacroix and copied many anatomical studies, especially those of hands.[3] Of Maurice's four studies of hands examined in this essay, only the three in red chalk—Figures 1b, 1c, and 1d above—are drawn *d'après nature*.[4] Figure number 1a (my numbering), in charcoal, is a counter-proof of no. 1c; it is a mirror image, not a depiction of a right hand. (All four figures are shown again below; and Figure 1b is shown again twice at the end of this essay, renumbered 7a and 8b).

Are all these drawings based on the same model? Finding them gathered in this way suggests so, as do certain details—especially the shape of the fingernails, which are cut short. However, the morphology of the thumb shows a slight difference in all the drawings. Numbers 1b and 1d, which have paper and chalk of identical quality, are similar to each other, forming one pair; numbers 1a and 1c form another.

How might we proceed in identifying the model? In terms of the posture of the thumb, our point of reference will be the red chalk drawing, no. 1b. We can compare it against the few duly authenticated portraits of Chopin that depict his hands in some detail.[5] Another important source is the posthumous mold of Chopin's left hand by the sculptor Auguste Clésinger, the son-in-law of George Sand.[6] In addition, we can examine descriptive details in memoirs by those in Chopin's circles.

We now turn to three Chopin portraits: the lithograph by Maria Wodzińska (Figure 2), a Polish noblewoman and Chopin's student, to whom he was briefly engaged, which is based on her own watercolor (1836); the painting by Ary Scheffer (1847), which has disappeared, although a photograph of it remains (Figure 3); and the drawing by Henri Lehman (19 April 1847) (Figure 4).[7] Ironically, the daguerreotype by Louis-Auguste Bisson (ca. 1847) (Figure 5) is of little use in this context; the photographer's lens is focused on the hands in the foreground, which appear swollen with dilated veins. In any case, rounded nails and long, narrow fingers characterize the studies created ten years earlier by Wodzińska, as well as the one by Scheffer; Lehmann lightly accentuates the joints of the phalanges. All these elements align with the sketch no. 1b by Maurice Sand-Dudevant.

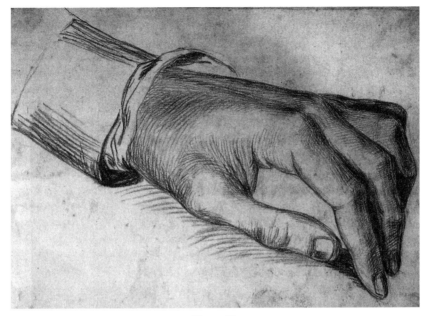

Figure 1b

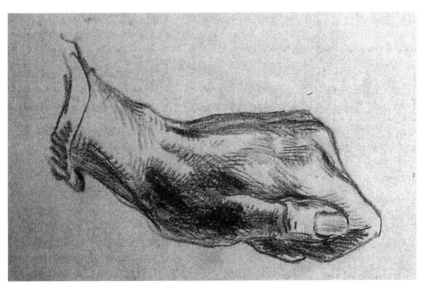

Figure 1d

Figures 1b and 1d. Maurice Sand-Dudevant, paired sketches,
red chalk on paper, both of identical quality.

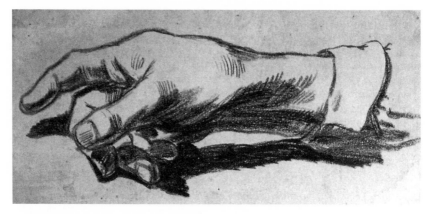

Figure 1a

Figure 1c

Figures 1a and 1c. Maurice Sand-Dudevant, paired sketches,
charcoal and red chalk, mirror images.

Figure 2. Maria Wodzińska, portrait of Fryderyk Chopin, lithograph, 1836.

Figure 3. Ary Scheffer, *Portrait de Frédéric Chopin*,
photograph of an oil painting that has disappeared, 1863.

Figure 4. Henri Lehmann, *Portrait of Frédéric Chopin*,
pencil with white highlights in chalk, 19 April 1847.

Figure 5. Louis-Auguste Bisson, Fryderyk Chopin, daguerreotype (ca. 1847),
since disappeared. Photograph by Czesław Olszewski (1936).

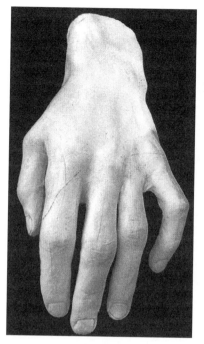 

Figure 6a   Figure 6b

Figure 6a. Auguste Clésinger, plaster cast of the left hand of Chopin, 1849.
Musée de la vie romantique, Paris.

Figure 6b. Albert Graefle, left hand of Chopin as molded by Clésinger,
pencil drawing, 19 October 1849.

    This sketch bears the greatest affinity with the cast of Chopin's left
hand made by Clésinger several hours after the pianist's death (Figures
6a, 7b, and 8a), when Clésinger also made his first version of Chopin's
mask (there are two).[8] It is also worth mentioning the two sketches
signed by Albert Graefle (Figures 6b and 9) and dated 19 October 1849.
Clésinger's plaster, made in the short interval after the pianist's death,
served as the model; therefore, in seeking to identify Maurice's model,
Graefle does not count as a primary source.[9] Finally, let us consider the
following question: Why a mold of (only) the left hand? Lacking any
direct documentation on the matter, it is fair to speculate that this may
not have been the choice of the sculptor and mold-maker. Material con-
straints may have made it difficult, if not impossible, to access the right
hand—for example, because of the orientation of the death bed.

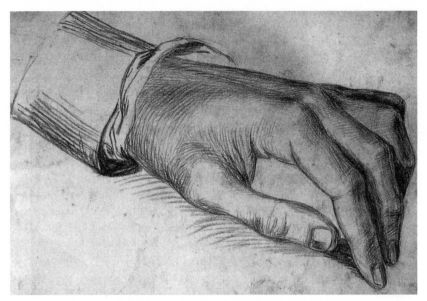

Figure 7a

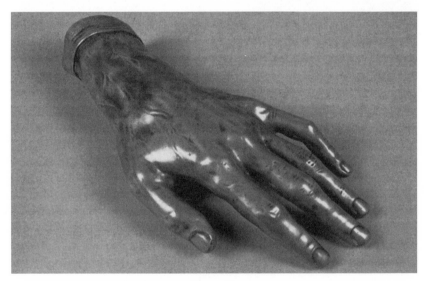

Figure 7b

Figure 7a (same as 1b). Maurice Sand-Dudevant, sketch of left hand, red chalk (private collection, France); compare with bronze cast (7b).

Figure 7b. Auguste Clésinger, bronze cast of the left hand of Chopin, 1849, Musée de la vie romantique, Paris; compare with sketch of left hand (7a).

Clésinger's first plaster casts, given to those close to the deceased, are especially useful as models for comparison: namely, the plaster casts in the collection of Jane Stirling (Royal Manchester College of Music)[10] and the bronze cast given by Aurore Lauth-Sand to the Musée Carnavalet (currently held in the Musée de la vie romantique, Paris),[11] which is reproduced here (Figure 7b). If the fingers of the mold in sketch no. 7a (1b) appear to be relatively "spatulate" (as per Alfred Cortot, *In Search of Chopin*),[12] the hand's profile shows it at rest but ready to play; the free, poised thumb stands in opposition to the other fingers; the phalanges are bulged and the fingernails cut short like a pianist's. There can be little doubt as to Maurice's model. The red chalk of Maurice Sand (7a/1b) suggests what the mold shows more completely: a strongly independent fifth finger at the opposite extremity of the hand, responding in some way to the robust development of the thumb (one can observe the importance of the latter in the other drawings). This morphological singularity of the little finger, the hand's outer bound, was highlighted in another sketch by Maurice Sand (Figure 10): as Chopin gives a lesson to Pauline Viardot, he places his left hand on the top of a pianino.

At this point, it is worth recalling the master's considerations on the art of touch in his *Esquisses pour une méthode de piano*. The constitution of the fingers and the hand were foundational:

> Each finger's power is determined by its shape. The thumb has the most power, being the broadest, shortest, and freest; the fifth [finger] as the other extremity of the hand; the third as the middle and the pivot; then the second . . . and then the fourth, the weakest one, the Siamese twin of the third, bound to it by a common ligament, and which people insist on trying to separate—which is impossible and, fortunately, unnecessary.[13] As many sounds as there are fingers—everything is a matter of knowing good fingering.[14]

But the most striking point of commonality between the drawing and the plaster is the position of the hand itself, which appears to be shaped by an unseen keyboard. It was Chopin who wrote in his *Esquisses*:

> Find the right position for the hand by placing your fingers on the keys E, F♯, G♯, A♯, B: the long fingers will occupy the high [black] keys, and the short fingers the low [white] keys. Place the fingers occupying the high keys all on one level

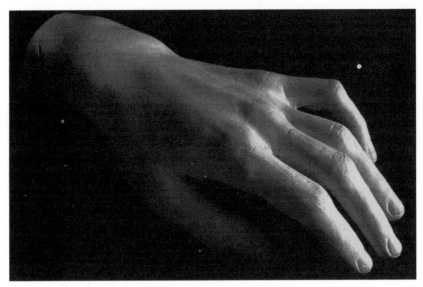

Figure 8a

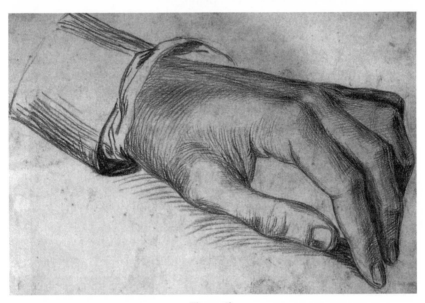

Figure 8b

Figure 8a. Auguste Clésinger, bronze cast of the left hand of Chopin, 1849,
compare with sketch (8b).

Figure 8b (same as 1b and 7a). Maurice Sand-Dudevant, sketch of left hand, red chalk
(private collection, France); compare with bronze cast (8a).

and do the same with those occupying the white keys, to make the leverage relatively equal; this will curve the hand, giving it the necessary suppleness that it could not have with the *fingers straight*.[15]

Through the position of Chopin's hand (which might have been manipulated after his death), the mold illustrates the master's own pedagogical principle, perfectly—albeit unsettlingly—memorializing his paradigm. Even if the fingers of sketch no. 8b (1b) appear too close for striking E–F♯–G♯–A♯–B (1–2–3–4–5), the posture of the pianist is captured. Chopin most likely posed for Maurice.

In a sense, the sketch of Maurice Sand confirms *in vivo* Clésinger's impressions of a hand "such as that at last eternity transforms into itself," to paraphrase Mallarmé.[16] All these representations show a relatively small hand, superbly proportioned, and ideally shaped for the keyboard—or even sculpted by it. These qualities are noted in the accounts of Chopin's close friends, followers, and colleagues, who highlighted his exceptional flexibility: "His fingers seemed to be without any bones; but he would bring out certain effects by elasticity," observed one fine pupil, Eliza Peruzzi.[17] It is precisely this ability for extraordinary extension, allowed by his flexibility, that most struck his contemporaries. Karol Mikuli—a disciple of Chopin who passed along the legacy of his master for nearly half a century in Lwów—spoke of "his hand . . . that of a born pianist, not so much large as extremely supple, permitting him to arpeggiate the most widely spaced harmonies and to stretch wide spans in the sorts of passages he himself had most daringly introduced into piano playing" (recall that the Etude, Op. 10, No. 1, was written when he was nineteen).[18] For his part, the pianist and composer Stephen Heller recounted, "It was a wonderful sight to see one of those small hands expand and cover a third of the keyboard. It was like the opening of the mouth of a serpent which is going to swallow a rabbit whole."[19] At last, we come back to Solange Clésinger, who heard all the moments at Nohant, to describe the poetic impact of a cosmic creation: "Under the flexible and responsible fingers of Chopin's pale and frail hand the piano became the voice of an archangel, an orchestra, an army, a raging ocean, a creation of the universe, the end of the world."[20]

Chopin's thoughts on technique, and therefore his pedagogical principles, proceed from his wondrous discovery of a close connection between the way the hand is constituted and the morphology of the keyboard, a word whose etymological root—*clavis* (Latin), or "key"—is not

Figure 9. Albert Graefle, left hand of Chopin as molded by
Clésinger, pencil drawing, 19 October 1849.

insignificant. The allocation of white keys and black keys is, for the piano,
like the keywork of wind instruments. Perhaps better yet:

> One cannot overpraise the genius who presided over the
> construction of the keyboard, so well adapted to the shape of
> the hand. Is there anything more ingenious than the higher
> [black] keys—destined for long fingers—so admirably serv-
> ing as points of pivot.[21]

Thus, "Between the hand and the tool begins a friendship that will never
end. One transmits to the other its living heat and molds the other per-
petually. . . . I do not know if there is a break between the manual order
and the mechanical order—I am not very sure of it—but, at the end of
the arm, the tool does not contradict the man; it is not a hook of iron
screwed to a stump; between them, there is the god in five persons that
traverses the scale of all dimensions: the hand of the mason in cathe-
drals, the hand of the illuminators of manuscripts"—and the hand of the

Figure 10. Maurice Sand-Dudevant, Chopin giving a lesson to Pauline Viardot, pen-and-ink sketch, Nohant, June 1844. Erroneous date in the hand of George Sand.

prince of pianists, we might add to this magnificent text by art historian Henri Focillon.[22]

As we all know, Chopin composed at his instrument. The medium of his thoughts, his hand on the piano was, so to speak, the alpha and omega of his creation and his interpretation. Apt indeed is the praise of his compatriot Witold Lutosławski, who declared: "No composer in the whole history of music has created such strength and indissoluble cohesion, a mysterious connection of three elements: hand, keyboard, and the sensation of the music through sound."[23]

NOTES

1. The owner of these documents obtained them directly from Madame Christiane Sand. The identity of the model has not been mentioned. I thank the owner for sharing these images with me and for authorizing their reproduction.

2. Concerning the date of 1845 affixed at the bottom of one of the anatomical drawings, see Christiane Sand and Sylvie Delaigue-Moins, *Maurice fils de George Sand* (Lancosme, Tours: Editions du patrimoine, 2010), 87.

3. See the numerous reproductions of studies of hands in ibid., 70–73.

4. Translator's note: The French expression *d'après nature* has no direct equivalent in English; it means that the image is seen in unaltered form, as if from the perspective of a viewer who is actually present.

5. See Mieczysław Idzikowski and Bronisław Edward Sydow, *Les portraits de Fryderyk Chopin* (Kraków: Polskie Wydawnictwo Muzyczne, 1953); and their "Autour de Frédéric Chopin: Sa correspondance, ses portraits," *La Revue musicale* 229 (1955): 97–150. See also Robert Bory, *La vie de Frédéric Chopin par l'image* (Geneva: Jullien, 1951); and Ernst Burger, *Frédéric Chopin: Eine Lebenschronik in Bildern und Dokumenten* (Munich: Hirmer Verlag, 1990).

6. Le Musée de la musique in Paris holds a plaster mold (E. 1919) that allegedly is of Chopin's right hand, but its authenticity has never been established.

7. The pencil drawings of Chopin at the piano by Eliza Radziwiłł (dated 1826, though in fact they were done in 1829) and by Jakob Götzenberger (October 1838) do not permit a detailed study of the right hand. It is the same for the oil portrait by Antoni Kolberg (1848), which has since disappeared (though it was photographed).

8. See Czesław Sielużycki, "Prace chopinowskie rzeźbiarza Jean-Baptiste-Auguste Clésingera: Studium dokumentacyjne i porównawcze" (The Works Concerning Chopin of the Sculptor J.-B.-A. Clésinger: Documentary and Comparative Study), *Rocznik Chopinowski* 16 (1984): 119–51.

Gastone Belotti, in his monumental *F. Chopin l'uomo*, 3 vols. (Milan-Rome: Sapere Edizioni, 1974), hypothesizes that Clésinger made two successive molds of Chopin's left hand: the first in 1847–48, and the other just after Chopin's death (3:1360–61, and 1404). He bases his claim on two casts: the plaster at the Musée de la vie romantique, which he dates to the end of 1847–48, and the posthumous bronze, requested by Princess Marcelina Czartoryska, then offered by her to the Princes Czartoryski Foundation, Kraków (inventory XIII-518). This hypothesis is untenable because it is disproved by all sources and documented arguments.

From a postmortem mold Clésinger created many casts in plaster and bronze that show the same left hand in exactly identical postures. In my opinion, it could be that the exemplar in bronze held by Princess Czartoryska (Figure 8a)—which very well might be a first cast (Sielużycki)—resulted from the sculptor Clésinger creating a work based on his mold, as it depicts several veins and visible nerves that do not appear in the first plaster casts—unless, of course, there was a second mold.

9. Graefle's sketches come from the Fryderyk Chopin Museum, Warsaw, M/132 and M/133.

10. Reproduction in Peter Willis, *Chopin in Manchester* (Newcastle upon Tyne: Elysium Press, 2011), 37.

11. Inventory number: 1989-178.

12. Alfred Cortot, *In Search of Chopin*, trans. Cyril and Rena Clark (London and New York: P. Nevill, 1951), 21.

13. In 1848, Chopin complained half-jokingly, "What has remained for me is a large nose and an *inept* fourth finger." (Emphasis in original.) *Chopin's Polish Letters*, trans. David Frick (Warsaw: Fryderyk Chopin Institute, 2016), 446.

14. Jean-Jacques Eigeldinger, *Chopin: Pianist and Teacher, As Seen by His Pupils*, ed. Roy Howat, trans. Naomi Shohet, Krysia Osostowicz, and Roy Howat (Cambridge: Cambridge University Press, 1986), 195.

15. Ibid., 194.

16. This quote paraphrases the opening line "Tel qu'en Lui-même enfin l'éternité le change," from Mallarmé's "Le tombeau d'Edgar Poe."

17. Cited in Frederick Niecks, *Frederick Chopin as a Man and Musician*, 2 vols, 3rd ed. (London: Novello, 1902), 2:339.

18. Eigeldinger, *Chopin: Pianist and Teacher*, 275. Translation amended slightly.

19. Niecks, *Frederick Chopin*, 2:96.

20. Eigeldinger, *Chopin: Pianist and Teacher*, 281.

21. Ibid., 192.

22. Henri Focillon, "Éloge de la main," *La vie des formes*, 5th ed. (Paris: Presses universitaires de France, 1964), 110–11.

23. Zbigniew Skowron, ed. and trans., *Lutosławski on Music* (Lanham, MD: Scarecrow Press, 2007), 205.

Afterword

Chopin and the Consequences of Exile

LEON BOTSTEIN

In Memory of Samuel Wyszewiański (1916—2005) and
Kamilla Sikorska-Wyszewiańska (1920—2005)

In exile in 1976, well before the fall of Communism in Poland, the Polish poet Czesław Miłosz observed that a writer who embraces exile, whether "as a result of banishment or his own decision," inevitably finds that no one in his place of exile treats issues that are matters of "life or death" to him with any significant concern. Nonetheless, within a vacuum of genuine empathy and understanding for what really matters, the exiled artist adjusts gradually, for "incidental reasons," to the society in which he lives, and his knowledge of everyday life in the country of his origin changes from the "tangible to the theoretical." Cut off from the homeland, the exile engages in a "constant reassessment of tradition in search of vital roots" and a "critical observation of the present."[1]

Amid this process, a "moral torment" sets in and consumes the exile, particularly the voluntary exile. This torment is tied to an "estrangement" that does not abate by contact with other exiles. Inevitably, the exiled artist "senses his native tongue in a new manner." In exile Miłosz realized that, as a Pole, his language and origins were that of "poor relations" within a European "family" that once promised but failed to be a shared home.[2] Yet the recognition that he could not bridge that barrier—compounded by a sustained separation from his Eastern European roots—propelled him onto an uncharted path of idiosyncratic self-invention as a writer.

Most commentary on the consequences of exile concerns writers and scholars.[3] But Miłosz's experience bears a resemblance to the career of Fryderyk Chopin, who lived in voluntary exile in Paris from his native Poland for eighteen years, from 1831 to his death in 1849.[4] Chopin's medium was music; specifically, wordless instrumental music for the piano. Yet Chopin understood music as a form of declamation, analogous to language. Music, whether from a text or freely improvised, possessed a grammar and syntax that communicated meaning.[5] During his career in exile, Chopin became famous as the distinctly Polish "poet" of his nation. The eloquence and sentiments audible in his music were construed as giving voice to Poland, revealing its unique "melancholy" soul.

With the exception of fellow Poles in Paris, whose company gave him only slight relief from a sense of estrangement, Chopin the exile, as Miłosz surmises, was surrounded by few who truly understood what was at stake for him. A form of "moral torment" lingered. In response, Chopin pursued the path of invention as a composer, using his "native tongue" in a new manner to express an imagined vision of his homeland by means of a "reassessed" tradition.

From the very start of his career in Paris and particularly after the 1851 publication of Franz Liszt's influential book about him (co-authored with Carolyne zu Sayn-Wittgenstein), Chopin was seen both as an exile who was quite at home in Paris as well as the authentic voice of a nation. Since Chopin was cut off from his homeland, he supplanted the "tangible" with a wary construct, an aesthetic invention in music that in implicit and explicit ways offered an account of the character, sensibilities, and aspirations of "Polishness," which then took hold inside and outside his native Poland.

Chopin, as a composer, eluded the exiled writer's most daunting challenge. He never lost contact with his native language—music—and its audience. Musical culture in the first half of the nineteenth century was, by reason of the restricted social class of its participants and the structure of its rituals, from notation and criticism to performance, strikingly international. In Warsaw, patriotic Polish teachers and contemporaries helped shape the musical language and practices Chopin acquired, first as a prodigy and then as a young man. But their teachings and the musical life in the Warsaw of Chopin's youth also provided him with influences that ranged from J. S. Bach, Mozart, and Beethoven to Rossini, Weber, and Hummel.[6] Such knowledge deepened the young Chopin's recognition—bold patriotic assertions and usages of distinctly Polish elements by his teacher Józef Elsner and other Polish musicians notwithstanding—that as a Pole he was, by comparison to the French and the Germans, still from the "periphery," a place once considered the image of "exterior darkness."[7]

The transnational continuity and solidarity of an aristocratic domination of musical culture did not, however, compensate for Chopin's struggle with isolation and, above all, exile's "moral torment." His response, audible in his music after 1831, was to rethink the traditions he had acquired in his Warsaw years, and to define his allegiance to Poland within music whose surface character was one of unmistakable originality and subjective intimacy. Chopin's torment indeed "transformed," in Miłosz's terms, his sense of his native tongue in ways that came to be seen as generically representative of human feelings and also irreducibly Polish. Three sources of influence account for this transformation after 1831: (1) Poland, as refracted in Chopin's fragmentary memories; (2) the fashions and styles he encountered in Paris; and (3) Chopin's mature engagement with the tradition represented by Bach, Mozart, and Beethoven, Chopin's ambivalence toward Beethoven's legacy notwithstanding.[8]

Chopin's capacity to express solitude and loneliness, and to exemplify the Romantic notion of the subjective in art, deepened because of the personal toll exile exacted from him. Alfred Cortot characterized this burden as a "psychic contraction" that erected a barrier to Chopin's ability to make close friends. Chopin, despite his extensive socializing in Paris and his legendary charm and wit, believed himself "destined to live and die alone, surrounded by people indifferent to his fate who meant nothing to him."[9]

Biography, particularly the dubious arena of psychobiography, is certainly seductive, but it is limiting as an approach to understanding works of art. But it remains significant that Chopin never forged bonds of intimacy during his years of exile that matched those he had developed in Warsaw, even during the years with George Sand in the context of a complex and poorly understood relationship.[10] Chopin's contemporaries in Paris recognized that he masked his inner feelings under a veil of stylized politeness, chivalric grace, and easy humor. As he confessed to his closest and oldest friend, Tytus Woyciechowski, the sense of "loneliness and abandonment" never left him. Chopin's elegant camouflage of mistrust and dislike earned him Marie d'Agoult's acid description as an "oyster sprinkled with sugar."[11]

The Shadow of Poland's History

Chopin's status and experience as an exile and his posthumous reception mirrored a quintessentially Polish reality. The peculiar nature of the Polish exile in the nineteenth century derived from the exceptional nature of Polish history: its decline from an earlier status as a great European power before the eighteenth century; its dismemberment and partition by powerful neighbors; the particular severity of Russian and Prussian domination; repeated failures at armed insurrection; and the remarkable allegiance of its people, despite foreign occupation, to the Polish language and a peculiarly fervent brand of Roman Catholicism. Poland's humiliation also lent the ideal of Poland a legendary connection to political dreams of individual liberty, as well as of heroic deeds on behalf of an aristocratic construct of the idea of democracy. In Chopin's lifetime, Poland as a sovereign political entity remained a memory, an illusion, and a dream, interrupted briefly by dubious compromises. Poland was seen throughout Europe as the stuff of tragedy and an object of rhetorical enthusiasm that ranged from compassion to condescension and even contempt.

Modern nationalism and coherent and reductive formulations of national identity took shape after the French Revolution. Romanticism nurtured them. But they flourished, primarily after 1848, and therefore after Chopin's death. The unique aspect of Polish national sentiment throughout the nineteenth century was that a vision of Poland remained a persistent, yet to be realized dream. As such, it became an internationally fashionable, if not controversial, political ideal in Chopin's lifetime. Although aristocratic egalitarian and chivalric traditions dating back to the seventeenth century remained at the core of this dream's various iterations, the nineteenth century's image of the distinctiveness of Poland's people and culture was shaped disproportionately by exiles, and particularly by three writers who all had interactions with Chopin: Adam Mickiewicz, Zygmunt Krasiński, and Juliusz Słowacki.

In contrast, exiled Russian writers of the mid-nineteenth century—Ivan Turgenev and Alexander Herzen, for example—fled or were banished from a regime within a powerful and imposing sovereign nation. In their case, a fluid political and cultural dynamic emerged between exiled voices and a vibrant internal community of writers and artists at home. Other Eastern European communities, such as the Bohemian, Moravian, and Hungarian, harbored no myth of lost greatness comparable to the Polish. They remained intact entities within the dynastic Habsburg monarchy with their own distinct continuous histories.

Poland was, throughout the nineteenth century, a simmering and depoliticized community, suffering particularly under the Prussian and Russian occupations. Russia, after 1831, and Prussia later in the century were determined to integrate and absorb their Polish provinces. They suppressed the Polish language, Catholicism, and culture through a policy of forced Russification in the East and, later, Germanization in the West. Casting a shadow on this powerlessness was Poland's mythologized memory of its glorious past, particularly of Vienna in 1683 when Poland, then a great European power led by King Jan III Sobieski, successfully defended Western Christendom against the Ottoman threat.[12]

Polish exiles in the early nineteenth century, Chopin prominent among them, were less in dialogue with counterparts in their homeland than they were with one another. It would be their dreams of Polish independence and their interpretations of history rather than their critique of an extant regime that became defining elements of a modern Polish national identity and character.[13] Art—literature and music—became surrogates for politics. Ignacy Jan Paderewski, the legendary pianist, composer, and renowned interpreter of Chopin, recalled that it was during a speech at a series of concerts in Lwów in 1909 that he made his "first real entrance into politics, the very beginning of a career" that included becoming, after the First World War, the first prime minister of an independent Poland.[14]

Schumann and Liszt popularized the idea of Chopin's music as being expressive of the Polish national spirit and soul. Liszt located a distinctly Polish "melancholy," *żal,* a sensibility of suffering unique to Poland's fate, at the heart of Chopin's music.[15] But Schumann and Liszt misconstrued and mischaracterized Chopin's achievement. Overtly Polish genres—the mazurka and polonaise, for example—do not typify the general character of Chopin's output. Chopin's idiosyncratic use of classical genres (sonatas, concertos, and a trio), and his focus on single-movement structures—ballades, scherzos, impromptus, waltzes, preludes, and etudes—were not essentially Polish but variants on the early-Romantic preference for temporally dense, poetic narratives in music.

Chopin's music never expressed anything concrete, and certainly nothing collective, historic, or inherited, despite his use of Polish dance forms and occasional folkloristic melodies. The mazurka may have been of Polish origin, but Chopin's elaboration followed a well-established pattern. He gave that dance form a novel poetic character that diminished its cultural specificity and lent it stature as a musical genre. Non-Polish composers, notably Czech and French, went on to use the mazurka as redefined by Chopin. The Polonaise had its pre-history as a musical genre outside of Poland, as examples by Weber and Ferdinand Ries among others attest, before Chopin's remarkable deployment of it.[16]

Schumann and Liszt's appeals to some Polish essence in Chopin derived from their need to isolate the uniqueness and striking rhetorical and emotional power of Chopin's music. They felt compelled to demarcate and contain Chopin's astonishing originality and alluring distinctiveness in relation to themselves as composers. The Polish explanation—the appeal to exoticism—fit. Its plausibility was enhanced by a shared European conceit that it was improbable that someone from Poland could attain greatness as a composer without some peculiar advantage. Their view took hold. Chopin may have fashioned his originality out of cosmopolitan Classical and Romantic musical traditions, but his expressive rhetoric successfully passed as being rooted in the character of Poland and its national feelings of loss, oppression, and isolation.

Liszt's characterization was the most persuasive, in and outside Poland, because he construed Chopin's music as a signifier of the confrontation between the defeat of Poland and Polish pride in the nobility of its history and the pathos of its martyrdom. For Liszt, Chopin's music justified art as politics, particularly the politics of resistance. Liszt elaborated Schumann's famous quip from decades earlier that Chopin's works were dangerous to Tsar Nicholas I and were "guns buried in flowers."[17] The highly vaunted Polish melancholy Liszt sensed was the voice of an exile. Exile inspired a captivating individuality and that individuality gained a unique historical significance as the sole example of instrumental music becoming a constituent of an invented and widely disseminated national ethos.

Vladimir Nabokov, for whom exile and memory were lifelong obsessions, described one's personal past as "a constant accumulation of images" from which we select and which we seek to retain through memory. "The act of retention," he wrote, "is the act of art, artistic selection, artistic blending, artistic re-combination of actual events." Music, as an art form in time, is in Nabokov's terms a "fluid medium for the culture of metaphors."[18] Only small fragments of the remembered past lurk beneath the aesthetic transformation by the artist in exile, who, through estrangement and nostalgia, fashions something that never existed.[19] Nabokov's description illuminates how Chopin's fragments of a remembered past were reconfigured to create sonic "metaphors" that became a surrogate for a national political ideology. An exile that began, in Chopin's case, as a personal and professional journey assumed a political symbolism that in turn influenced the trajectory of his career and aesthetic inspiration. And the exilic achievement—the "re-combination of actual events," the artistic blending and selection—became appropriated posthumously as political.

Chopin's momentous innovations vindicate Nabokov's and Miłosz's characterizations of the aesthetic consequences of exile. Chopin pioneered the use of musical time to generate a flexible discursive and narrative form. He bent predictable dance forms, such as the waltz and mazurka, into vehicles of formal experimentation and ambiguity. Chopin's arresting harmonic juxtapositions and overlapping and irregular phrase structures extended the musical rhetoric and vocabulary of musical expression for future generations. Form in Chopin emerged less from past models and practices than from his distinct realization of the Romantic impulse to use music as a structure for the expression of contemplation and the succession of feelings.[20]

Chopin deployed clock time duration with an uncanny control so that musical time ran parallel to an individual's experience of inner dialogue. Chopin's allegiance to non-explicit programmatic music, his unique interest in novel short forms and genres, his residual link to musical Classicism and in particular Bach and Mozart, his ambivalent debt to Beethovenian drama and his distaste for the theatricality of Berlioz, as well as his foregrounding of the solitary individual at the piano (and the intimacy of musical communication this generated) can be explained through his ambition to universalize his emotional experiences as a Polish exile.

Therefore Chopin's significance as an inventor of a national voice did not deter his exceptional international influence on nineteenth-century harmonic language, melodic rhetoric, and form well beyond the realm of piano music. Chopin's wide-ranging impact on subsequent composers and their publics—from the United States to Russia—was not limited by any overriding sense that he was exotic or foreign. This disjunction between Chopin as quintessentially Polish and Chopin's international influence was encouraged by the fact that the political entity of Poland did not exist before it emerged as an independent nation in 1918. Uniquely within European politics, Poland remained a Romantic aspiration whose content was defined by aesthetic and metaphysical ideals. Appropriation by Russian, German, Austrian, and French composers, performers, and publics was encouraged by this political nonexistence. Chopin represented no competitive political "other": no actual Polish national framework existed, and therefore no functioning symbiosis between politics and culture.[21] The political within the attribution of meaning in Chopin's music was associated with powerlessness and the experience of exile. His music was a nostalgic projection, an act of imagining life *not* in exile.

An eloquent expression of this universalist view of Chopin, in which the notion of his music as expressive of Poland is subordinated, was articulated by the pianist who did more than any other to spread Chopin's reputation during the nineteenth century, Anton Rubinstein. In his 1892 "Conversation on Music," Rubinstein argued that Chopin

> was the greatest of those whom we have spoken until now, have intrusted [*sic*] their most intimate, yes, I may almost say, most beautiful thoughts to the Piano-forte—but the Pianoforte-Bard, the Pianoforte-Rhapsodist, the Pianoforte-Mind, the Pianoforte-Soul is Chopin. Whether the spirit of this instrument breathed upon him or he upon it—how he wrote for it, I do not know; but only an entire going-over-of-one-into-the-other could call such compositions to life.

Tragic, romantic, lyric, heroic, dramatic, fantastic, soulful, sweet, dreamy, brilliant, grand, simple; all possible expressions are found in his compositions.[22]

Chopin's piercing, so to speak, of the illusions of community and coherence as a solace against the inevitability of human isolation and unrequited aspiration was in a way the musical answer to Balzac's exposure of the "human comedy" in prose.

A closing caveat: since the ideology of nationalism as we have come to understand it through critics such as Edward Said was at best nascent during Chopin's lifetime, Said's way of construing exile has severe limitations.[23] For example, Chopin never truly contemplated returning home. He probably was out of favor with the Russians, but not enough to make a visit impossible. He missed his family and friends, but not enough to sacrifice his ambition for an international pianistic career and for fame as a composer. After his first trip in 1829 to Vienna, he found Warsaw limiting as a field of endeavor. He wished to take his place among the elite within a cosmopolitan cultural community—in Vienna, Paris, leading centers of German culture, or in London and perhaps even St. Petersburg, the cultural capital of the Russian oppressors he despised.

Chopin's patriotism involved a fierce commitment to the idea of, if not political independence, at least genuine autonomy for Poland; it was rooted in a love of its landscape, history, language, and people. But it was removed from partisan politics, and therefore from both leading factions within the Paris émigré community. Chopin openly confessed to being no revolutionary and took refuge in language, customs, and culture, within a circumscribed aristocratic circle, an elite community defined by social status and breeding that included fellow artists and musicians. And he did so always at some remove.

Chopin therefore never looked at non-exiles with resentment, as writers exiled from modern nation-states or aspiring nation-states often do. He socialized with the large Parisian Polish exile community and cherished the chance to speak Polish, but most of his social life in Paris was not spent with Poles but with the social, economic, and artistic elite of Paris. Apart from Chopin's fear of social unrest in the 1830s and '40s, and his distaste for the poverty and grittiness of Paris, he relished his new surroundings and the elegant, sophisticated milieu in which he traveled, to an extent that dismayed Mickiewicz.[24] Chopin's response to Poland's fate in the 1830 November Uprising was certainly one of sorrow and anger. Yet his lingering nostalgia was benign and familial, one of isolation, not of a "distorting loss."[25]

The sense of loss in Chopin's case was not remotely akin to feeling cut off from "one culture, one home, one setting," a phrase that suggests rather a late nineteenth- and twentieth-century construct of national consciousness. That said, Said's perception that an exile acquires a "contrapuntal" perspective from the experience of exile that enables him to achieve the artistic leap from imitation to originality and to transcend the limits of inherited practices and styles remains valid, and aptly characterizes the ambition Chopin exhibited in his years in Paris.

Chopin was not in the strict sense a political exile. When he left Poland for what he thought would be an extended but not permanent sojourn, he did so knowing that at home he would most likely find himself caught in some violent political conflict in which he would have had to choose not only which side among many he would ally himself with but also face a choice between participating in or escaping from politics altogether. Launching an international career was a means to avoid an unpalatable dilemma.

Given the acute condescension toward Polish culture that was widespread in Western Europe, an attitude rooted in a mix of ignorance and arrogance, and the desire among Poles to assert their greatness and equality (if not superiority) despite political powerlessness, the idea that Chopin, their equivalent of Mozart, could travel abroad and claim honor, pride, and distinction for Poland through his artistry was readily embraced as a patriotic act not only by Chopin's family and friends but by his teacher Elsner as well. This rationalization was only partially successful. After the defeat of the November Uprising, Chopin was required to register in Paris. Faced with the choice of identifying himself as a voluntary émigré or an involuntary political exile, he chose the former. He was, after all, not a veteran of the Uprising, only a sympathizer. But unease at his own behavior did little to discourage his self-image and public image as a patriot.

Chopin's "moral torment" in exile was rendered even more complex because in contrast to the majority and the most prominent members among the large community of Polish exiles in Paris in the 1830s and '40s (over five thousand arrived after 1831), his medium was not words but the piano and "sounding forms." He showed no interest in writing the first great Polish national opera. His music was not, by and large, theatrical. It did not seek to reach a large audience in the sense of the public concert and theater audience; its widest and most immediate reach was through international publication. His music was not overtly narrative or descriptive, in the manner pioneered by Berlioz and Liszt. Chopin's commitment to music as an autonomous medium—coherent in the sense of a language, albeit imprecise in the linguistic sense—was consistent. This aesthetic credo created a counterpoint with Chopin's experience as a Polish exile; Chopin's path to originality was marked by these two competing demands on his image of himself and his ambitions. The comparative opacity of music as a means of communication permitted him to shield contradictions and complexities—and his inner self—from view.

Although many of his contemporaries, among them Felix Mendelssohn and Ferdinand Hiller, kept their own distance from the dramatic Romanticism of Berlioz and Liszt, and ascribed to instrumental music clarity and precision of expression, particularly of subjective emotional responses to the external world and the human experience, Chopin's music was explicitly poetic in character, and resistant to the model of prose. And despite its overt associations with Polish elements, it was never unambiguously polemical and political. Specificity of meaning was not so much inscribed in the text as imposed by individuals who harbored little doubt about the precision and clarity of their understanding.

There was even the oportunity to remain hazy and inarticulate in one's embrace of Chopin's musical fabric without seeming insipid. As Heine put it with his characteristic and biting sarcasm when attempting to characterize George Sand's obsession with Chopin, "She is seeking God and nowhere is God so readily found as in music. As is commonly believed, music does not provoke dissent and is never inane, because it never needs to be astute. It is everything one could possibly want from it. It saves us from a mind that torments, without robbing us of spirituality."[26]

Chopin's project can be compared with that of another Polish exile from a subsequent generation: Joseph Conrad. Employing an astonishing array of non-European characters and settings, Conrad would use the prose novel to undermine the conceits of European superiority in the age of imperialism and colonialism, tearing off the masks of nationality, culture, race, and class, and revealing the essence of the human.

The example of Conrad suggests that comparisons are useful to understanding exile as a key to Chopin's style and originality. Three come to mind. First is Juliusz Słowacki (1809–1849), a Polish contemporary for whom Chopin harbored mixed feelings. The second is Conrad himself, who left Poland when he was sixteen. Conrad, like Chopin, retained a complex and deep attachment to the image of Poland; not surprisingly, he cherished a lifelong affection for the music of Chopin. Third is Heinrich Heine, whom Chopin knew in Paris and who wrote perceptively about the composer. Heine was an exile of a very different sort. Although the complexities of his exile resided in his status as both German and Jew, the Heine case sheds considerable light on Chopin.

Parallel Lives in Exile: Chopin and Juliusz Słowacki

The relationship between Chopin and Juliusz Słowacki needs to be considered in the context of a more senior master, Adam Mickiewicz, the most celebrated poet of Poland and an exile who arrived in Paris in 1832. Mickiewicz, more than a decade older than Chopin and Słowacki, has dominated the extensive scholarship on Chopin's relationship to Polish writers. The composer had read him with enthusiasm in his Warsaw years, and Mickiewicz's 1832 *Dziady* (Forefathers' Eve), notably Part III with its famous "Improvisation," written in exile, influenced Chopin's own "haunting" love of Poland and narrative, declamatory approach to form. Part III is the most political section and is tinged with expressions of guilt and nostalgia consistent with Mickiewicz's self-image as a fierce patriot. Although Mickiewicz wrote two famous works in exile, *Pan Tadeusz* and *Dziady III*, by the late 1830s (Mickiewicz died in 1855) exile had silenced him as a poet.

More revealing, however, may be the juxtaposition and contrast between Chopin and Juliusz Słowacki, Chopin's exact contemporary. Unlike Mickiewicz, Słowacki drew poetic inspiration from exile, much as Chopin did.[27] Słowacki could conjure the fantastic and shift moods and styles; he infused poetic language with a vivid forcefulness while never abandoning a certain Chopin-like mannered ornamentation. Słowacki experimented not only with poetic forms but also with subject matter, drawing inspiration from many non-Polish sources, including classical antiquity.

These were intentional departures from Mickiewicz's seemingly effortless poetic refinement. Słowacki was a vital figure in the evolution of modern Polish literature and politics, one of the three "bards" of Poland, and one particularly admired between 1863 and 1918, when Poland achieved independence. Among Słowacki's admirers were Joseph Conrad's father, Conrad himself, and Józef Piłsudski, the leading political figure of the interwar history of Poland. The Polish pianist and critic Jan Kleczyński first raised the notion of a Słowacki-Chopin comparison in 1870. He suggested affinities between Chopin's "caressing nocturnes" and Słowacki's poetry.[28]

Mickiewicz was a figure of universal veneration, Poland's Goethe and Byron, as George Sand argued.[29] But it was Słowacki who played a role in nineteenth- and early twentieth-century culture comparable to Chopin's. Słowacki, who also wrote powerfully for the theater, harnessed aesthetic Romanticism, including a profound engagement with Shakespeare, and formulated a distinct poetic and dramatic voice in exile that helped define the future character of his homeland.

Despite the weight of scholarly attention to a Chopin-Mickiewicz parallel and the personal antipathy between Chopin and Słowacki, the two contemporaries shared affinities and ambitions.[30] Chopin's innovative framing of the instrumental ballade may have been inspired by Mickiewicz's 1823 *Ballady i romanse* and even by his 1828 *Konrad Wallenrod*,[31] but the style, range and structure of Chopin's music after 1831 share traits with Słowacki's poetics rather than with the idealized, idyllic, and near novelistic poetic realism of Mickiewicz's 1834 masterpiece *Pan Tadeusz*, the culmination of his career as a poet.[32]

Słowacki's personality embodied Romanticism more in the manner of Berlioz. But despite Chopin's personal preference for Mickiewicz— who remained an object of obsessive rivalry for Słowacki[33]—Mickiewicz and Słowacki deserve to be paired as complementary parts of an organic whole, one that resembles the character of Chopin's music. The ennobled depiction of the real world in Mickiewicz, constructed on a neoclassical foundation, led to a reaction: Słowacki's intense, free-form, and individualized expressive power. Słowacki's work, on account of its biting criticism of Polish history and politics and novel style, was suggestive of a world yet to be realized. Like Chopin's, his Romantic modernism constructed a visionary image of Poland. Chopin's was more tied to nostalgia. Słowacki's—notably in the 1834 play *Balladyna*—was defined by fierce anger at the gap between a national rhetoric to be admired and the repeated historic failure of nerve on the part of Poland's protagonists.

Chopin did not possess a literary intellect. In contrast to Liszt, he was not a voracious reader and did not, like Brahms, leave behind a massive library. Only two books were listed among his effects at the time of his death. The wishes of hagiographical accounts of Chopin's life notwithstanding, he had little interesting to say about literature in general, even about the works of his French contemporaries. According to Alfred Cortot, after the end of his formal schooling Chopin did not have much "interest in the printed word."[34]

After music, Chopin's affinities ran rather toward the visual. Writing in 1830 to Tytus Woyciechowski, Chopin relied on visual metaphors to evoke the E-major Adagio of the E-Minor Concerto.[35] He maintained an interest in painting and landscapes. He prized visual elegance and was fastidious about his dress and the interior arrangements of his apartments. He was keen to remain in fashion. Despite his friendship with Delacroix, he preferred Ingres as a painter. His tastes favored the formal and decorative clarity and restraint of late Biedermeier style.[36] He was persuaded, rightly so, that beneath a non-theatrical economy of design, complexity and beauty could be expressed without indulging in the excesses of Romantic gesture.

Nevertheless, literary figures had a marked influence on Chopin's school years, according to the poet and essayist Jarosław Iwaszkiewicz, who pointed out the impact of poet Kazimierz Brodziński's lectures on literature, strongly endorsed by Elsner. Brodziński exhorted his students to emancipate Polish literature from dependence on French and German fashions, and seek its character and mission in the language, history, and mores of the Polish people. No work of art could achieve greatness and the sublime without being rooted in patriotic feelings. Elsner himself wrote a tract on the link between music and the Polish language and its distinct poetic character. Chopin took all this to heart.

Chopin's literary interests, such as they were, concerned poetry and poetic usage, not prose. He construed music as analogous to poetry. Music was "feelings" manifested in sound, and, like poetry, an "indefinite language," but a language nonetheless, capable of articulating thoughts not expressible in words.[37]

Słowacki, despite his works for the stage, was resolutely a poet. He wrote little prose, except for his remarkable letters to his mother.[38] Mickiewicz derided Słowacki for a certain absence of soul and faith—for cultivating style over substance and meaning. Słowacki in turn criticized *Pan Tadeusz* for its failure to pierce the veil of realism and the quotidian and to unleash the sublime and infinite. For Słowacki, poetry and music were uniquely adequate to evoke and approximate the intensity of thoughts and feelings.

Słowacki's dramatic, outspoken temperament and highly critical stance on Polish politics and history annoyed Chopin. Furthermore, Słowacki's most famous poem, "In Switzerland," was inspired by his infatuation, however platonic, with Maria Wodzińska, whom Chopin had at one time sought to marry. An accomplished musician himself, Słowacki resented Maria's admiration for and attraction to Chopin.[39] Despite this absence of personal affinity within an overlapping circle of friends that included critic Maurycy Mochnacki,[40] deeper aesthetic concerns connected the two artists. Chopin never aspired to produce in music an epic equivalent of either *Pan Tadeusz* or *Forefathers' Eve*. Słowacki's work—even the completed drama *Kordian*—is less a coherent epic than a drama composed of distinct poetic fragments with marked contrasting sections more reminiscent of Chopin. And in Słowacki there is an unmistakable lyric originality in poetic usage and electrifying shifts in mood suggestive of Chopin.

Słowacki and Chopin also shared a sense of guilt and shame for their distance from the actual political struggle, feelings they displaced onto their artistic work.[41] Słowacki was in Warsaw during the 1830 November Uprising but did not participate. He left on an official mission for the provisional government, never to return. The contradiction between overt, active patriotism and introspective nationalistic reverie lent the language used to express the love of country in both Chopin and Słowacki an unrelenting resemblance to the language of personal love and desire—for one's mother (more prominently in Słowacki's case), one's friend (in Chopin's case, Tytus Woyciechowski), and for the "beloved." Both artists blurred the boundary between the intimate and the political.

The torment of Chopin's exile and distance from the struggle for independence was expressed in nostalgia and pessimistic skepticism. Słowacki was far more explicit. He was a poet of ideas.[42] His dramatic writings treat the history of Poland with philosophical and moral criticism, damning the older generation for its excessive chivalric rhetoric, high ideals, and practical failures. Both artists shared frustration and anger against the Russians, a self-justificatory distance from direct action, and a righteous suspicion of politicians. But Słowacki took direct aim at Polish leaders past and present and at the self-congratulatory and grandiose claims of Polish national pride. Słowacki also took ironic exception to the facile displacement of the political into the aesthetic and private, particularly among Poles in Paris. In Canto III of his 1841 poem *Beniowski*, he wrote, "Look, right after blood rained down in Poland in November, new poets grow like mushrooms. How sadly each poet weeps buckets of tears to remember. . . . Each has his own language but is crippled in every extremity . . . should their plots contain thunder and lightning, the censor puts an end to them, lest they inspire fear."[43]

Słowacki's lifelong bête noir in this respect remained Mickiewicz. The younger poet saw himself as Poland's poetic equivalent of Achilles, and Mickiewicz as its Hector. Mickiewicz's use of poetry was seen as exhortative, affirmative, and heedlessly glorifying. Słowacki sought to be daring, aggressive, and arresting. Like Chopin he wanted to transform the fate of Poland into a moral parable of humanity. Whereas Mickiewicz, suffering the torment of exile differently, retired to teaching and a domestic life, his greatest work behind him, Słowacki kept on fighting through his poetry. With candid self-awareness, Mickiewicz wrote in *Pan Tadeusz*: "Shame on us, who fled in times of pest / And timid souls who took refuge in the West." In the drama *Kordian*, which was a direct response to Mickiewicz's *Forefathers' Eve*, Słowacki crafted a picture of Polish inaction and indecision, the inability to seize the moment.[44] He criticized fiercely the Romantics' privileging of the aesthetic: art was an insufficient surrogate for politics when it came to bringing about freedom and justice in a world caught between good and evil.

Chopin shared this ambivalence about the conceits of Romanticism as an aesthetic movement with political importance. A tinge of Słowacki's pessimism lingers in his music, often buried beneath the melancholy Liszt ascribed to it, as do echoes of Słowacki's fiery temperament. The beauty of Mickiewicz's poetry and its formulation of patriotic allegiance may have inspired Chopin, but its expression in music, particularly in the shifts in mood, suggest rather Słowacki's complex amalgam of experimentalism, anger, and aspiration.

Frederick Niecks, one of Chopin's first major biographers, argued that in music Chopin rendered the soul "sensible." Niecks characterized him as a "pre-eminently lyrical" composer for whom "subjectivity" was the "beginning and end." Even though Chopin "abhorred" the music of Berlioz and Liszt, he was "a tone poet, and as such had something to communicate, Chopin must be in one way or another a composer of 'programme' music."[45]

The "something" Chopin communicated was more than an idealized expression of the Polish soul, character, and nation. A sense of resignation about the political consequences of patriotism can be heard, comparable to Słowacki's evocation of the pathetic status of martyrdom and its poetic glorification in the wake of concrete failure and defeat. But Chopin did not share Słowacki's radical concerns for social and economic reform, or empathy with the plight of the vast majority of poor, oppressed, and illiterate Polish peasants.

Much of Polish patriotism of the early nineteenth century was trapped in the tradition of an aristocratic idealism that promised freedom and democracy only to the *szlachta* class, members of a gentry that was remarkably large—10 percent of the population. A small elite within that group, the aristocracy, dominated the wealth of the land. Chopin was in sympathy with their traditions and therefore was more at home in the émigré circle of the Hôtel Lambert, the political camp of Prince Adam Czartoryski, than he was among the Polish social radicals in Paris. In exile, he focused on becoming accepted within elite Parisian circles; he did not want to be seen as yet another importunate Polish émigré.

Chopin compensated for his nonpartisan distance from political reality by devoting himself to his art—celebrating the use of Polish elements and his fame as the voice of Poland. All the same, writing to Julian Fontana in 1848, Chopin advised him to stay away from Poland. There was going to be no breakthrough, no Poland rising from the ashes. Three emotions define the "something" mentioned by Niecks that Chopin sought to evoke through his music: (1) the experience of exile and isolation, and its attendant idealized nostalgic vision of home; (2) the guilt of non-participation and the absence of sacrifice, frequently expressed in displaced rage; and (3) a mistrust of politics, particularly anti-aristocratic utopian radicalism.

These three emotions appear as well in two verses from Słowacki's 1839 *Agammemnon's Tomb*:

O Poland, as long as your angelic soul
Remains captive inside a thick skull,
As long as you allow the executioner to hack your body,
Your sword will not inspire the terror of revenge
As long as a hyena hovers over you,
You will face, a tomb, opened-eyed.

O Poland, you are still lured by baubles.
The peacock of nations you have been—and the parrot.
And now you are another's servant.
Though I realize these words
May not resound too long in your heart,
Where an idea does not remain even for even single hour.
This I tell you and I am sad—and am myself completely guilty.[46]

Poland, Słowacki charged, did not even retain the power to curse. In a moment of searing self-criticism, he described the consequence of his voluntary exile: "I have no dignity—I have fled from martyrdom." Poland, as a nation, was a slave that glorified its martyrdom and then celebrated it in art. These convictions undercut the highly sentimental and depoliticized construct of *żal*, the melancholy so frequently associated with Chopin and his Polish identity. The elusive, intense personal confessional impulse beneath the elegant surface of Chopin's music echoes Słowacki. Yet this authorial meaning, however precise, did not interfere with the capacity of performers and listeners to render Chopin personal in their own manner.[47]

Chopin's political skepticism in the early 1830s was further deepened in the 1840s by the spread of a messianic interpretation of the unique character of Poland and its tragic history. Mickiewicz had already articulated a version of this in *Forefathers' Eve*: Poland's destiny as the instrument of European redemption in modern times. Poland was the bulwark against Russian barbarism, the antidote to Prussian rigidity, French superficiality, and Anglo-American materialism. Having been martyred, Poland would rise again and lead the way to a redeemed Europe defined by freedom, justice, and spirituality. Mickiewicz wrote in the preface to Part III:

For half a century now, Poland has been the scene of such ceaseless, unflagging, inexorable cruelty at the hands of the tyrants who oppress Her, and such illimitable devotion and endurance on the part of Her suffering peoples, as the world has not seen since the days of the persecuted Christians. It seems as if these Kings possessed a Herod-like presentiment of the manifestation of a new light appearing upon the earth, and of their own imminent downfall, while the people believe ever more strongly in their renewal and resurrection.[48]

In contrast to Mickiewicz, the resolutely anti-clerical Słowacki quickly abandoned his brief flirtation with Polish messianism, whose high point occurred when its most powerful voice, the charismatic Andrzej Towiański, arrived in Paris.[49] Towiański created a sensation with sermons and public appearances. The government of Louis Philippe maintained a cautious attitude to the Polish émigré community and was wary of the impact on Parisians of its radical factions and their constant agitation for armed struggle and social reform. Towiański was expelled. Chopin was repelled from the start by the movement and its utopian vision of the Polish nation of the future, which included not only its transformation from a feudal rural state but also a "unification" with the Jews of Poland so that Jews could become a "homogeneous" part of Poland. In his overt philo-Semitism, Towiański stood side by side with Mickiewicz and Słowacki.[50]

Chopin's anti-Semitic sentiments ran deep.[51] They are evident in his correspondence from a young age. Particularly offensive to him were Jews who had assimilated and passed as equals in polite society. He once confessed that he would rather deal with a real orthodox Jew than a Jew who appeared integrated and cosmopolitan. He was offended by Leo Herz's use of Polish themes and accused him of being a sort of musical Uncle Tom who vulgarized these melodies, cheapening them by transforming them into the kind of exotic entertainment that Polish nobility demanded of Jews on their lands.[52] Chopin's anti-Semitism was rooted in his self-image as an aristocrat and as a superior soul rather than in some more elaborate racial theory, except perhaps for his adherence to a suspicion of Jews in matters of money and business. Anti-Semitism did not interfere with his admiration for and friendship with Alkan or even Heine, although there are tinges of it in his relationships with Moscheles and Meyerbeer. Chopin never seems to have considered that the Jews of his era were in a sense also exiles: a distinct population that struggled against pervasive political and social oppression.

In the end, Chopin and Słowacki took refuge in their art. Słowacki made politics a recurrent subject, but he would become famous for his poetic virtuosity, not primarily the overt content of his work, just as Chopin's musical ambitions as a composer dwarfed his allegiance to a theoretical construct of Poland. In both cases, exile, in placing of the artist outside of the two communities—homeland and foreign home—offered an undefined space in which to pursue a wholly individual course. Political idealism expressed in art offered respite from the self-image as pariah. Chopin achieved more stability in exile than Słowacki, but in the work of both, distance, anger, and loss and tinges of irony found unique aesthetic formulations. Chopin and Słowacki vindicate the critic Sigurd Burckhardt's perception that "great creators" are set apart by their ability to "sustain, often for a long time and without letup, the pain of disorder."[53]

For all the veneration routinely accorded Mickiewicz, future generations of Polish poets, writers, and musicians turned to Słowacki and Chopin. Chopin's influence on Polish culture and national self-definition deepened over time.[54] So did the influence of Słowacki. In 1905, the German-Jewish literary critic Gustav Karpeles, in a volume titled *Slavic Journeys*, singled out Słowacki's influence on contemporary writers as unique. The young, he argued, "only accepted Słowacki, the Polish Heine, and recited with great fondness those poems that condemned the old Poland."[55] Słowacki was the poet from the past who influenced literary modernism, just as Chopin did in music. Both had fashioned a novel aesthetic that carried within it a visionary Polish self-image. Słowacki "was the only one among the great poets of the Romantic era who dared during its heyday to shake off the yoke of extreme foreign influence."[56] Not surprisingly, Józef Piłsudski insisted that Słowacki's remains be brought back from exile and reburied in Poland, in a place of honor next to Mickiewicz. Since no other modern European nation's self-image and identity was so influenced by contemporary émigré artists from the past, it is perhaps no coincidence that Słowacki and Chopin, both Romantic innovators in exile, shared the same dream. Knowing full well that they would die in exile, they wanted their hearts returned and buried in Poland.[57]

The causal link between voluntary exile and the character of the work produced in exile connects their work. Formulating a distinct aesthetic identity in the context of being uprooted from a coherent but politically dismembered community that one intuitively grasps though its language customs and mores (including music), required entering a new context in which one remains a foreigner. In Chopin's case, the artistic outcome of exile was equally dependent on the destination. Paris itself colluded with his decision not to return. It also shaped Chopin's compositional trajectory, particularly the exclusive focus on the piano. Paris was the capital of opera and of the piano and Chopin, owing to his father's French heritage, spoke the language. The musical culture he encountered there helped define what Liszt aptly characterized as music of an "entirely new expressiveness" and "a harmonic structure as original as it is learned." Perhaps only in a context rife with competing aesthetic movements could Chopin perfect a "profundity" hidden behind "charm," "ingenuity," and grace, resulting in an "elusive poetry that is so idealized and fragile that it scarcely seems to belong to this world." These attributes had unique positive and negative stimuli (consider, for example, Chopin's exposure to Berlioz and Bellini) from within the place of exile. The intersection of exposure to Parisian tastes with characteristics such as grace and charm from the locus of exile shaped by refracted memory residues from the distant homeland to generate a unique synthesis.[58]

All this hinged on a common attribute: Słowacki and Chopin left Poland imbued, from childhood, with the same construct of patriotism specific to Poles of their generation. They were brought up suffused with myths concerning the loss of independence and autonomy, as well as a sense of foreboding and oppression. The vision of Poland Słowacki carried with him into exile was sharply drawn. Chopin's remained one of sentiment and aspiration. But in their aesthetic breakthroughs they found the means to rob the shame of political failure framed in their memories of distant victory, and point a path into the future for the culture and language of Poland.

The Legacy of a Childhood in Exile: Joseph Conrad

The peculiar nature of Polish identity and patriotism made its reappearance in the career of the only other Polish exile to achieve international stature as an artist in the nineteenth century, Joseph Conrad.[59] Just as the uprising of 1830 became pivotal in Chopin's life, the failed uprising of 1863 played an important role in Conrad's life.[60]

Chopin came from a family of szlachta on his mother's side only. His father, although of French birth and descent, was an ardent Polish patriot, a veteran, and an admirer of Tadeusz Kościuszko. Conrad's ancestors were proudly szlachta on both sides. His father, Apollo Korzeniowski, was an outspoken, charismatic but failed man of politics—a writer and organizer for Polish independence.[61] Supported enthusiastically by his wife, he suffered imprisonment and was exiled along with his family by the Russians—all for the Polish cause. Conrad never forgot that his parents had died as martyrs for a hopeless Romantic political illusion and was convinced that their forced exile had fostered absurdly passionate political illusions and diminished his father's grasp of reality. He was determined not to follow his parents' path.

Chopin left Poland when he was twenty, tasked with the goal of placing Poland on a cultural par with the other nations of Western Europe; he was Poland's most promising musical talent. Conrad, on the other hand, left as an obscure orphan on the brink of maturity who as yet had exhibited little in the way of talent, let alone genius.[62] The uncertainty of his fate can easily be blamed on the intensity with which his father sacrificed domestic tranquility, comfort, and stability for the ultimately doomed cause of Polish independence and social reform. Despite his ambivalent feelings about his father—a mix of resentment and glorification—Conrad proudly remembered that at age six he had described himself to his grandmother as a "Pole, Catholic and Gentleman."

But like Chopin, Conrad never overcame the mix of loss, fragments of memory, and guilt associated with leaving Poland. He once observed, "I can't think of Poland often. It feels bad, bitter, painful. It would make life unbearable." Conrad's accent and manners remained distinctly Polish and he never entirely abandoned the use of his native language. He followed Polish politics and, among other things, relished listening to Chopin. His status as a Polish exile was not immaterial to him, even when he exhibited both reticence and anger about it. He recognized its significance to his career as a writer in English. As he put it in an interview to a Polish journalist during his visit to Poland on the eve of the First World War:

> The immortality of Poland? No one doubts it. English critics—and after all I am an English writer—whenever they speak of me add that there is something incomprehensible, inconceivable, elusive. Only you can grasp this elusiveness, and comprehend what is incomprehensible. This is Polishness, Polishness which I took from Mickiewicz and Słowacki. My father read *Pan Tadeusz* to me and made me read it aloud. Not just once or twice. I used to prefer *Konrad Wallenrod*, *Grażyna*. Later I preferred Słowacki. Do you know why Słowacki? *Il est l'âme de toute la Pologne, lui.*[63]

Słowacki, Chopin, and Conrad are linked by their shared distrust of political action, partisan commitments, and dreams of democratic or social utopias, a distrust only deepened in exile. The image of Poland Conrad carried with him was an extension of Chopin's and Słowacki's. It was dreamlike—an "incomprehensible, inconceivable" and "elusive" ideal of a free state led by aristocratic individuals, each imbued with virtues of loyalty and courage. In contrast to the crass materialism and violence of modern politics, a Polish state was envisioned capable of offering all individuals, particularly artists, the hope of unfettered self-realization. Faced with the improbability of such a political vision, the torment and guilt of voluntary exile felt by Conrad became transformed into a credo of artistic creation centered on the candid observation of human nature. Conrad's ambition was to harness the peculiar strangeness of the exiled Polish sensibility to express a de-mythologizing universality in which the criteria of judgment derived from the Polish paradox: the confrontation between the tragic outcome of history and the unique humanism of traditional aristocratic Polish idealism, heroism, and solidarity. The latter had already found its voice in the work of the exiled Mickiewicz and, despite his resentments, in Słowacki.

As astonishing and unexpected as Conrad's mastery of the English language was, the counterpoint of exile did not leave its primary mark on his prose style, which is perhaps why Nabokov remained so dismissive of him.[64] Conrad's foreignness has often been credited with lending his prose its engaging character, but his great breakthrough was based on his shrewd manipulation of established traditions of prose realism. Conrad used the story and the novel to reveal the elusive, inconceivable, and incomprehensible constant in life beneath the detailed particularities of human experience—the tragic terror of self-awareness that might well be called a universal "Polishness."

Conrad's status as exile permitted him an unsentimental perspective on imperialism and colonialism. Using his experiences at sea, he brought to life an astonishing range of places and characters with spellbinding craft. If Chopin fashioned a new language of subjective expression in music, Conrad defined the limits of Romanticism's celebration of human autonomy and subjectivity. Yet he never abandoned the ideal his father had cherished—that the coherent homogeneous community, the one from which he had fled, was, if rendered free, the only plausible and proper condition of life. Only in community could the virtues of loyalty and fidelity find expression. But beneath the stark contrasts in cultures, personalities, and mores Conrad depicted—and despite the reality of shared national characteristics, even among the English—an inescapable and tragic existential predicament prevailed whose recognition no individual could evade. Europeans, in the end, could lay claim to no moral priority and no cultural superiority.

Conrad's ambition to describe his own self-representation as an artist further recommends a comparison to Chopin. In 1897, he declared in the preface to *The Nigger of the 'Narcissus'*: "I stand or fall as an artist in prose."

For Conrad, music held the highest status as the "art of arts." Music exemplified the purpose of all art, whether achieved through words, images, or sounds. That purpose was to "reach the secret spring of responsive emotions." Conrad the artist sought to engage all readers, not only the English public, much as Chopin the composer sought international recognition. Conrad was determined to "make you hear, make you feel—it is before all—to make you see. . . . If I succeed you shall find there according to your desserts: encouragement, consolation, fear, charm—all you demand; and, also that glimpse of truth for which you had forgotten to ask."[65] Beneath the alluring detail and within the illusion of realism was the need to confront an invariable, shared, and daunting truth.

Conrad believed that the "only valid justification for the worker in prose" was to aspire to the power of music, which he characterized as "the perfect blending of form and substance." As if to echo Chopin's attention to the craft of composition, Conrad required of himself an "unremitting never discouraged care for the shape and ring of sentences."[66] Through his command of the prose form, Conrad could engage the reader sufficiently deeply to come to grips with the irreconcilable contradictions of human nature.

Conrad's success in creating a unique style, form, and voice was comparable to Chopin's. Like Chopin, he invented himself artificially through the act of writing.[67] Using the traditions of prose writing in both English and Polish, Conrad fashioned a persona in exile that never shed its elusive character.[68] His protean originality permitted readers a wide range of subjective responses. As with Chopin, the impact of the exile experience found its end point in an artistry that transcended cultural and national lines.

The Essence of Exile: The Case of Heinrich Heine

The third prism through which we may view the career and achievement of Chopin is the parallel path followed by one of the most celebrated and studied artists in exile, Heinrich Heine. He was of course not Polish but a German Jew, albeit a converted one.[69] Heine, as Ernst Pawel aptly put it, was a man whose lifelong destiny was to be the "quintessential outsider." Baptism notwithstanding, he never escaped being viewed and even celebrated within his native world as a Jewish pariah.

Heine fled German-speaking Europe in May 1831 and arrived in Paris a few months before Chopin. He remained in that city for the rest of his life (he died in 1856), taking only two brief trips back to Germany. His exile was far less voluntary than Chopin's, as his writings, radical revolutionary sympathies, and political activities led him into conflict with the authorities in various German states. His works were censored and, not unreasonably, he feared imprisonment if he returned to Germany. Heine's Parisian friends included practically the entire elite of Paris, including Chopin and Karl Marx.

Unlike Chopin, Heine saw himself as a key participant in the political struggles of his homeland. Germany may have still been a disparate group of independent states, but it already exerted real industrial and political force, unlike Poland. The question in Germany was one of social and economic justice and reform and unification, not independence: a struggle against both lingering feudalism and the more novel bourgeois rapacity. The sins of industry and the capitalist marketplace were a subject that intensely occupied George Sand and many of her friends, many of them adherents of Saint-Simon who fancied themselves utopian socialists. Chopin was tone-deaf to these debates.

For all his social concerns, Heine at his core was a poet. By the time he settled in Paris, he was already acknowledged as one of Germany's finest and most popular lyric voices. His poetic instincts were decidedly musical. Like music, poetry was a "blessed and secret world" in which the poet, as scholar Ritchie Robertson put it, was "king in the realm of thought" and "ruler in a dream world."[70] In Paris, Heine and Chopin became acquainted. They traveled in many of the same circles, encountering each other mostly in elegant salons. While in Paris, Heine dabbled in criticism, much of it on music and the theater. The true meaning of Heine's sardonic and elegant journalistic opinions has been questioned on account of his complex motivations, including personal enmities, need for money, and his political beliefs, but he never wavered in his admiration of Chopin. His enthusiasm was genuine.

This was due in part to Heine's turn, after 1840, against the direction of musical Romanticism represented by Liszt and Berlioz and his affinity for Chopin's lyricism, Classicist impulses, as well as lack of theatrical bombast. Goethe's death in 1832 left Heine as the leading poetic voice of Germany and he continued the late Goethe's defense of poetic restraint, refinement, and form, but in his own way. At the same time, in exile, Heine never lost his sharp wit and instinct for satire and polemic, qualities foreign to Goethe's spiritual gravity.

Liszt was the first to suggest that Heine possessed a particularly keen insight into Chopin and his music: "Chopin and Heine understood each other intuitively, so that to any murmured question the musician replied with surprising passages on the keyboard. . . . After Chopin had answered, they . . . remained silent and sad, seized with homesickness."[71] Liszt fashioned these phrases using Heine's own words. But it was Liszt, not Heine or Chopin, who drew attention to the shared sense of exile as the source of their special bond.

Liszt explained Chopin's uniqueness as a composer primarily in terms of his status as "an essentially Polish poet" who "individualized" in himself "the poetic sense of a whole nation": as if the reimagining of an idealized homeland in exile provided Chopin with all the inspiration he required to realize uncommon beauty and compositional originality. As Liszt observed, Heine recognized in Chopin a reflection of his own fate. Heine's internal exilic status as a Jew in Germany as well as his Parisian exile shaped the characterization of the "flying Dutchman" in his 1833 satiric novel, *Aus den Memoiren des Herrn von Schnabelewopski*. The seafaring Van der Decken, condemned to be cast adrift on the ocean without intimacy and home, became the model for Wagner's later opera.

But Heine and Chopin had more than loss and isolation in common. As exiles they both embraced Paris and its culture as the epitome of an ideal cosmopolitan capital. Heine relished Paris as a place where an outsider who was an artist could become a genuine defining insider (as Chopin discovered, particularly during his notorious liaison with George Sand). Chopin, far more than Heine, achieved this rarefied insider status in Paris. Homesickness was a state of mind that coexisted with an allegiance to place, status, and security achieved in a new home. A return to their national community was never envisaged as a practical possibility, and only desired in the abstract.

Liszt once reproached Heine for the sharp criticism of his own music and style of performance. Heine had characterized it as the work of a "cranky, strange, disfigured" (*verschrobenen*) and "unsettled" (*unbequemen*) character. Liszt countered by asking if it was not true that their entire generation of artists was living in a moment of history that, understood in terms of its political and social instability, could be aptly described as unsettled and disfigured. Was not everyone living in times "between a past that we no longer wish to emulate and a future that we still do not know"? Could not Heine himself be characterized similarly?[72]

Liszt challenged Heine's use of the status of exile as a privileged source of legitimization for a less theatrical, less grandiose Romantic aesthetic, one contained by an allegiance to pre-Romantic traditions represented best by Raphael, Mozart, and the post–Sturm und Drang Goethe.[73] Heine's answer holds a clue to Chopin's rejection of the dramatic and spectacular Romanticism of contemporaries such as Berlioz and even his friend Delacroix. For Heine (and Chopin), the aesthetic realm was idealized as a realm with the potential to transcend the quotidian without a total denial of reality. Through the discipline of Classical restraint, poetry and music could express the sublime without explicitly mirroring the disfigurement and unsettled nature of external reality. Rather, art could be an ideal, critical and contradictory response to this reality. In Heine's late lyric poetry and in Chopin's music from the mid-1830s, the modern became original without either ceasing to be modern or becoming learned, academic, and even regressive.[74] In their modernist distinctiveness, Classical discipline revealed common ground.[75]

In formal terms, Heine and Chopin both tempered Liszt's extroverted, rebellious Romantic impulse. By linking the present with an imagined past that could be emulated, this rigorous aesthetic transfiguration enabled the work of art and its creator—particularly the exile—to overcome national distinctions and local conditions. Aesthetic discernment, nurtured in exile, ennobled the artist, reader, performer, and listener. It defined the cosmopolitan, the individual possessed of a universal sensibility. In the Paris of Heine and Chopin, exotic particularity—whether Polish, Jewish, or Hungarian-Gypsy—was integrated into a new construct of the human community in which the exiled artist became the ideal protagonist.

In the end Heine, for all his sustained revolutionary commitments, subordinated politics to the primacy of the aesthetic, even though his destiny to die in exile was rooted in an unrelenting desire to challenge political authority. Yet even when the overt subject of his poetry was political, the power of the experience of exile enabled him to harness the suffering and anger caused by politics in forms whose surface beauty and formal economy triumphed over systems of ideology and justified the aristocracy of the cosmopolitan artist. In Chopin's forms, harmonic daring, and refined pianism Heine sensed a musical achievement parallel to his own achievement in poetry.

Consider Heine's most famous and often quoted remarks on Chopin that highlight Chopin's cosmopolitan stature, his amalgam of identities, his status as an exile, and the nature of his art. Heine articulates parallels to himself:

> It would not be fair were I not to mention here a pianist who, along with Liszt, is truly celebrated. Chopin, who not only shines as virtuoso through his technical perfection, but also achieves greatest things as a composer. He is a human being of the highest order. Chopin is indeed the darling of an elite that looks in music for the highest spiritual enjoyment. His

fame is of the aristocratic kind; he gives off the scent of the praise of good society, but his refinement is in his person.

Chopin was born to French parents in Poland and enjoyed part of his education in Germany. The influences of these three nations gave his personality a most extraordinary aspect— namely, he appropriated the best of what distinguishes each of these people: Poland gave him his chivalric spirit and his sense of historical suffering; France gave him his facile charm, his grace; Germany gave him his Romantic profundity. . . . But nature itself gave him a delicate, slender, somewhat frail figure, a most noble heart, and his genius. Yes, one has to grant Chopin genius, in the full meaning of the word; he is not only a virtuoso, he is also a poet; he can show us that the poetry that lives in his soul can be brought into view. He is a poet of sound, and nothing compares to the pleasure he gives us when he sits at the piano and improvises. Then he is nei- ther Pole nor French nor German but rather reveals his truly elevated origins. We realize then that he comes from the land of Mozart, Raphael, Goethe—his true homeland is the dream- land of poetry. When he sits at the piano and improvises, I feel as if a fellow countryman from the beloved fatherland is visiting and telling me all the curious things that happened in my absence. . . . At times I would like to interrupt him with questions: And how fares the beautiful mermaid, who knew so well to wind her silver veil flirtatiously around her green locks? Does the white-bearded god of the seas still pursue her with his foolish and stale love? Are the roses of our land still standing proudly in their flaming color? Do the trees still sing so beautifully in the moonlight?[76]

The two exiles Heine and Chopin are leading citizens of an imagined polity—a community of artists, the true basis of cosmopolitan society. That, and not the place from which they came, is their true home. And its world is the world of the aesthetic imagination, defined in terms of the poetic and the musical. The poetic remained the key vehicle for the pro- found expression of the human. Chopin's case demonstrated that it was not sufficient to win over the public and succeed in the commerce of art, particularly in terms of technical perfection: "Chopin is not satisfied that the skillfulness of his hands is applauded approvingly by other hands." Chopin, Heine concludes, "strives for higher laurels, his fingers are but the servants of his soul, and it is his soul that is celebrated by people who listen, not with ears alone but with their soul."[77]

As the modern equivalent of Mozart, Goethe, and Raphael,[78] Chopin harnessed the traditions of his art in a new way, but at a price that Heine struggled to conceal. The cosmopolitan was a construct reinforced by the Parisian social life Chopin and Heine shared. But it was not genuinely political and hardly masked the void created by the escape from reality necessitated by exile into the "dreamland" of the poetic. Heine, and to a lesser extent Chopin, recognized that the aesthetic was, at best, a weak substitute for the political. The feeling of exile and the sense of responsibility for one's remove from the native community were never fully camouflaged or amalgamated into a stable meta-political self-image of the artist as the true constituent of cosmopolitanism—a fact that became painfully acute to both men during moments of social unrest in the streets in the 1830s and particularly in 1848.

For Heine, all the superficial markers of things Polish in Chopin's music did not, in the end, make the work Polish in Liszt's sense. It was a transcendent synthesis of distinct cultural influences. The music could therefore express the elevated "wistful melancholy" of the artist as citizen of a supranational world. This points to the affinity that can be found between Chopin's melancholy and the emotional tone of Heine's later lyric poetry—particularly *Romanzero*, written between 1848 and 1851.

But the similarities between Heine the poet and Chopin the composer diverge in terms of their reception. The Chopin-like character of Heine's late poetry would be contrasted, negatively, with Goethe's. Heine's poetry and prose from his years in exile were attacked for the very reasons Chopin's music was lauded: its "dreamland" fantastic surface, its distance from the real, and its ironic fictional sensibility. Contemporary and posthumous critics claimed that Heine's originality rested in the deleterious transposition of a French "charm and grace" into German lyricism, depriving the German of its authentic indigenous character. Heine corrupted his native language by appropriating a French (and thus superficial) sensibility.[79]

In contrast, Chopin's transformations of Polish materials into an original style embedded in European musical practices did not earn Chopin derision or prevent his music from being embraced as authentically Polish.[80] Heine's lyricism did indeed depart from an essentialist definition of German poetics. But the pronounced difference in the posthumous reputations of these two Parisian exiles also certainly owed something to Heine's Jewishness. Chopin became a defining element in all matters Polish. Had he been Jewish, would his posthumous fate have been more like Heine's, the exiled rebel and iconoclast who became a figure of ambivalence, accused of corrupting the spiritual essence of the German? Even so, Chopin was not entirely exempt from being viewed by critics with condescension as superficial (i.e., French) and less profound than the great German masters.

Heine and Chopin were subject to similar criticicsms. It was alleged that Chopin's distinctive style and capacity to express "an unusual grand subjectivity" masked a fatal flaw beneath its seductive beauty of sudden contrasts, sharp dissonances, and folklike simplicity. Mortiz Veit pointed to that same flaw in Heine's case with these words: "Swept into the midst of the enticing bustle of cosmopolitanism, corruption and excessive delicacy," Heine "poisoned the innocence of his heart." The poetry's mannered surface masked its ultimate insincerity.[81]

Such doubts about Chopin were expressed by Ludwig Rellstab in the mid-1830s, J. W. Davidson in the 1840s, and in the 1890s most forcefully by William Henry Hadow.[82] This critique of Chopin, and the suspicion directed at Heine, suggested that perhaps Paris and its self-consciously cosmopolitan conceits had corrupted the otherwise spontaneously exotic Polish musical poet and the otherwise gifted German lyric poet. Chopin's work was often dismissed in German criticism as a species of "salon music." Paris, the symbol of refinement and superiority in matters of style and fashion, if not the pretentious conceits of the artist,[83] was said to have limited if not ruined Chopin's genius. So did an excessive concern with criteria of grace and surface elegance associated with aristocratic circles, and Chopin's avoidance of the long forms of instrumental music. The reception history of Chopin as fundamentally Polish then became a rebuttal used by Chopin's defenders.

This critical approach had its most memorable articulation in Nietzsche's remarks on Chopin. Much as Nietzsche welcomed the relief he brought to a ponderous, heavy, and obscure German aesthetic, Chopin, he thought, had lived too long under the spell of a dangerous French influence. Too many of his works revealed the irresistible narcotic of an overrefined culture. They appear elegant and lavishly clothed but mask a pale, suppressed interior, deprived of indispensable and healthy sunlight.[84] Artur Schnabel's coldness to Chopin may have had its origins in this attitude.

These caveats aside, the later work of Chopin and of Heine share virtues in the use of lyricism, economy, and restraint to express an existential condition of searing sadness.[85] That condition has two dominant sides. The first is the fantasy and anger directed at powerlessness and the sorrow of isolation. The richness of "natality" is seen as being beyond reach.[86] The second is memory transfigured through classical cosmopolitan aesthetics. The resultant synthesis is an idealized remembrance of the past that presents itself as universalized human subjectivity propelled by the recognition of the absence of a homeland. Exile is refracted through the lens of the embrace of an aristocratic cosmopolitanism. Longing and dreaming and a sense of isolation pervade the lyricism of human subjectivity. Two separate fragments from Heine's *Romanzero* reveal these two sides, which are equally dominant in Chopin.

The first fragment, from Book I, comes at the end of a poem whose overt subject is ancient Mexico, where anger and impotence are made manifest through melodic lyricism. The peculiar self-reflection imposed by exile is displaced into an imagined exotic home, placed ironically within the frame of a "new" world (America never presented itself as an option for Heine because of his contempt for its "boorish" egalitarianism). Rage and resentment are turned both inward and outward, driven by the exile's dark view of human nature. Heine's pessimistic, unvarnished view of humanity was common among exiles like Słowacki and Conrad and can be detected in Chopin's music.

Heine's Mexico is of course a placeholder for Germany. Living in it, Heine writes: "Yes, a devil I will become, and as comrades I greet you . . . teach me all your horrors, and your beautiful art of deceit! My dear Mexico, I can no longer rescue you, but avenge you with fury I will, my beloved Mexico."[87]

In the second example, taken from Book II of *Romanzero*, the poet muses on where the exile might possibly find a home. In a poem titled "And Now, Where?" Heine concludes, "I gaze into the heavens sadly, where thousands of stars shimmer, but nowhere can I catch a glimpse of my own star. Perhaps in heaven it lost its way within the golden labyrinth, just as I have become lost in the chaos of the earth."[88] The star is the artist as protagonist of the subjective, a self-definition that illuminates the ambivalent and unstable interactions of both Chopin and Heine with their Parisian surroundings, their underlying mistrust, and, in Chopin's case, a preference for the rhetoric and illusions of romantic desire, love, and companionship rather than the daunting proximity of real intimacy. Ultimately, the suspicion of inauthenticity and insincerity derives from the unrelenting sorrow brought on by distance from any semblance of a political community or a sense of home—the prerequisite for human friendship and intimacy.

The synthesis of a cosmopolitan aesthetic with the distance of exile inscribed in Chopin's music permits its remarkable appropriation and adaptation by performers and listeners, and the repeated transfer of its subjectivity away from its original authorial intention.[89] This explains the wide variation in and seemingly never-ending controversy surrounding the proper performance practice of Chopin. A plasticity in modes of Chopin interpretation illuminates the equally persistent controversy over the meaning and merit of Heine's poetry.

Exile's Tragic End: Chopin and the Jews of Poland in the Twentieth Century

In the first volume of his all too vivid embellished autobiography, the pianist Arthur Rubinstein described a youthful and close friendship in Berlin with "Frederic Harman," whom Rubinstein describes as a young Polish composer from Warsaw. Harman was actually Juliusz Edward Wertheim, a distinguished Polish Jewish musician. It was Wertheim who persuaded Rubinstein that Chopin was more than a "young sick romantic figure who wrote sentimental music for the piano, elegant and difficult" but empty except for its unrelenting melancholy. Rubinstein had previously sympathized with those Germans who derided Chopin as "salon music," but Wertheim revealed to him "the real authentic Chopin."

Wertheim, although hampered technically, played Chopin differently. He did so without the often "arbitrary exaggeration of expression and tempo" that Rubinstein remembered from Paderewski's playing. His more modernist, disciplined approach revealed the "true accent" of the music, an accent that distanced Chopin from the superficiality of the aristocratic salon and exposed "earthy" Polish rhythms. Chopin's music suddenly gave voice to deeply populist and patriotic emotions accessible to the modern concert audience.[90]

Rubinstein heard Chopin re-politicized. The cause of the success of this transposition, Rubinstein recalled, was an act of aesthetic re-evaluation and self-recognition. Chopin, in Wertheim's studied respect for the logic and form of his music, and shorn of any apparent personalized self-indulgence, revealed a musical mirror of "my innate love of Poland." This curious anecdote foregrounds three distinct but related facets in the reception history of Chopin during the early twentieth century, the era that witnessed the birth of modernism in music and the rebirth of Poland as an independent political entity.

First, the wordless sounds of Chopin (his songs never had a significant following) emanated from a single instrument, the piano, whose mass distribution between 1830 and 1914 assured its primacy in the rapidly expanding musical culture of an industrialized Europe and North America. This almost exclusive focus on the piano, which during Chopin's lifetime was considered a barrier to his being considered one of the greatest composers in music history, became an asset by the end of the century. By then, the piano had become the defining and most comprehensive medium of musical literacy. Chopin was the composer who most fully commanded its capacity to communicate musical thinking, in terms of melodic invention, harmonic color and plasticity, and variation in rhythm. Chopin achieved all this with uncommon control over sonority and counterpoint, and a striking accessible transparency of form. Profundity inhabited his dance forms and other musical equivalents of short poetic frameworks, giving voice to intimate individual feelings. During the fin de siècle, an era marked by the rejection of the post-Wagnerian musical aesthetics of late Romanticism dominant in Mahler and Richard Strauss, Chopin—reinterpreted as a master of Classicist restraint and economy—eluded the derision of the modernists and acquired a resilient respectability, earning the allegiances of Debussy, Reger, Schoenberg, Heinrich Schenker, and Scriabin.[91]

For professionals and amateurs of the piano alike, self-expression appeared most fully realized through Chopin's music. It provided an almost complete range of secret personal meanings compatible with public display. The ubiquity of the piano allowed the essence of Chopin to became a normative standard for instrumental music as a medium of individual, personal communication. It helped that a significant amount of Chopin's music was playable by amateurs. The prominence of the piano in homes of all classes and in public spaces, from hotel lobbies and restaurants to schools, allowed the sound of Chopin to became a defining element of the modern cultural consciousness of intimacy, Hollywood included.[92] His works constituted a compact but democratically accessible compendium of and guide to the musical expression of feelings.

Insofar as Chopin's music evoked something distinctly Polish, that distinctiveness was subordinated to its overarching virtuosity of melodic and harmonic invention. To the non-Polish public, the Polish element had been absorbed into a universal rhetoric of expressiveness. In other cases of European "national" music—Bartók, Rimsky-Korsakov, Dvořák, and Smetana, for example—the national element stemmed from constructed musical mirrors of recognizable folk elements from pre-industrial times. The music elaborated sentiments and self-images that had a prior visual and literary presence in a national narrative. Music translated national sentiment into sound and thereby added a recognizable, unifying musical element to modern national identities; it exploited familiar, irreducible exoticisms, both at home and abroad.

By the end of the nineteenth century, the sustained political absence of a Polish nation and the regional divergences within Poland resulting from the tripartite partition left a near-vacuum of reductive secular markers of national self-recognition. The one exception was Chopin, who posthumously filled that vacuum. Only in Poland did a single composer's style and language shape its literate elite's unifying image of the country. Rather than expressing a preexisting national sensibility in music, Chopin invented it. Shaped in exile, Chopin's "theoretical" Poland (to use Miłosz's term) was a hazy, inaccessible spiritual object of loss and desire. By the turn of the century Chopin's music had reconfigured it into a successful, romanticized construct of a nation.

A second facet was that despite special pleading concerning the authentic "folk" sources and folklike national elements in Chopin's music, particularly during the era of Communist Poland, the politicization of Chopin as the voice of Poland was successful precisely because Chopin's music rendered folk elements less evidently "folk." He fashioned a more universal language of personal confession and emotions, veiled in music of uncommon originality but reminiscent of tradition, readily comprehensible, and adaptable by any individual. Each person seated at the piano, each listener, could identify with Chopin's sentiments. They could bend Chopin to their own experience.

The startling irony is that as this persuasive cosmopolitan plasticity of Chopin's musical language of subjectivity succeeded throughout Europe and North America (and now Asia), it also gained a powerful symbolic presence as the political credo for modern Poles in the twentieth century. Chopin's exilic distance offered modern Polish nationalism a distinct unifying voice that sounded universal and sidestepped the thorny issues of social class (tensions between landed gentry and poor peasants), the ravages of the rapid industrialization of Poland, the political instability after independence in 1918, regional tensions derivative of the years of partitions, the role of the Church in politics and, most poignantly, the connection between Polish nationalism and the place of the Jews in Poland.

Chopin's life story, his patriotism, and self-identification as an aristocrat, with family links to szlachta, all helped. His music was, Rubinstein notwithstanding, neither earthy or folklike (the Mazurka, Op. 24, No. 2 is an exception), nor was it a transparent and condescending aestheticizing of the traditions of common people. It was immediately accessible music of suggestion and aspiration that could unify a nation and define a national ideal that bridged gaps of class and status. Chopin opened up wide access to a refined aesthetic and an emotional intensity rooted in an idealized Polish aristocratic heritage and culture. His work offered the aesthetic equivalent of a national historical narrative linking the worlds of the ancient families of Radziwiłł and Czartoryski to those of Józef Piłsudski and, ultimately, those of Władysław Gomułka, Lech Wałęsa, and Jarosław and Lech Kaczyński.

The third and final facet concerns the special place Chopin took on as the authentic bearer of Polish national identity among the not insignificant population of urban Jews in the major cities of Poland, particularly Warsaw and Rubinstein's native Łódź. The elite of Polish Jews, like their better- known counterparts in Germany, sought to assimilate, and so they did; they played an outsized role in modern Polish economic life and culture.[93] Love of Chopin defined a love of Poland precisely on account of this music's cosmopolitan transformation of folk markers of the Polish. Since Chopin's medium was music it had more impact than Mickiewicz's poetry, particularly the sympathetically drawn Jewish character Jankiel in *Pan Tadeusz*. The music's capacity to engage the personal in a universal manner assured its efficacy politically among those who were not Catholic, and in other reductive senses, not authentically Polish. The sound of Chopin as evocative of the essence of Poland was sufficiently persuasive and humanistic enough to blunt the brute facts of persistent, pervasive, and deadly anti-Semitism throughout all classes of Polish society—a feature of modern Polish identity that survives to this day.

Chopin became the pervasive emblem of solidarity with Polish nationalism among Jews. Nowhere is this more pronounced than in the attitudes of the seemingly endless stream of great Polish Jewish pianists for whom Chopin defined their credo as artists and citizens. Consider, to name but a few, Ignaz Friedman, Leopold Godowsky, Moritz Rosenthal, Josef Hofmann, Mieczysław Horszowski, and Arthur Rubinstein.[94] These Chopin interpreters of Polish-Jewish descent were so visible and influential that the self-styled "prophet" of Chopin, the Russian-German pianist Vladimir de Pachmann, felt he needed to go to great lengths to prove he had no trace of Jewish parentage.[95]

The allegiance to Chopin as the true expression of the Polish soul on the part of assimilated Polish Jews was a necessary refuge for them. The extraordinary and tragic persistence of anti-Semitism in Poland, the dominant place Catholicism played in defining Polish identity, and the widespread economic and social resentment Polish Jews faced in the late nineteenth and early twentieth centuries, made Chopin indispensable for those Jews seeking acceptance in Polish society. Music in Poland had been an unusually fertile field for assimilation and acculturation, as music had been after 1800 for all European Jews, notably in German-speaking Europe. The synthesis within Chopin of a transnational rhetoric of subjective expression and the articulation of an idealized spiritual and shared national consciousness was a unique oasis of ambiguity, if not neutrality. It permitted Polish Jews to assert patriotism without shame, without opening themselves to accusations of self-hate or betrayal of their Jewish origins and status. Playing Chopin provided Polish-Jewish pianists and their Polish-Jewish listeners the opportunity to display their genuine allegiance to Poland in public and in private.

This link between Chopin and the fragility and ultimate tragedy of Jewish life in Poland is eloquently expressed in the case of the Polish-Jewish pianist Władysław Szpilman, a survivor of the Warsaw Ghetto and author of a memoir that was turned into the celebrated film *The Pianist,* directed by Roman Polanski, himself a Polish-Jewish survivor. The film (as opposed to the memoir) opens with Szpilman playing Chopin on the radio. It ends as it began, with Szpilman's awkward and astonishing return to normalcy after the war, back in the studio, once again playing Chopin. Chopin's music justified his choice of an undiminished attachment to Poland.

What Chopin provided the educated Polish Jew—so well epitomized by Szpilman—was a false consolation. That consolation lay in a reality implied by the music but left unrealized, an illusion sustained by the music: a possible release from the status of a pariah—a form of exile within a community—that existed in Poland. Chopin's music signified to the acculturated Polish-Jewish community in the interwar years, during Polish independence, how in an idealized Poland the individual Jew might assume an equal place as a citizen. The Jew in a Polish political community defined by Chopin would therefore obtain, through aesthetic taste, the basic human equality and freedom necessary to share and express intimacy and solidarity.

As Chopin's music begins to sound at the start and the closing moments of Polanski's film, this false consolation is both evoked and unmasked. What lingers is nonetheless a vision of an idealized human community, imagined and created in exile: a vision contingent on Chopin's music's unique capacity to express in musical language the most deeply felt individual experiences of isolation, loss, and longing, as well as a fantastic vision of a unified, humane community with a shared history and destiny.

NOTES

1. Czesław Miłosz, "Notes on Exile," in *To Begin Where I Am: Selected Essays*, ed. and with an introduction by Bogdana Carpenter and Madeline G. Levine (New York: Farrar, Straus and Giroux, 2001), 13–19. I would like to thank Halina Goldberg, Jonathan Bellman, Cecile Kuznitz, Byron Adams, and Christopher Gibbs for their invaluable advice, corrections, and criticism.

2. Czesław Miłosz, *Native Realm: A Search for Self-Identification*, trans. Catherine S. Leach (Garden City, NY: Doubleday, 1968), 2.

3. See David Kettler, *The Liquidation of Exile: Studies in the Intellectual Emigration of the 1930s* (London and New York: Anthem Press, 2011).

4. This essay relies on the following books on Chopin's life: Tadeusz A. Zieliński, *Chopin: Sein Leben, sein Werk, seine Zeit*, trans. from the Polish by Martina Homma and Monika Brockmann (Mainz: Schott, 2008); Jim Samson, *Chopin* (Oxford and New York: Oxford University Press, 1996); Mieczysław Tomaszewski, *Frédéric Chopin und seine Zeit*, trans. Małgorzata Kozłowska (Laaber: Laaber, 1999), and *Chopin: Ein Leben in Bildern* (Mainz: Schott, 2009); Ernst Burger, *Frederic Chopin: Eine Lebenschronik in Bildern und Dokumenten* (Munich: Hirmer, 1990); Jarosław Iwaszkiewicz, *Chopin* (Kraków: Polskie Wydawnictwo Muzyczne, 2010); and Adam Zamoyski, *Chopin: Prince of the Romantics* (London: HarperCollins, 2010).

5. See Notes in Jean-Jacques Eigeldiner, *Chopin: Pianist and Teacher, As Seen by His Pupils*, ed. Roy Howat, trans. Naomi Shohet, Krysia Osostowicz, and Roy Howat (Cambridge: Cambridge University Press, 1986), 195. See also Leonard G. Ratner, *Classic Music: Expression, Form, and Style* (New York: Macmillan, 2000); and Danuta Mirka, ed., *The Oxford Handbook of Topic Theory* (Oxford and New York: Oxford University Press, 2014).

6. See Halina Goldberg, *Music in Chopin's Warsaw* (New York: Oxford University Press, 2008).

7. These phrases from Miłosz's *Native Realism* (9) are used with irony to indicate that in the 1830s Poland was looked on by elites in Germany, France, and England as marginal in cultural terms. That Chopin was well trained and versed in composition was a surprise to audiences and colleagues in Vienna and Paris at the start of his sojourn abroad. Being Polish and yet equal to others from more "advanced" centers added to the novelty of his early career.

8. Chopin heard much opera, especially in Paris, and met the leading composers. He sought out scores (e.g., famously Mozart's *Requiem*) and as a teacher and pianist was constantly in contact with music by past masters. See the recollections by pupil Karl Mikuli and others quoted in Jean-Jacques Eigeldinger, *Chopin: Pianist and Teacher, As Seen by His Pupils*, ed. Roy Howat, trans. Naomi Shohet, Krysia Osostowicz, and Roy Howat (Cambridge: Cambridge University Press, 1986), 275–78.

9. See the letter from Chopin to Tytus Woyciechowski, 25 December 1831, in which he refers to himself as being "happy on the outside" but "inside something is killing me . . . some forebodings, anxiety." *Chopin's Polish Letters*, trans. David Frick (Warsaw: Fryderyk Chopin Institute, 2016), 258. Chopin was periodically given to hyperbole and bouts of self-pity in his letters, as if to reassure those back home that he suffered from not being with them and at home.

10. Jonathan Bellman correctly suggests that other close relationships from the Paris years are poorly understood and merit closer scrutiny, including Chopin's friendship with the Marquis de Custine and Charles Valentin Alkan. See Jonathan D. Bellman, *Chopin's Polish Ballade: Op. 38 as Narrative of National Martyrdom* (Oxford and New York: Oxford University Press, 2010); see also Pierre Azoury, *Chopin Through His Contemporaries: Friends, Lovers, and Rivals* (Westport, CT: Greenwood Press, 1999).

11. Alfred Cortot, *In Search of Chopin*, trans. Cyril Clarke and Rena Clarke (Mineola, NY: Dover, 2013), 174.

12. See for example Andrzej Chwalba, *Historia Polski, 1795–1918* (Kraków: Wydaw-nictwo Literackie, 2000); and Czesław Miłosz, *The History of Polish Literature*, 2nd ed. (Berkeley: University of California Press, 1983).

13. A partial exception to this description was the part of Poland—Galicia—that was a dominant area within the Habsburg Empire. The Austrian approach to local regional languages and cultures was far more tolerant than that of Russia and Prussia. Divided loyalties therefore emerged in the Polish regions of the Habsburg Empire and dimin-ished the Galician influence on Polish nationalism, even casting suspicion on its elite as collaborative and insufficiently committed to the cause of Polish independence. This was the view of many committed late nineteenth-century Polish nationalists, including Joseph Conrad's father, Apollo Korzeniowski. See Larry Wolff, *The Idea of Galicia: History and Fantasy in Habsburg Political Culture* (Redwood City, CA: Stanford University Press, 2010); and the catalogue *Mythos Galizien* for the 2015 exhibition of the same title at the Wien Museum (Vienna: Metroverlag).

14. Ignace Jan Paderewski and Mary Lawton, *The Paderewski Memoirs* (New York: Da Capo, 1980), 375. See also Marek Zebrowski, *Celebrating Chopin and Paderewski* (Warsaw: Ministry of Foreign Affairs, 2010).

15. Meirion Hughes, ed. and trans., *Liszt's Chopin: A New Edition* (Manchester: Manchester University Press, 2010), 83–84. Another useful scholarly edition is *The Collected Writings of Franz Liszt*, vol. 1: *F. Chopin*, ed. and trans. Janita R. Hall-Swadley (Lanham, MD: Scarecrow Press, 2011).

16. Consider, for example, Ries's 1833 Introduction and Polonaise.

17. Schumann's phrase comes from the May 1836 review of the Chopin Piano Concertos, in Robert Schumann, *Gesammelte Schriften über Musik und Musiker* (Leipzig: Breitkopf und Härtel, 1914), 1:167. On the Schumann-Chopin relationship, see Klaus Wolfgang Niemöller, "Chopin im Davidsbund Robert Schumanns: Aspekte einer kom-plexen Beziehung," in *Chopin im Umkreis seiner Freunde*, ed. Irene Poniatowska (Warsaw: Neriton, 1997), 15–54.

18. Vladimir Nabokov, *Strong Opinions* (New York: Vintage Books, 1990), 186.

19. Halina Goldberg, "Nationalizing the *Kujawiak* and Constructions of Nostalgia in Chopin's Mazurkas," *19th-Century Music* 39/3 (Spring 2016): 223–47.

20, See Alina Witkowska and Ryszard Przybylski, *Romantyzm* (Warsaw: Wydawnictwo Naukowe PWN, 2007), 599–602; and Charles Rosen, *The Romantic Generation* (Cambridge, MA: Harvard University Press, 1995), 410–71.

21. Such as Serge Rachmaninoff, Alexander Scriabin, Claude Debussy, Johannes Brahms, Max Reger, and many lesser talents.

22. Anton Rubinstein, *A Conversation on Music* (New York: DaCapo Press, 1982), 74–76.

23. See Edward W. Said, *Reflections on Exile and Other Essays* (Cambridge, MA: Harvard University Press, 2000), 173–86.

24. See the classic work on the poor in Paris, Louis Chevalier's *Laboring Classes and Dangerous Classes in Paris During the First Half of the Nineteenth Century*, trans. Frank Jellinek (New York: Howard Fertig, 1973); also Christophe Charle, *A Social History of France in the 19th Century*, trans. Miriam Kochan (Oxford: Berg, 1994); David H. Pinckney, "The Revolutionary Crowd in Paris in the 1830s," *Journal of Social History* 5/4 (Summer 1972): 512–20; and Theodor Zeldin, *France 1848–1945*, vol. 2: *Intellect, Taste, and Anxiety* (Oxford: Oxford University Press, 1977).

25. See the famous Stuttgart diary entry, in *Chopin's Polish Letters*, 231–34. Chopin's habit of concealing his feelings makes it hard to assess to what extent there might have been some measure of loss. He seemed more intent on presenting himself as a patriot who was nonetheless not obsessed or paralyzed by the loss of his homeland. See the fine

essay by Jolanta T. Pekacz, "Deconstructing a 'National Composer': Chopin and Polish Exiles in Paris 1831−49," *19th-Century Music* 24/3 (Fall 2000): 161−72.

26. H. H. Houben, ed., *Gespräche mit Heine* (Potsdam: Rütten & Loening, 1948), 394.

27. On Słowacki, see the introduction by Peter Brang and the afterword by Ulrich Schmid in Juliusz Słowacki, *Des Dichters grösster Ruhm: Ausgewählte Lyrik*, trans. Christoph Ferber (Mainz: Dieterich'sche Verlagsbuchhandlung, 1997), 7−15 and 119−39, respectively; the introduction to *Poland's Angry Romantic: Two Poems and a Play by Juliusz Słowacki*, ed. and trans. Peter Cochran, Bill Johnston, Mirosława Modrzewska, and Catherine O'Neil (Newcastle-upon-Tyne: Cambridge Scholars Publishing, 2009), 1−30; and Miłosz, *History of Polish Literature*, 232−43.

28. See Jan Kleczyński, "Fryderyk Szopen," *Tygodnik Ilustrowany* (1870), in *Chopin and His Critics*, ed. Irena Poniatowska (Warsaw: Fryderyk Chopin Institute, 2011), 70.

29. See George Sand, "Essai sur le drame Fantastique: Goethe-Byron-Mickiewicz," *Revue des deux mondes* (1839).

30. See Ferdynand Hoesick, *Słowacki i Chopin* (Warsaw: Trzaska, Evert i Michalski, 1932).

31. See Jonathan D. Bellman's brilliant discussion of this question, in his book *Chopin's Polish Ballade: Op. 38 as Narrative of National Martyrdom* and Jim Samson, *Chopin: The Four Ballades* (Cambridge: Cambridge University Press, 1992). See also Matti Asikainen, "Utwory Mickiewicza jako źródło inspiracji ballad g-moll i F-dur Chopina," in *Zeszyty Naukowe* 32 (Gdansk: Akademia Muzyczna, 2000): 7–42; and Asikainen, "'Mickiewicz of the Piano': The National Style of the Ballades," in *Interdisciplinary Studies in Musicology: Materials from the First Scholarly Conference, Poznań, 23−24 November 1991*, ed. Jan Stęszewski and Maciej Jabłoński (Poznań: Ars Nova, 1993), 81–90.

32. Iwaszkiewicz suggested, for example, that there is an affinity between the poetic strategies in Słowacki's *Samuel Zborowski* and the ballade-like ending of the B-Minor Sonata. See Iwaszkiewicz, *Chopin*, 208−10.

33. Słowacki lost no opportunity to parody and respond to Mickiewicz's *Forefathers' Eve* in his 1834 *Kordian*, as Zygmunt Krasiński suggested as early as 1840. Słowacki's works are filled with direct responses to Mickiewicz, often left in fragmentary form.

34. Cortot, *In Search of Chopin*, 153.

35. *Chopin's Polish Letters*, 160.

36. See, for example, Oskar Fischel and Max von Boehn, *Die Mode: Menschen und Moden im 19 Jahrhundert*, vol. 2: *1818–1842* (Munich: F. Bruckmann, 1907); Colette Lehmann, *Mobilier Louis-Philippe Napoleon III* (Paris: Editions Ch. Massin, n.d.); Janine Leris-Laffargue, *Restauration Louis-Philippe* (Paris: Editions Ch. Massin, 1994); Anthony Sutcliffe, *Paris: An Architectural History* (New Haven and London: Yale University Press, 1993), 76–82; and Rainer Haaff, *Louis-Philippe: Bürgerliche Möbel des Historismus* (Stuttgart: Arnoldsche Buchhandlung, 2004).

37. See Appendix 1 in Eigeldinger, *Chopin: Pianist and Teacher*, 190–98.

38. See Ryszard Przybylski, *A Swallows' Shadow: An Essay on Chopin's Thoughts*, trans. John Comber (Warsaw: Fryderyk Chopin Institute, 2011). Słowacki's letters offer a striking contrast to Chopin's correspondence, which, special pleading to the contrary, is both less revealing and eloquent than the correspondence of Mozart or Mendelssohn, for example. Słowacki's account of his travels from Naples to the Holy Land is in poetic form.

39. Iwaszkiewicz, *Chopin*, 164−66.

40. On Mochnacki, see Halina Goldberg's essay in this volume. See also Zieliński, *Chopin: Sein Leben, sein Werk*, 214−16; Tomaszewski, *Frédéric Chopin*, 52−54; and Słowacki's reference to him in his poem *Beniowski*, in *Dzieła*, vol. 3: *Poematy* (Wrocław: Wydawnictwo Zakładu, 1949), 201.

41. In contrast, Mickiewicz suffered imprisonment by the Russians.

42. Słowacki did write a mystical tract in 1844 on the "Genesis from the Spirit."

43. Julius Słowacki, in *Poematy*, 147; an English version of the poem is included in *Poland's Angry Romantic*, 171–305.

44. Julius Słowacki, *Kordian*, trans. Gerard T. Kapolka (Chicago: Green Lantern Press, 2010), v–xviii. For Mickiewicz, see *Pan Tadeusz* (New York: Hippocrene Books, 1992), 578-79.

45. Friedrick Niecks, *Programme Music in the Last Four Centuries* (London: Novello, n.d.), 211–17.

46. The Polish text is found in *Dzieła*, 3:74–75; the translations are mine. An alternative English version is in *Poland's Angry Romantic*, 162, 164.

47. This issue raises the question of performance practice in Chopin's time and posthumously. Wilhelm von Lenz underscored Chopin's desire that the performer make the work his or her own and not imitate. See Wilhelm von Lenz, *The Great Piano Virtuosos of Our Time from Personal Acquaintance* (New York: Schirmer, 1909), 27–74. And then there is the vexed understanding of "tempo rubato" in Chopin. See the compact and helpful discussion of this in Franz Kullak, *Der Vortrag in der Musik am Ende des 19. Jahrhunderts* (Leipzig: Leuckart, 1898), 118–20, which outlines the use of tempo rubato to vary expressive intent. Also see Rene Leibowitz, "Was kann man von Chopin lernen?" in *Musik-Konzepte 45: Fryderyk Chopin* (Munich: Edition Text und Kritik, 1985), 52–57.

48. Adam Mickiewicz, *Forefathers' Eve*, trans. Charles S. Kraszewski (London: Glagoslav Publications, 2016), 171.

49. Słowacki joined Towiański's group in 1842 and left it in 1843.

50. On Towiański, see Harold B. Segel, ed., *Stranger in Our Midst: Images of the Jew in Polish Literature* (Ithaca, NY, and London: Cornell University Press, 1996), 14–15. Słowacki's sympathetic attitude to the Jews can be gleaned from his experimental fragment from the 1840s "Chorus of the Israelite Spirits" (Chór Duchów Izraelskich), in *Liryki i Inne Wiersze*, in *Dzieła*, 1:140–41.

51. See Jeffrey Kallberg's excellent and provocative contrasting analysis of this issue in his contribution to this volume.

52. Chopin to his family, 28 May 1831, in *Chopin's Polish Letters*, 225. The Yiddish expression *majufes* derives from the Song of Songs 7:7. The Hebrew phrase means "how beautiful." The term in Chopin's time referred to the opening of a song sung on the Sabbath eve. The common belief among Poles was that this Sabbath song, "Ma Yofis," had a special melody. It was alleged that the landed nobility on whose land many Jews lived and for whom Jews worked would request that Jews sing this song for their entertainment. Therefore "to sing 'Ma Yofis'" to a gentile came to mean to act obsequiously or slavishly. To act as a *mayofesnik* meant to cringe and be servile.

53. Kettler, *The Liquidation of Exile*, 106.

54. Magdalena Dziadek, "Chopin in Music Criticism before the First World War," in *Chopin and His Critics*, 21–47.

55. Gustav Karpeles, *Slawische Wanderungen* (Berlin: Allgemeiner Verein für Deutsche Literatur, 1905), 211.

56. Ibid.

57. See Eva Gesine Baur, *Chopin oder Die Sehnsucht: Eine Biographie* (Munich: Deutscher Taschenbuch Verlag, 2012), 512–13.

58. See Jean-Jacques Eigeldinger, *L'univers musical de Chopin* (Paris: Fayard, 2000); and William G. Atwood, *The Parisian Worlds of Frédéric Chopin* (New Haven and London: Yale University Press, 1999). The phrases are from *Liszt's Chopin*, 111–12.

59. On Conrad, see the three volumes by Zdzisław Najder, trans. Halina Najder: *Joseph Conrad: A Life* (Rochester, NY: Camden House, 2007); *Joseph Conrad: A Chronicle* (New Brunswick, NJ: Rutgers University Press, 1983); and, as editor, *Conrad Under Familial Eyes* (Cambridge: Cambridge University Press, 1983). See also Jeffrey Meyers,

Joseph Conrad: A Biography (New York: Cooper Square Press, 2001); and John Batchelor, *The Life of Joseph Conrad: A Critical Biography* (Oxford and Cambridge: Blackwell, 1996).

60. The brutality of the 1863 defeat and its legacy in Poland can be observed in Stefan Żeromski's 1912 novel *The Faithful River*, trans. Bill Johnston (Evanston, IL: Northwestern University Press, 1999).

61. Conrad was named after Mickiewicz's heroic protagonists.

62. Conrad left Poland to evade the military service Russia demanded of children of political prisoners. Conrad retained a lifelong antipathy to the Russians.

63. Najder, *Conrad Under Familial Eyes*, 199

64. Nabokov, *Strong Opinions*, 139.

65. Joseph Conrad, *The Nigger of the 'Narcissus': An Authoritative Text, Backgrounds and Sources, Reviews and Criticism*, ed. Robert Kimbrough (New York: W. W. Norton, 1979), 147.

66. Ibid., 146.

67. See Edward W. Said, *Joseph Conrad and the Fiction of Autobiography* (New York: Columbia University Press, 2008).

68. Conrad read with interest the prose of Bolesław Prus. See Najder, *Joseph Conrad: A Life*, 463; and Najder, *Joseph Conrad: A Chronicle*, 400.

69. Meyerbeer, a contemporary whom Heine championed in the 1830s, did not convert. Early in his career, Heine did write a fascinating travel piece on Poland, "Über Polen." See Heinrich Heine, *Sämtliche Schriften*, vol. 2 (Munich: Hanser, 1976), 69–95. On Heine, see Jeffrey L. Sammons, *Heinrich Heine: A Modern Biography* (Princeton: Princeton University Press, 1979); and Laura Hofrichter, *Heinrich Heine*, trans. Barker Fairley (Oxford: Clarendon Press, 1963).

70. See Richie Robertson, *Heine* (New York: Grove Press, 1988), 99. The quotes are from Heine's poem "Der Apollogott" (The God Apollo), in *Heinrich Heine und die Musik*, ed. Gerhard Müller (Leipzig: Reclam, 1987), 185–89.

71. *Liszt's Chopin*, 90.

72. Franz Liszt, *Sämtliche Schriften*, vol. 1: *Frühe Schriften*, ed. Rainer Kleinertz (Wiesbaden and Leipzig: Breitkopf & Härtel, 2000), 173.

73. Chopin's attitude to Mozart was best expressed, in his last years, in the conversations he had with Delacroix; see *Delacroix: Journal 1822–1863* (Paris: Plon, 1996), 183, 189–192.

74. As was said about the music of Cherubini, for example. See Katharine Ellis, *Music Criticism in Nineteenth-Century Paris* (Cambridge: Cambridge University Press 1995), 88; and Chopin's passing comment from 1831 in a letter to Elsner, in *Chopin's Polish Letters*, 251–54.

75. One could speculate that the allegiance to a Classicist aesthetic in both Chopin and Heine derived from a particular social and political insecurity: Chopin's Polish identity, representing a "peripheral" culture in the world of music, and Heine's status as a Jewish poet writing in German.

76. There are factual errors in Heine's account, such as the "education in Germany" and the "French parents." See the sources: *Sämtliche Schriften*, vol. 3 (Munich: Hanser, 1978), 353; *Heinrich Heine und die Musik*, 106–7; and Michael Mann, *Heinrich Heines Musikkritiken* (Hamburg: Hoffmann and Campe, Heinrich Heine Verlag, 1971).

77. Ibid.

78. Mozart was Chopin's ideal, as he eloquently expressed to Delacroix. The comparison with Raphael has a long history in Chopin reception, including Balzac's phrase of "Raphael-like perfection" in the novel *Le cousin Pons* and Nietzsche's description of Chopin matching "the princely elegance of Raphael," in *Menschliches, Allzumenschliches*, vol. 2, No. 159, in *Werke*, ed. Karl Schlechta, vol. 1 (Munich: Hanser 1954), 937.

79. The classic and most famous example of this critique was Karl Kraus's 1910 attack on Heine, *Heine und die Folgen* (Munich: Langen, 1910).

80. It was also influenced by an array of foreign models, ranging from John Field and Bellini to Ferdinand Ries, and in the waltzes (despite claims to the contrary) to the Viennese Lanner and Strauss. See Eric McKee, *Decorum of the Minuet, Delirium of the Waltz: A Study of Dance-Music Relations in ¾ Time* (Bloomington: Indiana University Press, 2012); and Andrzej Koszewski, "Das Wienerische in Chopins Walzer," in *Chopin Jahrbuch 1963*, ed. Franz Zagiba (Vienna: Verlag Notring der wissenschaftlichen Verbände Österreichs, 1963), 27–42.

81. Quoted in George F. Peters, *The Poet as Provocateur: Heinrich Heine and His Critics* (Rochester, NY: Camden House, 2000), 23–24.

82. See Poniatowska, *Chopin and His Critics*, 217–20, 451–53, 526, 535–36.

83. See Mary Gluck, *Popular Bohemia: Modernism and Urban Culture in Nineteenth-Century Paris* (Cambridge. MA: Harvard University Press, 2005). See also Ellis, *Music Criticism in Nineteenth-Century Paris*, 145–48, 158–59.

84. Friedrich Nietzsche, *Ecce Homo*, in *Werke* 2, 1091–93.

85. See Jeffrey Kallberg, *Chopin at the Boundaries: Sex, History, and Musical Genre* (Cambridge. MA: Harvard University Press, 1996).

86. The concept of "natality" is being used here in the sense elaborated by Hannah Arendt in *The Human Condition* (Chicago: University of Chicago Press, 1958).

87. Heine, *Sämtliche Schriften*, vol. 6/1 (Munich: Hanser, 1985), 7–172, at 75.

88. Ibid., 102.

89. See Nicholas Cook, *Beyond the Score: Music as Performance* (Oxford and New York: Oxford University Press, 2013), esp. 157–66; and Cook, "Time and Time Again: On Hearing Reinecke," in *Music in Time*, ed. Suzannah Clark and Alexander Rehding (Cambridge. MA: Harvard University Press, 2016), 3–32.

90. Arthur Rubinstein, *My Young Years* (New York: Alfred A. Knopf, 1973), 86–87; also Harvey Sachs, *Rubinstein: A Life* (New York: Grove Press, 1995), 58.

91. Hugo Leichtentritt's two-volume *Analyse von Chopins Klavierwerken* (Berlin: Hesse, 1921–22) exemplifies the modernist embrace of Chopin. Schenker deeply admired Chopin (he studied with Chopin's student Karol Mikuli). He was most concerned about the distortion and sentimentalizing of Chopin by performers and amateurs. See Hellmut Federhoffer, *Heinrich Schenker: Nach Tagebüchern und Briefen* (Hildesheim: Olms, 1985), 4, 196; and Federhoffer, ed., *Heinrich Schenker als Essayist und Kritiker* (Hildesheim: Olms, 1990), 106, 159.

92. Ivan Raykoff, *Dreams of Love: Playing the Romantic Pianist* (Oxford and New York: Oxford University Press 2014), 153–73.

93. See Alexander Hertz, *The Jews in Polish Culture*, ed. Lucjan Dobroszycki, trans. Richard Lourie (Evanston, IL: Northwestern University Press, 1988), 232–33. For description of the rapid economic development in Poland and the role of the Jews, see for example Samuel Wyszewiański, "La naissance et le premier développement de l'industrie textile de Pabianice (Pologne), 1823–1865" (PhD diss., University of Geneva, 1939).

94. See, for example, Allan Evans, *Ignaz Friedmann: Romantic Master Pianist* (Bloomington: Indiana University Press, 2009), 9–27; Josef Hofmann, *Piano Playing* (New York: Dover, 1976), 86–90.

95. Edward Blickstein and Gregor Benko, *Chopin's Prophet: The Life of Pianist Vladimir de Pachmann* (Lanham, MD: Scarecrow Press, 2013), 4–5. Polish Jews—Róża Etkin and Bolesław Kon—were among the earliest winners of the Chopin competitions.

Index

Page numbers followed by "n" indicate chapter endnotes.
Page numbers in italics refer to figures and musical excerpts.

Nocturnes, Op. 27, 16, 21
Nocturne, Op. 27, No. 1, C-sharp Minor, 99, 218, 234, 235, 282
Nocturne, Op. 27, No. 2, D-flat Major, 154, 165, *167*
Nocturne, Op. 32, No. 1, B Major, 23, 93–99, *95, 96*, 263
Nocturne, Op. 37, No. 1, G Minor, 154, 285, *286*
Nocturne, Op. 37, No. 2, G Major, 233–34, 240
Nocturne, Op. 48, No. 2, F-sharp Minor, 154, *155*, 234
Nocturne, Op. 55, No. 1, F Minor, 22
Nocturne, Op. 55, No. 2, E-flat Major, 65
Nocturne, Op. 62, No. 2, E Major, 73, 84n33
Nocturne, Op. 72, No. 1, E Minor, 233

Piano Concerto No. 1, Op. 11, E Minor, 56, 73, 151, 272, 276, 277, 326
Piano Concerto No. 2, Op. 21, F Minor, 41n25, 64, 69f, 171, 251, 272
Polonaise, B-flat Minor, 153
Polonaise, Op. 26, No. 1, C-sharp Minor, 64, 151
Polonaise, Op. 40, No. 1, A Major ("Military"), 151, 218–21, *219, 220*, 223, 225
Polonaise, Op. 40, No. 2, C Minor, 221–25, *222, 223*
Polonaise, Op. 44, F-sharp Minor, 235
Polonaise, Op. 53, A-flat Major, 151
Polonaise-Fantaisie, Op. 61, A-flat Major, 99, 151, 173, 215, 246, 260, 262
Polonaise for piano and cello, Op. 3, C Major, 56
Preludes, Op. 28, 23, 69, 85, 89–93, 260
Prelude, Op. 28, No. 1, C Major, 69, *97*
Prelude, Op. 28, No. 2, A Minor, 99, 137–40, *138*, 144n60
Prelude, Op. 28, No. 8, F-sharp Minor, 69
Prelude, Op. 28, No. 15, D-flat Major ("Raindrop"), 99, 105–6, 147
Prelude, Op. 45, C-sharp Minor, 256, 260

Rondo, Op. 1, C Minor, 53, 82n18
Rondo, Op. 16, E-flat Major, 262
Rondo, Op. 73, C Major, 129
Rondo à la krakowiak, Op. 14, F Major, 55, 151, 272

Rondo à la mazur, Op. 5, F Major, 53, 68–69, 73

Scherzos, 66
Scherzo, Op. 39, C-sharp Minor, 73
Scherzo, Op. 54, E Major, 73, 234–35, 240
"Sketch for a Method" (*Esquisses pour une méthode de piano*), 287–90, 307–9
Sonata, Op. 4, C Minor, 75
Sonata, Op. 35, B-flat Minor (Funeral March), 39, 73, 84n33, 99, 137, 147, 168
Sonata, Op. 58, B Minor, 64, 76, 236–37, 279
"Śpiew z mogiły" (Hymn from the Tomb), 254

Trio for piano, violin, and cello, Op. 8, G Minor, 54

Variations brillantes, Op. 12, B-flat Major, 73
Variations on Mozart's "Là ci darem la mano," Op. 2, B-flat Minor, 56, 153, 256, 272

Waltz, Op. 34, No. 2, A Minor, 279
Waltz, Op. 70, No. 2, F Minor, 265–66, *266, 267*, 275

Index of Names and Subjects

Adam, Louis, 59, 276, 284; *Méthode de piano du Conservatoire*, 273–74, 282–83
Aeolian harp, 36, 105, 106
Alexander I, 5, 53, 213, 214
Alkan, Charles-Valentin, 93, 97, 128, 141n22, 331; *Trois morceaux dans le genre pathétique*, 93
Allanbrook, Wye Jamison, 231
Arne, Thomas Augustine, 159
Auber, Daniel, 110, 157, 251, 276
Auenbrugger, Leopold, 119n2
Augustus III, 192

Baader, Franz von, 28–29
Bach, Carl Philipp Emanuel (C. P. E.), 195–98, *196, 197*, 201, 283
Bach, Johann Sebastian, 74–75, 149, 272, 276, 316, 321
Baculard d'Arnaud, François-Thomas-Marie de, 86–87

Niemcewicz, Julian, *Historical Chants*, 4, 40n11
Nietzsche, Friedrich, 342
nightingale image, 110–14, *113*
Nirenberg, David, 128, 130, 134, 142n24
nocturne, 15, 69–70, 154, 232–34
Nodier, Charles, 24, 88
noise libel, 130–36
Norblin, Jean Pierre, 188, *189*
nostalgia, 16–17, 20–23, 245–46
Novalis (Friedrich von Hardenberg), 26, 27, 28, 93
November Uprising (1830–31), 1, 5, 32, 46, 157, 214, 229n83, 322, 323
Nowakowski, Józef, 278

obertas, 73, 83n32
Offenbach, Jacques, 232
Ogiński, Prince Michał Kleofas, 193, 203, 209, 211–13, *214*
Okołow, Jerzy, 52, 82n16
Onslow, George, 61, 83n28
opera: improvisation on arias, 251; operatic narrative as inspiration for Chopin, 152–57; ornamentation and embellishment, 155–56, 157; in Paris, 6; piano-vocal scores of, 153; Polish national, rise of, 3–4. *See also specific operas*
ornamentation: Chopin on Sontag and, 276; Chopin's pianism and, 274, 290; improvisation and, 249, 255–57; operatic, 155–56, 157
Orpheus image, 110, 114–17

Paderewski, Ignacy Jan, 319, 344
Paër, Fernando, 186n18, 277
Paganini, Nicolò, 273, 276, 277
Paris: Chopin's arrival in, 5–6, 56–57, 271; as European capital of music, 5; French school of pianism, 276, 282–87; improvisation renounced in, 251–52; pianists active in, 271; Polish Romantics in, 34
pas de bourrée, 192
patriotism. *See* nationalism and nationality, Polish
pedal, use of, 79
Philipp, Isidor, 282
pianism and pianistic contexts and influences: anti-Judaism and, 133–34; Chopin as unicum, 290–91; "Cult

of Chopin," 147; fantasies as story and, 158–67; Liszt compared to Chopin, 279; operatic narrative and vocalism, 152–57; performances in France and, 277–82; sensitivity and elegance vs. noisiness, 132–36; Sikorski on, 57–62, 76–79; "Sketch for a Method" (Chopin), 287–90, 307–9; touch, articulation, and pedagogy in the French school, 276, 282–87; vernacular dance genres and, 149–52; in Warsaw, 272–77. *See also* Chopin, hands of
piano, popular ascendance of, 345
Piast (the Wheelwright), 50, 81n12
Piłsudski, Józef, 325, 332, 347
Pleyel, Camille, 105, 126, 127, 260, 282
Pleyel, Marie, 271
Pleyel piano, 105, 109
Poland: Chopin's "theoretical" Poland, 346; as crucified Christ, in Mickiewicz, 116–17, 224–25, 330–31; exile and shadow of history of, 317–24; Galicia and the Habsburg Empire, 350n13; historical overview of, 1–3, 317–18; nationalism and romanticism in, 3–5, 32–34 (*See also* nationalism and nationality, Polish; Romanticism); as puppet state, 213; as Romantic aspiration, 321. *See also* exile; Warsaw
Polanski, Roman, 347
polonaise (dance form): C. P. E. Bach polonaise, 195–98, *197*; choreography of, 192–94; cultural associations of, 150–52, 202–8; German, 203; Grabowiecki polonaise, *198*, 198–99; heroic, 208–11, *210*, 218, 221–25; historical overview, 191–92; Kościuszko Polonaise, 4, 174, *176*, 177, 180, 229n74; Kozłowski's "Grom Pobedï razdavaisya!"(Thunder of Victory, Resound!), 209–11, *210*; Kurpiński's "Witaj Królu" (Welcome King), 214–15, *216–17*; melancholy, 203, 211–13, 222–24, 229n74; musical characteristics of the Polish ballroom polonaise, 194–202; Norblin's *Dancing the Polonaise*, 188, *189*; Ogiński's Polonaise in F Minor, 213, *214*; Polonaise of May the Third, 4, 7, 9, 174; pre-history outside Poland, 319; Russian model, 214–15, 218; as

Contributors

Jonathan D. Bellman is professor of music history and literature and head of academic studies in music at the University of Northern Colorado. His previous books include *The "Style Hongrois" in the Music of Western Europe* (1993), *The Exotic in Western Music* (1998), *A Short Guide to Writing About Music* (2000; 2nd ed. 2007), and *Chopin's Polish Ballade: Op. 38 as Narrative of National Martyrdom* (2010). He has published articles on Chopin and musical style in general in such journals as *Historical Performance, 19th-Century Music, Early Music, Journal of Musicology, Musical Quarterly, Keyboard Perspectives,* and *The Journal of Musicological Research.*

Leon Botstein is president and Leon Levy Professor in the Arts of Bard College, author of several books, and editor of *The Compleat Brahms* (1999) and *The Musical Quarterly.* The music director of the American Symphony Orchestra and conductor laureate of the Jerusalem Symphony Orchestra, he has recorded works by, among others, Szymanowski, Hartmann, Bruch, Dukas, Foulds, Toch, Dohnányi, Bruckner, Chausson, Richard Strauss, Mendelssohn, Popov, Shostakovich, and Liszt. Beginning in the summer of 2018, he will assume the position of artistic director of the Grafenegg Academy in Austria.

John Comber, a freelance translator and writer from Wales, has lived in Poland for twenty years. He specializes in music-related translation, including the multi-volume *History of Music in Poland* for Sutkowski Edition, the source commentaries to the Fryderyk Chopin Institute's facsimile edition of Chopin's works, and countless academic texts, as well as librettos, song lyrics, and poems. The Fryderyk Chopin Institute is his major client. He has also worked for the Polish National Opera, Warsaw Chamber Opera, PWM Edition, Polish National Radio Symphony Orchestra, ISPAN, the Polish President's Office, and universities across Poland.

Jean-Jacques Eigeldinger, professor emeritus at the University of Geneva, has published numerous books and articles on Chopin, the best known being *Chopin vu par ses élèves / Chopin: Pianist and Teacher*, the foundation-text addressing Chopin's pianism. His more recent books—*Chopin et Pleyel, L'univers musical de Chopin*, and *Chopin: Âme des salons parisiens*—situate the composer within nineteenth-century culture and aesthetics, and his annotated editions of performance texts include Chopin's own incomplete piano method and interpretive essays by Chopin's "grand-student" Raoul Koczalski. Eigeldinger is also one of the editors of *The Complete Chopin—A New Critical Edition* (Peters Edition, London).

Halina Goldberg is professor of musicology at the Jacobs School of Music at Indiana University, and affiliate of the Sandra S. Borns Jewish Studies Program, Polish Studies Center, and Russian and East European Institute. Much of her scholarship is interdisciplinary, engaging the areas of cultural studies, music and politics, performance practice, and reception, with special focus on nineteenth- and twentieth-century Poland and Eastern Europe, Chopin, and Jewish studies. She edited *The Age of Chopin* (2004) and is author of *Music in Chopin's Warsaw* (2008; paperback edition 2013; Polish translation 2016).

Jeffrey Kallberg is William R. Kenan, Jr. Professor of Music and Associate Dean for Arts and Letters at the University of Pennsylvania. He has published widely on the music and cultural contexts of Chopin, including in his book *Chopin at the Boundaries: Sex, History, and Musical Genre*. He is also founder and general editor (with Anthony Newcomb and Ruth Solie) of the Cambridge University Press monograph series, New Perspectives in Music History and Criticism.

David Kasunic is an associate professor of music history at Occidental College in Los Angeles, California. His research has focused on Chopin's compositional relationship to French and Italian opera and contemporary singing practice. His work on tubercular singing in Verdi's *La traviata* appeared in the article "Tubercular Singing" in *Postmodern Culture* and was supported by a residency at the University of California Humanities Research Institute. His current research seeks to understand Chopin's piano technique in the context of dance, and to develop a mode of analysis that will link piano technique to compositional craft, and body movement to sound.

Anatole Leikin is professor of music at the University of California, Santa Cruz. His scholarly articles have been published in various musicological journals and essay collections worldwide, and his critically acclaimed books—*The Performing Style of Alexander Scriabin* and *The Mystery of Chopin's Préludes*—were recently published by Ashgate Publishing and reprinted by Routledge. Professor Leikin has performed extensively as a solo and chamber pianist, fortepianist, and harpsichordist; he has also recorded the piano music of Scriabin, Chopin, and Cope. He currently serves as an editor for *The Complete Chopin—A New Critical Edition* (Peters Edition, London).

Eric McKee is professor of music theory at Penn State University, where he has taught since 1992. McKee's research interests include Schenker's concept of tonal form, phrase rhythm, topic theory, and dance-music relations. He was awarded a fellowship from the American Council of Learned Societies for his research on the dance music of Chopin. He is the author of *Decorum of the Minuet, Delirium of the Waltz: A Study of Dance-Music Relations in ³⁄₄ Time* (2013). His articles have appeared in *Music Theory Spectrum*, *Music Analysis*, *In Theory Only*, *College Music Symposium*, and *Theory and Practice*.

James Parakilas is the James L. Moody, Jr. Family Professor of Performing Arts at Bates College. His publications include *Ballads without Words: Chopin and the Tradition of the Instrumental Ballade* (1992), *Piano Roles: 300 Years of Life with the Piano* (2000), and *The Story of Opera* (2012), as well as "Disrupting the Genre: Unforeseen Personifications in Chopin," *19th-Century Music* 35/3 (Spring 2012) and "'Nuit plus belle qu'un beau jour': Piano, Song, and the Voice in the Piano Nocturne," in *The Age of Chopin: Interdisciplinary Inquiries*, ed. Halina Goldberg (2004).

John Rink is professor of musical performance studies at the University of Cambridge, and fellow and director of studies in music at St. John's College, Cambridge. His research interests include Chopin studies, performance studies, theory and analysis, and digital applications in musicology. He has produced seven books on Chopin and on musical performance, and he has directed the AHRC Research Centre for Musical Performance as Creative Practice, *The Complete Chopin—A New Critical Edition*, Chopin's First Editions Online, and the Online Chopin Variorum Edition. He performs regularly as a pianist and lecture-recitalist, specializing in the use of historic pianos.

Sandra P. Rosenblum holds degrees from Wellesley and Harvard, and is the author of *Performance Practices in Classic Piano Music: Their Principles* *and Applications* (1988), a foundational and highly influential text for the discipline of piano performance practices. Since then she has published articles on Chopin (and other topics) in such venues as the *Polish Music Journal, The Journal of Musicological Research*, and *Journal of the Conductors' Guild,* and contributed chapters to *The Age of Chopin* (ed. Halina Goldberg, 2004) and *Keyboard Perspectives IX* (ed. Annette Richards, Westfield Center for Historical Keyboard Studies, 2016).

Virginia E. Whealton is a PhD candidate in musicology at Indiana University-Bloomington. In her dissertation, "Travel, Ideology, and the Geographical Imagination: Parisian Musical Travelogues, 1830–1870," she investigates how Parisian musicians used prose travelogues and travel-inspired compositions to craft their public personae and contribute to sociopolitical discourse. Her research has been supported by a Mellon Innovating International Research and Teaching Fellowship, among other grants. She has presented at numerous venues, including the Fryderyk Chopin Institute, and in 2012 she published a review article on the new translation of Liszt's book *F. Chopin* in the *Journal of the American Liszt Society*.

OTHER PRINCETON UNIVERSITY PRESS
VOLUMES PUBLISHED IN CONJUNCTION WITH
THE BARD MUSIC FESTIVAL

Brahms and His World
edited by Walter Frisch (1990)

Mendelssohn and His World
edited by R. Larry Todd (1991)

Richard Strauss and His World
edited by Bryan Gilliam (1992)

Dvořák and His World
edited by Michael Beckerman (1993)

Schumann and His World
edited by R. Larry Todd (1994)

Bartók and His World
edited by Peter Laki (1995)

Charles Ives and His World
edited by J. Peter Burkholder (1996)

Haydn and His World
edited by Elaine R. Sisman (1997)

Tchaikovsky and His World
edited by Leslie Kearney (1998)

Schoenberg and His World
edited by Walter Frisch (1999)

Beethoven and His World
edited by Scott Burnham and Michael P. Steinberg (2000)

Debussy and His World
edited by Jane F. Fulcher (2001)

Mahler and His World
edited by Karen Painter (2002)

Janáček and His World
edited by Michael Beckerman (2003)

Shostakovich and His World
edited by Laurel E. Fay (2004)

Aaron Copland and His World
edited by Carol J. Oja and Judith Tick (2005)

Franz Liszt and His World
edited by Christopher H. Gibbs and Dana Gooley (2006)

Edward Elgar and His World
edited by Byron Adams (2007)

Sergey Prokofiev and His World
edited by Simon Morrison (2008)

Brahms and His World (revised edition)
edited by Walter Frisch and Kevin C. Karnes (2009)

Richard Wagner and His World
edited by Thomas S. Grey (2009)

Alban Berg and His World
edited by Christopher Hailey (2010)

Jean Sibelius and His World
edited by Daniel M. Grimley (2011)

Camille Saint-Saëns and His World
edited by Jann Pasler (2012)

Stravinsky and His World
edited by Tamara Levitz (2013)

Franz Schubert and His World
edited by Christopher H. Gibbs and Morten Solvik (2014)

Carlos Chávez and His World
edited by Leonora Saavedra (2015)

Giacomo Puccini and His World
edited by Arman Schwartz And Emanuele Senici (2016)